Edgar J. Treischl
Practice R

Edgar J. Treischl

Practice R

An interactive textbook

DE GRUYTER

Author
Dr. Edgar J. Treischl
Researcher at the Chair of Empirical Economic Sociology
School of Business and Economics
Friedrich-Alexander-University Erlangen-Nuremberg
Findelgasse 7/9
90402 Nuremberg
Germany

ISBN 978-3-11-070496-9
e-ISBN (PDF) 978-3-11-070497-6
e-ISBN (EPUB) 978-3-11-070508-9

Library of Congress Control Number: 2022949290

Bibliographic information published by the Deutsche Nationalbibliothek
The Deutsche Nationalbibliothek lists this publication in the Deutsche Nationalbibliografie; detailed bibliographic data are available on the internet at http://dnb.dnb.de.

© 2023 Walter de Gruyter GmbH, Berlin/Boston
Cover image: StudioM1 / iStock / Getty Images Plus
Printing and binding: CPI books GmbH, Leck

www.degruyter.com

Supplementary material

Practice R is a textbook for the social sciences. The corresponding R package PracticeR gives access to the book's tutorials, provides further materials, and templates to help the reader learn R (see Chapter 2).

For more information, please scan the QR code or visit the PracticeR website: https://edgar-treischl.github.io/PracticeR/

Contents

List of figures —— IX

Part I: **The first steps**

1   Introduction —— **3**

2   First steps in R —— **10**
2.1   Introducing R and RStudio —— **10**
2.2   Base R —— **23**
2.3   Data types and structures —— **30**

3   Data exploration —— **43**
3.1   Categorical variables —— **44**
3.2   Continuous variables —— **53**
3.3   Explore effects —— **60**

4   Data manipulation —— **69**
4.1   The five key functions of dplyr —— **70**
4.2   Data manipulation with dplyr —— **80**
4.3   Workflow —— **95**

Part II: **The basics**

5   Prepare data —— **111**
5.1   Data import and export —— **112**
5.2   Missing data —— **136**
5.3   Categorical variables —— **147**

6   Analyze data —— **154**
6.1   Linear regression analysis —— **155**
6.2   Develop a linear regression model —— **162**
6.3   Visualization techniques —— **179**

7   Visualize research findings —— **193**
7.1   The basics of ggplot2 —— **195**
7.2   The applied grammar of graphics —— **215**
7.3   Extensions of ggplot2 —— **236**

VIII —— Contents

8   Communicate research findings —— **248**
8.1   The basics of rmarkdown —— **249**
8.2   Create a document —— **255**
8.3   Create a template —— **261**

Part III: Beyond the basics

9   GitHub —— **277**
9.1   The Git(Hub) basics —— **278**
9.2   Install Git —— **281**
9.3   GitHub and RStudio —— **284**

10   Automate work —— **292**
10.1   Reports —— **293**
10.2   Text —— **306**
10.3   Emails —— **313**

11   Collect data —— **324**
11.1   PDF files —— **325**
11.2   Web scraping —— **342**
11.3   APIs —— **353**

12   Next steps —— **363**

Session info —— **376**

Bibliography —— **378**

Index —— **384**

List of figures

Fig. 1.1   Example tutorial —— **4**
Fig. 1.2   Gapminder bubble chart —— **8**

Fig. 2.1   The R console —— **11**
Fig. 2.2   Panes of RStudio —— **13**
Fig. 2.3   Auto-completion in RStudio —— **14**
Fig. 2.4   The Files pane —— **16**
Fig. 2.5   The Plots pane —— **17**
Fig. 2.6   The Tutorial pane —— **20**

Fig. 3.1   Pie chart vs Pac-Man —— **48**
Fig. 3.2   Pie chart pitfalls —— **49**
Fig. 3.3   Illustration of a box plot —— **58**

Fig. 4.1   The five dplyr functions —— **70**
Fig. 4.2   Structure of an R script —— **100**
Fig. 4.3   Section menu in RStudio —— **101**
Fig. 4.4   Snippet preview —— **107**

Fig. 5.1   Data import window —— **113**
Fig. 5.2   Long (A) and wide (B) data —— **125**
Fig. 5.3   Mutating joins —— **131**
Fig. 5.4   Full join (A) and inner join (B) —— **131**
Fig. 5.5   Left join (A) and right join (B) —— **132**
Fig. 5.6   The mechanisms of missing values —— **139**
Fig. 5.7   The naniar package —— **147**

Fig. 6.1   Linear association —— **156**
Fig. 6.2   Explained and unexplained variance —— **160**
Fig. 6.3   Anscombe's quartet —— **162**
Fig. 6.4   Power analysis —— **167**
Fig. 6.5   Simpson's paradox —— **169**
Fig. 6.6   The Datasaurus —— **180**
Fig. 6.7   Regression diagnostics overview —— **182**

Fig. 7.1   Global common era temperature reconstruction —— **193**
Fig. 7.2   Scatter plot example —— **195**
Fig. 7.3   Standard themes —— **199**
Fig. 7.4   Shape types in R —— **205**
Fig. 7.5   ColorBrewer palettes —— **208**
Fig. 7.6   The esquisse addin —— **214**
Fig. 7.7   The Export menu —— **214**
Fig. 7.8   Geoms for continuous variables —— **219**

Fig. 8.1   Create a new R Markdown document —— **250**

https://doi.org/10.1515/9783110704976-201

X —— List of figures

Fig. 8.2   Render a document —— **251**
Fig. 8.3   The structure of an R Markdown document —— **252**
Fig. 8.4   The visual markdown editing mode —— **256**
Fig. 8.5   Menu of the visual markdown editing mode —— **256**

Fig. 9.1   GitHub code changes —— **277**
Fig. 9.2   GitHub Desktop —— **284**
Fig. 9.3   Create a GitHub repository —— **285**
Fig. 9.4   GitHub quick setup —— **286**
Fig. 9.5   Clone repository —— **287**
Fig. 9.6   Git pane —— **288**
Fig. 9.7   Push with the Git pane —— **288**
Fig. 9.8   Track changes of code —— **291**

Fig. 10.1   Interactive interface to knit documents —— **300**
Fig. 10.2   An automated scatter plot —— **309**
Fig. 10.3   Preview of an email —— **313**
Fig. 10.4   Preview of an improved email —— **317**
Fig. 10.5   The cronR package —— **322**

Fig. 11.1   Preview regular expressions —— **329**
Fig. 11.2   Firefox's developer mode —— **345**
Fig. 11.3   The GitHub API —— **355**
Fig. 11.4   The plumber API —— **361**

Fig. 12.1   The shiny app —— **373**

Part I: **The first steps**

1 Introduction

R is a programming language and a powerful tool to analyze data, but R has a lot more to offer than statistics. To mention just a few options, R has many capabilities to visualize data, to collect data (e.g., from a website), or even to create interactive dashboards. From this perspective it is no wonder why R has a huge fan base. Unfortunately, learning R can be though. People who struggle may say that the data handling is complicated, some complain that R lacks a graphical interface, and probably all agree that beginners face a rather steep learning curve. Regardless of our perception, the best way to learn R is by means of practice. For this reason, this book introduces R, focuses on the most important steps for applied empirical research, and explains how to use R in practice. After reading and working on the materials in this book, you will be able to *prepare* and *analyze* data, make *visualizations*, and *communicate* key research insights.

Who should read this book? Overall, the book introduces R and is written for people with no prior knowledge about it. However, Practice R is a textbook for the social sciences, and it is assumed that the reader has prior knowledge in statistics and quantitative methods. Practice R might not be the first choice if you have yet to learn what a *standard deviation*, *Pearson's r*, or a *t-test* is. The same applies for topics of quantitative empirical research. I presume that the reader has knowledge about research designs, is familiar with the difference between cross-sectional and longitudinal data, and other aspects that intermingle with statistics, seeing that quantitative methods are a substantial part of the social science curriculum. Of course, this does not mean that only (social science) students can profit from reading the book. A diverse audience – holding the assumed prior knowledge – may use Practice R to become a proficient R user.

To support you, the book is accompanied by an R package. An R package is a software add-on and extends the capabilities of R. In our case, the `PracticeR` package gives you access to tutorials to practice the discussed content, it provides the code of this book, and also further materials (e.g., a template to create reports) that are supposed to boost your skills. We will learn how to install R packages in the next chapter, but keep in mind that all materials of the book become available once the `PracticeR` package is installed.

Let me outline the idea of the tutorials and how they are related to the content of the book. The tutorials summarize the content and aim to familiarize you with the core concepts. The interactive tutorials are integrated in R and run on your computer. By clicking on the Run button, R code will be executed, and the tutorial shows the results. Don't mind if something goes wrong, you can reload and start over at the click of a button. As an illustration, Figure 1.1 shows a screenshot of the Basics of Data Manipulation (Chapter 4) tutorial. It summarizes how to filter, arrange, and select data. Irrespective of the topic, each tutorial probes you to apply the discussed content. The exercises in the tutorials aim to increase your coding skills and they are ordered as-

https://doi.org/10.1515/9783110704976-001

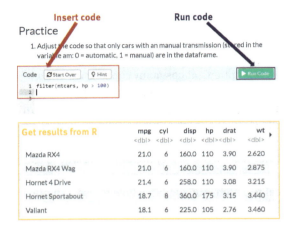

Fig. 1.1: Example tutorial

cendingly by difficulty. Sometimes I'll ask you to adjust the R code, which gives you a better understanding of how the code works. In most instances I will challenge you with typical data analyzing problems. In the more advanced steps, you are supposed to transfer the discussed content to a similar or a new concept. Don't worry, hints are provided to solve the exercises and the tutorials include the solutions. Now that the scope is set, we can divulge the content of Practice R.

The content

Part I lays the foundation and outlines the first steps to work with R:
- Chapter 2 introduces R and RStudio, which is an integrated development environment to work with R. The chapter contains the most important steps to understand how R behaves and outlines in depth how RStudio substantially helps us to increase our R skills. We install both software packages and we discover some of the cool features of RStudio. Next, I give a concise introduction of base R – the programming language – which is essential for subsequent steps. Moreover, the chapter makes you familiar with data types and structures.
- In Chapter 3 we start to explore data. We examine variables, we calculate and visualize descriptive statistics, and we explore how variables are related. We estimate the correlation between two variables, visualize the effect, and interpret the effect size. Data exploration is crucial when we start to work with data. For this reason, this chapter also highlights packages and ways to get a quick overview of new and unfamiliar data. For example, some packages implement graphs to examine several variables at once; others can generate a PDF report with summary statistics

for all variables of a particular data set. Thus, we explore variables, and we get in touch with packages that help us to discover unfamiliar data.

– Chapter 4 focuses on data manipulation steps and introduces the `dplyr` package (Wickham, François, et al., 2022). The latter is the Swiss pocketknife for manipulating data. I introduce the main functions of the package and we will focus on typical steps to prepare data for an analysis. Before we can dive into this topic in the second part, we should take one step back. The last part of this chapter highlights strategies to increase the workflow and, consequently, the efficiency of our work. For example, you may wonder how much R code you need to remember to become an efficient R user. The last section outlines in detail why there is no need to memorize code and introduces strategies to handle (complicated) code.

Part II introduces the basics to analyze data, visualize results, and create reports:

– Chapter 5 outlines the data preparation steps required before we can start to analyze data. We learn how to import data and how to cope with problems that may occur. Depending on the data, the import step may induce errors, but the same may apply during the data cleaning steps, and we should consider the concerns of missing (and implausible) values. Finally, I introduce the main functions from the `forcats` package (Wickham, 2022a). The package is made for *categorical variables* and is a good supplement to our data manipulation skills since categorical variables are often used in social sciences.

– We analyze data in Chapter 6. There is a broad range of possibilities to analyze data with R, however, we apply a linear regression analysis, because it is the workhorse of social science research. First, I give an non-technical introduction for people with a different educational background. Next, we run an example analysis that we will improve step by step. We learn how to develop the model, we examine interaction effects, and we compare the performance of the estimated models. To compare models and to examine the assumption of a linear regression analysis, we also focus on visualization techniques.

– To visualize research findings, Chapter 7 concentrates on the `ggplot2` package (Wickham, Chang, et al., 2022). The package can be quite demanding in the beginning, but we will learn that creating a graph without much customization is far from rocket science. We first focus on typical steps to create and adjust a graph (e.g., adjust a title). Next, we increase the theoretical knowledge by exploring how `ggplot2` works behind the curtain. Ultimately, there are a lot of packages that extend the possibilities of `ggplot2`. The last section highlights some of these possibilities.

– Chapter 8 focuses on reporting. After the analysis and the visualization step, we need to summarize the findings in a document and the `rmarkdown` package makes it possible to create text documents with R (Allaire, Xie, McPherson, et al., 2022). An `rmarkdown` file contains text, graphs, or tables, just like any other text document. However, it is code-based and also contains output from R. Thus, we create tables and graphs with R and include them in the `rmarkdown` document. Using code to create the report increases the reproducibility of the work and we avoid introducing errors, because we eliminated the need to transfer output from R into a word processing software.

Part III completes the basics and focuses on topics that – at first glance – seem less related to applied empirical research, but that will add to your skill set:

- Chapter 9 introduces Git, a version control system for code, and GitHub, a host for Git-based projects. Think of Git/GitHub as a sort of cloud for code. Suppose you changed a code, but you made a mistake. A version control system lets us travel back in time to find out where the error occurred. GitHub marks changes of the code and forces us to explain – in a few words – what happens to the code when we make an update. GitHub has more advantages, but I guess the example makes clear that a version control system is very valuable if you work with code on a regular basis. Chapter 9 gives a short introduction, we learn the basics to send (receive) code to (from) GitHub, and we connect RStudio with your GitHub account.
- Chapter 10 outlines the advantages of dynamic reports and highlights that whenever possible we are not supposed to repeat ourselves, instead we can automate the boring manual stuff. Say we made a report with R, but the data for the report gets an update. There is no need to manually re-estimate the results, re-create graphs, or tables – create a dynamic report and let R recreate and update the document. Chapter 10 introduces dynamic reports and discusses further steps to automate the reporting process (e.g., to send reports automatically via email).
- Chapter 11 demonstrates that we can collect data with R. Consider you work with a data set that lacks an important variable. Maybe you find this information on a website or in a PDF report; or suppose you want to retrieve data from a social media platform – your R skills help you in all those instances. The last chapter highlights the possibilities of collecting data and underlines the main steps to retrieve data from a PDF file, a website, and a web server.
- Finally, Chapter 12 outlines possible next steps and demonstrates that there are many cool packages and features to discover. This chapter introduces topics, packages, and frameworks, that would otherwise not find a place in an introductory book and we explore the next steps in connection to data preparation, analysis, visualization, and reporting.

Practice R contains only a selection of the possibilities that R offers. Maybe you have to prepare or analyze data, beyond what is covered in the book. Fortunately, R has a large and helpful community and you can find a lot of information on the web. This book introduces R and focuses on the main aspects of applied research, which is why I skip some of the more sophisticated topics. Using info boxes, the book covers additional topics and guidelines on where to find more information. Irrespective of the content, Practice R was written with several guiding principles in mind.

Guiding principles

Practice R applies some rules or guiding principles that should help you to learn R. Let's outline a few things about the R code, the data, and learning strategies before we start with the installation of R and RStudio.

In this book R code will be printed in the running text or via the *console* (#>). In the running text, R code is typeset. Most of the time, R code and the output that the code creates will be printed via the R console. For example, we can use R as a calculator. R returns results via the console. Moreover, I add comments that describe what the code does with a hash tag (#) :

```
# Use R as a calculator:
1 + 2
```

```
#> [1] 3
```

R comes with a lot of implemented data sets for teaching purposes. I will use those and toy data sets to introduce new concepts. Such data sets are clean and well prepared for demonstrating how code works. For example, the next console displays a part of the mtcars (Motor Trend Car Road Tests) data set. It contains fuel consumption (mpg) and further design and performance variables about cars.

```
# R comes with built-in data, for example, the mtcars data:
```

```
#>                    mpg cyl disp  hp drat    wt  qsec vs am gear carb
#> Mazda RX4         21.0   6  160 110 3.90 2.620 16.46  0  1    4    4
#> Mazda RX4 Wag     21.0   6  160 110 3.90 2.875 17.02  0  1    4    4
#> Datsun 710        22.8   4  108  93 3.85 2.320 18.61  1  1    4    1
#> Hornet 4 Drive    21.4   6  258 110 3.08 3.215 19.44  1  0    3    1
#> Hornet Sportabout 18.7   8  360 175 3.15 3.440 17.02  0  0    3    2
#> Valiant           18.1   6  225 105 2.76 3.460 20.22  1  0    3    1
```

I use such data because they are small and clean. Even though we might not be interested in their content, they let us focus on how the code works, rather than what each variable measures. The same applies to toy data sets – it's fake data and just an illustration of what the data may look like. More importantly, you must not download, nor import a data set to apply the code. A toy data set also has advantages when it comes to learning a new programming language. Toy data makes it possible to show you how the data is generated, which establishes a deeper understanding of how data needs to be prepared, and what the code actually does.

Toy data makes it easier to grasp the logic behind the code, but it will also help you apply your skills to real data. Suppose you execute code, but R returns an error.

Don't get disappointed or frustrated, because we all make mistakes when we write code. However, by using a toy data set first, you can be sure that the code does not contain typos or other mistakes when it works. Unfortunately, you still have to figure out why you get an error with the real data, but that's a different story. Thus, we will often learn the principles with clean data, but then you need to apply the knowledge to a real data set.

Many R packages provide access to data. For example, do you know the Gapminder project? To generate empirical insights about different areas of social life, the Gapminder project collected a broad data set and they created interactive graphs to visualize their findings. Hans Rosling, Anna Rosling Rönnlund, and Ola Rosling initiated the project, and they show us, for example, that income is associated with life expectancy worldwide. The bubble charts from the Gapminder data are very famous to show this association: the graphs display how life expectancy and income (gross domestic product per capita) are related but differ between continents. Figure 1.2 shows the bubble chart for the year 2007 that I made with the ggplot2 package.

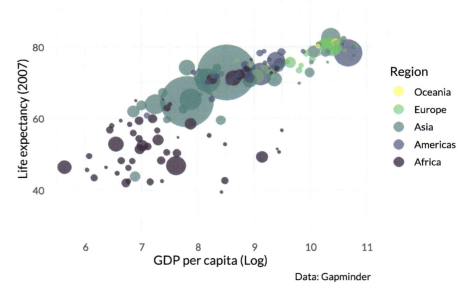

Fig. 1.2: Gapminder bubble chart

Regardless of the bubble chart, the gapminder R package gives you access to the data that I used for this graph. Or consider the PracticeR package. It contains data from the General Social Science survey that we will prepare and analyze. In Chapter 4, I will provide more information about the data and I introduce further data sources (e.g.,

European Social Survey). Thus, even though I use toy data to illustrate how code works, there are many opportunities to apply and extend your R skills.

Finally, let me give you some advice regarding your R learning strategy. Try to understand what the code does and how R "thinks". At some point, code will get longer, more complicated, and it will become harder to capture what is happening under the hood. Please, do not feel intimidated – we will work on several strategies to work with code, many R packages provide cheat sheets with the most important commands, and you need not memorize code to create awesome things with R. We will circle back to this point in Chapter 4, since in the beginning the R code will not be complicated. Maybe one recommendation is already worth emphasizing: There is a simple solution to help your future self understand what code does, add descriptive comments if you start to write code.

```
# I add comments for important steps
# Do the same for your future self
# Try to be explicit and outline what the code does
```

A last piece of personal advice: Play around with the code. The PracticeR package gives you access to the code of each chapter. Please, do not just copy the code without also applying and fooling around with it. Trust me, you will gain deeper insights if you write code and apply the discussed concepts. For example, use a different data set and rerun the discussed steps. Sometimes I will outline more than one solution giving you an idea that there are always several ways to solve a problem. But what will your document look like if you fooled around and tried a lot of things? The document gets messy, and you may wish to have a clean version as a summary of the chapter. For this reason, going beyond the convenience, I included the code of each chapter in the PracticeR package.

There are more guiding principles. For example, all chapters are supposed to start in a similar way. Before we dive into the topic of a chapter, I outline in more detail what the section contains and highlight which data set and which packages are needed. But before I can stick to this rule, we need to get in touch with R.

2 First steps in R

Learning R is a tough cookie. Most students in the social sciences have little programming background, which is one of the reasons why some struggle to learn R. This book will not cover how to program in detail, but introduces the basics of the R programming language (base R). To this end, this chapter is your savior, yet also the dragon you must slay in order to make the first substantial steps with R. Why is that?

– In Section 2.1, I show you how to install R and RStudio. This chapter will be a savior because we work with RStudio, which is an integrated development environment (IDE) for R. RStudio has many cool features that supports us to write code, get help, or import files. This section outlines in detail its most important features: We learn how to send code to R and we will examine the differences between R and RStudio which will help you to learn and conquer R. We will take advantages of RStudio, which is why I skipped some of the typical and sometimes complicated first steps (e.g., to import data, see Chapter 5) when it comes to analyzing data. RStudio simplifies such tasks, but unfortunately this does not mean that this chapter will be a piece of cake, since you must defeat base R in order to progress.

– Section 2.2 will emphasize why knowledge about base R is useful to speed up the learning curve. R is an object-oriented programming language and we need to learn some of the core basics first. For example, we will create objects, we will manipulate them, and we will write a simple function with R. Depending on your prior experience, this might be the toughest section of the book, because learning the core basics of R seems vaguely related to the typical steps of applied research. The good news is, I try to cut this part down to its core, since I believe that learning by practice is the most efficient way.

– In Section 2.3, we apply our base R skills. I will outline more details about data types and structures and we learn how to filter data. In the social sciences, we are often interested in sub-groups and examine, for example, if there are any significant differences between these groups. To prepare a subgroup analysis, we need to learn how data can be sliced by applying our base R knowledge.

2.1 Introducing R and RStudio

R is an open-source software for Windows, Mac, and a variety of UNIX systems. Go online and install the latest R distribution for your system with the installer from the R Project website.

```
# Download and install R:
# https://www.r-project.org/
```

https://doi.org/10.1515/9783110704976-002

The comprehensive R archive network (CRAN) provides several servers to download the installer. As outlined on their website, CRAN is "a network of ftp and web servers around the world that store identical, up-to-date, versions of code and documentation for R". Choose one of the CRAN servers, but make sure to download an executable installer which contains everything to start with. Execute the file, install R and, after the installation is finished, go to the Windows Start Menu (or the application folder on Mac) and open R. As Figure 2.1 displays, the *R console* opens and you can interact with R if you insert code into the console after the prompt (>).

```
R version 4.0.3 (2020-10-10) -- "Bunny-Wunnies Freak Out"
Copyright (C) 2020 The R Foundation for Statistical Computing
Platform: x86_64-w64-mingw32/x64 (64-bit)

R is free software and comes with ABSOLUTELY NO WARRANTY.
You are welcome to redistribute it under certain conditions.
Type 'license()' or 'licence()' for distribution details.

  Natural language support but running in an English locale

R is a collaborative project with many contributors.
Type 'contributors()' for more information and
'citation()' on how to cite R or R packages in publications.

Type 'demo()' for some demos, 'help()' for on-line help, or
'help.start()' for an HTML browser interface to help.
Type 'q()' to quit R.

> 1 + 2
[1] 3
> print("Hello World")
[1] "Hello World"
>
```

Fig. 2.1: The R console

Do me favor: Test if everything works by using R as a calculator. As Figure 2.1 also illustrates, use your keyboard, type a mathematical equation into the console and press enter. R solves the equation and returns the result via the console. Maybe this sounds like a weird task, but it underlines that R has no graphical interface; R is a programming language. As long as we do not install any other software, we can only use the console to work with R. The next console shows several examples of how to use R as a calculator.

```
# Basic operations: +,-,*,/
5 * 5
```

```
#> [1] 25
```

```
# Powers
3^2
```

```
#> [1] 9
```

```r
# Square root
sqrt(16)
```

```
#> [1] 4
```

```r
# Natural logarithm
log(1)
```

```
#> [1] 0
```

```r
# Exponential function
exp(1)
```

```
#> [1] 2.718282
```

We apply functions to work with R in the same way as we apply exponential or other mathematical functions. To give you another prominent example, use the `print()` function and let R print the text string "Hello World". Do not forget the parentheses of the function and the quotation marks around the text string ("Hello World"). Otherwise, R does not know which words it should print.

```r
# Let R talk
print("Hello world")
```

```
#> [1] "Hello world"
```

Perhaps you are wondering why you should examine such code? It demonstrates the differences between R and RStudio and you should use R at least once to get a feeling for these differences. A lot of people work with RStudio because it provides major advantages to R. To name a few: RStudio makes it easier to read code because it contains a code editor that displays code in colors (syntax highlighting); RStudio provides several features for data visualization; and RStudio makes it convenient to import data. As an open-source software, RStudio is free to use for non-commercial purposes and in Practice R we work only with it. But enough of the flattering. Go to the RStudio website to download and install the latest desktop version for your operating system.

```r
# Install RStudio (from Posit):
# https://posit.co/downloads/
```

After the installation is done, open RStudio and you will see a similar window as Figure 2.2 displays. To make the introduction a bit smoother, Figure 2.2 highlights the different panes (windows) in RStudio with text labels and colored boxes. There are only three panes the first time you open RStudio: The *R console*, the *Environment*, and the *Files and more* pane. The panes on the right side contain further panes, which we will discuss in the end. First, we will focus on the code pane and the R console.

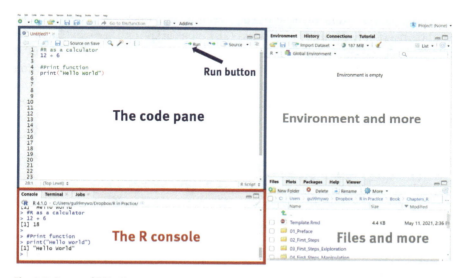

Fig. 2.2: Panes of RStudio

2.1.1 The Code pane and the R console

We run code from an *R script* and RStudio has integrated a code pane for this purpose. RStudio sends the code to R and you can see the results in the R console. After you have created a new R script, RStudio looks exactly like Figure 2.2. To create a new R script click on *File* in the tool bar, choose *New File* and then select *R script*. After you have created the script, the code pane appears and shows an empty R script.

How do we work with an R script? Of course, you may use the console as well, but an R script makes your code reusable. As Figure 2.2 highlights, RStudio has a *Run button* in the code pane to execute code. For instance, use RStudio as a calculator and insert one of the mathematical equations in the R script. Next, click inside the line of code that should be executed and then press the Run button. RStudio executes the code and jumps to the next line. Do not forget to click inside the line before you push the Run button. Alternatively, select an entire line of the code that is supposed to be executed solitarily. RStudio runs this selected code as well, but does not jump to the next line (of code).

14 —— 2 First steps in R

There is also a helpful shortcut to execute code. Click inside the line of code and press <Ctlr/Cmd> + <Enter> on your keyboard. Try to memorize this shortcut because it is faster than clicking a button. I assure you, the shortcut will become second nature.

```
# Run code via the shortcut (Windows/Mac):
# Press: <Ctlr/Cmd> + <Enter>
```

Can you do me a second favor? Run the print() function once more, but this time in RStudio. Insert only the first four letters – just type 'prin' and see what happens. RStudio shows code suggestions and explanations, as Figure 2.3 displays. RStudio suggests all kinds of code that start with these letters and the *auto-completion* function helps us finish the line. R does not make our lives easy in terms of writing code, but RStudio does by providing suggestions to complete the code. Alternatively, press <TAB> to activate the auto-completion.

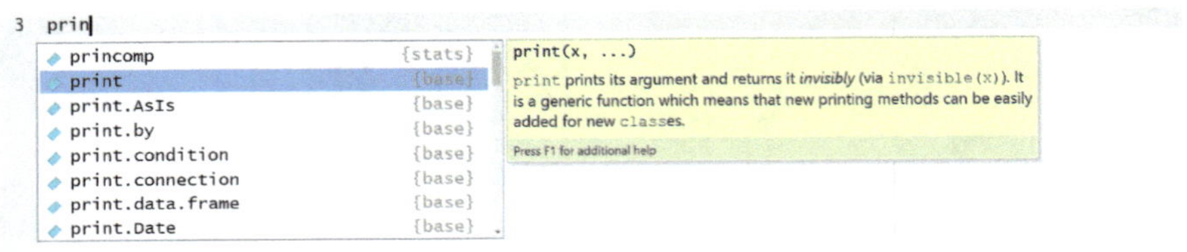

Fig. 2.3: Auto-completion in RStudio

Auto-completion is amazing and works for characters (e.g., quotation marks) as well. RStudio automatically adds the second if you insert the first parenthesis of the print function. I guess you are less excited than I am: Imagine writing code but the code returns an error due to a missing parenthesis. Thus, you need to check whether the code contains both opening and closing parenthesis of the entire script. I can tell from my experience that this really is a tedious task. I made such mistakes many times when I started to learn a programming language and auto-completion reduces such pain.

Error messages give you some insights as to why the error occurs: For instance, characters in the print function need to be enclosed by quotation marks. But what does R return if we forget them?

```
# Do not forget the quotation marks ("" or '') to print a string
print(Hello)
```

```
#> Error in print(Hello): object 'Hello' not found
```

R searches the Hello object and does not know that we wanted to print a string. Error messages are often cryptic and hard to decipher – especially, but not exclusively, for beginners. Do not feel discouraged by a cryptic error message. We will deal with typical error messages in the tutorial of this chapter, but keep in mind that R will print a plus sign (+) if the code is not complete. Say we run print("Hello" without the closing parenthesis. R waits patiently until it gets one. At some point this might be the reason why nothing seems to happen if you run the code, go to the console and press the Escape key (<ESC>) to abort.

R has a great community, which is why you will often find a solution if you search the web. Unfortunately, R is also a frequently appearing letter of the alphabet which makes it necessary to combine the key words with R (e.g., regression analysis in R) to get the search results that you are actually looking for. Moreover, RStudio may also display an error message next to the code or highlight a potential problem. Feel free and use R directly if such features seem irrelevant, but RStudio helps us a lot to reduce the pain of learning R.

The smaller panes on the right side contain several tabs. Most of them outline their purpose with their name. We will talk about those further panes later, but as a new R user we should at least get in touch with several tabs of the Files and more pane: The next subsections introduce the Files, the Plots, the Packages, the Help, and further panes.

2.1.2 The Files pane

The Files pane shows the files of your working directory. The latter points to the path on your computer where R searches for and exports files to (e.g., to import data, export a graph). You probably have no idea which working directory you currently use. R returns the current working directory if you run the getwd() function.

```
# The getwd() function returns the current working directory
getwd()
```

```
#> [1] "C:/Users/Edgar/R/Practice_R"
```

At the moment, RStudio shows you the path and the files of the default working directory, which can be changed in the settings of RStudio. As Figure 2.4 displays, the files pane shows you the path on your computer that leads to this directory (in the head of the pane) and makes it possible to navigate from one folder to another. Later, we will import data and export graphs, which will make it necessary to adjust the working directory. However, even now it would be nice if you have access to all your R scripts in one place (e.g., all scripts for this book). Create a new folder for your R scripts.

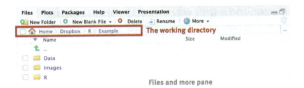

Fig. 2.4: The Files pane

Next, you can set the working directory manually by using the `setwd()` function with the path to your working directory. Depending on your operating system and your folder, the path to the folder may look like the paths displayed in the next console, but hold on, there is no need to insert paths manually.

```
# Windows
setwd("C:/Users/Edgar/R/Scripts")
# Mac
setwd("~/R/Scripts/")
```

RStudio sets your working directory without the hassle of writing down the entire path. Navigate to your directory via the Files pane, press the *More* button and click on *Set as working directory*. Now, look at your console. RStudio runs the `setwd()` function and inserted the chosen path. Certainly, you do not want to repeat that step the next time you open your script. So, copy your code from the console and paste it into your script.

Maybe you do not realize it yet, but setting a working directory manually can be painful. Every typo in the path leads to an error. What happens if you move the folder to a new place? You get an error message because the path is no longer valid. If your script points to your working directory, please make sure that you put the command at the top of your script. Putting the working directory in a prominent position makes it easier for your future self and other people to adjust it. We learn how to improve this awkward situation by using projects in RStudio (Chapter 4), which makes it possible to work without the hassle of setting a working directory manually.

In addition, the files pane also comes with several convenient functions. You can create a new folder, delete or rename files, all without leaving RStudio. The *More* button lets you copy and move files, copy the folder path to the clipboard, or opens the folder in a new window to name just a few options. Thus, create a structure and manage your files directly from RStudio. Create several folders in your working directory and save your R scripts in a folder named `R`, your data comes into the `data` folder, and so on. A simple structure helps to increase our workflow and stay organized. In Chapter 4, we talk about this topic in more detail.

2.1.3 The Plots pane

As the name reveals, graphs are displayed in the Plots pane. For example, the barplot() function creates a bar graph. Copy the code from the next console and execute it. The bar graph depicts random numbers that I have included in the code. Never mind how the code works, we will cover that in the next sections. As Figure 2.5 illustrates, the Plot tab shows up with the graph after the code is executed.

```
# Copy and run the following code to generate a bar plot!
barplot(c(a = 22, b = 28, c = 33, d = 40, e = 55))
```

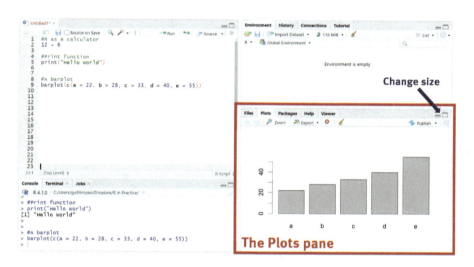

Fig. 2.5: The Plots pane

What else can we do with the plots pane? For example, sometimes the preview is too small to see the details of a graph properly. RStudio has a small button to zoom in – it opens a new window that lets you adjust the size. Or consider the export menu; at some point we will save a graph as a file and RStudio has integrated an export function. We learn more about those possibilities when we focus on visualizations (Chapter 7). For the moment just keep in mind that such options exist.

We can zoom in to get a larger view of a graph, but RStudio gives you a lot of freedom to arrange and resize each pane. Adjust the size of a pane manually by drawing it smaller (or larger). For now this might be a fun fact, but at one point you may wish to have a larger pane to examine a graph or more space for the script. The same applies

18 —— 2 First steps in R

for the integrated tutorials, which we can adjust in size as well. To get access to the book's tutorials and materials, we need to learn how to install R packages.

2.1.4 The Packages pane

Packages aim to improve R and its functionality. The Packages pane lists all packages that are installed on your computer. If you have installed R for the first time, the packages tab lists only core R packages; further packages need to be installed manually. Use the code `install.packages("name")` to download and install a package from CRAN. By running the `install.packages()` function, R searches the package, downloads the files, and installs them locally.

```
# Install a package with:
# install.packages("package_name")
# Caution: The package name needs to be enclosed in quotation marks
```

The next console prints the code to install the `palmerpenguins` and `tidyverse` packages. The `palmerpenguins` package shares data about penguins (Horst et al., 2022); and the `tidyverse` package includes several packages (e.g., `dplyr`, `ggplot2`, `forcats`) to analyze data (Wickham, 2022d). After the installation of a package, the R console may return some cryptic information. The next output shows what my console returned.

```
install.packages("palmerpenguins")
install.packages("tidyverse")

#>Try URL 'https://cran.rstudio.com/bin/4.0/palmerpenguins_0.1.0.tgz'
#>Content type 'application/x-gzip' length 3001738 bytes (2.9 MB)
#>==================================================
#>downloaded 2.9 MB

#>The downloaded binary packages are in
#>   /var/folders/0v/T//Rtmp4z29r0/downloaded_packages
```

Cryptic, but it seems as though the packages were installed, because R returns the installation path of the package, how large the package is, and further details of the download and installation process. R has finished the installation process if you see the prompt again. After the installation is done, search within the Packages pane, both packages should now be listed there. Give it a try and install the `palmerpenguins` and the `tidyverse` packages on your own machine. We need both packages anyway.

There is second important command to make a package available each time you start or restart R. You must load a package with the `library()` function before you can use it. Remember, you have to install a package only once, but each time you start a new R session, you must load it with the `library()` function. Often, R does not return anything after you have loaded a package; everything works fine as long as R does not return an error message.

```
# Packages need to be installed only once
# But: Load a package each time you start a new R session!
library(palmerpenguins)
```

Some packages return start-up messages. Consider the message from the `tidyverse` package. It shows which packages are loaded (attached) and their possible conflicts with other packages and base R.

```
library(tidyverse)
```

```
#> Attaching packages --------------------------------- tidyverse 1.3.1

#> v ggplot2 3.3.6      v purrr   0.3.4
#> v tibble  3.1.7      v dplyr   1.0.9
#> v tidyr   1.2.0      v stringr 1.4.0
#> v readr   2.1.2      v forcats 0.5.1

#> Conflicts ------------------------------------ tidyverse_conflicts()
#> x dplyr::filter() masks stats::filter()
#> x dplyr::lag()    masks stats::lag()
```

There are many R packages and some packages have identical function names. For example, the `dplyr` package has a `filter()` function, but so does the R `stats` package. R picks the function that was loaded last. To differentiate between those functions, we separate the package name and the function with two colons (e.g. `dplyr::filter`). In Practice R, you will see the same notation occasionally to make it clear which package and function we are talking about.

Installing packages is not complicated but can be tricky. Suppose you try to install a package. R tells you that several other packages are needed and asks for permission to automatically install them. Unfortunately, this process sometimes fails. You will get an error message when the required package is (still) not installed. In this situation you need to install the dependencies on your own. In other instances, you need to update some of the packages that are already installed, and R asks for your permission to update. Please do so and get the latest CRAN version. RStudio helps you also with this task. The Packages pane has an Update button which shows all packages that can be updated. Before we can continue and inspect further panes, you need to install the PracticeR package, which gives you access to the materials and tutorials of this book.

The Practice R package

The PracticeR package is not available on CRAN, which is why you cannot install it directly, but you can download it from GitHub. GitHub is a version control system and gives people access to code. To install a package from GitHub, you must install the devtools package first, because the latter makes it possible to install a package from GitHub (Wickham, Hester, Chang, et al., 2022).

```
# The devtools package let you install packages from GitHub
install.packages("devtools")
```

Next, use the install_github() function from the devtools package to install the PracticeR package. The function needs the web address of the package. In our case, the following code installs the PracticeR package.

```
# Install the PracticeR package
devtools::install_github("edgar-treischl/PracticeR")
```

After the package has been installed, go the *Environment and more* pane. You will find the *Tutorial* pane which shows all available tutorials, including the tutorials from the PracticeR package. Figure 2.6 guides your way to the tutorial pane. Click on a corresponding *Start tutorial* button to run one of the tutorials. This runs the code that creates the tutorial and starts the tutorial in the pane (or you can open the tutorials in a browser). After you have finished the tutorial, you have to click on the *Stop* button in the tutorial pane to stop the code from running in the background.

Fig. 2.6: The Tutorial pane

In addition to the tutorials, the `PracticeR` package also has some convenient functions. Use the `show_script()` function to get the source code of Practice R. The function copies the code for each chapter, opens a new tab in RStudio, and inserts the code in a new script. If the function gets no valid input, it returns an error message with all available script names.

```
# Load a chapter script with show_script()
library(PracticeR)
show_script("chapter02")
```

R is an open-source software and some of the described code (and packages) may change in the future. For this reason, the `show_script()` function downloads the latest version of the source code that is discussed in this book. In consequence, the source code may slightly differ compared to the printed version, but I will mention it in the script if an update occurred.

Of course, you can download all book materials from the `PracticeR` website. However, there is no need to Google the website or copy the link to the `PracticeR` website manually. All important links of the book are available via the `show_link()` function, which returns the link in the console and opens a new browser window with the link. For example, insert `pr_website` and inspect the `PracticeR` website. In this book I set the option `browse` to `FALSE`, which prevents the browser for being opened and returns the link only. If the function gets no valid input, it returns an error message with all available key words.

```
# Show_link opens a browser with the link
show_link("pr_website", browse = FALSE)
```

```
#> [1] "https://edgar-treischl.github.io/PracticeR/"
```

2.1.5 The Help pane

Sometimes we have no clue how code works and this is where the Help pane and help files come into play. Use the help pane to search for unfamiliar code. All functions come with a help file that contains a description and further information (e.g., options). Scroll down the help file, because it usually includes examples at the end of the document. The code illustrates how a function works and such examples often make it easier to apply them. You may run examples from the online help with the `example()` function. For instance, consider some example bar plots.

```
# Run examples from the online help (press ESC to abort)
example(barplot)
```

Moreover, ask R for help. You can activate the help pane if you add a question mark (?) before the code itself (e.g., ?barplot). Alternatively, search for a keyword within the help files, as the next console summarizes.

```
# Ask for help
?barplot
# Search for keywords
help.search("keyword")
```

Vignettes and RStudio's Addins provide even more help. The next info box introduces both briefly and discusses the addin from the pkgsearch package (Csárdi & Salmon, 2022).

ℹ **Vignettes and Rstudio's Addins**

There are additional sources that support you to work with R, among them are package *vignettes* and RStudio's *Addins*. Vignettes are extremely useful to get a deeper understanding about a package. They are written from the author's perspective and intend to show in detail how a package works. Vignettes can be viewed in RStudio and you have access to the described code as well. So far, we have not yet systematically dealt with a package, and I will highlight several vignettes in the course of the book, but you should be aware that such resources exits. The browseVignettes() function displays all available vignettes from a package in your browser; the vignette() function returns a specific vignette in the viewer; and the edit() function opens the script and lets you copy and paste the code of a vignette. You are not familiar with the dplyr package (which is a part of the tidyverse), but you can use the package anyway to inspect how vignettes work.

```
#Browse vignettes from a package:
browseVignettes("dplyr")
#Inspect a vignette in the viewer by calling its name:
vignette("dplyr")
#Edit the code from a vignette:
edit(vignette("dplyr"))
```

Moreover, some R packages provide Addins for RStudio, which let you run advanced code and functions without writing the code. For example, the pkgsearch package has a graphical interface to search for packages on CRAN. This might not be necessary now, but imagine you have no idea whether there is a package for a specific task. The addin let you search packages, explore new packages, and shows the top packages on CRAN. Thus, such addins provide a convenient way to work with RStudio and run code by clicking on a button. After the corresponding package is installed and RStudio is restarted, addins will be listed in the RStudio's addins menu.

2.1.6 Further panes

The *Environment and more* pane encompasses several panes – it contains the *Environment*, the *History*, and the *Connections* panes. We will not discuss them in detail, but a few words may clarify their purpose.

The Environment pane shows information about the working environment. The environment pane is tricky to explain since we have not created any objects yet. We will come back to this point later, but note that the pane lists objects, for example, a data set that we have imported in an active session. This pane also helps us to import data and get rid of objects from the workspace.

The History pane lists code that has been executed. Since we just started to work with R, your history pane is (almost) empty. However, a long working session is not required to understand why a history pane is valuable. Say we analyze data. We tried to achieve something new, but at some point the code crashes. Or suppose you deleted the code by accident. The history pane makes it possible to go back in time. We retrieve code that worked or we can try to figure out where the mistake came from. Moreover, you can also travel back in time with the arrow keys. Click into the console and press the <arrow up> button on your keyboard once or several times to inspect the history.

The Connections pane is not important for us in this book, because it lets us connect RStudio with different applications. Suppose you work with an online database. To retrieve or to send data to the database, the connections pane helps to connect your local computer with the database.

We come back to the functions of RStudio's panes later, but let me outline what happens if you close RStudio as last tip. Save your script and close RStudio. Be prepared, there might be a pop-up that asks you if you want to save your work space in an .RData file in your working directory. We will learn more about why it is not useful to save our work space in Chapter 5, but in terms of reproducibility it should be enough to say that we want R to start as a blank slate. Our old work from the past should be gone for good if we start new, because otherwise it may interfere with the most recent analysis. If you get bothered by the pop-up, go to RStudio settings (Tools > Global Options) and remove the check mark from restoring the work space at start up and tell RStudio that it never should save the work space on exit. Since we have established a basic understanding of RStudio, we can now focus on base R.

2.2 Base R

R is a programming language and offers more possibilities than being software alone. You can achieve great things without having a proper background as a programmer, but a basic understanding of base R is nonetheless important. It can be abstract and frustrating to learn base R. Please, do not worry, I try to cut this part down to its core. However, we need some basics about *objects* and *functions*.

2.2.1 Objects

R is an object-oriented programming language which means that we must understand which types of objects exist and how we manipulate them with the help of functions. In R, we create new objects by using the *assignment operator* (<-). Suppose we analyzed data and we want to have access to these results in a later step. We create the object by assigning the results of a calculation to the object (e.g., `result`).

```
# The object result refers to 5*5
result <- 5 * 5
result
```

```
#> [1] 25
```

R does not print the result of the assignment and lists your objects in the environment pane. You must call the object once more, as the previous console shows, or use parenthesis as the next console illustrates. Furthermore, we may overwrite the object by rerunning the code and instead of a number, the object may also refer to a character string.

```
# R does not print the result of the assignment
(result <- "Hello from the other side!")
```

```
#> [1] "Hello from the other side!"
```

We use the assignment operator not to save numbers; technically more accurate, we create a binding that refers to the number, even though I say that we saved the object to keep things as simple as possible. We create a binding to all sorts of objects, such as the code to make a graph, the binding to data that we import, or save a calculation result as an object. In all these instances, we use the assignment operator.

By assigning values to objects, we can manipulate them. As the next output shows, we may run basic calculations: assign numbers to objects (a and b), build the sum of these objects, and save the `result` again. Now, the object contains the result of the simple computation, but the same applies if you import data or if you assign a graph to an object.

```
# AB(C) of the assignment operator
a <- 5
b <- 6
```

```
# The result
```

```
result <- a + b
result
```

```
#> [1] 11
```

We create new objects, manipulate them, or compare them. By applying mathematical operators, R compares the objects and returns a Boolean expression that indicates whether the comparison is TRUE or FALSE. To this end, we compare whether an object is less than (or equal to), greater than (or equal to), exactly equal to, or not equal to.

```
# Compare objects:
# Is a less (<) than (or equal to =) b
a <= b
```

```
#> [1] TRUE
```

```
# Is a greater (>) than (or equal to =) b
a >= b
```

```
#> [1] FALSE
```

```
# Is a equal to (==) b
a == b
```

```
#> [1] FALSE
```

```
# Is a not equal to (!=) b
a != b
```

```
#> [1] TRUE
```

R provides us with the corresponding results of the binding each time we call the object. Especially during advanced analysis steps, we often save the results as a new object. The assignment operator seems a bit bulky in the beginning but assigning objects will become second nature. Maybe an RStudio shortcut helps to increase the learning process.

```
# Assign like a Pro, press:
#<Alt> + <-> (Windows)
```

```
#<Option> + <-> (Unix/Mac)
# The assignment operator will appear out of nothing
```

One last recommendation regarding object names. It is up to you how objects are named, but R is case sensitive (a versus A) and has restrictions for object names. A name may contain letters, numbers, points, and underscores, but cannot start with a number or contain special characters (e.g., $). Perceive this restriction as an important convention, since it forces us to provide a specific and descriptive name for an object (and the same applies for variable names). The make.names() function illustrates this point. It returns syntactically valid names and underlines that R does not allow numbers and special characters.

```
# No numbers
make.names(names = "1.wave")
```

```
#> [1] "X1.wave"
```

```
# No special characters as names
make.names(names = "income_$")
```

```
#> [1] "income_."
```

```
# Even if a name is valid, try to provide a descriptive, short name
make.names(names = "an_object_should_describe_its_content")
```

```
#> [1] "an_object_should_describe_its_content"
```

2.2.2 Functions

Depending on the type of object, we use different functions to manipulate them. This sounds complex, but applying functions in R is not difficult. We have already applied functions such as print(). Within the parentheses of each function, we must provide the input for the function (here a text string) and options (optional arguments) of the function, separated by commas. For example, the quote option lets us determine how strings are printed.

```
# RStudio suggests also the input of a function (e.g. object name)
my_string <- "Hello"
print(my_string, quote = FALSE)
```

```
#> [1] Hello
```

Let's see what this means by exploring base R functions. Say we need a running number. The *combine* (`c()`) function helps us with this task, because we can combine several objects to a running number (`running_number`). By applying the `c()` function, all values within the parentheses are combined to an *atomic vector*, a one-dimensional data array.

```
# Combine function
running_number <- c(1, 2, 3, 4, 5, 6, 7, 8, 9, 10)
running_number
```

```
#>  [1]  1  2  3  4  5  6  7  8  9 10
```

Objects, functions, or the assignment operator are not made to scare you. They will help you to do very useful things. For example, some functions reduce your workload. I generated the running number by hand. I was overambitious, since it is foolish to type each number tediously by hand. The next console shows the last example again, but this time I provide a list of numbers and R does the work for me. R counts from one to ten and all we have to do is set a starting and an endpoint within the `c()` function.

```
# Set a start and endpoint
running_number <- c(1:10)
running_number
```

```
#>  [1]  1  2  3  4  5  6  7  8  9 10
```

A *sequence* and a *repetition* function work in similar ways and we can let R do the boring stuff again. R creates a sequence from zero to ten with the `seq()` function and we can adjust the increment of the sequence with the `by` option.

```
# The sequence function
seq(0, 10, by = 2)
```

```
#> [1]  0  2  4  6  8 10
```

In terms of a repetition, the `rep()` function returns each element a certain number of times. The `times` option tells R how many times the repetition loops through the cycle, while the `each` option tells R how often each element is repeated.

```
# Repeat five times
rep(1:2, times = 5)
```

```
#>   [1] 1 2 1 2 1 2 1 2 1 2
```

```
# Repeat each element five times
rep(1:2, each = 5)
```

```
#>   [1] 1 1 1 1 1 2 2 2 2 2
```

Such tasks seem artificial, because I did not make up a cover story as to why we need to repeat those numbers. It's almost like I said that the function repeats a string, say rep("I am working like a machine!"). When do we need such a repetition? For example, sometimes we need to generate a group number and we can use the repetition function to give all observations of a group a unique indicator, without repeating ourselves. Thus, such functions will help us to reduce the workload. However, functions have more to offer than counting or repeating – we can use them for many different tasks.

Writing a function seems complicated, especially if you have only limited programming experience. The good news is that there is no need to write functions – R and a lot of R packages provide functions which are user-friendly and ready to use. The bad news is that we still need to learn how to write a function because it will help to understand how they work.

Suppose that we want to write a *mean* function. We must tell R what the function should do with each element of the *input vector*. The next output shows you first what the basic code looks like. We tell R that our function should use the input x and we must specify what exactly should happen with each element of x within the *body* (the braces) of the function. Apparently, my first attempt is not working, since I describe only with words what the function should do. However, this gives us the room to focus on the code structure of a function:

```
# The basic structure of a non-functioning function:
```

```
my_fun <- function(x) {
  #  build the sum of x, divided by n
}
```

The next console shows you how a function works based on three steps. First, I create a toy data set instead of talking about a *vector*. It is not necessary to save the input before we write a function, but it helps to visualize that each element of x will enter the function instead of talking about a vector. In the second step, I generate the function. It only returns each element (return(x)) and I assign it as an object (the return_input function). In the last step, I apply the function with the data from the first step.

```r
# 1. The input
data <- c(3, 2, 1, 5, 8, 12, 1)

# 2. Create a function
return_input <- function(x) {
  return(x)
}
# 3. Call and feed the function
return_input(data)
```

```
#> [1]  3  2  1  5  8 12  1
```

In order to calculate the mean, we have to get familiar with two other mathematical functions. The sum() function creates the sum (of a vector), and we count the elements of the vector with the length() function. Applying these functions is not complicated and the next console illustrates how they work. We can hand over some data as input or use the c() function to insert example values. The latter approach shows also that functions can be combined.

```r
# Build the sum
sum(c(1, 2, 3))
```

```
#> [1] 6
```

```r
# The length
length(c(1, 2, 3))
```

```
#> [1] 3
```

Now that we have prepared all steps, we can fill in the ingredients for the mean_function. Instead of returning each x, we have to divide the sum by its length to get the mean and feed it with example data.

```r
# The mean_function
mean_function <- function(data) {
  mean <- sum(data) / length(data) # save and create mean
  return(mean)
}

mean_function(data)
```

```
#> [1] 4.571429
```

Eureka! We improved the first function and now it returns some useful information. Of course, calculating a mean is probably not what you expected from this chapter, and I am sure that you can anticipate how we calculate a mean without writing a function first. The mean() function has been implemented for this purpose. This is not the main point here; we learned how functions work. We can even improve our first result and let R round the values for us. Put the mean() function inside the round() function and by adjusting the digits option, it lets us determine the number of digits that should be returned. This improves the first approach significantly.

```
# The "real" mean
round(mean(data), digits = 2)
```

```
#> [1] 4.57
```

Writing a function is not rocket science. It seems complicated because we are not used to writing functions, using *loops* (to run code repeatedly), or applying other coding tricks. Many core concepts from base R seem more complicated than they are. Using the assignment operator, working with objects, and writing functions is not witchcraft. I learned it and you will succeed at it as well. However, if it was witchcraft, a quote from *Harry Potter* may underline my point of view: "Every great wizard in history has started out as nothing more than we are now: students. If they can do it, why not us?" (Rowling, 2014).

Also, please keep in mind that R has fantastic packages which is why you won't have to dig deep every time you work with R. To be honest, some programming skills help to generate a deeper understanding on how R works, especially if you create something new or advanced. For this reason, we learned how to write a function, but we will not work on our programming skills in general terms. Instead, we will learn core concepts and how to apply them by focusing on specific tasks. To achieve this goal, we need to increase our knowledge about data types and structures first.

2.3 Data types and structures

We learn how to analyze data in the next chapters. We learn how to import, clean, and manipulate it. We will even save our results for the afterlife by creating reports with R. Before we work with data, we need to talk about *data types* and *data structures* in R. A data set may contain different data types, for example:

- Integers (int: 5, 9)
- Real numbers (doubles or dbl: 3.23, 7.44)
- Dates (dates: 2021-01-07) and times (times: 17:04:55 CEST)

- Strings and character vectors (chr: "Hello world")
- Factors (fctr for categorical variables: male, female)
- Logical (lgl: TRUE, FALSE)

However, if you are not sure what kind of object (or data type) you examine, inspect it with the class() function.

```
# Inspect the class of vector x
x <- "Hello world"
class(x)
```

```
#> [1] "character"
```

```
x <- c(TRUE, FALSE)
class(x)
```

```
#> [1] "logical"
```

So far, I have just played around with vectors; I did not explain where these values came from, nor what they illustrate. Working with vectors – and toy data – is useful to understand the main logic behind applied steps. Many packages for data manipulation and analysis will do the hard job for us, but some knowledge about base R helps us to understand how R handles vectors and other *data structures* (e.g., when we import data).

A vector is an example of how data may look like in R. More precisely, it is an example of a one-dimensional data structure. In principle, you could add another dimension and create a matrix or a multidimensional array. Since our goal is applied data analysis, we will mainly work with *data frames* and *tibbles* in this book, but I will also briefly introduce *lists*.

2.3.1 Data frames

Suppose we imported a data set and each row has information about one observation unit (e.g., person, etc.) and each column represents a value of a variable. With the words from the authors of the tidyverse, we say that such a data set is tidy. As Wickham and Grolemund outline: "There are three interrelated rules which make a data set tidy:
1. Each variable must have its own column.
2. Each observation must have its own row.
3. Each value must have its own cell." (Wickham & Grolemund, 2016, p. 149)

32 —— 2 First steps in R

Of course, data must not be tidy and is often messy compared to this description. Nonetheless R has different types of data structures, so let us first explore what a data frame is. Based on the R base logic, we get a data frame (df) if we extend a vector and combine multiple vectors as one object. This sounds complicated: First, we need two vectors of identical length (an identical number of elements) in order to create a data frame. We can apply the c() function to create two example vectors. Next, we combine those vectors with the data.frame() function:

```r
# Create two vectors of identical length
sex <- c("Men", "Women")
age <- c(19, 28)

# Combine them as data.frame
df <- data.frame(sex, age)
df

#>      sex age
#> 1    Men  19
#> 2  Women  28
```

Why do we spend so much time making a data frame, instead of learning how to import data? There are several reasons why we focus on data structures: You will work with different data, and some analysis steps may differ depending on the data structure. Furthermore, knowledge of data structures will reduce your struggle to learn R. Regardless of the language you learn, at some point the code is not running and you will get an error message. If you have no idea what the error means, you copy the message and turn to Google for some help. It is likely that someone else had the same problem and often you will see a reproducible example (*reprex*). A reprex includes a small amount of data and all steps that are necessary to reproduce the error. This gives other people the chance to understand and fix the problem. Thus, you need to understand how a data frame can be generated to follow these leads.

Even though learning how to create a data frame is not vital in the beginning, it is important to understand the logic behind it and you should be aware that you will encounter different data types and structures. Now that we clarified what a data frame is, let me outline the difference between a data frame and a tibble.

2.3.2 Tibble

The short answer is, that a tibble is essentially a data frame, but with some advantages compared to regular data frames. Create a tibble with the corresponding tibble()

function from the `tidyr` package (which is a part of the `tidyverse`). It works the same way as with a data frame and the functions returns the data if we do not assign it.

```
# Create a tibble
library(tidyr)
tibble(
  sex = c("Men", "Women"),
  age = c(19, 28)
)
```

```
#> # A tibble: 2 x 2
#>   sex      age
#>   <chr> <dbl>
#> 1 Men      19
#> 2 Women    28
```

Another form of tibble is a transposed tibble (*tribble*). Transposed tibbles are very useful in creating small snippets of data and are very popular because they are easy to read. People provide tribbles for reprexes, or you can add a tribble if you share your code but not your data. As the console shows, the first line of a tribble is like the head of a table and contains the variable names; each variable starts with the tilde (~) operator, observations are separated with a comma until the last value of the last row.

```
# Transposed tibbles
tribble(
  ~sex, ~age,
  "Men", 19,
  "Women", 28
)
```

```
#> # A tibble: 2 x 2
#>   sex      age
#>   <chr> <dbl>
#> 1 Men      19
#> 2 Women    28
```

In our case there are only minor differences between a tibble and a data frame, which is why I speak most of the time about data frames even if it is a tibble. However, a tibble prints the data type after the variable name, which is a useful feature if you are inspecting unfamiliar data. Moreover, the first line of the console returns the size of the tibble and your console displays only the first ten rows.

34 —— 2 First steps in R

I guess you cannot appreciate the last feature yet. Suppose you inspect a data frame and you call it by its name. R will return the entire data in the console. You scroll up and down to get an idea of what the data contains, and you get frustrated if you cannot find the line with the variable names. Obviously, I am talking about myself, but the tibble returns only the first ten lines (unless the default printing option is changed).

This is a nice feature, but we must examine how the `data.frame()` function behaves in terms of recycled vectors to see the real strength of a tibble. I claimed that vectors need to be of identical length to create a data frame. Look at the next console, I was wrong. It is possible to create a data frame with vectors of different lengths because R recycles vectors.

```
# R recycles vectors
data.frame(a = 1:6, b = 1:3, c = 1:2)
```

```
#>   a b c
#> 1 1 1 1
#> 2 2 2 2
#> 3 3 3 1
#> 4 4 1 2
#> 5 5 2 1
#> 6 6 3 2
```

Base R recycles vectors and because b and c fits nicely into vector a – more precisely, two and three times – we do not get an error message. R recycles vectors b and c and reiterates two and three times to build the data frame. Look what happens if we try to make a tibble with the same vectors:

```
# A tibble does not recycle vectors, unless ...
tibble(a = 1:6, b = 1:3, c = 1:2)
```

```
#> Error:
#> ! Tibble columns must have compatible sizes.
#> * Size 6: Existing data.
#> * Size 3: Column `b`.
#> i Only values of size one are recycled.
```

Nothing. The last code did not even run! Instead, we produced an error – the console warns us that the tibble columns must have compatible sizes and that only values of size one are recycled. I am pretty sure that this example sounds artificial. You probably ask yourself why you would create a data frame (or a tibble) anyway?

How about an example: Suppose we generate a new variable and we need an indicator for six different groups. Thus, we assign numeric values for each group, but unfortunately we made a mistake and assigned only two values instead of six. In a worst-case scenario, we may not even realize the mistake because R recycles the vector without a warning. R recycles vectors because it has advantages in terms of programming and how fast R executes code. However, we do not want to recycle the vectors because this may introduce mistakes. Thus, tibbles support us to manage data frames and a vector will not be recycled unless it has the exact same length or if we assign each element the same (constant) value. Tibbles are also handy when it comes to variable names, which we will explore later (see Chapter 5.1). Instead, we get in touch with lists.

2.3.3 Lists

Lists are much more flexible than data frames or tibbles and can contain any kind of object. As the next output illustrates, lists are created with the `list()` function and in our case it contains three different objects: a running number with integers and two vectors, one with letters, and one with names. Each object of this list has a different length. Thus, a list makes it possible to combine heterogeneous input in one object.

```
# A list may combine heterogeneous input
my_list <- list(
  "numbers" = 1:10,
  "letters" = letters[1:3],
  "names" = c("Bruno", "Justin", "Miley", "Ariana")
)
my_list

#> $numbers
#>  [1]  1  2  3  4  5  6  7  8  9 10
#>
#> $letters
#> [1] "a" "b" "c"
#>
#> $names
#> [1] "Bruno"  "Justin" "Miley"  "Ariana"
```

Lists are very flexible, but harder to handle in terms of data management – especially when we try to retrieve or manipulate data. Most of the time we work with data frames and tibbles, but you need to be aware that different data structures behave differently. To this end, we will discover ultimately how we slice data and get access to single values of a data frame, a tibble, and a list.

36 —— 2 First steps in R

Slice data

Let's pretend we wanted to do some operations depending on whom we observe. First I use a column vector with the names of persons, which makes it easier to grasp the logic behind it.

```
# How do we slice a vector?
x <- c("Bruno", "Justin", "Miley", "Ariana")
```

To get access to values of x, we must index or slice it with brackets. For instance, x[1] returns the first element of x, x[2] the second one, and so on. Of course, we can apply other tricks from base R to retrieve values faster. For example, x[-3] returns all names except from the third element or x[2:3] slices the vector from the second to the third element. Slicing is not complicated in the case of a one-dimensional vector, and the next console shows the results of the discussed steps.

```
# The first element
x[1]
```

```
#> [1] "Bruno"
```

```
# The third element
x[3]
```

```
#> [1] "Miley"
```

```
# All elements except the third
x[-3]
```

```
#> [1] "Bruno"   "Justin" "Ariana"
```

```
# From the second to the third element
x[2:3]
```

```
#> [1] "Justin" "Miley"
```

Slicing gets more complicated with a data frame, but there is no difference between tibbles and data frames. Say we have observed the name, birth year, and sex of the following persons:

```
#Example data
df <- tibble::tribble(
    ~names, ~year,     ~sex,
    "Bruno",  1985,   "male",
    "Justin", 1994,   "male",
    "Miley",  1992, "female",
    "Ariana", 1993, "female"
)
```

We need to specify which *row* and *column* to slice. The first number refers to the row; the second number refers to column. Thus, df[1, 1] returns the first element of the first row and column.

```
# The first row and the first column
df[1, 1]
```

```
#> # A tibble: 1 x 1
#>    names
#>    <chr>
#> 1 Bruno
```

However, if you do not provide a number, all rows and columns are returned. As the next console shows, df[1,] returns the first row, but all columns of the data frame; while we get all rows of the first column with df[, 1].

```
# The first row
df[1, ]
```

```
#> # A tibble: 1 x 3
#>    names  year sex
#>    <chr> <dbl> <chr>
#> 1 Bruno  1985 male
```

```
# The first column
df[, 1]
```

```
#> # A tibble: 4 x 1
#>    names
#>    <chr>
#> 1 Bruno
```

```
#> 2 Justin
#> 3 Miley
#> 4 Ariana
```

Of course, we can apply the same tricks as we have seen before. We can provide a starting and an endpoint or call all rows except the one we mark with a minus (-) sign.

```
# Start and endpoint
df[1:2, ]
```

```
#> # A tibble: 2 x 3
#>    names    year sex
#>    <chr>   <dbl> <chr>
#> 1 Bruno    1985 male
#> 2 Justin   1994 male
```

```
# All elements except the first row
df[-1, ]
```

```
#> # A tibble: 3 x 3
#>    names    year sex
#>    <chr>   <dbl> <chr>
#> 1 Justin   1994 male
#> 2 Miley    1992 female
#> 3 Ariana   1993 female
```

The next console highlights a special case: we can slice an entire column vector with the dollar ($) sign and the column name; keep this in mind because we apply the same principle when we refer to variables in later steps.

```
# Get (slice) a column vector with $
df$names
```

```
#> [1] "Bruno"  "Justin" "Miley"  "Ariana"
```

Unfortunately, slicing a list is a bit trickier because it has a nested structure. Consider the my_list once more:

```
# Consider what my_list contains
my_list
```

```
#> $numbers
#>  [1]  1  2  3  4  5  6  7  8  9 10
#>
#> $letters
#> [1] "a" "b" "c"
#>
#> $names
#> [1] "Bruno"  "Justin" "Miley"  "Ariana"
```

If we index on the highest level, R returns the corresponding element of the list. Thus, `my_list[1]` returns the first list, not the vector.

```
# my_list[1] returns the first element (list), not the vector!
my_list[1]
```

```
#> $numbers
#>  [1]  1  2  3  4  5  6  7  8  9 10
```

Provide additional brackets if you want to extract the vector:

```
# Get the values of the first list
my_list[[1]]
```

```
#>  [1]  1  2  3  4  5  6  7  8  9 10
```

To make this point clearer, suppose you must extract the first three elements of the first list:

```
# First three elements of the first list
my_list[[1]][1:3]
```

```
#> [1] 1 2 3
```

Say we make a mistake and execute `my_list[1][1:3]` instead. R returns the first list, but the list contains only one object due to the slicing, the list of numbers. To put it differently, the first list has only one element – the list of numbers – the second and the third element of the list do no longer exist (R returns NULL) because we slice it.

```
# You need to take the nested structure of a list into account
my_list[1][1:3]
```

```
#> $numbers
#>  [1]  1  2  3  4  5  6  7  8  9 10
#>
#> $<NA>
#> NULL
#>
#> $<NA>
#> NULL
```

Slicing data and knowledge about base R really help us to handle and to analyze data, but this probably seems abstract in the beginning. Let me give you one last example to illustrate how slicing and knowledge about base R supports us in analyzing data. The palmerpenguins package is made for teaching purposes and contains a data set with variables about three different penguin species. We may use the penguins data and get in touch with the penguin species Adélie, Chinstrap, and Gentoo.

Say we want to analyze each species separately listed in the penguins data and from the summary statistics section we know that there are 152 observations for Adelie. Thus, we slice the data and create a new data frame with Adelie penguins only. Instead of referring to numbers, the species column should only contain observations for Adelie.

```
# Slice/subset of the data
adelie_data <- penguins[penguins$species == "Adelie", ]
```

Did it really work? We may inspect the new data frame to see if it worked. The nrow() function is also useful in this situation because we know how many observation the new data frame should have. It returns the number of rows and let us check the new sample size. The counter part of the number of rows function is the ncol() function, which does essentially the same for columns.

```
# Number of rows
nrow(adelie_data)
```

```
#> [1] 152
```

```
# Number of columns
ncol(adelie_data)
```

```
#> [1] 8
```

Next, we would do the analysis, but that is not the reason why I showed you this example. In R there are always several ways to approach a task or a problem, and the programming background helps us elaborate on our understanding of how R works instead of applying packages first. There are many packages that provide functions to work with R, and the latter will increase our skills as well. Consider how the `filter()` function from the `dplyr` package works. I will introduce the package in Chapter 4 systematically. The next console shows how we can use the `filter()` function without slicing the data. Can you tell me what the next code does just from reading the code out loud?

```
# The dplyr::filter function
library(dplyr)
adelie_data <- filter(penguins, species == "Adelie")
```

We apply a filter and include only observations where the species is equal to Adelie. That's closer to how humans think and easier to learn in the beginning. However, we sliced data to get a better understanding about the R principles. Some of you may not feel confident how base R works, but as the last example illustrates, there are many packages that provide convenient functions to work with. In the next chapters we will get in touch with different packages that help to improve your skills, without going into the programming details. Overall, objects, functions, and other aspects about base R may seem to have little to do with your goal, working with data. Be patient, we will get in touch with the first steps to explore (unfamiliar) data in the next chapter, but first let me summarize this chapter.

Summary

Congratulations, you have achieved the most challenging part when it comes to learning R: the first steps and base R. Keep in mind that R is an object-oriented programming language and we create objects with the assignment operator (<-). Everything can be an object: we assign values to an object, but also graphs, data, or functions. Depending on the object, we can apply different functions and adjust how a function behaves by tweaking available options.

We also focused on data types and structures and I highlighted differences between data frames, tibbles, and lists. There is no need to memorize how to make them, since you will get in touch with them sooner or later. However, remember that different data structures behave differently when it comes to analyzing data. We may need a different approach depending on the examined data structure. Luckily, we will work with tibbles and data frames most of the time, but I sliced data to illustrate this point.

If you still don't know what to think about base R, be aware that I feel your struggle. I learned R as a student and many R packages we use today on a daily basis were not available (or well known) at that time. Thus, I started my journey also with base R. In several sessions I learned about objects, functions, or how data can be sliced. However, I know from my personal experience that learning base R is tough and can be disappointing. Students come to class and expect to learn how to deal with data right away. Instead they learn abstract concepts and do not get in touch with data. This is not how I want to conceptualize introduction classes, and Practice R is also not meant to show you all the ins and outs of base R.

I tried to cut it down to the most important principles, but at some point you start to analyze data and will run into an error. In that case it is very useful to have some understanding about base R, because you will see solutions in base R when you google for an error. Fortunately, there are many excellent packages that help you to master R and you will come across such solutions as well. These packages are often more user-friendly than base R and we use them if they offer a simple and elegant solution to analyze data, even though base R provides the most stable solutions.

3 Data exploration

Data exploration is an important step to analyze data. What does the data look like, what kind of variables do we observe, and what about missing and implausible values? There are a lot of questions when we start exploring data. The good news is that there exists an easy way to find answers. Get in touch with and explore the data. This chapter gives an overview about the typical first steps.

Suppose you examine if participants sex has an effect on life satisfaction (happiness). We start by exploring how the variables are measured. How many men (women) do we observe? How is the outcome variable distributed and which preparation steps do we need to analyze the data? Of course, the measurement of the variables determines which analysis we apply, but the logic to explore and prepare data is roughly the same.

Talking about data analysis, I assume that you are familiar with statistic measures. Can you explain what a median, a standard deviation, or a correlation expresses? If the answer is no, consider reading a statistics textbook first, because I will not outline what those measurements mean. Please, do not feel offended. Students in the social sciences attend statistics classes and there is not much we can practice with R if I introduce statistical concepts. There are a lot of excellent books that cover the statistical background (e.g., see Bruce et al., 2020; Rajaretnam, 2015).

Overall, we apply two strategies. First, we use base R to explore the data, to estimate summary statistics and we make graphs. In Chapter 7, we will systematically work on our visualization skills and get in touch with ggplot2, a package which provides many opportunities to create visualizations. With base R you can create a lot of graphs with little effort, which is why we start with this graphical approach. Second, there are many R packages that focus on data exploration steps and they help us tremendously to get a quick overview on unfamiliar data. For example, instead of creating a bar plot to depict one variable, those packages provide functions to create a bar plot for each categorical variable of the data frame. Thus, we explore variables, estimate statistics, and use visualization to explore data in this chapter.

- In Section 3.1, we focus on categorical variables. We make tables and graphs to explore how R handles categorical variables and we gain our first insights into factor variables in general terms.
- In Section 3.2, we apply similar steps with numerical outcomes. We get in touch with built-in functions to calculate summary statistics, make tables to inspect several statistics at once, and we visualize numerical variables with histograms and box plots.
- In Section 3.3, we make first attempts to analyze the data. We explore whether one independent variable (x) has an effect on a dependent variable (y) by making cross tables. In terms of numerical outcomes, we examine correlation coefficients, scatter, and correlation plots.

https://doi.org/10.1515/9783110704976-003

You need to install several packages for this chapter. For instance, the `correlation` package helps us to explore correlations; the `corrplot` package provides nice graphs to depict correlations; and the `summarytools` package creates tables very efficiently. Make sure that you have installed and loaded the following packages.

```
# Setup of chapter 3
# Remember you can install packages via: install.packages("name")
library(correlation)
library(corrplot)
library(DataExplorer)
library(effectsize)
library(forcats)
library(PracticeR)
library(summarytools)
library(tibble)
```

3.1 Categorical variables

In this chapter we work with the General Social Survey, which is a cross-sectional study that observes adults in the United States since 1972. I included the data for the year 2016 (gss2016) in the `PracticeR` package. We installed the `PracticeR` package in the first section. After the package is installed and loaded, the gss2016 data is available. The latter is a large survey with many variables, and therefore, we use the smaller subset (gss5) that I prepared for this chapter with the following variables only:
- Respondent's age: gss5$age
- Respondent's sex: gss5$sex
- Respondent's ethnic background: gss5$race
- General happiness: gss5$happy
- Total family income: gss5$income

Before we start with categorical variables, how can we explore (new) data? For example, the `glimpse()` function helps us to get in touch with the data. As the next output shows, it returns an overview of the data, the number of observations (rows), and the number of variables (columns). It shows us a preview of each variable – after the $ sign – and the type of data (e.g., <fct>).

```
# Take a glimpse at your data frame!
df <- PracticeR::gss5
glimpse(df)
```

```
#> Rows: 2,867
```

```
#> Columns: 5
#> $ age    <dbl> 47, 61, 72, 43, 55, 53, 50, 23, 45, 71, 33,~
#> $ sex    <fct> Male, Male, Male, Female, Female, Female, M~
#> $ happy  <fct> Happy, Happy, Happy, Happy, Happy, Happy, H~
#> $ race   <fct> White, White, White, White, White, White, W~
#> $ income <dbl> 26, 19, 21, 26, 26, 20, 26, 16, 20, 20, 1, ~
```

As the output shows, the data contains several categorical variables. Among them, factor variables such as sex or happy. The data also has numerical outcomes, such as age and income. Remember that you can activate the help pane (?gss5) for more information about code and data.

An alternative way to explore data is the str() function. It essentially returns the same as the glimpse() function, but the latter has a nicer output. However, the str()function makes it literally apparent that we inspect the structure of the data, not the data itself. For example, we use the str() function to examine the structure of a variable from the data frame. In the last section we sliced data and we learned that the same principle applies if we want to apply a function to one variable of a data frame. Type the name of the data frame, insert the dollar ($) sign, and the name of the variable. Luckily, the auto-complete function from RStudio shows all variable names if we type the name of a saved object (here a data frame) and the dollar sign.

```
# Inspect the structure of a variable with $
str(df$sex)
```

```
#>  Factor w/ 2 levels "Male","Female": 1 1 1 2 2 2 1 2 1 1 ...
```

The head() function is also useful to inspect data: it returns the head – the first six elements (lines) – of a data frame. Sometimes it is sufficient to see the first six elements, but we can adjust how many elements are returned by changing the n argument within the function.

```
# head shows the first 6 rows of the data as default
head(df, n = 3)
```

```
#> # A tibble: 3 x 5
#>     age sex    happy race  income
#>   <dbl> <fct> <fct> <fct>  <dbl>
#> 1    47 Male  Happy White     26
#> 2    61 Male  Happy White     19
#> 3    72 Male  Happy White     21
```

46 —— 3 Data exploration

The head() function also has a counterpart, the tail() function which returns the
last (six) elements as default. Instead of looking only at a few lines, we can inspect
the entire data with View(). The function opens a new tab with the data set. The next
console prints only the code to inspect the data:

```
# View the data set
View(gss5)
```

Now that we have a first overview about the data, we will focus on categorical variables.
We may count how often each category appears and display the result with a bar graph
(or another visualization). For example, how many male (female) participants are listed
in the gss5 data? As the next output shows, categorical variables are often stored as a
string or *factor variable* and we must count how often each category – or *level* – appears.

```
# The first five observations of sex
df$sex[1:5]
```

```
#> [1] Male    Male    Male    Female Female
#> Levels: Male Female
```

By exploring the variable only, we have no idea how many men or women we observed.
How do we count such strings? The table() function counts and creates a very simple
table, but unfortunately it returns only absolute values.

```
# A simple table
table(df$sex)
```

```
#>
#>    Male Female
#>    1276   1591
```

Creating such a table is easy, but the table is not very informative. The function does
not display frequencies or the sum by default. The summarytools package lets us create tables more efficiently (e.g., see Comtois, 2022). It provides functions to generate
frequency and cross tabulations, as well as tables for descriptive statistics. To explore
how many males (females) we observe, the freq() function creates a frequency table. It
returns, for example, absolute and relative frequencies, an indicator for missing values
(Not Available: <NA>), and the percentage of valid observations.

```
# A frequency table
library(summarytools)
freq(df$sex)


#> Frequencies
#> df$sex
#> Type: Factor
#>
#>                Freq    % Valid    % Valid Cum.    % Total    % Total Cum.
#> ------------ ------ ---------- --------------- ---------- ---------------
#>         Male   1276      44.51           44.51      44.51           44.51
#>       Female   1591      55.49          100.00      55.49          100.00
#>         <NA>      0                                  0.00          100.00
#>        Total   2867     100.00          100.00     100.00          100.00
```

Next, we create a bar plot to visualize the counting result. We may use different visualizations to explore categorical data, but a bar plot is the classic approach visualizing
nominal and ordinal variables.

3.1.1 Bar plots

As the next console shows, I apply first the `table()` function and save the results as an
object (`count_sex`). Next, I use the `barplot` function and insert the object. The result of
the `barplot()` is displayed on the left side of the next output. For the sake of illustration,
I adjusted several arguments of the second `barplot()` function on the right side. For
instance, the `main` argument inserts a title, `xlab` adds a label for the x-axis, and `ylab`
for the y-axis.

```
# Count sex
count_sex <- table(df$sex)

# Left bar plot
barplot(count_sex)

# Right bar plot
barplot(count_sex,
  main = "Sex",
  ylab = "Count"
)
```

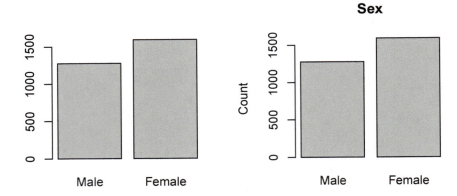

Of course, a bar graph is not the only way to visualize a categorical variable, but a very popular one. The same applies to pie charts, but in many instances they are a rather flawed choice when it comes to exploring data, especially if the variable includes a lot of categories. The next info box on pie charts outlines the main concerns about them.

Data exploration is more fun and goes a lot faster if we use packages that are made for data exploration purposes. There are several packages you may want to consider if you start to explore data. Let's say we want to get a quick overview of all categorical variables. That is a job for the plot_bar() function from the DataExplorer package, which returns bar graphs for all categorical variables (Cui, 2020).

Pie charts

As Figure 3.1 shows, approximately 80 percent of all pie charts look like Pac-Man which underlines that pie charts are both, popular and infamous. Why do many people – including myself – dislike pie charts?

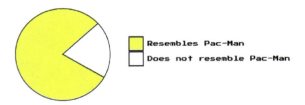

Fig. 3.1: Pie chart vs Pac-Man

I am kidding, but pie charts are infamous because they make it hard to interpret values. A pie chart does not display the numbers that we actually compare. Look at Figure 3.1. I claimed that 80 percent of the observed pie charts look like Pac-Man. However, 80 percent of 360 degrees is 288 degrees. So, pie charts do not display the observed numbers – they display angles of a circle. Angles are harder to interpret since (most of the time) the angles don't correspond with the underlying numbers.

To compare angles is especially difficult if there are many categories. Figure 3.2 shows a second example. The graph display two pie charts based on fake data that summarize the number of fruits in 2010 and 2020. At the bottom of the graph, the same numbers are displayed as bar plot. If we would examine this data with pie charts only, we may miss a significant pattern. As the bar plots highlight, the order of the fruits changed completely and turned around between 2010 and 2020. In this example pie charts are a bad design choice, since they do not reveal the pattern. Keep in mind that there is no visualization that suits all purposes. It is our task to be aware of these limitations and the potential pitfalls of a graph.

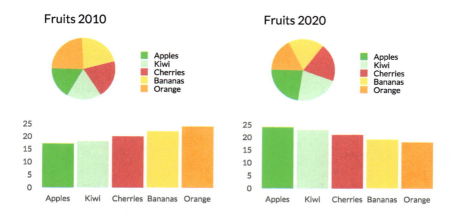

Fig. 3.2: Pie chart pitfalls

Depending on the data, such a plot may become quite large. If you work with a large data set, you may want to slice the data, to get a clearer picture of individual variables and I slice the output every now and then to create a smaller output for this book. Since we use a small data frame, there is no need to filter or slice the data. In our case the function returns a bar graph for participant's sex, their happiness, and their ethnic background.

```
# Plot several bar graphs
library(DataExplorer)
plot_bar(df)
```

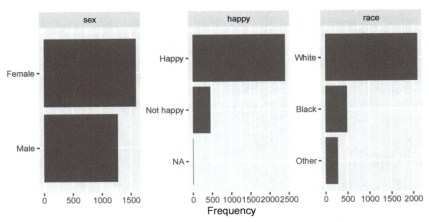

Before we can go on to explore a data set, we should first learn more about factor variables in order to work with categorical variables.

3.1.2 Factor variables

Categorical variables are often saved as factor variables. Look at our bar plot examples: We get a text label for each graph because the variables are factor variables. Sometimes you will encounter categorical variables without labels, or you will see labels that are not optimal for our purposes (e.g., abbreviations such as f for females and m for males). Thus, we need to know how R deals with factor variables to explore or manipulate categorical variables.

In the case of participant's sex, there are two levels defined and the data indicates whether a person is either female or male. Since sex is a factor variable, missing values (NA) are automatically excluded and a bar plot displays those text labels and not a numerical indicator for each group. Often we have no idea what the variable contains when we start to explore unfamiliar data. The levels() function displays all levels of a factor variable.

```
# Inspect the levels of a factor variable
levels(df$sex)
```

```
#> [1] "Male"    "Female"
```

Factor variables have advantages in terms of computational power, and we can even include them in an analysis without generating numerical indicators. Unfortunately, they can also be confusing if you are not used to working with strings or characters. Maybe you know that statistics software packages often store categorical variables as integers. R works differently since we can work directly with strings. Nonetheless, R also handles factor variables as integers. The `typeof()` functions returns the storage mode of an object and in the case of a person's sex, the letters are actually stored as integers.

```
# typeof returns the storage mode
typeof(df$sex)
```

```
#> [1] "integer"
```

We can create a factor variable by hand, which deepens our understanding of how R deals with them. The next console illustrates how to create a factor variable with fruit names. If R knows that `fruit` is a factor variable, only unique levels (fruits) are returned and R sorts the levels alphabetically.

```
# Create an example factor variable
fruit <- factor(c("pear", "apple", "apple", "cherry", "apple"))
fruit
```

```
#> [1] pear   apple  apple  cherry apple
#> Levels: apple cherry pear
```

Imagine that we conducted a survey. We let the participants rate political topics (e.g., climate crisis), and ask them whether a topic is of low, medium, or high importance. We need to take the sorting of this rating into account and sort the data in an ascending (descending) way. The next console shows an illustration for an ordinal rating. I generated a `rating` variable with three levels (`low`, `medium`, `high`), but R sorts the ratings alphabetically.

```
# Create a rating variable
rating <- factor(c(
  rep("low", 10),
  rep("high", 2),
  rep("medium", 7)
))
# Inspect the order
levels(rating)
```

```
#> [1] "high"   "low"    "medium"
```

52 —— 3 Data exploration

Such an order makes it complicated to read a table or to interpret a bar plot. To sort the variable correctly, we need to specify the desired order using the `levels` option in the `factor()` function.

```
# Set the levels
rating <- factor(rating,
  levels = c("low", "medium", "high")
)

levels(rating)

#> [1] "low"    "medium" "high"
```

Suppose a data set contains participant's sex, but the variables indicate whether a person is female (F) or male (M). This is obviously a messy factor variable. Numerical labels and abbreviations can be very confusing, even if we know what those letters refer to. At least text labels are easier to read if we generate a table with such variables.

```
# A messy factor variable
sex <- factor(c(
  rep("F", 10),
  rep("M", 7)
))
# A messy table
table(sex)

#> sex
#>  F  M
#> 10  7
```

The `table` function does not return fancy tables anyway, but we have a really hard time reading such a table, graph, or output if we mix up abbreviations and values. It is better to include the levels and the corresponding `labels` for each category in the `factor()` function.

```
# Create or adjust the labels
sex <- factor(sex,
  levels = c("F", "M"),
  labels = c("female", "male")
)
```

```
table(sex)
```

```
#> sex
#> female    male
#>     10       7
```

This is a simple illustration, but labels work regardless of how many levels (or observations) we examine. We increase our skills to handle factors with the `forcats` package in Chapter 5.3, instead we focus now on continuous variables.

3.2 Continuous variables

Base R has built-in functions to calculate summary statistics and we already estimated a `mean()` in Chapter 2. There are corresponding functions to estimate other summary statistics. For instance, finding the minimal value with the `min()` function, estimating a `median()` instead of the mean, or calculating the standard deviation with `sd()`.

```
# Minima
min(c(1, 5, 6, 8, 11))
```

```
#> [1] 1
```

```
# Median
median(c(1, 5, 6, 8, 11))
```

```
#> [1] 6
```

```
# Maxima
max(c(1, 5, 6, 8, 11))
```

```
#> [1] 11
```

```
# Standard deviation
sd(c(1, 5, 6, 8, 11))
```

```
#> [1] 3.701351
```

54 —— 3 Data exploration

Estimating summary statics is a piece of cake, but what happens if you apply one of the summary statistics functions to explore the gss5 data without any data preparation steps? What is the average age of the observed people?

```
# Mean age
mean(df$age)
```

```
#> [1] NA
```

R tells us that the value is not available (NA). Try it with another function and the results remain the same: R returns NA. Inspect the data one more time – it has missing values and we cannot apply the summary functions without first dealing with this problem. The summary functions return NA if a variable has a missing value.

```
# Missing values
min(3, 5, 6, 8, NA)
```

```
#> [1] NA
```

To apply one of the functions, we must provide a logical indicator to state that missing values (na.rm) should be removed (TRUE).

```
# The na.rm argument removes missing values
mean(df$age, na.rm = TRUE)
```

```
#> [1] 49.15576
```

Keep in mind, excluding missing values may have strong implications and may distort estimation results. It is fine to remove missing values when we explore data, but dropping missing or implausible values is a serious concern and can be interpreted as data falsification. We will elaborate on our knowledge to assess under which circumstances it is (not) okay to drop missing values and revisit this topic in Chapter 5.

The base R functions to estimate summary statistics are straight forward, but they return only one result at a time. To get a better intuition about the distribution of a variable, we need to take all of them into account. The summary() function returns the entire range and the number of missing values. How is age distributed?

```
# Summary statistics of one variable
summary(df$age)
```

```
#>    Min. 1st Qu.  Median    Mean 3rd Qu.    Max.    NA's
```

```
#>    18.00   34.00   49.00   49.16   62.00   89.00       10
```

As the `summary()` function shows, participants are on average 49 years old, with a
minimum of 18 and a maximum of 89, while this information is not available (NA) in
ten cases.[1] Moreover, the `summary()` function returns a summary for all variables of a
data frame.

```
# Summary statistics of the first four variables
summary(df[1:4])
```

```
#>       age               sex              happy           race
#>  Min.   :18.00   Male   :1276   Happy     :2407   White:2100
#>  1st Qu.:34.00   Female :1591   Not happy : 452   Black: 490
#>  Median :49.00                  NA's      :   8   Other: 277
#>  Mean   :49.16
#>  3rd Qu.:62.00
#>  Max.   :89.00
#>  NA's   :10
```

Calculating summary statistics is no big deal, but what if you want to create a table for
a report with all summary statistics? How do we calculate the summary statistics for
several variables without much effort? There are different packages that help you to create a descriptive statistics table without calculating any statistic by hand. For instance,
the `descr()` function from the `summarytools` package returns summary statistics for all
numerical variables with very little programming effort. As the next console shows, the
`descr()` function only expects a data frame as input and returns descriptive statistics
for all numerical variables which we will use to generate a table (see Chapter 8).

```
# The descr() function returns descriptive summary statistics
library(summarytools)
descr(df,
  stats = c("min", "mean", "sd", "max")
)
```

```
#> Descriptive Statistics
#> df
#> N: 2867
```

---

[1] Sometimes you wish for a fine-grained result to inspect how a variable is distributed. The `quantile()`
function lets you adjust the probabilities and split the range of the variable, for example, in ten percent
increments.

```
#>
#>                    age    income
#> -------------  -------  --------
#>        Min     18.00      1.00
#>        Mean    49.16     17.37
#>        Std.Dev 17.69      5.83
#>        Max     89.00     26.00
```

Furthermore, you can adjust which summary statistics are returned with the `stats` option. If you do not provide input for the `stats` option, the function returns the entire list of all computed summary statistics (e.g., for all numerical variables of `gss2016` data). Next we get in touch with histograms and box plots.

3.2.1 Histograms

A common way to visualize the distribution of a continuous variable is a histogram. The bars of a histogram do not represent distinct groups, instead they visualize the frequency. The histogram splits the range of a numerical variable into sections (bins or breaking points) and depicts the frequency of the estimated bins.

In base R we use the `hist()` function. The next console shows you two examples which I made to explore how people's age is distributed. On the left side you can see the result of the basic `hist()` command. Additionally, I adjusted several options of the `hist()` function on the right side. Even though we will not systemically learn how to customize graphs in this chapter, we have to at least discuss the most important parameters of the histogram. The number of bins (the option `breaks`) determines how the distribution is shaped because it defines how many bins should be used. If you increase (decrease) the number of bins manually it may not match exactly with the graph due to the underlying algorithm used to create the histogram. In addition, I set the `freq` argument to `FALSE` in order to examine the density instead of the frequencies; I add a title (`main`); and a label for the axis (`xlab`).

```r
# Left histogram
hist(df$age)

# Right histogram
hist(df$age,
  breaks = 6,
  freq = FALSE,
  main = "Density",
  xlab = "Age"
)
```

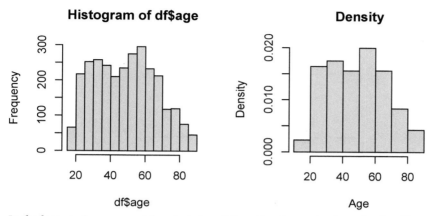

In the last section we used the plot_bar() function to create a bar plot for all categorical variables. The plot_bar() function has siblings to display continuous variables. For example, the plot_density() function returns density plots and the plot_histogram() returns histograms. As the next console shows, we get a histogram for age, income, or for all continuous variables if we do not restrict the data.

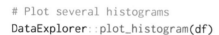

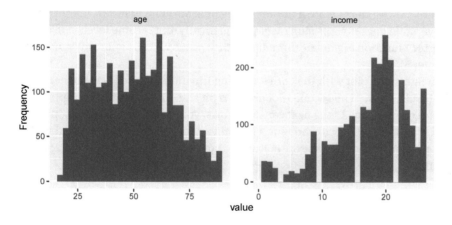

3.2.2 Box plots

A box plot displays the variation of the variable without making an assumption of the underlying statistical distribution. With the help of boxes and whiskers, it splits the range of a variable to depict the statistical dispersion. Figure 3.3 shows an example which underlines how boxes and whiskers are interpreted. The box represents the interquartile range (i.e., the difference between the 75th and 25th percentiles of the data), the whiskers point to the minimum and maximum of the distribution, while potential outliers are displayed as dots.

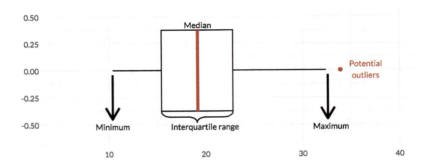

Fig. 3.3: Illustration of a box plot

Box plots are useful to compare groups. Which group has a higher (lower) median, which one a wider range, and what about outliers? For instance, do men have a higher income than women? Actually, income is a factor variable in the gss2016 data, but it has many levels, which is why we can perceive it as quasi-numerical. In order to use such a variable, we may create a numerical income variable first. So, keep in mind that our variable does not measure income numerically, but income levels. I used the as.numeric() function to prepare the data and the income variable is already numerical (see Chapter 5).

We create a box plot with the corresponding function in base R, as the next plot on the left side shows. The second plot on the right side illustrates several options of the boxplot() function. As the next console shows, you can make several box plots to compare groups if you provide an independent variable (e.g., sex), separated with a tilde (~) operator. In addition, use the horizontal option to align the boxes horizontally or vertically.

```
#Left box plot
boxplot(df$income,
        horizontal = TRUE)

#Right box plot
boxplot(income~sex,
        data=df)
```

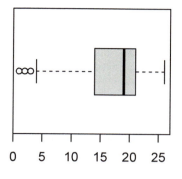 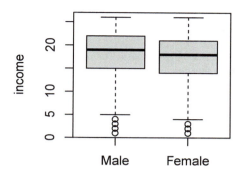

Box plots are made to visualize the summary statistics, but they have limitations regarding the representation of data. The underlying distribution of each group might be very different, but we merely see the distribution based on the displayed boxes and not the data. Furthermore, the number of observations could be unevenly distributed within groups and a visual representation of the data is not included. For instance, we could display both boxes and data points in one graph and add the number of each group in the graph (which we may make with `ggplot2`, see Chapter 7). Thus, graphical procedures to visualize data have their limitations. This is the case for box plots, but applies to other visualizations as well.

We explore variables to get familiar with the data, yet we can also create a report for the entire data. For example, the `create_report()` function from the `DataExplorer` package generates an automated HTML report with statistics and graphs. The report shows the structure of the data, the number of missing values, and even a correlation analysis. Such a document is awesome if you have little knowledge about the data. Moreover, the `create_report()` function comes with several options to adjust the report. Maybe you wish a PDF instead of an HTML file (via `output_file`); or you want to give the exported file a proper name (via `output_format`). The `create_report()` function saves the file in the working directory.

```r
# Create a data report
library(DataExplorer)
create_report(insert_data,
  output_file = "my_report.pdf",
  output_format = "pdf_document"
)
```

The graphs from `DataExplorer` and other packages look different than the base R graphs, because many packages use `ggplot2` to create graphs. If you are not happy with the look and feel of base R graphs, read the next info box and inspect the `ggblanket` package (Hodge, 2022).

The ggblanket package

Chapter 7 focuses entirely on visualization and we need a complete chapter to introduce the ggplot2 package because it implements a theoretical position, plus there are many cool package extensions that wait to get discovered. Moreover, we did not start with ggplot2 because the code to create and customize a graph can become complex and base R provides many graphs to explore data quickly.

However, if you are not happy with the look and feel of base R graphs, inspect the ggblanket package. It provides functions to simplify the visualization process, for many standard graphs with ggplot2. As the next console illustrates, the package provides several gg_* functions, for example, to make a bar graph or a histogram.

```
library(ggplot2)
library(ggblanket)
# Left plot
gg_bar(df, x = sex)
# Right plot
gg_histogram(df, x = age)
```

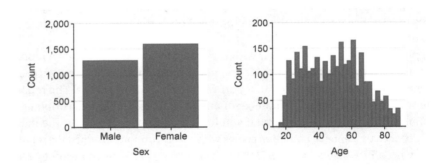

The package makes it convenient to create graphs and it returns ggplot2 objects. In consequence, all knowledge that we are going to acquire in Chapter 7 can also be applied to graphs that are made with the ggblanket package. The same applies to graphs from DataExplorer and other ggplot2 extensions. As long as they return ggplot objects – and the class() function reveals what kind of object a package returns – we can apply our acquired knowledge.

3.3 Explore effects

To explore effects implies that we examine the effect of an independent variable (x) on a dependent variable (y). In other words, we start to analyze data. Maybe you are wondering why we explore effects when this book has a chapter about data analysis. We focus on numerical outcomes in Chapter 6 only and learn how to apply a linear regression analysis in R. You might be tempted to run a regression or another analysis technique before you have explored the variables. This is a bad idea, because you miss the opportunity to learn more about the data and its potential pitfalls (such as missing values, outliers, etc.).

For this reason, we first explore effects in this section. We start simple and generate a cross table to examine categorical outcomes and differences between groups. Next, we extend our knowledge to numerical outcomes and determine whether two variables are related, calculate correlation coefficients for two and more variables, and use scatter plots to visualize the effect.

3.3.1 Categorical outcomes

Suppose we examine life satisfaction (happy) and we ask whether male or female persons are happier. The happy variable has two levels, which makes the interpretation a piece of cake.

```
# The levels of happy
levels(df$happy)
```

```
#> [1] "Happy"     "Not happy"
```

Actually, I created a binary variable and I collapse two levels of the happy variable (Very Happy and Pretty Happy from the gss2016 data). In Chapter 5, we learn how to manipulate factor variables in detail with the help of the forcats package, but a first glimpse does not harm. I collapsed levels with the fct_collapse() function, as the next console illustrates with toy data.

```
# Collapse level of a factor variable with fct_collapse
x <- c("Pretty Happy", "Not happy", "Very Happy")

forcats::fct_collapse(x,
  Happy = c("Pretty Happy", "Very Happy")
)
```

```
#> [1] Happy     Not happy Happy
#> Levels: Not happy Happy
```

So, we use the latter example to highlight why a cross table (contingency table) might not be fancy but worth starting with. The table() function creates a cross table if we include a second variable.

```
# A simple table
table(df$sex, df$happy)
```

```
#>
#>          Happy Not happy
#>   Male    1082       191
#>   Female  1325       261
```

Again, the table is not very informative because it returns absolute values only. The ctable function from the summarytools package returns a simple cross table with row (r) proportions (prop) as the default. As the next console shows, obviously, there seems to be no significant difference if we compare women and men in terms of happiness.

```
# A cross table
summarytools::ctable(
  x = df$sex,
  y = df$happy,
  prop = "r"
)
```

```
#> Cross-Tabulation, Row Proportions
#> sex * happy
#> Data Frame: df
#>
#> -------- ------- --------------- ------------- ---------- ---------------
#>          happy           Happy    Not happy          <NA>          Total
#>    sex
#>   Male             1082 (84.8%)  191 (15.0%)   3 (0.2%)   1276 (100.0%)
#>   Female           1325 (83.3%)  261 (16.4%)   5 (0.3%)   1591 (100.0%)
#>   Total            2407 (84.0%)  452 (15.8%)   8 (0.3%)   2867 (100.0%)
#> -------- ------- --------------- ------------- ---------- ---------------
```

It becomes more complicated if more groups or levels are included, but the interpretation of a cross table is straight forward when both variables are binary. We can adjust the default and print column (c) or total (t) proportions by adjusting the prop option. Moreover, the function can even return the chi-square statistic, the odds ratio, and the relative risk if you add the corresponding options.

Keep the numbers of the cross table in mind, because we could visualize the results of the cross table with the help of a mosaic or spine plot. The width of the boxes on a mosaic plot is proportional to the number of observations within each category that we observe. Use the spineplot() function, insert the variables, and define the relationship by using the tilde (~) operator. The dependent variable is on the left side, while the independent variable is on the right side of the tilde.

```
# Boxes are proportional to the number of observations
spineplot(happy ~ sex,
  data = df
)
```

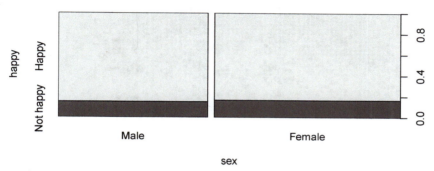

As the spine plot shows, we observe slightly more women than men, but the proportions are almost the same and we do not observe any substantial differences. The actual strength of a spline plot becomes visible if there is a substantial effect between groups (see Chapter 7.3 for an example). Ultimately, we use scatter plots and estimate the correlation coefficient to explore an effect on a continuous outcome.

3.3.2 Continuous outcomes

After we have explored the variables and checked the distribution, you may examine whether two continuous variables are associated with each other. The gss5 data contains participant's age and income and we may assume that older participants have a higher income. A scatter plot is the standard graph to explore the association between two numerical variables. The plot() function depicts each observation of *x* and *y* in a coordinate system with a dot (or another symbol via the pch option) if we insert two numerical variables. Furthermore, the abline() function includes a linear regression line, which gives us an impression of how the variables are related to each other. To put it simply, the regression line shows us the expected value of *y* for a given *x* (see Chapter 6 for more information about regression analyses). In addition, we may use a different color (col) for the regression line, which often makes it easier to see the line.

```
# Create a scatter plot (with filled circles and without a frame)
plot(
  y = df$income, x = df$age,
```

```
    pch = 20, frame = FALSE
)
# And a red regression line
abline(lm(income ~ age, data = df),
    col = "red"
)
```

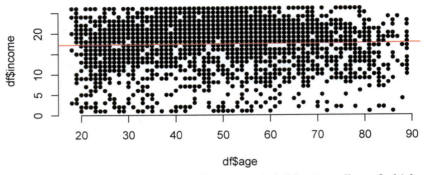

As the scatter plot shows, there is no linear trend visible. Regardless of which preliminary conclusion we may arrive at, scatter plots are very useful to explore linear trends, yet sometimes it can be tricky to tell if variables are correlated and, if so, how strong the association is.

A correlation coefficient ranges from -1 to 1 and quantifies the strength of a linear effect. The corresponding function in R is cor(). Insert *y* and *x* into the function and it returns Pearson's r by default. Furthermore, the cor function does not know what to do if we have a missing values problem. As the next console shows, we can use only complete observations by adding the use option. Excluding data is fine if you start to explore data, but we must soon expand our knowledge about missing values!

```
# By default, the cor function returns Pearson's r
cor_value <- cor(df$income, df$age, use = "complete")
cor_value
```

#> [1] 0.01747172

There is not even a moderate correlation between *x* and *y* and we cannot predict a person's income if we know their age. How did I come to this conclusion? A lot of students in the social sciences learn the rules to interpret effect sizes proposed by Cohen (1988). Cohen differentiates between *very small* (r < 0.1), *small* (0.1 <= r < 0.3), *moderate* (0.3 <= r < 0.5) and *large* (r >= 0.5) effects. Such rules are arbitrary, but they provide a convention to determine the effect size.

There is a convenient way to assess whether the effect is small, moderate or large. Let R – respectively the `effectsize` package – do that job for you (Ben-Shachar et al., 2022). The `interpret_r()` function returns the effect size. Insert a value or the corresponding correlation coefficient. With the `rules` option, you can apply different rules to assess the effect. Let's stick to Cohen's (1988) rules and the last example to see how it works. We have saved the correlation coefficient as `cor_value`. Just insert the object into the `interpret_r()` function.

```
# The effect size package interprets r
library(effectsize)
interpret_r(cor_value, rules = "cohen1988")
```

```
#> [1] "very small"
#> (Rules: cohen1988)
```

The `cor()` function is easy to apply but it does not evaluate whether the association is statistically significant and we had to tweak the options to adjust for missing values. The `correlation` package makes our life easier when we need to estimate correlation coefficients (Makowski, Wiernik, et al., 2022). For instance, suppose we examine the results of a survey that includes several items to measure a latent variable based on several indicators (e.g., environmental consciousness). We get a very quick overview about each variable and how they are related if we use the `correlation` package instead of base R.

The `correlation()` function excludes non-numerical data, returns the statistical significance, and we can inspect the results for an entire data frame (correlation matrix). The next console shows the function with the build-in `mtcars` data set. The `gss2016` data contains only a limited number of numerical variables. The `mtcars` data set contains many numerical variables which makes it easier to see the real strength of the approach. The next console illustrates it with three numerical variables from the `mtcars` data.

```
# Estimate several correlation coefficients on the fly
library(correlation)
correlation(mtcars[1:3])
```

```
#> # Correlation Matrix (pearson-method)
#>
#> Parameter1 | Parameter2 |     r |            95% CI | t(30) |          p
#> ----------------------------------------------------------------------
#> mpg        |        cyl | -0.85 | [-0.93, -0.72] | -8.92 | < .001***
#> mpg        |       disp | -0.85 | [-0.92, -0.71] | -8.75 | < .001***
#> cyl        |       disp |  0.90 | [ 0.81,  0.95] | 11.45 | < .001***
```

Unfortunately, the more variables we include, the more complicated it becomes to inspect each coefficient. We have to check each coefficient, assess the effect size and determine if there is a small, moderate or large correlation between two variables. Some of the variables are positively associated; others are negatively associated, which makes it difficult to inspect each coefficient with such a table.

The corrplot package lets us create a correlation plot (Wei & Simko, 2021), which depicts correlation coefficients with the help of color. As the next console shows, we can use the corrplot() function to depict the correlation of the numerical variables from the mtcars data. In order to do so, we calculate a correlation matrix (corr_matrix) with the cor() function first, which creates a matrix with all correlation coefficients. Next, we insert the objects in the corrplot() function for the default plot on the left side. The plot on the right side shows several options.

```
# Left plot: A correlation plot example
library(corrplot)
corr_matrix <- cor(mtcars)
corrplot(corr_matrix)
```

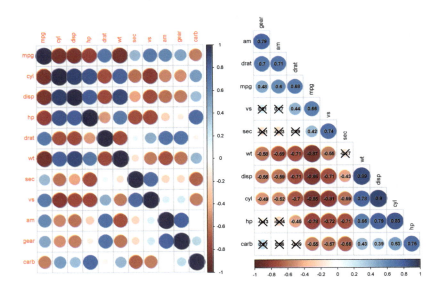

As the plot on the right side shows, the package offers a lot of options. For example, the order option lets you sort the variables (e.g., in accordance with their effect size); estimate p-values (p.mat) to see if a correlation is (not) significant; we can display the entire matrix or only upper or lower triangular matrix (type); and adjust whether the coefficients on the diagonal (diag) are displayed. Consider the help files for more information and the next console for the discussed options.

```r
# Estimate p-values
p_values <- cor.mtest(mtcars, conf.level = 0.95)

# Right plot
corrplot(corr_matrix,
  order = "AOE",
  p.mat = p_values$p,
  type = "lower",
  diag = FALSE
)
```

Ultimately, keep in mind that a correlation does not express whether two variables are related. A correlation coefficient of zero implies only that there is no linear association between the variables. In a similar sense, we cannot say that x is a cause for y even if the correlation is large. We observe only the co-variation of the examined variables. We will deepen those concerns and increase our knowledge about causality – at least a bit – in Chapter 6. Before we summarize the chapter, the next info box outlines data exploration tips for Excel users by introducing the rpivotTable package (Martoglio, 2018).

The rpivotTable package   **i**

Do you belong to the dark side of data exploration? Have you ever used Excel to explore data? As luck would have it, R integrates several features of the dark side, which makes your decision easier in terms of data exploration. Don't get me wrong, I am not saying that Excel has no raison d'être, no right to exist, but people often claim that data management steps are easier to apply with Excel. You can literally see the data and exploring data is as easy as the click of a button. Give the rpivotTable package a try. The package creates a graphical interface which lets you interact with data in the same way as with pivot tables in Excel. Insert a data frame in the rpivotTable() function and it will open an interface in the viewer.

Such tools are awesome when exploring unknown data quickly. I might sound like a James Bond villain because I did not mention it in the beginning of this chapter. Can you believe it, there are graphical interfaces for R which let you work with R just by clicking on a button? However, clicking buttons may create a huge problem soon, which is the reason why I did not introduce interfaces.

Let me explain: Suppose you analyzed data with Excel. After three months the data gets an update. Are you still able to remember all data preparation steps that you made? Without code, you cannot reproduce your work and in absence of a script that does the work for you, you will have to remember and repeat all these (manual) steps. Moreover, it is not only about reproducibility. Say you sent the analysis to a colleague who realized that you made a mistake. The mistakes force you to rerun the applied steps. If your script shows each step, it becomes easier to narrow down where the problem might be coming from. Certainly, it's up to you which side appears shinier, but it's a bit more than Excel-bashing from my side. Using a graphical interface will get you in touch with data, but using code will make your work reproducible. You can see each step and, if you are lucky, see the errors as well.

---

68 —— 3 Data exploration

Summary

This chapter introduced typical steps to explore data. We examined categorical and continuous variables and we started to discover how variables are related. Keep in mind that graphs are especially valuable to explore data, variables and effects, even if our first steps are preliminary in nature. Furthermore, I outlined that, besides functions and graphs from base R, several packages to explore data are worth to consider. We used the `summarytools` to create frequency and cross tables; the `DataExplorer` package to visualize categorical and numerical variables; and the `correlation` package to estimate several correlation coefficients efficiently. Those packages are not the only ones available to explore data and I did not dissect all the functions that they provide, I just highlighted some of the possibilities to explore data quickly. Inspect the packages (e.g., vignettes, website) for more information. In addition, check out the `GGally` and the `skimr` packages which also provide ideas and functions to explore data (Schloerke et al., 2021; Waring et al., 2022).

Data exploration steps lay the groundwork for the next stages of applied research. Exploring data helps us to get familiarized with the data, we get to know how the variables are measured, and which analyses we may apply. In the next step we focus on data manipulation steps in order to prepare variables for an analysis.

4 Data manipulation

The last chapter of Part I focuses on data manipulation steps. Up to this point we have explored data and applied statistics. To become more efficient using R, you have to transfer the acquired knowledge and apply it in different contexts. To prepare you for this journey, Part II concentrates on the entire process of applied research, but before we start over, this last chapter will focus on typical steps of data manipulation. You can perform many typical steps of data manipulation with the dplyr package and with the knowledge of base R that we have learned so far.

- In Section 4.1, we learn the five key functions of the dplyr package (Wickham, François, et al., 2022). For instance, suppose the data is large, which is why we can't work with the entire data set. The dplyr package helps you to focus on a narrow data frame by introducing a filter() function that is more user-friendly than base R solutions.
- Section 4.2 introduces additional features from the dplyr package. Most of the time we work with data that was compiled by someone else. This implies that you have to prepare data and generate new variables based on the values of other variables. For example, a nominal variable contains several group levels, but we want to compare only two of them. This section focuses on such steps and introduces additional functions from the dplyr package to manipulate data. Moreover, in this section we use actual survey data and I will introduce further data sources which give an idea where to apply your dplyr skills next. Before we start to analyze data on a regular base, the last section concentrates on how we work with R.
- Section 4.3 tries to increase the efficiency of our workflow and discusses how we can improve working with R. Talking about workflow and efficiency might sound boring, and you probably did not expect such a topic. However, some workflow aspects are so essential, that I believe, we need to discuss them before we can dig deeper. I give you some recommendations regarding scripts that will help you to structure and reuse your work, I outline the advantages of RStudio's projects, and I introduce code snippets which aim to reduce the time and effort applying code.

You need to load the dplyr package which is included in the tidyverse package. In case you are not following the course of the book, install it with install.packages(). Moreover, this chapter needs the following packages.

```
# Setup of Chapter 4
library(dplyr)
library(magrittr)
library(PracticeR)
library(tidyr)
```

https://doi.org/10.1515/9783110704976-004

```
library(tibble)
library(usethis)
```

4.1 The five key functions of dplyr

Figure 4.1 highlights the key functions (or verbs) from the dplyr package based on an illustration of a small data set where boxes represent the cells of a data set. Figure 4.1 (A) displays the raw data. It contains three persons (ID) and we observed their sex and year of birth.

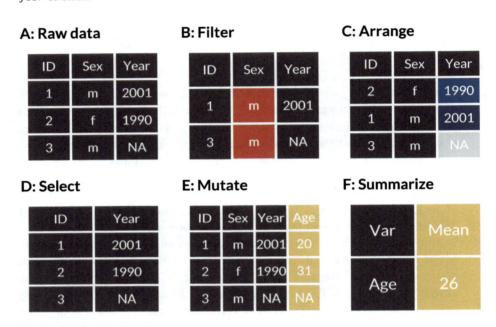

Fig. 4.1: The five dplyr functions

There are five key functions to manipulate data: (1) Apply a *filter* and subset the data. As Figure 4.1 (B) shows, we may examine male (m) persons only by using a filter() first. (2) *Arrange* data. Figure 4.1 (C) illustrates that we can arrange() the years in ascending (or descending) order. (3) *Select* variables, especially if a data set contains so many variables that it is hard to see what is going on in the first place. Create a smaller data set and, as Figure 4.1 (D) depicts, select one or several variables from the raw data. The last two key functions are mutate() and summarize(). (4) *Mutate* new variables. For example, estimate how old the participants are (in 2021) based on the year of birth and mutate() a new age variable (see Figure 4.1 [E]). (5) *Summarize* the data. Figure 4.1

(F) highlights that we can estimate the average age of the participants or use other functions to summarize the data.

So, let's see how this works by using the implemented `mtcars` data set. To understand what we are actually doing, we should first briefly inspect the data. As the next output shows, the data comprises fuel consumption and other aspects about cars. For instance, `mpg` contains how many miles per gallon a car runs and `cyl` is the number of cylinders of the car's engine. All eleven variables are numerical with thirty-two observations. Moreover, I used the `as_tibble()` function to convert the data frame (`df`) to a tibble, which makes the output a bit nicer.

```
# The mtcars data set
df <- tibble::as_tibble(mtcars)
head(df)
```

```
#> # A tibble: 6 x 11
#>     mpg   cyl  disp    hp  drat    wt  qsec    vs    am
#>   <dbl> <dbl> <dbl> <dbl> <dbl> <dbl> <dbl> <dbl> <dbl>
#> 1  21       6   160   110  3.9   2.62  16.5     0     1
#> 2  21       6   160   110  3.9   2.88  17.0     0     1
#> 3  22.8     4   108    93  3.85  2.32  18.6     1     1
#> 4  21.4     6   258   110  3.08  3.22  19.4     1     0
#> 5  18.7     8   360   175  3.15  3.44  17.0     0     0
#> # ... with 1 more row, and 2 more variables: gear <dbl>,
#> #   carb <dbl>
```

Often we work with larger data sets that have a lot more variables and observations. Working with a large data set needs more computational power and there is always a risk that you lose overview. In such a case we may use a `filter()` which helps us to focus only on those variables we are interested in.

4.1.1 Filter

Use the `filter()` function to create a subset of the data based on values of variable(s). Insert the data and outline the filter condition(s). We can use any mathematical arguments to filter the data. For instance, restricting the data and creating a data frame that contains cars with more than 100 horsepower (`hp > 100`).

```
# Use one or more conditions to filter the data
filter(df, hp > 100)
```

72 —— 4 Data manipulation

```
#> # A tibble: 23 x 11
#>    mpg   cyl disp    hp  drat    wt  qsec    vs    am
#>  <dbl> <dbl> <dbl> <dbl> <dbl> <dbl> <dbl> <dbl> <dbl>
#> 1  21      6   160   110  3.9   2.62  16.5     0     1
#> 2  21      6   160   110  3.9   2.88  17.0     0     1
#> 3  21.4    6   258   110  3.08  3.22  19.4     1     0
#> 4  18.7    8   360   175  3.15  3.44  17.0     0     0
#> 5  18.1    6   225   105  2.76  3.46  20.2     1     0
#> # ... with 18 more rows, and 2 more variables: gear <dbl>,
#> #   carb <dbl>
```

The dplyr package filters the data depending on the specified conditions and returns a new data frame. Now only cars with hp > 100 are included, but we can use any condition to filter the data. For example, our research question may only apply to a certain age group and we can use a filter to get rid of observations that we do not want to include in the analysis.

The next console shows several examples to highlight how logical and relational operators can be implemented and combined to filter data.

```
# Filter with logical and relational operators (see Chapter 2)
# Cars with automatic transmission only (equal to: ==)
filter(mtcars, am == 0)


#>                     mpg cyl  disp  hp drat    wt  qsec vs am gear carb
#> Hornet 4 Drive     21.4   6 258.0 110 3.08 3.215 19.44  1  0    3    1
#> Hornet Sportabout  18.7   8 360.0 175 3.15 3.440 17.02  0  0    3    2
#> Valiant            18.1   6 225.0 105 2.76 3.460 20.22  1  0    3    1
#> Duster 360         14.3   8 360.0 245 3.21 3.570 15.84  0  0    3    4
#> Merc 240D          24.4   4 146.7  62 3.69 3.190 20.00  1  0    4    2
#> Merc 230           22.8   4 140.8  95 3.92 3.150 22.90  1  0    4    2


# Cars with manual transmission only (not equal to: !=)
filter(mtcars, am != 0)


#>                   mpg cyl  disp  hp drat    wt  qsec vs am gear carb
#> Mazda RX4        21.0   6 160.0 110 3.90 2.620 16.46  0  1    4    4
#> Mazda RX4 Wag    21.0   6 160.0 110 3.90 2.875 17.02  0  1    4    4
#> Datsun 710       22.8   4 108.0  93 3.85 2.320 18.61  1  1    4    1
#> Fiat 128         32.4   4  78.7  66 4.08 2.200 19.47  1  1    4    1
#> Honda Civic      30.4   4  75.7  52 4.93 1.615 18.52  1  1    4    2
#> Toyota Corolla   33.9   4  71.1  65 4.22 1.835 19.90  1  1    4    1
```

```
# And combine conditions
# Cars with automatic transmission and (&) large horsepower
filter(mtcars, am == 0 & hp > 200)


#>                       mpg cyl disp  hp drat    wt  qsec vs am gear carb
#> Duster 360           14.3   8  360 245 3.21 3.570 15.84  0  0    3    4
#> Cadillac Fleetwood   10.4   8  472 205 2.93 5.250 17.98  0  0    3    4
#> Lincoln Continental 10.4   8  460 215 3.00 5.424 17.82  0  0    3    4
#> Chrysler Imperial    14.7   8  440 230 3.23 5.345 17.42  0  0    3    4
#> Camaro Z28           13.3   8  350 245 3.73 3.840 15.41  0  0    3    4

# Cars with large horsepower OR (|) high consumption
filter(mtcars, hp >= 250 | mpg > 25)


#>                 mpg cyl  disp  hp drat    wt  qsec vs am gear carb
#> Fiat 128       32.4   4  78.7  66 4.08 2.200 19.47  1  1    4    1
#> Honda Civic    30.4   4  75.7  52 4.93 1.615 18.52  1  1    4    2
#> Toyota Corolla 33.9   4  71.1  65 4.22 1.835 19.90  1  1    4    1
#> Fiat X1-9      27.3   4  79.0  66 4.08 1.935 18.90  1  1    4    1
#> Porsche 914-2  26.0   4 120.3  91 4.43 2.140 16.70  0  1    5    2
#> Lotus Europa   30.4   4  95.1 113 3.77 1.513 16.90  1  1    5    2
```

Keep in mind that the dplyr package never modifies, but creates a new data frame. Use the assignment operator (<-) to save the results.

4.1.2 Arrange

Sometimes we need to arrange or sort the data, and whilst doing so we might even realize that we made mistakes during the data manipulation step. Suppose we grade an exam. The data contains the points pupils gained in a test and we must create a new variable with their grades depending on their test score. Arrange the data to see if the pupils get the right grades – arranged data makes it easier to spot possible problems from the manipulation step.

Use the arrange() function to sort or arrange the order of single or several variables. For example, we can arrange the cars from the lowest to the highest value of horsepower.

```
# Arrange in an ascending order
arrange(df, hp)


#> # A tibble: 32 x 11
```

```
#>      mpg   cyl  disp    hp  drat    wt  qsec    vs    am
#>    <dbl> <dbl> <dbl> <dbl> <dbl> <dbl> <dbl> <dbl> <dbl>
#> 1   30.4     4  75.7    52  4.93  1.62  18.5     1     1
#> 2   24.4     4 147.     62  3.69  3.19  20       1     0
#> 3   33.9     4  71.1    65  4.22  1.84  19.9     1     1
#> 4   32.4     4  78.7    66  4.08  2.2   19.5     1     1
#> 5   27.3     4  79      66  4.08  1.94  18.9     1     1
#> # ... with 27 more rows, and 2 more variables: gear <dbl>,
#> #   carb <dbl>
```

Add a second variable and R will sort the data accordingly; or use desc() to sort the data in a descending order:

```
# Arrange in a descending order
arrange(df, desc(hp))
```

```
#> # A tibble: 32 x 11
#>      mpg   cyl  disp    hp  drat    wt  qsec    vs    am
#>    <dbl> <dbl> <dbl> <dbl> <dbl> <dbl> <dbl> <dbl> <dbl>
#> 1   15       8   301   335  3.54  3.57  14.6     0     1
#> 2   15.8     8   351   264  4.22  3.17  14.5     0     1
#> 3   14.3     8   360   245  3.21  3.57  15.8     0     0
#> 4   13.3     8   350   245  3.73  3.84  15.4     0     0
#> 5   14.7     8   440   230  3.23  5.34  17.4     0     0
#> # ... with 27 more rows, and 2 more variables: gear <dbl>,
#> #   carb <dbl>
```

4.1.3 Select

The select() function helps us to focus on a subset of the data. The mtcars data is neither messy nor big, but we can learn the principles of column selection anyway. Use select() and specify which variables (e.g., mpg, hp) we want to keep from the data. The dplyr package returns a new data frame that contains the selected variables only.

```
# Select mpg and hp
select(df, mpg, hp)
```

```
#> # A tibble: 32 x 2
#>      mpg    hp
#>    <dbl> <dbl>
#> 1   21     110
#> 2   21     110
```

```
#> 3   22.8      93
#> 4   21.4     110
#> 5   18.7     175
#> # ... with 27 more rows
```

Now your base R skills come into play. Remember, you can select several columns without typing each of their names. Just choose a starting and endpoint and combine them with a colon. For example, you can select all columns between two variables.

```
# Select variables by providing a start and an endpoint
select(df, mpg:hp)
```

```
#> # A tibble: 32 x 4
#>      mpg   cyl  disp    hp
#>    <dbl> <dbl> <dbl> <dbl>
#> 1   21       6   160   110
#> 2   21       6   160   110
#> 3   22.8     4   108    93
#> 4   21.4     6   258   110
#> 5   18.7     8   360   175
#> # ... with 27 more rows
```

Maybe we want to select all columns except the variables shown in the last output. This is not a complicated task. We exclude them with the minus (-) sign. Thus, select all variables expect all columns between mpg and hp.

```
# Reverse the selection
select(df, -(mpg:hp))
```

```
#> # A tibble: 32 x 7
#>     drat    wt  qsec    vs    am  gear  carb
#>    <dbl> <dbl> <dbl> <dbl> <dbl> <dbl> <dbl>
#> 1   3.9   2.62  16.5     0     1     4     4
#> 2   3.9   2.88  17.0     0     1     4     4
#> 3   3.85  2.32  18.6     1     1     4     1
#> 4   3.08  3.22  19.4     1     0     3     1
#> 5   3.15  3.44  17.0     0     0     3     2
#> # ... with 27 more rows
```

To manipulate variables implies that we have to focus on the variables that we need to prepare for the analysis and select() helps us to generate a narrow data frame,

76 —— 4 Data manipulation

but it returns a new data frame even if we select one variable (column vector). We can examine if an object is a data frame with the is.data.frame() function.

```
# Select returns a data frame
hp <- select(df, hp)
is.data.frame(hp)
```

```
#> [1] TRUE
```

However, sometimes we want to select the vector and not a data frame. This is the difference between select() and pull(). The select() function returns a data frame, while pull() extracts a column vector, as the next console illustrates.

```
# Use pull to extract a variable/column vector
hp <- pull(df, hp)
is.vector(hp)
```

```
#> [1] TRUE
```

There are more tricks on how to select variables, especially regarding variable strings and running numbers. For example, some data sets contain several variables to measure one construct, or there are several index variables with a running number. Hopefully those variable names all start with the same string, so you can select them by adding starts_with("var_") in the select function. The dplyr package checks the variables names and includes variables whose name starts with the corresponding string. A similar function exists for the last letters. Instead of looking at the first string characters, the option ends_with("string") checks the end of the string. Or if the variables in your data contain a running number, say the variables from var1 to var10, the option num_range("var", 1:10) includes all ten variables.

4.1.4 Mutate

Raw data often does not contain variables that are prepared for the analysis. In this case, we need to transform the data and generate a new variable that depends on the values of other variables. Here mutate() comes into play, which adds a new variable (or column). First, we need a narrow data set, otherwise we cannot see the added variables in the output of the console. Let's select the variable hp and assign the result as a new data frame (df_small).

```
# Create a small(er) subset
df_small <- select(df, hp)
head(df_small)
```

```
#> # A tibble: 6 x 1
#>       hp
#>    <dbl>
#> 1    110
#> 2    110
#> 3     93
#> 4    110
#> 5    175
#> # ... with 1 more row
```

For instance, let's assume we have to report how much kilowatt (kw) a car's engine has, but the data contains only the gross horsepower (hp) of a car. We can extend the data frame and generate the new variable kw by multiplying hp with a conversion factor.

```
# Mutate and create new variables
conversion <- 0.74570

mutate(df_small,
  kw = hp * conversion,
  hp_new = round(kw * 1.34102, 2)
)
```

```
#> # A tibble: 32 x 3
#>       hp    kw hp_new
#>    <dbl> <dbl>  <dbl>
#> 1    110  82.0    110
#> 2    110  82.0    110
#> 3     93  69.4     93
#> 4    110  82.0    110
#> 5    175 130.     175
#> # ... with 27 more rows
```

The mutate() function extends the data and calculates a new variable. We can even generate a second variable which depends on the values of the first variable. Look at the variable hp_new. I had no idea how to transform horsepower into kilowatt, so I used Google to find the conversion factor. To assess the approach, I reversed the calculation and saved the results as an additional variable. Thus, you can generate several variables

78 —— 4 Data manipulation

on the fly. In terms of data manipulation, we must check whether our data manipulation steps really work out. As the output shows, we can use other R functions (see Chapter 2) as well. Thus, use arithmetic operators (e.g., +, -), logical comparisons (e.g., <, ==), and functions (e.g., log) to generate new variables.

Each time we extend the data set, we will extend the output, which makes it harder to spot the variable and errors of the data manipulation step. Fortunately, mutate() has a counterpart function called transmute(). As default, mutate() keeps all variables, transmute() keeps only variables that are listed in the function and the new ones. As the next console shows, use mtcars instead of the smaller data frame and create the kw variable one more time, but now with transmute(). We get the same results, even though we skipped the selection step.

```r
# Transmute keeps only new (or listed) variables
transmute(mtcars,
  hp,
  kw = hp * conversion
)
```

```
#>                      hp        kw
#> Mazda RX4           110   82.0270
#> Mazda RX4 Wag       110   82.0270
#> Datsun 710           93   69.3501
#> Hornet 4 Drive      110   82.0270
#> Hornet Sportabout   175  130.4975
#> Valiant             105   78.2985
```

4.1.5 Summarize

We can calculate measurements of central tendencies (e.g., the mean) with the summarize() function, which collapses vectors into a single value. For instance, let's calculate the average horsepower of the cars.

```r
# Summarize variables
df |>
  summarize(mean_hp = mean(hp))
```

```
#> # A tibble: 1 x 1
#>     mean_hp
#>       <dbl>
#> 1      147.
```

You may wonder what the pipe operator (|>) does? To start, it is enough to know that we can combine several data manipulations steps without repeating the data name. The pipe operator (|>) makes sure that we send the data to the next step and chains those functions together. This point becomes clearer if we start to combine data manipulation steps, for example, to estimate a mean for groups.

Let's say we believe that cars with different transmissions (am: 0 = automatic, 1 = manual) differ in terms of horsepower. To this end, we must group and assign the data first with the `group_by()` function; in a second step, we estimate the mean. The function splits the data based on the values of am. After this step, we can use `summarize()` one more time to estimate group-specific means.

```
# Group by variables
compare_group <- group_by(df, am)

# And summarize for the groups
summarize(compare_group, hp_mean = mean(hp))

#> # A tibble: 2 x 2
#>       am hp_mean
#>    <dbl>   <dbl>
#> 1      0    160.
#> 2      1    127.
```

This goes way easier with the pipe (|>). The pipe is a key element in `tidyverse`, it was first introduced by the `magrittr` package and many people work with the pipe in R. As the package vignette describes, the pipe has two aims: "Decrease development time and improve readability and maintainability of code. Or even shortr [sic]: make your code smokin' (puff puff)" (see Bache & Wickham, 2022). It puts the steps of your analysis forwards, so you can combine several lines of code in one command. Sure, in our example we have only two lines of code, but even in this case it is easier to read if you get used to the pipe. Just think, *next* or *then* if you see a pipe.

Starting with R version 4.1.0, the native pipe (|>) is included in R, which has the same purpose as the `magrittr` pipe (%>%). Regardless of which one you prefer, we chain one function after another with the pipe. First we send the data in the preparation step, then we group the data, and next we call the summary function for which we estimate the group-specific mean.

```
# Use the pipe operator to combine steps
df |>
  group_by(am) |>
  summarize(
```

```
    mean_hp = mean(hp)
  )

#> # A tibble: 2 x 2
#>       am mean_hp
#>    <dbl>   <dbl>
#> 1      0    160.
#> 2      1    127.
```

I hope these examples made dplyr, the pipe, and how functions can be chained a bit clearer. In the next section, we will we apply the dplyr verbs and extend our knowledge about the package. To this end, we manipulate data and focus on typical steps that are necessary prior to analyzing data.

4.2 Data manipulation with dplyr

Most of time you will lay your hands on data that was pulled together by someone else and you have to prepare the data for your own purposes. For example, you want to analyze if there are any differences between male and female, but the corresponding sex variable holds only zeros and ones instead of text labels. How can you transform the variable? Or, assume we have to restrict the analysis sample to persons aged between 18 and 65, but the data set contains only birth years. Accordingly, we may create a new variable with labels, calculate respondent's age in order to restrict the analysis sample, or we create any other variable needed for the analysis. This section focuses exactly on such steps.

We learned in the last section how to use mutate() and transmute(). Both functions help us to create new variables and we can combine them with further functions to create new variables. We first focus on how we can manipulate variables. I will demonstrate how to apply the if_else() function to create a new variable that checks a condition. Next, we learn how to create complex conditions with case_when(). Finally, we talk about how we recode the values of a variable.

This time, we will not work with a tiny data set. We will increase our mutating skills with gss2016 data from the PracticeR package. As the help file outlines, the data contains an extract from the General Social Survey 2016, with a long list of variables. Among them, respondent's age, sex, and their happiness.

```
# The gss2016 data
library(PracticeR)
head(gss2016)
```

```
#> # A tibble: 6 x 33
#>    year     id ballot     age childs sibs  degree race  sex
#>    <dbl> <dbl> <labell> <dbl>  <dbl> <lab> <fct>  <fct> <fct>
#> 1  2016     1 1           47      3 2     Bache~ White Male
#> 2  2016     2 2           61      0 3     High ~ White Male
#> 3  2016     3 3           72      2 3     Bache~ White Male
#> 4  2016     4 1           43      4 3     High ~ White Fema~
#> 5  2016     5 3           55      2 2     Gradu~ White Fema~
#> # ... with 1 more row, and 24 more variables: region <fct>,
#> #   income16 <fct>, relig <fct>, marital <fct>,
#> #   padeg <fct>, madeg <fct>, partyid <fct>,
#> #   polviews <fct>, happy <fct>, partners <fct>,
#> #   grass <fct>, zodiac <fct>, pres12 <labelled>,
#> #   wtssall <dbl>, income_rc <fct>, agegrp <fct>,
#> #   ageq <fct>, siblings <fct>, kids <fct>, ...
```

In the last chapter we used implemented data which makes it easier to understand the logic behind a function. Unfortunately, this does not mean that it becomes easier to apply it in other instances and, as next step, you need to apply your knowledge to data that was not created for teaching purposes. For this reason we learn how to manipulate the gss2016 data in the next subsection, but you may use other data to apply and increase your dplyr knowledge. As the next info box outlines, a lot of data is available to apply your skills.

4.2.1 Manipulate, but check!

To err is human and we all make mistakes when we write code. A typo in the data preparation step may affect your analysis substantially. Maybe you have forgotten one little character, or sometimes you are not cautious enough and include a false character by accident. Use select() to create a narrow data frame and inspect how your data preparation steps affect the data. In this section we will also learn how to change the order of variables with the relocate() function. Both functions help us to get an overview of the data and to examine whether each preparation step worked out. Before we increase our data mutating skills, let me first outline why it is important to inspect data carefully.

82 —— 4 Data manipulation

ℹ **Apply your skills**

So far, we used data from the General Social Survey (GSS) which examines residents of the United States and it includes many behavioral and attitudinal questions. The GSS is conducted since 1972 and you can download many different waves from their website. Go and visit their website to find out more about the GSS and its topics.

```
# The General Social Survey
# https://gss.norc.org/
```

Maybe you have no specific interest in the United States, what about East Asia (e.g. East Asian Social Survey) or South America (e.g., Latinobarómetro)? Or consider the European Social Survey (ESS). The latter is also a cross-sectional survey that measures behavior and attitudes on various topics for many European countries. After a short registration, the data is free of charge for non-commercial use. Again, visit the ESS website (or from any other mentioned survey) to inspect the documentation of the data, the topics, and the variables they include.

```
# The European Social Survey
# https://www.europeansocialsurvey.org/
```

Your data preparation skills will grow if you prepare data on a regular basis, but especially if you work with data that was not prepared for the scientific community. The R community has established a weekly challenge to prepare, analyze, and visualize data. The #TidyTuesday project publishes a new raw data set for a broad range of topics. For example, they examined bee colony losses, student mobility, and the pay gap in UK in 2022. Thus, there are a lot of resources, data, and inspiration available to apply your dplyr skills. You can find more information about #TidyTuesday on their GitHub website:

```
PracticeR::show_link("tidy_tuesday")
```

Suppose we want to examine how old the survey respondents are and we create a binary variable that indicates whether a person is older than the respondents' mean age. We start by creating a variable that stores the mean age. We already know how to achieve the first step, but let's have a look at the output. Can you spot the new age variable?

```
# First attempts ...
gss2016 |>
  mutate(age_mean = mean(age)) |>
  head()

#> # A tibble: 6 x 34
#>    year    id ballot     age childs sibs  degree race  sex
#>   <dbl> <dbl> <labell> <dbl>  <dbl> <lab> <fct>  <fct> <fct>
```

```
#> 1   2016     1 1           47      3 2      Bache~ White Male
#> 2   2016     2 2           61      0 3      High ~ White Male
#> 3   2016     3 3           72      2 3      Bache~ White Male
#> 4   2016     4 1           43      4 3      High ~ White Fema~
#> 5   2016     5 3           55      2 2      Gradu~ White Fema~
#> # ... with 1 more row, and 25 more variables: region <fct>,
#> #   income16 <fct>, relig <fct>, marital <fct>,
#> #   padeg <fct>, madeg <fct>, partyid <fct>,
#> #   polviews <fct>, happy <fct>, partners <fct>,
#> #   grass <fct>, zodiac <fct>, pres12 <labelled>,
#> #   wtssall <dbl>, income_rc <fct>, agegrp <fct>,
#> #   ageq <fct>, siblings <fct>, kids <fct>, ...
```

Apparently not: age_mean is not even displayed in the console since we are now working with a large data set that was not created for teaching purposes. By default, each new variable is appended on the right side of the data, which is why I used a narrow data frame in the last section to show you how mutate() works. Depending on the data set, the console may not display all the variables, but we must check if all data preparation steps worked out. Moreover, even if the new variable is displayed, sometimes we need to visually compare variables to make sure that we did not introduce an error. Comparing variables is tricky if there are a lot of variables listed between them.

As we know, we can select variables and create a smaller data frame that contains only core variables needed for an analysis.

```
# Select variables that are needed ...
gss2016 |>
  select(age, income_rc, partners, happy) |>
  mutate(age_mean = mean(age)) |>
  head()
```

```
#> # A tibble: 6 x 5
#>      age income_rc   partners  happy         age_mean
#>    <dbl> <fct>       <fct>     <fct>            <dbl>
#> 1    47 Gt $170000 <NA>       Pretty Happy        NA
#> 2    61 Gt $50000  1 Partner Pretty Happy        NA
#> 3    72 Gt $75000  1 Partner Very Happy          NA
#> 4    43 Gt $170000 <NA>       Pretty Happy        NA
#> 5    55 Gt $170000 1 Partner Very Happy          NA
#> # ... with 1 more row
```

My first attempt to create the variable did not work, because the age variable has missing values. Keep in mind that data often contains missing and implausible values. Both may have serious implications for the analysis, which is why we will figure out how to deal with the problem of missing values in Chapter 5. In this chapter we heroically and unrealistically assume that we can exclude them without any severe consequences to at least learn more about data manipulation.

The tidyr package lets us exclude missing values with the drop_na() function (Wickham & Girlich, 2022). It drops all observations with missing values (NA), or for a specific variable if you include the variable name inside the function. For example:

```
# An example data
missing_example <- data.frame(x = c(1, NA, 3, NA))

# Drop_na drops NA
tidyr::drop_na(missing_example, x)


#>   x
#> 1 1
#> 2 3
```

Thus, apply the drop_na() function and combine it with the other steps to generate the mean variable.

```
# Combine steps ...
df <- gss2016 |>
  select(age, income_rc, partners, happy) |>
  drop_na() |>
  mutate(age_mean = mean(age))

head(df)


#> # A tibble: 6 x 5
#>     age income_rc  partners   happy          age_mean
#>   <dbl> <fct>      <fct>      <fct>             <dbl>
#> 1    61 Gt $50000  1 Partner  Pretty Happy       47.5
#> 2    72 Gt $75000  1 Partner  Very Happy         47.5
#> 3    55 Gt $170000 1 Partner  Very Happy         47.5
#> 4    53 Gt $60000  1 Partner  Very Happy         47.5
#> 5    23 Gt $30000  1 Partner  Very Happy         47.5
#> # ... with 1 more row
```

Both age variables are now visible, and we have created a new variable with the mean. However, we wanted to create a binary variable that indicates if a person is older than the average. Thus, we need to compare age and age_mean, but unfortunately, there are many variables between them, which makes it difficult to compare them visually. We can relocate() variables to a new column. The option .after lets us determine where the variable will be relocated.

```r
# Relocate variables to get a better overview
df |>
  relocate(age_mean, .after = age)
```

```
#> # A tibble: 1,619 x 5
#>      age age_mean income_rc   partners  happy
#>    <dbl>    <dbl> <fct>       <fct>     <fct>
#> 1     61     47.5 Gt $50000  1 Partner Pretty Happy
#> 2     72     47.5 Gt $75000  1 Partner Very Happy
#> 3     55     47.5 Gt $170000 1 Partner Very Happy
#> 4     53     47.5 Gt $60000  1 Partner Very Happy
#> 5     23     47.5 Gt $30000  1 Partner Very Happy
#> # ... with 1,614 more rows
```

The relocate() function moved the variable to the second column, right *after* age. Before we continue, meet the counterpart of the .after option, because sometimes we need to relocate .before another variable. Furthermore, there is no need to relocate each time we generate a new variable, since we can also integrate this step in the mutate() function.

```r
# Instead of selecting variables, create a variable list
varlist <- c("income_rc", "partners", "happy", "age")
```

```r
# Include relocate in the mutate step
df |>
  select(all_of(varlist)) |>
  drop_na() |>
  mutate(age_mean = round(mean(age), 2), .before = age)
```

```
#> # A tibble: 1,619 x 5
#>   income_rc   partners  happy        age_mean   age
#>   <fct>       <fct>     <fct>            <dbl> <dbl>
#> 1 Gt $50000  1 Partner Pretty Happy      47.5    61
#> 2 Gt $75000  1 Partner Very Happy        47.5    72
#> 3 Gt $170000 1 Partner Very Happy        47.5    55
#> 4 Gt $60000  1 Partner Very Happy        47.5    53
```

86 —— 4 Data manipulation

```
#> 5 Gt $30000  1 Partner Very Happy        47.5    23
#> # ... with 1,614 more rows
```

It is super easy to introduce mistakes when we work with data. Thus, make sure that you can see what is going on when you manipulate variables. The `select()` function – but also `transmute()` and `relocate()` – helps us to get an overview. Since it is much easier now to compare age with `age_mean`, let us learn how we create a variable that indicates whether age is above (below) average with the `if_else()` function.

4.2.2 If else

The `if_else()` function is inspired by an `if else` statement from base R. An `if else` statement checks a condition and assigns a value depending on whether the condition is (not) fulfilled. Say we need to check how many chocolate bars we have. The following `if else` statement checks our chocolate bar stock and prints a message, depending on the value of the stock. Currently we have three chocolate bars on the shelf, which is why R picks the `else` condition.

```
# The chocolate bar stock
chocolate <- 3
```

```
# If else statement
if (chocolate > 5) {
  print("Don't panic, there is enough chocolate!")
} else {
  print("Jeeez, go and get some chocolate!")
}
```

```
#> [1] "Jeeez, go and get some chocolate!"
```

You may wonder what an `if else` statement has to do with our initial plan. Let me first introduce the `if_else()` function from the `dplyr` package.[1] Say we have observed two female participants and one male participant.

```
# Example data
sex <- c("f", "m", "f")
sex
```

---

[1] The function is also inspired by `ifelse()` function from base R. Both functions essentially do the same thing, but we can include the `if_else()` function in the data manipulation steps.

```
#> [1] "f" "m" "f"
```

The variable contains characters, but we wish to recode the variable into a binary indicator. Just as the `if else` statement, the `if_else()` functions checks a condition and depending on whether the condition applies, returns a value. Let's see how it works based on the example `sex` data:

```
# The dplyr::if_else function
if_else(sex == "f", 0, 1)
```

```
#> [1] 0 1 0
```

The first person is female, therefore `if_else()` returns zero. The second person gets one since the `if` condition (`sex == "f"`) is not met. The `if_else()` function works the same way if we check numerical values and assign characters.

```
# if_else with numerical input
sex <- c(0, 1, 0)
if_else(sex == 0, "female", "male")
```

```
#> [1] "female" "male"   "female"
```

Let's see how `if_else()` helps us to create a variable that indicates if a person is older than the mean average. All we must do is adjust the condition:

```
# Insert if_else in the mutation step
df |>
  select(age, age_mean) |>
  mutate(
    older = if_else(age > age_mean, "older", "younger"),
    .after = age_mean
  )
```

```
#> # A tibble: 1,619 x 3
#>      age age_mean older
#>    <dbl>    <dbl> <chr>
#> 1     61     47.5 older
#> 2     72     47.5 older
#> 3     55     47.5 older
#> 4     53     47.5 older
#> 5     23     47.5 younger
```

#> # ... with 1,614 more rows

To create the indicator variable, I first created a variable with the mean value, but this step was redundant and I included it only to illustrate that we should be cautious whether our code works. There is no need to calculate the mean first, since we can chain the discussed steps and apply it with the gss2016 data. Moreover, we probably do not want to create a binary indicator, but a logical vector, as the next output illustrates.

```
# Chain steps with gss2016 data
gss2016 |>
  drop_na(age) |>
  transmute(age,
    older = if_else(age > mean(age), TRUE, FALSE)
  )
```

```
#> # A tibble: 2,857 x 2
#>      age older
#>    <dbl> <lgl>
#> 1     47 FALSE
#> 2     61 TRUE
#> 3     72 TRUE
#> 4     43 FALSE
#> 5     55 TRUE
#> # ... with 2,852 more rows
```

The if_else() function makes it easy to create new variables, but what if we want to check several conditions? Let me introduce the case_when() function for this purpose.

4.2.3 Case when

Often, we need to restrict the analysis sample to certain characteristics. Suppose we need to restrict the analysis sample to adult persons excluding pensioners. Thus, we need to create a variable that tells us if a person is younger, older, or in between the age range. We can use the case_when() function if several conditions are involved.

As the next console shows, I created a new variable (older_younger), which indicates if a person's age is older, younger, or in-between. The function checks a condition: in the first argument it checks if age is smaller or equal to 17, and in the last if age is greater than or equal to 65. It returns the corresponding values (e.g. younger) when a condition is true, which is separated in the code by the tilde (~) operator.

```
# First case_when attempt
df |>
  transmute(age,
    older_younger = case_when(
      age <= 17 ~ "younger",
      age > 17 & age <= 64 ~ "in-between",
      age >= 65 ~ "older"
    )
  )
```

```
#> # A tibble: 1,619 x 2
#>     age older_younger
#>   <dbl> <chr>
#> 1    61 in-between
#> 2    72 older
#> 3    55 in-between
#> 4    53 in-between
#> 5    23 in-between
#> # ... with 1,614 more rows
```

Identifying persons within our age range illustrates the real strength of the case_when() function since we can combine several conditions and variables to create a new variable. Consider the second argument, the variable needs to identity persons who are older than 17 and younger than 65.

However, we do not need that step as long as our data does not contain missing values. The case_when() function uses the logic of the if else statements and run the code in order. In a similar sense, instead of defining which values are in between, we can add TRUE ~ "in-between" and all other observations get the corresponding label. Toy data illustrate this point.

```
# The case_when logic
x <- data.frame(age = c(17, 77, 51, 24))

x |>
  transmute(age,
    older_younger = case_when(
      age <= 17 ~ "younger",
      age >= 65 ~ "older",
      TRUE ~ "in-between"
    )
  )
```

```
#>   age older_younger
#> 1  17       younger
#> 2  77         older
#> 3  51    in-between
#> 4  24    in-between
```

The last example showed you how to apply the `case_when()` function with a single variable. You can, however, combine several variables, use any mathematical operator, or even create the wildest of combinations. For example, maybe we want to compare older and younger persons with a high score on the happiness variable compared to all other persons. This is an erratic example, but it outlines that we can combine several conditions and variables.

The next time you need to extract a range from a numerical variable, I hope you remember the `between()` function. The latter represents a special case. The `between()` function checks whether the observation of a numerical vector lies *between* a range, which makes my last attempts obsolete.

```
# Between selects observations between a certain range
df |>
  transmute(age,
    age_filter = between(age, 18, 65)
  )
```

```
#> # A tibble: 1,619 x 2
#>     age age_filter
#>   <dbl> <lgl>
#> 1    61 TRUE
#> 2    72 FALSE
#> 3    55 TRUE
#> 4    53 TRUE
#> 5    23 TRUE
#> # ... with 1,614 more rows
```

Please do not feel offended that we learned the `case_when()` function first, because it is ever so flexible when creating new variables. However, we can separate all persons within a certain age range with just one line of code by means of the `between()` function. Moreover, add a filter to finally restrict the analysis sample.

```
# Restrict the analysis sample
df |>
  transmute(age,
```

```r
    age_filter = between(age, 18, 65)
  ) |>
  filter(age_filter == "TRUE")
```

```
#> # A tibble: 1,351 x 2
#>      age age_filter
#>    <dbl> <lgl>
#> 1     61 TRUE
#> 2     55 TRUE
#> 3     53 TRUE
#> 4     23 TRUE
#> 5     32 TRUE
#> # ... with 1,346 more rows
```

4.2.4 Recode

We can resolve many data manipulation steps with the discussed functions but depending on your taste and prior experience, you may desire to know how to simply replace values. To replace values works in principle the same way and we can use the `ifelse` function to replace the values of a binary indicator.

```r
# Recode with if_else
sex <- c("m", "f", "m")
sex <- if_else(sex == "m", "male", "female")
sex
```

```
#> [1] "male"   "female" "male"
```

Or with the help of the `case_when()` function should we want to replace several categories. Nevertheless, the `dplyr` package also has a dedicated `recode()` function. Consider two examples of a binary indicator for `sex`. The first variable comes as characters (`sex`), the second one as integers (`sex_num`).

```r
# Example df
df <- tibble::tribble(
  ~sex, ~sex_num,
  "m", 1,
  "f", 2,
  "m", 1,
  NA, NA
)
```

Use `recode_factor()` to recode a character variable into a factor variable or `recode()` in case of the numerical input.

```
# Recode a factor variable
recode_factor(df$sex, m = "Men", f = "Women")
```

```
#> [1] Men    Women Men    <NA>
#> Levels: Men Women
```

```
# Recode a numerical variable
recode(df$sex_num, `1` = 1, `2` = 0)
```

```
#> [1]  1  0  1 NA
```

To replace values implies that we need to be sure about what we replace. All those previously created variables had only two levels, which made it easy to understand the code. However, consider the next example. Instead of recoding directly, we may use `if_else()` to recode and to create a new variable. This makes missteps easier to spot and we can exclude variables that we no longer need in a next step.

```
# Create new variables to check if any errors are introduced
df |>
  select(sex) |>
  mutate(sex_new = if_else(sex == "f", "female", "male"))
```

```
#> # A tibble: 4 x 2
#>   sex   sex_new
#>   <chr> <chr>
#> 1 m     male
#> 2 f     female
#> 3 m     male
#> 4 <NA>  <NA>
```

4.2.5 Additional features

The last section introduced functions from the `dplyr` package, which will help you to overcome many typical problems in manipulating data. The package has more to offer than I can possibly outline in one chapter, which is why I focused on typical steps of applied social science research. It is also an excellent idea to inspect the package's website and vignettes if you are faced with a problem that I did not discuss. This last section highlights that you can solve many problems with the `dplyr` package, especially if you combine them with functions from other packages (of the `tidyverse`) and with your base R skills. For illustration purposes, we use toy data and the `mtcars` data set once more.

In the last chapter we calculated summary statistics, but now that we have a basic understanding of `dplyr`, we can use `summarize()` to calculate several means or other measures of central tendencies for numerical variables.

```
# Calculate a mean
summarize(mtcars,
  mpg = mean(mpg),
  cyl = mean(cyl),
  disp = mean(disp)
)
```

```
#>        mpg    cyl     disp
#> 1 20.09062 6.1875 230.7219
```

Unfortunately, we have to repeat ourselves. We must call the mean function each time and write down each variable. This goes way easier with `across()`, which lets you select variables and apply a function such as `mean()`.

```
# Calculate a mean across variables
summarize(mtcars, across(mpg:disp, mean))
```

```
#>        mpg    cyl     disp
#> 1 20.09062 6.1875 230.7219
```

We can even improve this step and include the `everything()` function which selects all available variables.

```
# Give me everything (if possible)
summarize(mtcars, across(everything(), mean))
```

```
#>        mpg    cyl     disp       hp     drat      wt     qsec      vs      am
#> 1 20.09062 6.1875 230.7219 146.6875 3.596563 3.21725 17.84875 0.4375 0.40625
#>       gear   carb
#> 1 3.6875 2.8125
```

Did you realize that the `mtcars` data set has row names? The car's models are listed as row names, but not as a variable.

94 — 4 Data manipulation

```r
# rownames
head(mtcars)
```

```
#>                   mpg cyl disp  hp drat    wt  qsec vs am gear carb
#> Mazda RX4        21.0   6  160 110 3.90 2.620 16.46  0  1    4    4
#> Mazda RX4 Wag    21.0   6  160 110 3.90 2.875 17.02  0  1    4    4
#> Datsun 710       22.8   4  108  93 3.85 2.320 18.61  1  1    4    1
#> Hornet 4 Drive   21.4   6  258 110 3.08 3.215 19.44  1  0    3    1
#> Hornet Sportabout 18.7  8  360 175 3.15 3.440 17.02  0  0    3    2
#> Valiant          18.1   6  225 105 2.76 3.460 20.22  1  0    3    1
```

The row names may contain some useful information, but we have no access as long as they are not a part of the data. The `tibble` package is a part of the `tidyverse` and it includes the `rownames_to_column()` function. The function inserts the row names as a column in the data.

```r
# Augment your dplyr skills with further packages
mtcars |>
  tibble::rownames_to_column(var = "car") |>
  head()
```

```
#>                 car  mpg cyl disp  hp drat    wt  qsec vs am gear carb
#> 1         Mazda RX4 21.0   6  160 110 3.90 2.620 16.46  0  1    4    4
#> 2     Mazda RX4 Wag 21.0   6  160 110 3.90 2.875 17.02  0  1    4    4
#> 3        Datsun 710 22.8   4  108  93 3.85 2.320 18.61  1  1    4    1
#> 4    Hornet 4 Drive 21.4   6  258 110 3.08 3.215 19.44  1  0    3    1
#> 5 Hornet Sportabout 18.7   8  360 175 3.15 3.440 17.02  0  0    3    2
#> 6           Valiant 18.1   6  225 105 2.76 3.460 20.22  1  0    3    1
```

Of course, most of the time you will not work with row names, but this is an illustration of how we have not examined all the possibilities that `dplyr` and other packages of the `tidyverse` provide to manipulate data.

It goes without saying that sometimes you will be faced with a problem that `dplyr` (and other packages) do not explicitly cover. In such cases, you need to integrate your R skills into the data preparation steps. For example, say you want to create a unique identifier (e.g., a running number) for each observation. Is there a function that creates such a variable? Maybe, but don't forget your base R skills: use the `nrow()` function and `mutate()` to count the number of rows. You may even `arrange()` the data first and give it a running number according to a sorted variable.

```r
# Include your base R skills
mtcars |>
  select(mpg) |>
  arrange(mpg) |>
  mutate(running_number = 1:nrow(mtcars)) |>
  head()
```

```
#>                    mpg running_number
#> Cadillac Fleetwood 10.4              1
#> Lincoln Continental 10.4             2
#> Camaro Z28         13.3              3
#> Duster 360         14.3              4
#> Chrysler Imperial  14.7             5
#> Maserati Bora      15.0              6
```

The dplyr package gives you many possibilities to manipulate data, especially if we combine it with other packages and your base R skills. We will extend our knowledge about dplyr and other packages to prepare data in Chapter 5. From my opinion, learning dplyr is often easier than achieving the same task with base R or another data manipulation approach, but many roads lead to Rome and, as the next info box outlines, different approaches (e.g., dplyr vs. data.table, see Dowle & Srinivasan, 2022) have different strengths to prepare data. Before we further improve our data preparation skills, the next section discusses several topics on how to increase your work efficiency and workflow.

4.3 Workflow

You might be wondering why I talk about workflow before we learn how to analyze data in detail. Most of the R code in the first part was not very complicated. We will, however, make some substantial progress in the second part of Practice R. The more advanced things we perform with R, the more complex the code will become. Other people, and your future self, may find it difficult to understand what the code does, but we can learn some tricks to make the code easier to write, read, and thus, faster to understand when revisited.

Increasing the workflow implies that we get better using R step by step. This is a learning process. It depends on what you are trying to achieve and on your prior experience. Perceive your first R code as like small children who learned how to walk. The code is not the most elegant and some parts are probably a bit shaky. That's okay. It is exactly how we learn new things and improve ourselves.

96 —— 4 Data manipulation

ℹ Data manipulation approaches

There are several approaches to work with data in R. Instead of using `dplyr`, we could achieve the same task with base R. Consider the next examples which compare the code of both approaches. The next console shows that the equivalent of the `filter()` function is the `subset()` function; the differences between both approaches are minimal.

```
#Dplyr: filter data
mtcars |> filter(am == 0)
#Base: subset data
subset(mtcars, am == 0)
```

Maybe it's hard to believe, but in some instances solutions from base R are easier to apply. Suppose we need to extract a vector from a data frame. Instead of using the `pull()` function from `dplyr`, we only need to extract the vector and assign the object.

```
#Dplyr: Pull a vector
mtcars |> pull(hp)
#Base: Extract the vector
hp <- mtcars$hp
```

Thus, keep in mind that there are always several approaches and that you will come across base R, as well as other packages to manipulate data. However, `dplyr` is pretty verbal and often easier to apply than base R. On the other side, base R provide the most stable solution (code), even though it is harder to apply. For example, consider the variable names of the `mtcars` data.

```
colnames(mtcars)
```

```
#> [1] "mpg" "cyl" "disp" "hp" "drat" "wt" "qsec" "vs" "am" "gear" "carb"
```

The next console illustrates a complicated base R solution. Say we want to give the variable hp a proper name. In base R we need to assign a new label for the column vector, but only for the variable name that we want to change, which is why we need to slice it and then assign a new value. The `dplyr` is much easier, since we can integrate this step when we select data (see Chapter 5 for more information).

```
#Base: Assign horsepower in the names column
names(mtcars)[names(mtcars) == "hp"] <- "horsepower"
#Dplyr: Change a variable name during the select step
mtcars |> select(horsepower = hp)
```

This chapter focused on `dplyr` because it's the Swiss pocketknife for manipulating data and not difficult to apply, but there are other approaches as well. For example, the `data.table` package provides fast solutions to work with large data sets.

Let me give you an example. Suppose you calculate some simple statistics, say the mean for a series of x variables, shown in the following console. This task is a piece of cake, because you know how to apply the mean() function.

```
# A small df
df <- tibble(
  x1 = c(3.3, 3.5, 3, 4.4, 5.4),
  x2 = c(3.1, 7.2, 8, 5.5, 4.3),
  x3 = c(3.4, 3.1, 6, 6.2, 8.8)
)

mean(df$x1)

#> [1] 3.92
```

Thus, you calculate the mean, next you do the same for x2, and so on. This is a simple example, but it illustrates that the code is not elegant and error prone, considering that we repeat ourselves numerous times. How can we improve? Of course, we could use our dplyr skills, but the colMeans() function calculates the means for all columns with one line of code.

```
# Column means
colMeans(df)

#>   x1   x2   x3
#> 3.92 5.62 5.50
```

This is a substantial improvement compared to the repetitive task, but there is still room for improvement. What happens if we need to estimate the median instead of the mean? We can apply a function – such as the median or the mean – over a list or a vector with lapply(), which returns a list with our results. We can also use sapply(), which does essentially the same as lapply(), but sapply() tries to simplify the results. If possible, it will return a vector instead of a list. Let's see how this works for our simple application:

```
# Apply a function over a list or a vector
lapply(df, mean)

#> $x1
#> [1] 3.92
#>
```

```
#> $x2
#> [1] 5.62
#>
#> $x3
#> [1] 5.5
```

```
# Simplify the result, if possible
sapply(df, mean)
```

```
#>   x1   x2   x3
#> 3.92 5.62 5.50
```

Now it does not matter anymore which function we apply: we could calculate the standard deviation instead of the mean or the median. The code is also more elegant than repeatedly running the same code. Thus, start simple and revise the work from time to time. Catch up with your skill set and check whether you could improve the code and become more efficient. However, the last part of this chapter will not focus on code, but on tips and recommendations that aim to increase your coding skills in the medium to long term.

First, we focus on *scripts* and we learn how to create a useful structure that helps us stay organized – especially when a script becomes larger and harder to understand. Next, I will introduce *RStudio projects*, because a project provides the environment to stay organized. Finally, we get in touch with *code snippets* which help us to manage complicated code.

4.3.1 Scripts

There are some general recommendations on how you should maintain code. The most important one is:

```
# Comments, comments comments!
# Add useful comments that describe what the code does
```

I introduced comments in the first chapter to highlight what the code does. What else can we learn about comments? Most obviously, comments will help your future self and other people to work with your scripts. Maybe you don't see just yet why using comments is crucial. Probably your code is super easy to understand and you can hardly imagine why some people should have problems to understand it. Of course, you understand what your script does if you open it again, say, a week later. What about a month, a year, several years from now? Comments help you to understand the meaning of the code and, in consequence, to be efficient.

Suppose, you want to perform an analysis based on an old script, but what happens if the script does not have enough comments and is messy? You have no idea how many times I believed that I could do a quick analysis because I did a similar one in the past. I open a confusing script with many steps, instead of a simple skeleton I could use as a basis. Like this, I first have to figure out what the code actually does. Only then can I try to run the script, but not without an error. Since I did not use the script for a long time, it is not unlikely that some of the packages have been updated and work slightly different now; or maybe my script was messy and I forgot to include all necessary parts. There are a lot of possible causes as to why I run into an error, and a good documentation cannot protect us against all odds. However, you are better equipped to reproduce your work with a good documentation, and most of the time troubleshooting will take a lot longer than the time you spent adding some useful comments.

What do I mean by *useful comments*? Try to be specific. Unspecific comments are okay if your steps to prepare data are short and straightforward. However, in most instances the steps to prepare data are the longest part of the script and you will quickly lose oversight if you do not provide enough guidance to your future self or other users. In the data preparation section of your script, you can use comments to make crucial steps obvious. For instance, you could write down why the preparation steps should be done in a certain way.

Don't get me wrong, you do not have to put every word on a gold scale, especially if the script is primarily for internal use. But even in such cases, it is worth considering which comments would be helpful to quickly explain the contents of the script. To help you with this task, RStudio makes it very convenient to use comments. You can turn multiple lines into comments, or even turn multiple lines of comments into code by applying a simple shortcut:

```
# Pro tip
# Turn multiple lines into comments and back again:
# Press: Ctrl/Cmd + Shift + C
```

Increase the readability of a script and give it a structure with sections for each substantial part. Hash tags (#) will help you to structure the script. A typical R script to analyze data may contain the following structure:

```
# 00 About ####
# 01 Packages ####
# 02 Data preparation ####
# 03 Data analysis ####
```

```
# 04 Visualization ####
# 05 Further ado ####
```

The script may first contain some information about the file. Try to provide some background information: who has written the script, when was it written, and what was the purpose.

Next, we typically load packages. It always is a good idea to load all necessary packages first. The future user needs to know whether the script will run with or without installing additional packages. It is okay if your scripts become messy while you are still busy defeating the (data) dragon. No matter what task you are trying to achieve, in the heat of the moment you might want to load the corresponding package right away should you find a solution for your quest. That's fine, but when the battle is over, go back and rearrange your script. Load all packages in the very beginning, because there is a huge chance that when you load your package somewhere later in the script, you might need their functions earlier. Try to stick to the rule that packages should be loaded before you do anything else. Having a separate section instantly shows which packages must be installed.

In the next steps you prepare the data and run the analysis. Preparing the data is often the longest and most difficult part. Particularly if we inspect older scripts, you will wonder about some of the steps if there are no descriptive comments. The chances are high that you will have forgotten what the data looks like and which steps are necessary to prepare the data. Finally, we may create a section for the data visualization or export – or anything else that was not included in the typical structure of the script.

Sections make your workflow efficient since you avoid searching the entire script when you are only looking for a chunk of code from the data preparation section. Or, if you use an old script as a template, it is much easier to go through a specific section and adjust it for the new purpose instead a screening the entire script. Creating a structure with hash tags also helps during the writing process of the script. Figure 4.2 shows what the proposed structure looks like in RStudio's code pane.

Fig. 4.2: Structure of an R script

There is a small arrow sign next to the number of the line in the script. RStudio automatically creates sections in the script if you add a hash tag (#) in front of the section name and at least four additional hash tags (or equal signs or dashes) at the end. Your code will be folded (indicated by the double arrow) if you click on the arrow sign and it appears again if you click once more. Thus, you can fold the code after you have finished the first section and concentrate on the incomplete parts. Sections help us to focus on a logical structure of the script and code folding makes working with longer scripts more convenient.

Moreover, sections make it possible to jump directly from one section to another with a mouse click. Figure 4.3 shows how RStudio has integrated a section menu that displays the structure of a script. A small window that displays the sections will pop up if you click on the button in the left corner of the script pane.

Fig. 4.3: Section menu in RStudio

Ultimately, your code style makes it easier (or harder) to read the script and grasp the meaning. This book uses in many parts the tidyverse code style because the style is implemented in RStudio, which makes it convenient to use in this book.[2] *The tidyverse style guide* by Hadley Wickham is available online.

```
# Visit the tidyverse style guide
# https://style.tidyverse.org/
```

To stick to and apply code styling rules is demanding. We must learn those rules, apply them consistently to improve the code, and undo any mistakes. This is a challenge, but the pain is worth the trouble because it increases our efficiency. Let me give you an illustration. The next console prints two versions of the same code. One applies the tidyverse code style, while the other is a messy code. Which one is easier to read?

```
#Compare code
# Version A:
df <-
  mtcars |>
```

---

[2] For example, the styler package inspects code, applies code style and converts the code accordingly (Müller & Walthert, 2022). The package comes with an convenient addin as well.

```r
  group_by(am) |>
  summarize(
    median_hp = median(hp),
    count = n(),
    sd = sd(hp),
    min = min(hp)
  )

#Version B:
df<-mtcars|>group_by(am)|>
  summarize(
    median_hp = median(hp), count = n(), sd = sd(hp), min = min(hp)
  )
```

I will not go into detail about the tidyverse code style: you can stick to the rules you encounter in this book, learn about other ways to style the code, or even create your own style. It is not important which style you prefer, but I do hope you agree that version A is easier to read than version B. Version A gives us a visual clue that several variables are generated and we can spot the content if we write each variable on a new line. Moreover, I deleted the white space around the pipe and the assignment operator; and I did not use a new line after the first pipe in Version B. Call me a monster, but hopefully you agree that the style of code increases its readability.

This gives you an idea what ugly code looks like and why we should stick to some conventions to increase the readability. In the long run, these habits will save more time than the one you spend writing comments, generating a structure, and sticking to a coding style. Since we did not apply any advanced analysis with R so far, I only discussed the most important aspects that I believe are helpful in the beginning, as well as in the long run. Of course, there is much more to discover to become efficient, such as RStudio projects.

4.3.2 Projects

RStudio projects contributes to increasing your work efficiency, because a project gives you the right environment for your work. We did not talk about projects so far and you have probably saved some of the discussed code as an R script somewhere on your hard drive. This is fine in the beginning, but one day, you will open a script, and it is very likely that you set the work directory and load data somewhere in the old script:

```r
# Set the working directory
setwd("/Users/edgar/my_scripts/")
```

```
# Import data
df <- read_csv("my_data.csv")
```

Note that I use an absolute path to set the working directory. If the folder exists, R will set my working directory to the folder my_scripts. In the second line of code, I used a relative path and R searches for my_data.csv wherever my working directory points to. So, what happens if you ever need to use another computer which has a different structure of folders? What if someone else runs the script? R will return an error.

Absolute paths may not work if you cannot guarantee that the directory exists. On the other hand, relative paths will work if you make sure that the working directory is set correctly. RStudio helps us to setup the working directory and a project gives you the environment for all files related to a certain project. If you use a project, there is no need to provide absolute paths anymore since the working directory is attached to your project. Moreover, your script still runs if you take the entire project folder and save it somewhere else on your computer, use a new computer, or give the project to someone else, because the working directory is set to the directory of the specific project.

Some may say that this is just a minor achievement since we only saved one line of code. Trust me, you will appreciate this when you search your hard disk for a considerable time to find data, or visualizations, or any project file. Maybe you are better than me at remembering where all your files live, but one day you will migrate to a new computer or something else will happen meaning that an absolute path will break. Therefore, I can only recommend creating a project. It gives you the chance to focus on a structure for project files. We can save R scripts in an R folder, save plots in the plots or whatever folder structure might best work for you. Thus, creating a specific project helps us to increase the reproducibility. Or in other words, it is a warm and cozy place for your script(s) and other file(s) related to your project.

Creating a new project is not a difficult task and RStudio has integrated a Project Wizard. There is a Project button in the right corner. Click the project button and create a new project or use the menu (File > New Project). In both instances, a new window opens with the project wizard and there are essentially three steps to create a new project:

1. First, decide if you want to create the project in a new or existing directory (see Chapter 9 for more information about version control).
2. Next, RStudio asks whether you want to create a special form of project (e.g., to create an R package), select a new project.
3. Finally, give the project a name and tell RStudio where your project should be saved. If you decided to create a new directory for the project – which is a very good idea – then RStudio creates a new folder and inserts a .Rproj file. The latter is saved in the project folder and contains the information about the project.

Besides the fact you can save all your documents that belong to each other in one place, working with projects has additional advantages. Each time you open a project, RStudio opens a fresh environment for your project. You can see that RStudio has opened a new instance after you created the project in the RStudio symbol which displays the project name as well. Thus, you can open several RStudio instances and code from one project will not interfere with code from another project.

Imagine you do not use RStudio projects but work on project A and B in one RStudio instance. You have loaded a package while working on project A, but you forgot to insert the same library in the script of project B. It is bitter, but you don't get any error because you have loaded it earlier, even though the library is never called in the script of project B. Thus, the script will not work the next time you open it. R tells you that some functions do not exist. Now, it is up to you to find out which package is missing. Maybe this sounds unrealistic, but I have seen this issue more than once and I have made the same mistake as well. You get an error if you have forgotten to update the script for project B, but only if each project runs its own R instance.

To this end, always restart R (Session > Restart R) one more time before you finish your script. You clean the entire environment by restarting R. This way, you make sure that your script runs without any errors the next time you open it. Restarting R several times is also useful if your script becomes longer, since you do not want to debug the entire script from the start to the last line of code when you are about to finish.

Sometimes you come across R scripts that start with the rm() function, which removes one, several, or all listed objects (rm(list=ls())) from the environment. Of course, we might be deemed to use code to remove objects, however, if you open your RStudio project, a new instance starts with a clean slate without any old ghost from a different project. The rm() function only removes objects that you have created, but there might be other objects that interfere with the analysis from packages that have been used in the beginning of the session. If you restart R, such dependencies become quickly visible and can be adjusted. In a similar sense, the use_blank_slate() function from the usethis package reminds us that we should not save the work space, nor load the work space from an earlier session (Wickham, Bryan, et al., 2022). It adjusts the settings, as the next console illustrates.

```
# Create a blank slate:
usethis::use_blank_slate()
#> Setting RStudio preference save_workspace to 'never'
#> Setting RStudio preference load_workspace to FALSE
```

Why not? It is our goal to create code that executes all necessary steps since our work needs to be reproducible. We should get the same results regardless of whether we rerun our script on a different day or on another computer. For such reasons, we definitely do not want to depend on obscure objects from the past. Go to the RStudio settings and remove the check mark from restoring the work space at start up and do not save the work space in an `.RData` file on exit (`Tools > Global Options`).

In larger projects, we may use one script to prepare the data, another one to run the analysis or visualize the results. Create a script for all steps, put them all in the same (R) folder, and use the `source()` function to run a script in the background.

```
# Use source to outsource your R script
source("R/my_script.R")
```

RStudio also helps you in terms of longer and probably more complex code chucks with code snippets.

4.3.3 Snippets

I still remember my first applied statistic course when I was a student. I learned how to use SPSS (Statistical Package for the Social Sciences) and a lot of students in the class were afraid. We had to memorize the code to pass the course, because SPSS had no auto-completion. Imagine it, with R code. We had to memorize that the `hist()` function returns a histogram.

```
# A simple histogram
hist(data$x)
```

Learning such a simple code snippet is no big deal, but what if the code snippet is getting substantially longer. Just for the sake of illustration, suppose you have to remember several options from the `hist()` function to adjust the plot. You need to memorize that you can adjust the title with the `main` option, add a label for the x-axis with `xlab`, fill the bars with a color (`col`), and examine the frequency or the density with the `freq` option. Look how complicated the code has become, and question yourself whether it makes any sense to memorize such code.

```
# A histogram with adjusted options
hist(mpg,
  main = "My title",
  xlab = "The x label",
  col = "darkgray",
  freq = FALSE
)
```

Your skills do not increase when you memorize such code snippets, but is it necessary to memorize as much code as possible to become an efficient user? All I can do today with SPSS is generate a frequency table or calculate a mean without the help of Google. Well, if I am honest, I have some serious doubts about the latter, too. Didn't I learn hard enough? The truth is that I am not an SPSS user. I only attended this particular course, and it should not come as a surprise that I cannot remember much.

I share this story because I truly believe that we do not have to memorize complicated code snippets to become an efficient R user. Irrespective of the programming language, one should never memorize code chunks. It is more important to understand what code does and how to use it, not how it is implemented. As you can recall, you can use the `help` function if you do not know how code works, you can read the vignettes, or google it. Often you will find that the code snippet for your purpose is only a few clicks away. Using such a code snippet also increases your skills because you will need to make a transfer in order to apply the code.

Unfortunately, searching for code snippets with Google takes time and reduces your work efficiency. Moreover, it is annoying if you do not find the right snippet and it becomes even more frustrating when you have to apply this strategy several times. Trust me, I am speaking again from my own experience. Luckily for you, there is a simple way to store and retrieve code snippets in RStudio.

Open RStudio, create a new script, type `fun` and press <TAB> on your keyboard. I hope you are as stunned as I was when I first discovered how snippets work in RStudio. The shortcut `fun` inserts the blank snippet to create a function. The snippet even assigns a `name` for the function as the next output shows.

```
# Insert fun and press TAB to insert the fun(ction) snippet
name <- function(variables) {

}
```

Snippets have predefined fields that need to be filled in. We can directly jump from one to another field by using <TAB> on the keyboard. After your snippet is inserted, the `name` of the function is preselected and you can directly insert a name for the function. If you click <TAB>, RStudio jumps to the second field (`variables`) and you can type again without using the mouse or any other devise. With the last <TAB> we enter the function's body. RStudio gives us a few pre-defined snippets to start with, but the best thing about snippets is that you can add your own.

Open RStudio's global options, go the second pane (`Data`), and scroll down the window. You will find a button to manage your snippets. Alternatively, use the `edit_rstudio_snippets()` function from the `usethis` package. It opens the document that saves all snippets.

```
# Use edit_rstudio_snippets() to edit your snippets directly
usethis::edit_rstudio_snippets()
```

The snippet document includes the snippet to create a function somewhere in between. As the next console shows, the fun snippet is defined as follows:

```
#The structure of the fun snippet
snippet fun
    ${1:name} <- function(${2:variables}) {
        ${0}
    }
```

To make a snippet is not difficult. Insert snippet, a name for your snippet, and then the code. Let us inspect how the fun snippet works. We must insert a dollar sign and a running number (${1}) for each snippet field. Thus, in the fun example, the first input refers to the ${1:name} where we are supposed to insert the name of the function. If you press <Tab> you jump to the second input ${2:variables} where we must insert the variables that the function handles and so on. All the rest of the code remains the same, although you may check the indentation before you test the snippet.

Let me give you one more piece of advice on how to use snippets efficiently. With the help of the snippet, it is easy to create code, since we must only remember the name of the snippet. At some point you will have several snippets and, if you picked your snippet name wisely, their name may immediately pop up, but you probably have to think twice after a long and tiresome day. Figure 4.4 shows you how RStudio's preview may help in this situation:

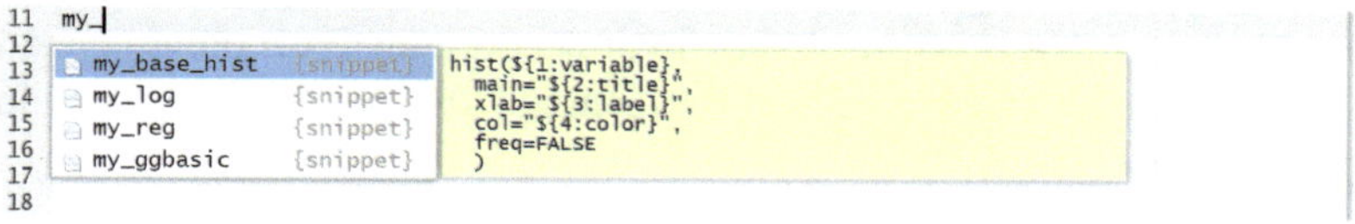

Fig. 4.4: Snippet preview

All your own snippets will show up if their name starts with the same prefix (e.g., my_) and you can scroll down the preview list to look for a snippet that did not come up instantly. Thus, instead of giving your snippets unique names, use a system that helps you to find the snippet (e.g., my_hist, etc.), even after a long day. Feel free to choose a system and names that are most appealing to you, but I do hope that the last example underlines that a consistent way of creating snippets will also improve your efficiency.

Thus, to become an efficient user, we should definitely remember what the hist() function does. Sometimes when we just want to explore the data, a quick-and-dirty version of the histogram is enough. However, it is time to start creating snippets if you have used Google several times to adjust the options of the `hist()` function or any other task.

Summary

Congratulations, mission accomplished! You are now able to manipulate data, which gives you the skills for your own missions. Of course, I know from personal experience that learning R can be awkward. Everyone makes a lot of mistakes in the beginning. It's pointless to say, but you will learn R by writing many lines of code, which will include an abundance of mistakes and errors. So, don't think of an error as something you are doing wrong – an error points to something you haven't achieved yet. R has a big community, and a lot of information is available online which helps you find a solution – or at least some hints – to solve the problem. Have a look at the `dplyr` cheat sheet available on the package website, which gives a compact overview of the possibilities at hand.

```
# The dplyr website
show_link("dplyr")
```

In addition, I tried to highlight the advantages of RStudio projects. Practice R focuses on applying R, which is why I did not start with projects in the beginning, and why I did not outline all advantages in great length. Start to use projects if you work with R on a regular basis. To mention some of the obvious advantages, it helps you to fix your working directory, it creates a new instance, and your file pane shows your project folder. Check out Chapter 2 of *What They Forgot to Teach You About R* by *Jennifer Bryan* and *Jim Hester*. They dedicate an entire chapter to project-oriented workflow. Or read Chapter 8 of *R for Data Science* by Wickham & Grolemund (2016) for more information about advantages of projects.

```
# What They Forgot to Teach You About R:
show_link("forgot_teach")
# R for Data Science
show_link("r4ds")
```

Part II: **The basics**

5 Prepare data

In the last chapter, we practiced data manipulation steps with implemented and prepared data. Unfortunately, data does not always come as clean as these examples imply. Data can be messy, and we have to apply many preparation steps before we can work with it. As a next step, it is a good idea to apply these concepts to a data set that is not made for teaching purposes. Working with toy data makes it easier to understand the logic, but at the end of the day you will close this book and import a data set. Therefore, we focus on some of the typical steps and pitfalls you may come across when you prepare data.

– In Section 5.1, we learn how to import (and export) data. This is not a difficult task, nonetheless it is not unlikely that you will run into problems during or right after this step. For instance, you get an error when you try to analyze a numerical variable, but some observations are stored as characters. Such mistakes are frustrating. We need to learn how the data is encoded and develop coping strategies for typical problems when cleaning the raw data. Thus, this section shows how to import different file formats and then focuses on typical problems that may arise when you start working with the imported data.

– In Section 5.2, we will increase our knowledge of missing data in theory and in practice. Often, we realize that values are missing or implausible when we explore the data. We need to deal with them, because missing values may seriously distort the estimation results. Our decisions about missing values, should we ignore them, may result in scientific misconduct and even data falsification. We will first lay a theoretical background under which circumstances missing values have a substantial effect on the analysis. Next, we use R to identify missing values, replace implausible and missing values, and we talk about patterns of missing values.

– In Section 5.3, we prepare categorical variables. This step is often needed before we run an analysis, and we already discussed how R handles factor variables in Chapter 3. In the social sciences we will often work with categorical variables, which is why we establish how the forcats package helps us to manipulate categorical variables in an efficient manner (Wickham, 2022a).

```r
# The setup of Chapter 5 #####
library(dplyr)
library(forcats)
library(janitor)
library(naniar)
library(readr)
library(tibble)
library(tidyr)
```

https://doi.org/10.1515/9783110704976-005

5.1 Data import and export

We can import data using different functions, depending on the file's format. For instance, many data sets can be downloaded as text files, often comma-separated value (*.csv) files. In this case, each observation is separated with a comma and the readr package lets us import csv and other text files (Wickham, Hester, & Bryan, 2022). As the next console illustrates, provide the name of a file to import, or the path that leads to the file if the data is not in the working directory.

```
# Import a csv file
library(readr)
my_data <- read_csv("path_to_the_file/data.csv")
```

Maybe you have never seen a csv file before. Maybe you are familiar with files saved in a format of other statistical software that is frequently taught in the social sciences (e.g., SPSS: *.sav file, Stata: *.dta file). I bet that you have at least worked with an Excel file (*.xlsx). The read_excel() function from the readxl package lets you work with an Excel file (Wickham & Bryan, 2022). Use the read_sav() function from the haven package to import an SPSS file; the haven package also provides a solution for Stata, as the next console illustrates (Wickham, Miller, et al., 2022).

```
# Import a stata (spss) file
haven::read_stata("my_stata.dta")
```

R even has its own data format (R data file: .rda), but the logic of the applied steps is (almost) identical regardless of the format. Before you continue to import data, consider that RStudio has several features that help us a lot with this task. For instance, RStudio has a *Data Preview*. The menu displays *Import Options* and we even see and get the code to import the data in the *Code Preview*. Let's inspect how the features are implemented.

The data preview shows how the data will be imported, which helps to figure out if something goes wrong. To see the data preview, go to the *Environment* pane and search for the Import button or use the toolbar (File -> Import Dataset). We can import text via R base or the readr package; import data from Excel; or files from statistic software such as SPSS, SAS, and Stata. A data import window will appear after you picked a format and Figure 5.1 shows a screen shot that illustrates the import window. I imported a csv file and picked the second option from the menu (the *From text (readr)* option). Irrespective of the imported file, the import window will only differ in terms of the displayed import options.

With the import window, we are able to examine the header, scroll up and down to inspect the data, and detect potential problems. For example, sometimes I try to import a text file that is not a csv file and, therefore, the file contains a different character to separate values. We will learn how to solve such a problem by tweaking the options in a minute, but with the help of the preview we quickly see if something went wrong. Of course, this is not a guarantee that everything works fine, but at least we get a sneak preview.

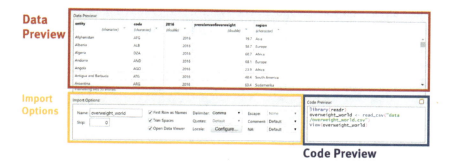

Fig. 5.1: Data import window

Import options lets us determine how the data is imported. RStudio has integrated several options at the bottom of the menu, depending on the format of the file. When importing a text file, you can select whether the first row includes a header with variable names. Should missing values not be coded as NA (not available), we must declare how they are saved in the file, and we have to adjust which delimiter is used to separate observations. The latter takes care of the fact that the information in a text file may not be separated by commas. Sometimes a file contains a tab (tab-separated values *.tsv) or other character delimiters to separate values. Talking about different file formats and options might be overwhelming. The good news is that you do not need to remember them in detail – it is enough to know that such options exists. Because of the next import feature, we don't even have to remember the code when importing data.

Examine the code preview at the bottom right of the menu. RStudio shows the code to import the file and there is no need to memorize the package, nor the function name. The code preview makes it comfortable to import data. The import menu shows the code to load the library, the function to import the data, and if you have adjusted options manually, it shows that code as well. As the next console illustrates, I imported data that contains the number of overweight people worldwide, and the code preview displays the following code.

```
# Copy the R code from the code preview
overweight_world <- read_csv("~/data/overweight_world.csv")
View(overweight_world)
```

114 ⸻ 5 Prepare data

RStudio suggests an object name and includes the code for the viewer, which helps you to inspect how the data was imported. Thus, use the import menu, but do not forget to copy the code to import the data. There is even a copy button in the code preview. For the next steps it is not necessary to import the same data, but I included the file (`overweight_world.csv`) in the `files` folder of the `PracticeR` package, which means that the file is already on your computer. The `system.file()` function returns the path to the file and the next console shows how you can import it.

```
# system.file returns the path of system files
overweight_path <- system.file("files", "overweight_world.csv",
  package = "PracticeR"
)
```

```
overweight_world <- read_csv(overweight_path)
```

In terms of the logical steps, there is no big difference between data import and export, but we are making a huge step into the future. For instance, we may want to export and save data after we have cleaned it; or maybe you created a new data frame with estimation results. Irrespective of the reason, use one of the `write_()` functions for this job. The following console shows how the code works in terms of a csv file and the `readr` package; it expects at least the exported object (e.g., the new data frame) and a string with the name. The function will export the file to the current working directory.

```
# Export data
write_csv(my_new_data, "my_new_data.csv")
```

I have barely touched the tip of the iceberg, and there is a lot more to learn about data export. How files and objects are exported largely depends on the file format. For instance, in the case of a csv file, we may need to tweak the options and adjust how missing values are handled (`na = "NA"`) or whether column names (`col_names`) are (not) included. It does not make much sense to learn all available options to export, but you should know that you can export files in different formats. Use the `write_dta()` function to export a file for Stata, or the `write_sav()` function if you require an SPSS file. Considering we have only explored the fundamentals, make sure that you inspect the help files before you start to export data.

I am focusing on files that you probably know or may use in the near future to analyze data, hence I don't provide a comprehensive list. There are more packages and possibilities to get access to data. To mention a few, work with *Google Sheets* and the `googlesheets4` package (Bryan, 2022), or use the `rjson` package (Couture-Beil, 2022) for JSON (JavaScript Object Notation) files. You may need the latter if you collect data from the web. Even if you will never use those packages, it is good to know that a lot of options exist. There is even the possibility of copying and pasting data into your R script. The next info box about the datapasta package outlines how the principle works (McBain et al., 2020).

The datapasta package   **i**

Imagine, you have found data on a website, but you cannot download it. Do you really want to copy and paste it all in an Excel sheet when you can include it straight into your R script in a nice and proper way? The datapasta package converts the copied data and inserts it from your clipboard as a tibble, a tribble, a data frame, or a vector. For example, consider the next console. I did not include this data manually, I copied it and let the datapasta package do its job.

```
#Datapasta to copy and paste data
tibble::tribble(
    ~Country, ~`2011`, ~`2012`, ~`2013`, ~`2014`, ~`2015`, ~`2016`,
   "Australia",    5.1,    5.2,    5.7,    6.1,    6.1,    5.7,
     "Austria",    4.6,    4.9,    5.3,    5.6,    5.7,      6,
     "Belgium",    7.1,    7.5,    8.4,    8.5,    8.5,    7.8,
      "Canada",    7.6,    7.3,    7.1,    6.9,    6.9,    7.1,
       "Chile",    7.1,    6.5,    6.1,    6.5,    6.3,    6.7
   )
```

Give it a try and go the PracticeR website (see next console). It contains an example website with tables that we will scrape in Chapter 11. However, there is no need for a sophisticated approach if we collect only one table. Insert first the tribble_paste() function from the datapasta package in your script, than go to the website and copy the table; ultimately go back to the R script and run the function. The function will automatically insert the data in the script when you execute it.

```
#Go to:
show_link("webscraping")
#Copy and paste via:
datapasta::tribble_paste()
```

Like this, you can copy and paste data from a csv, an Excel file, or even a website, all with the help of the datapasta package. The package even comes with an addin for RStudio which is why we don't need to remember the code. Just copy and insert it via the addin.

There are a lot of possibilities to import data and, at least in theory, it is simple. Unfortunately, there are several pitfalls when importing data, especially if the data is messy. Sometimes variable names are hard to work with because they contain special characters (e.g., $); or they have names that do not reveal what it measures (e.g. 2011). In general terms, raw data is often messy and we need clean it before we can prepare variables for an analysis. We need solutions for typical pitfalls that may occur during or after importing data. First, I focus on steps during the data import, which makes it necessary to increase our knowledge about *encoding*. Second, we talk about typical

116 —— 5 Prepare data

cleaning steps for raw data. Third, we learn how data can be *combined* since a data set can be split into several files.

5.1.1 Encoding

Suppose, you import data and run into an error. This happens if the data is messy, but even well-prepared data from official sources may contain some errors. The import menu shows how the data will be encoded and sometimes we see a problem right away, but what shall we do? Let me give you a few examples of what can go wrong if we import data, hopefully reducing your pain when you start working on your own.

Maybe you only recognize a problem after the data is imported. You have applied several preparation steps and starting all over again hurts. Suppose a numerical variable is encoded as a character vector, because some elements are characters, as the `class()` function reveals.

```
# A messy variable
x <- c("9", 9, 9, 2, 3, 1, 2)
class(x)
```

```
#> [1] "character"
```

We cannot apply a function for a numerical input if we do not convert the variable into a numerical vector. There are several `as.*` functions that transform the input into a different data type. Suppose we have a factor variable `x` and a numerical variable `y`. The `as.numeric()` function generates unique numerical values for each level, while the `as.character()` function makes a character vector from the numerical input.

```
# As numeric
as.numeric(x)
```

```
#> [1] 9 9 9 2 3 1 2
```

```
# As character
y <- c(3.11, 2.7)
as.character(y)
```

```
#> [1] "3.11" "2.7"
```

What happens if you need to adjust several variables because the data is a real mess? Consider the raw data from the last section. I used it to show that the amount of overweight and obese people increased worldwide. As the next console reveals, the data contains a column with the country name, an indicator for the prevalence of overweight people, and a year variable with strange variable names.

```r
# A real example, what a mess!
overweight_world <- read_csv("data/overweight_world.csv")
head(overweight_world)
```

```
#> # A tibble: 6 x 5
#>   entity      code  `2016` prevalenceofoverweight region
#>   <chr>       <chr> <dbl>                   <dbl> <chr>
#> 1 Afghanistan AFG    2016                    19.7 Asia
#> 2 Albania     ALB    2016                    58.7 Europe
#> 3 Algeria     DZA    2016                    60.7 Africa
#> 4 Andorra     AND    2016                    68.1 Europe
#> 5 Angola      AGO    2016                    23.9 Africa
#> # ... with 1 more row
```

Such a data frame emphasizes that we need cleaning steps before we run an analysis, at least to get rid of the odd variable names. We let readr decide how the variables are encoded, and in terms of encoding there were no errors. What shall we do if there is a mistake? In such cases it is convenient to know about the *column specification*. The specs() function returns the column specification that the readr package used to import the data.

```r
# Inspect the column specification
spec(overweight_world)
```

```
#> cols(
#>   entity = col_character(),
#>   code = col_character(),
#>   `2016` = col_double(),
#>   prevalenceofoverweight = col_double(),
#>   region = col_character()
#> )
```

The column specification contains the information on how the readr package encoded each column of the data. For example, the last variable region is a character column and readr made the right decision and declared the *column as characters* (col_character()). How does the package figures that out?

The readr package inspects the first one thousand observations of each variable and makes a guess about the stored information. In technical terms, different parsers are used to retrieve the information and we can apply the guess_parser() function to examine this procedure. As the next console illustrates, the guess_parser() returns the guess of the readr package for a character, a numerical, and a logical vector (Wickham & Grolemund, 2016, Ch. 11).

```
# Guess_parser reveals the parser to encode data
guess_parser(c("Hello world"))
```

```
#> [1] "character"
```

```
guess_parser(c("2000,5", "2005,44", "2010,3"))
```

```
#> [1] "number"
```

```
guess_parser(c("TRUE", "FALSE"))
```

```
#> [1] "logical"
```

Hopefully, the readr package makes the right guess. What if a variable is messy and contains first one thousand observations with characters? Or let's say that you received a newer version of the data and you want to make sure that a numerical variable will be imported as a numerical variable, regardless of what it contains. In this case, we must determine how variables are encoded.

Adjust the parser directly via the import menu. If you use RStudio to import data, you can see this information in the header of the preview and change it manually. Go back to the import menu and select *Data*. Click on the small arrow under the variable name in the import menu. A small pop-up menu appears that shows all available parsers. We can even exclude and skip the import of columns with the menu. After we have changed a parser or excluded a variable, look at how the code preview has changed. RStudio includes the column specification, as the next console illustrates.

```
# Adjust the column specification if it is necessary
overweight_world <- read_csv("data/overweight_world.csv",
  col_types = cols(
    code = col_skip(),
    `2016` = col_integer()
  )
)
```

I did not import several variables from `overweight_world` and I adjusted the column specification slightly. The years are now imported as integers. Thus, the code to import the data might have become more complicated, but we now are sure how the data will be imported. Maybe you are lucky, maybe you must never adjust how `readr` imports data, but remember that these possibilities exist should you run into an error.

What shall we do with missing values? We will focus in more detail on the problem of missing values in section 5.2, but we should take missing values into account while importing data. R expects missing values to be coded as NA, but accepts other characters as well. Say you import data from a spread sheet, but the missing values are just empty cells. Adjust how the data and missing values are imported with the RStudio import menu. For example, the na option of the `read_csv()` function lets you pick different NA indicators, even from empty cells in a spread sheet, while the `read_excel()` function automatically sets empty cells to NA.

```
# Refer to NA indicators with the na option
read_excel("data.xlsx",
  na = "99"
)
```

5.1.2 Cleaning variable names

It is up to you how variables are named, but R has certain restrictions for variable and object names. A name may contain letters, numbers, points, and underscores, but cannot start with a number or contain special characters. What happens if we import data that violates these restrictions? Suppose an Excel sheet contains a variable named `measurement 1` and a second one called `2016`. It is not allowed to start with a digit, but even the first variable breaks the rules since a blank space is included in the name. What happens if we create a data frame or import such data? We run into an error.

```
#This code returns an error:
data.frame(
  measurement 1 = 1,
  2016 = 1)
```

```
#> Error: unexpected numeric constant in:
#> "data.frame(
#>   measurement 1"
```

We may fix these problems by declaring the variables names as strings and put them in backticks:

120 —— 5 Prepare data

```
# Insert backticks
data.frame(
  `measurement 1` = 1,
  `2016` = 1
)
```

```
#>   measurement.1 X2016
#> 1             1     1
```

At least we can make a data frame out of this mess, but R inserts a point for the blank space and the letter x before the digits. A tibble is more convenient when it comes to variable names. A tibble does not change the name of the variables that violate the name restrictions:

```
# Tibble let us break name conventions
tibble(
  `measurement 1` = 1,
  `2016` = 2
)
```

```
#> # A tibble: 1 x 2
#>   `measurement 1` `2016`
#>             <dbl>  <dbl>
#> 1               1      2
```

We should stick to the rules and provide a meaningful name that outlines what the variable measures. In terms of the variable 2016, we are talking about a year which is obviously a better name that does not violate the rules. Moreover, even if we can create a variable with a blank space, we make our life more complicated since we need backticks to refer to the variable. In a nutshell, the rules are not supposed to make you struggle. On the contrary, if you give variables and objects names that explain what they measure – or in term of functions what they do – your future self and other people will thank you.

In the last section, I imported a data frame with a variable that consists of digits only, but I did not get an error message. In other words, we do not reproduce this error if we use the readr package to import data, because the package creates a tibble, not a data frame, as the is_tibble() function reveals.

```
# Is x a tibble?
tibble::is_tibble(overweight_world)
```

```
#> [1] TRUE
```

Sometimes implemented data is also not as clean and consistent as we wish. For example, the `iris` data provides measurements about flowers, but the variable names are stored in `Upper_Camel` case and single words of each variable are separated with a period. The `names()` function returns the column names.

```
# The iris data
names(iris)
```

```
#> [1] "Sepal.Length" "Sepal.Width" "Petal.Length" "Petal.Width" "Species"
```

There is nothing wrong with this style, but messy data may contain variables with an inconsistent style. For example, a mixture of:

```
#snake_case
my_var <- 1
```

```
#SCREAMING_SNAKE_CASE
MY_VAR <- 1
```

```
#camelCase
myVar <- 1
```

```
#Upper_Camel
MyVar <- 1
```

```
#kebab-case (hmm-mmmm)
my-var <- 1
```

Some people prefer `camelCase`, while other people use `snake_case` or a different style. Of course, it is up to you which style you prefer, as long as you apply one consistently. This sounds petty, but is the variable called `Sepal.Length`, `Sepal_Length`, or `sepal_length`? It is confusing if not all variables are named in a consistent way. It will increase your workload, because you must think twice how a variable is named. Moreover, it is error-prone because R is case sensitive and returns an error that a variable cannot be found if you apply the rules inconsistently. So, stick to one style.

Before we get rid of the inconsistent style of several variables, let's first learn how to rename a variable. There are several ways, but the `dplyr` package offers a convenient solution to rename a variable. Use the `rename()` function and give `dplyr` a new name for the old one.

```
# Rename variable: new_name = variable
dplyr::rename(iris, sepal_length = Sepal.Length)
```

However, there is no need to rename variables, because we can include this step if we select them.

```
# Include rename() in select
iris |>
  select(
    new_var = Sepal.Length
  )
```

```
#> # A tibble: 150 x 1
#>    new_var
#>      <dbl>
#> 1      5.1
#> 2      4.9
#> 3      4.7
#> 4      4.6
#> 5      5
#> # ... with 145 more rows
```

I picked the `iris` data because I prefer the `snake_case` rule, but the data applies a different style. Certainly, we could rename each variable, but to rename a bunch of variables is bothersome – at the very least it is a waste of time. How can we get rid of all `CamelCases` without spending too much time? Give the `clean_names()` function from the `janitor` package a try (Firke, 2021). Just like the janitor in a school, the package cleans the variable names – it converts them to the `snake_case` variables and we don't spend the entire day to clean each variable name manually!

```
# The janitor package cleans data
iris |>
  janitor::clean_names()
```

```
#> # A tibble: 150 x 5
#>    sepal_length sepal_width petal_length petal_width species
#>           <dbl>       <dbl>        <dbl>       <dbl> <fct>
#> 1           5.1         3.5          1.4         0.2 setosa
#> 2           4.9         3            1.4         0.2 setosa
#> 3           4.7         3.2          1.3         0.2 setosa
#> 4           4.6         3.1          1.5         0.2 setosa
```

```
#> 5              5          3.6         1.4         0.2 setosa
#> # ... with 145 more rows
```

You are no fan of the `snake_case` rule? Apply a different rule. The function returns `CamelCase` or other styles by tweaking the `case` option. Thus, the `janitor` package provides useful features to clean variable names without much effort. Of course, some inconsistencies may remain. Consider the next console with messy variable names. I created variable names that do not consistently apply a coding style. To examine how R will handle those variable names, use the `names()` function.

```
# Another messy data set
messy_data <- data.frame(
  firstName = 1:2,
  Second_name = 1:2,
  `income in €` = 1:2,
  `2009` = 1:2,
  measurement = 1:2,
  measurement = 1:2
)
names(messy_data)
```

```
#> [1] "firstName"      "Second_name"    "income.in.."    "X2009"
#> [5] "measurement"    "measurement.1"
```

As the console shows, I used `CamelCase`, but not all words start with a capital letter. I included a euro sign (€), which is not a good idea because special signs are excluded and the `income` variable gets two extra periods instead of the euro sign. Finally, I even used a name (`measurement`) twice! The good news is, `tibble()` returns an error message if a variable name is used twice and also gives some recommendations on how to fix the problem.

```
# Tibble checks duplicates and warns us
tibble(
  measurement = 1:2,
  measurement = 1:2
)
```

```
#> Error:
#> ! Column name `measurement` must not be duplicated.
#> Use .name_repair to specify repair.
#> Caused by error in `repaired_names()`:
```

```
#> ! Names must be unique.
#> x These names are duplicated:
#>   * "measurement" at locations 1 and 2.
```

What about the other variable names? Does the `clean_names()` function get rid of them? As the next console shows, all names are now consistent, but not all problems are solved. In a very similar way, it is likely that some inconsistencies and manual steps remain if you start to clean data.

```
# Janitor gets rid of many crude names
names(messy_data |> janitor::clean_names())
```

```
#> [1] "first_name"    "second_name"    "income_in"    "x2009"
#> [5] "measurement"   "measurement_1"
```

Sometimes we are lucky and a data set comes as one file, but sometimes the data might be split to several files. This is probable if we use data from a longitudinal study, which often stores waves in separate files. Or sometimes we need to combine a survey with data from other sources. In all of these examples we need to combine data, in order to prepare the data for the analysis.

5.1.3 Combining data

We need to acknowledge that data can be stored in a wide or a long format which makes it necessary to learn how to transform the data before we can combine it. The differences between *cross-sectional* and *longitudinal* data outline the reason why different data formats exist. Suppose we conducted a survey. In the first wave, we have observed two variables (x and y) for several participants (ID). In case of cross-sectional data, each row contains one observation and all variables get their own column. Say we have measured x two times, while y is a time-constant variable (e.g., participant's sex). Shall we append each observation of the second wave, or shall we create a new variable that indicates the time of the measurement?

In other words, shall we bring the data into the *long* or into the *wide* format. Figure 5.2 shows two small data sets, and each colored box represents a cell. If we append the second measurement, the data becomes longer and is stored in the *long format*. As Figure 5.2 (A) illustrates, the data contains two rows per person, which makes it necessary to include a key (ID) and a time (t) variable.

However, we may switch to the wide format, as Figure 5.2 (B) highlights. We include a separate column with a running number for each time-varying variable. We must ensure that both data sets have the same format when we are combining them. How can we transform data from long (wide) into the wide (long) format?

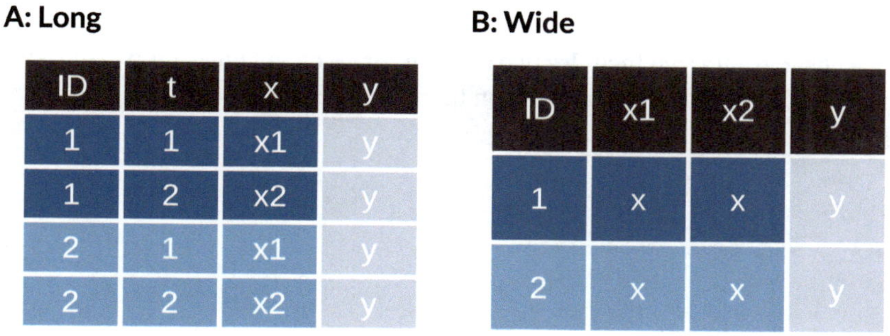

A: Long

ID	t	x	y
1	1	x1	y
1	2	x2	y
2	1	x1	y
2	2	x2	y

B: Wide

ID	x1	x2	y
1	x	x	y
2	x	x	y

Fig. 5.2: Long (A) and wide (B) data

Consider the `gapminder` data (Bryan, 2017). It contains information about life expectancy (`lifeExp`), the size of the population (`pop`), and the GDP per capita, (`gdpPercap`). Those variables are time varying, while variables such as `country` and `continent` are constant. The data comes in the long format and encompasses 142 countries and an observational period from 1952 up to 2007.

```
library(gapminder)
head(gapminder)
```

```
#> # A tibble: 6 x 6
#>    country     continent  year lifeExp       pop gdpPercap
#>    <fct>       <fct>     <int>   <dbl>     <int>     <dbl>
#> 1 Afghanistan Asia       1952    28.8   8425333      779.
#> 2 Afghanistan Asia       1957    30.3   9240934      821.
#> 3 Afghanistan Asia       1962    32.0  10267083      853.
#> 4 Afghanistan Asia       1967    34.0  11537966      836.
#> 5 Afghanistan Asia       1972    36.1  13079460      740.
#> # ... with 1 more row
```

Transforming and combining real data is often tricky because the data needs to be well prepared. Suppose we use the `country` name to match observations, but the key variable includes typos. In such cases, we can't match the observations. Or, suppose we match data but we do not observe the same time period for all included countries. In consequence, we introduce missing values which we will address in the last section of this chapter. First, we learn the principles to transform and combine data with clean data inspired by the `gapminder` data.

126 —— 5 Prepare data

From long to wide

Suppose we observe data that includes two different types of outcomes for two different countries: the GDP (gdp) and the population (pop) for Germany and the UK.

```
#A data frame (df) to illustrate:
df <- tibble::tribble(
    ~country, ~outcome, ~measurement,
   "Germany",    "gdp",          3.8,
   "Germany",    "pop",        83.24,
        "UK",    "gdp",          2.7,
        "UK",    "pop",        67.22
  )
```

Note that gdp is measured in billions of USD, while population indicates how many people live in each country, but measured in millions. Moreover, we do not know which measurement we observed without a variable name. This makes it clear why we would prefer a wide data set in this case.

The tidyr package helps us to transform the data from the long into the wide format (Wickham & Girlich, 2022): The pivot_wider() function has two main arguments, names_from and values_from. The first argument expects an input vector with variable names. It is the outcome in the minimal example. Furthermore, we must outline where the values of each variable come from (here measurement).

```
# tidyr::pivot_wider converts long data into the wide format
df |>
  pivot_wider(
    names_from = outcome,
    values_from = measurement
  )
```

```
#> # A tibble: 2 x 3
#>   country   gdp   pop
#>   <chr>   <dbl> <dbl>
#> 1 Germany   3.8  83.2
#> 2 UK        2.7  67.2
```

The pivot_wider() function comes with several options to adjust how the data is transformed. For instance, suppose the outcome variable is very obscure and does not outline what it measures at all. Instead, it only indicates the number of the outcome.

```
df <- tibble::tribble(
  ~country,  ~outcome, ~measurement,
  "Germany",        1,          3.8,
  "Germany",        2,        83.24,
       "UK",        1,          2.7,
       "UK",        2,        67.22
)
```

Nobody knows what a variable contains if the variable name consists only of numbers, so give the variable a name that reveals its content. We can set a prefix name (`names_prefix`) and append a running number for each variable. The `tidyr` package separates variable names with an underscore.

```
# Add names_prefix
df |>
  pivot_wider(
    names_from = "outcome",
    names_prefix = "outcome_",
    values_from = "measurement"
  )
```

```
#> # A tibble: 2 x 3
#>   country outcome_1 outcome_2
#>   <chr>       <dbl>     <dbl>
#> 1 Germany       3.8      83.2
#> 2 UK            2.7      67.2
```

We have examined one time-varying variable, but there might be several time-varying (and constant) variables. The next tibble accounts for this point and makes the data a bit more realistic. It contains several observations for each country (with random values of x and y) and a `time` variable for each measurement.

```
df <- tibble::tribble(
  ~continent, ~country, ~time,   ~x,    ~y,
    "Europe",     "UK",     1, 0.78, 0.77,
    "Europe",     "UK",     2, 0.63, 0.98,
    "Europe",     "UK",     3, 0.07, 0.18,
      "Asia",  "Japan",     1, 0.26, 0.69,
      "Asia",  "Japan",     2, 0.07, 0.11,
      "Asia",  "Japan",     4, 0.16, 0.13   )
```

We must include all time-varying variables in the `values_from` argument to transfer the data from long into the wide format.

```
# Include time-varying variables in values_from
df |>
  pivot_wider(
    names_from = time,
    values_from = c(x, y), names_sep = "_"
  )
```

```
#> # A tibble: 2 x 10
#>   contin~1 country   x_1   x_2   x_3   x_4   y_1   y_2   y_3
#>   <chr>    <chr>   <dbl> <dbl> <dbl> <dbl> <dbl> <dbl> <dbl>
#> 1 Europe   UK       0.78  0.63  0.07 NA     0.77  0.98  0.18
#> 2 Asia     Japan    0.26  0.07 NA     0.16  0.69  0.11 NA
#> # ... with 1 more variable: y_4 <dbl>, and abbreviated
#> #   variable name 1: continent
```

Did you notice that we generated missing values? Maybe you did not see it when the data was still in the long format, but there are no observations for Japan (in the third wave), while UK has missing in the fourth wave. All missing values are set to NA, but sometimes we need additional missing values indicators (e.g., for robustness test). Fill these gaps with the `values_fill` option, but keep in mind that the values are missing regardless of the indicator.

```
# Fill in missing values with, for example, 99:
df |>
  pivot_wider(
    names_from = time,
    values_from = c(x, y),
    values_fill = 99
  )
```

```
#> # A tibble: 2 x 10
#>   contin~1 country   x_1   x_2   x_3   x_4   y_1   y_2   y_3
#>   <chr>    <chr>   <dbl> <dbl> <dbl> <dbl> <dbl> <dbl> <dbl>
#> 1 Europe   UK       0.78  0.63  0.07 99     0.77  0.98  0.18
#> 2 Asia     Japan    0.26  0.07 99     0.16  0.69  0.11 99
#> # ... with 1 more variable: y_4 <dbl>, and abbreviated
#> #   variable name 1: continent
```

From wide to long

Let's pretend that we observed two countries and we measured *x* five times.

```
#Wide data frame
df <- tibble::tribble(
  ~continent,  ~country,  ~x1,   ~x2,   ~x3,   ~x4,   ~x5,
    "Europe", "Germany", 0.18, 0.61, 0.39,   NA, 0.34,
    "Europe",     "UK", 0.81, 0.35, 0.69, 0.22,   NA
  )
```

The `pivot_longer()` function transforms data from the wide into the long format. The function has three main arguments: (1) The `cols` argument expects columns that should be transformed. (2) The `names_to` argument needs the name for a new variable. This column will contain the measured outcome, but it does not exist in the data since we are going to collapse several columns of the data. Therefore, we need to provide a string with a new variable name. (3) The same applies to `values_to`. It creates a column for the measurement. As the next console shows, I picked the variable names `time` and `outcome` to illustrate how the code works but try to be more explicit than me.

```
# pivot_longer convert wide data into the long format
df |>
  pivot_longer(
    cols = c(`x1`, `x2`, `x3`, `x4`, `x5`),
    names_to = "time",
    values_to = "outcome"
  )
```

```
#> # A tibble: 10 x 4
#>   continent country time  outcome
#>   <chr>     <chr>   <chr>   <dbl>
#> 1 Europe    Germany x1       0.18
#> 2 Europe    Germany x2       0.61
#> 3 Europe    Germany x3       0.39
#> 4 Europe    Germany x4      NA
#> 5 Europe    Germany x5       0.34
#> # ... with 5 more rows
```

It is not necessary to list each variable, especially if the variables have a running number. Just provide a start and endpoint (`x1:x5`) instead of the complete list. Time-varying variables have often the same variable name with a running number to differentiate between the points of time. Instead of using a start and end point, we may use the

130 —— 5 Prepare data

`starts_with()` argument. This option includes all variables that start with a certain string. Moreover, the `names_prefix()` option will help us to get rid of the constant part of the variable name (x) and includes the running number only.

```
# Starts_with searches for variables strings
# Adjust prefixes with names_prefix
df |>
  pivot_longer(
    cols = starts_with("x"),
    names_to = "time",
    names_prefix = "x",
    values_to = "outcome"
  ) |>
  head()
```

```
#> # A tibble: 6 x 4
#>    continent country time  outcome
#>    <chr>     <chr>   <chr>   <dbl>
#> 1 Europe    Germany 1        0.18
#> 2 Europe    Germany 2        0.61
#> 3 Europe    Germany 3        0.39
#> 4 Europe    Germany 4        NA
#> 5 Europe    Germany 5        0.34
#> # ... with 1 more row
```

Again, the data has implicit missing values and there are no observations for Germany in the fourth wave, while the UK lacks the fifth measurement. We must decide what we do with those missing values. You can set `values_drop_na` to TRUE or FALSE.

To transform data can be tricky if even the mechanics seem simple. Make sure that you did not introduce any error and inspect the data carefully before you go on with the next steps. However, after the data has the same format, we are able to apply mutating and filtering joins to combine it. In the next step we discover several ways to combine data and we explore functions from the `dplyr` package that help us during the merging process.

Mutating joins

Figure 5.3 shows two small data sets (A and B) with colored boxes to illustrate how data joins work; each box represents one cell of the data and both contain two variables from three persons. In order to combine data, each data set needs a unique identifier variable. Here I gave each person a unique ID. In our case it is a running number, but we could use a character variable as well. Data set A contains variable x, while data set

B contains variable y. Note that both data sets differ in terms of the observed persons. Persons 1 and 2 show up in both data sets; while person 3 is not listed in data set B; and there is no information about person 4 in data set A.

Data A

ID	X
1	x1
2	x2
3	x3

Data B

ID	Y
1	y1
2	y2
4	y4

Fig. 5.3: Mutating joins

How can we join both data sets? Figure 5.4 shows you what the data looks like if you apply a *full join* (A) or an *inner join* (B). A full join creates a new data set with all possible combinations of both data sets. In our case it includes all persons and all observations of x and y. A full join may create a mess, especially if the data does not contain the same observation units. Keep in mind that depending on how we combine data, we need to deal with missing values either way. Figure 5.4 (B) shows the result of an inner join. The inner join combines data only for observations that appear in both data sets.

A: Full join

ID	X	Y
1	x1	y1
2	x2	y2
3	x3	NA
4	NA	y4

B: Inner join

ID	X	Y
1	x1	y1
2	x2	y2

Fig. 5.4: Full join (A) and inner join (B)

As Figure 5.5 further illustrates, we can also apply a *left join* (A) or a *right join* (B). Suppose you work with data set A. A left join adds the variables of data B that can be combined. In our example persons 1 and 2 get the corresponding values from data set B, while person 3 is set to NA since there is no information that we can add. A right join

132 —— 5 Prepare data

works exactly the other way around. We start with data set B and add all variables that can be combined from data set A.

A: Left join

ID	X	Y
1	x1	y1
2	x2	y2
3	x3	NA

B: Right join

ID	Y	X
1	y1	x1
2	y2	x2
4	y4	NA

Fig. 5.5: Left join (A) and right join (B)

Let us create two data frames to see how it works with dplyr. As the next console shows, I again created data frames for countries. The first data set contains the country name (as the identifier) and their gross domestic product (gdp); the second data frame contains the size of the population (pop) for some of the countries.

```
#Two example data sets
df1 <- tibble::tribble(
  ~country,   ~gdp,
  "Brazil",   1.44,
  "China",   14.72,
    "UK",    2.67
)

df2 <- tibble::tribble(
  ~country,   ~pop,
  "Germany", 83.24,
   "Italy", 59.03,
    "UK",   67.22
)
```

To combine them, insert both data frames into the inner_join() function and determine which variable should be used as the identifier with the by option.

```
# Inner join
inner_join(df1, df2, by = "country")
```

```
#> # A tibble: 1 x 3
#>   country   gdp   pop
#>   <chr>   <dbl> <dbl>
#> 1 UK       2.67  67.2
```

As the output shows, the combined data set contains only UK since the latter is the only observation that appears in both data frames. A full join reveals missing values and works the same way.

```
# Full join
full_join(df1, df2, by = "country")
```

```
#> # A tibble: 5 x 3
#>   country   gdp   pop
#>   <chr>   <dbl> <dbl>
#> 1 Brazil   1.44  NA
#> 2 China   14.7   NA
#> 3 UK       2.67  67.2
#> 4 Germany NA    83.2
#> 5 Italy   NA    59.0
```

Since Italy does not show up in the first data frame, the country is no longer included if we apply a left join. Or turn around and apply a right join:

```
# Left join
left_join(df1, df2, by = "country")
```

```
#> # A tibble: 3 x 3
#>   country   gdp   pop
#>   <chr>   <dbl> <dbl>
#> 1 Brazil   1.44  NA
#> 2 China   14.7   NA
#> 3 UK       2.67  67.2
```

```
# Right join
right_join(df1, df2, by = "country")
```

```
#> # A tibble: 3 x 3
#>   country   gdp   pop
#>   <chr>   <dbl> <dbl>
#> 1 UK       2.67  67.2
```

```
#> 2 Germany NA     83.2
#> 3 Italy    NA    59.0
```

The last examples only underlined that we create missing values, but if the data is not prepared, we may not combine it or create a real mess. Filtering joins help us to identify duplicates or observations that are (not) listed in a data set.

Filtering joins

Filtering joins do not create a new data frame; they return selected columns. Let's assume that you work with two similar data frames. Unfortunately, the data sets are messy and contain duplicates that we need to get rid of. We need to be aware of what the data contains in order to combine it: what have both data sets in common, why are the duplicates generated in the first place, and how can we get rid of them?

```
#Two messy data sets
df1 <- tibble::tribble(
    ~country,   ~gdp,
    "China",  14.72,
  "Germany",   3.85,
       "UK",   2.67
  )

df2 <- tibble::tribble(
    ~country, ~gdp,
   "Brazil", 1.44,
  "Germany", 3.85,
       "UK", 2.67
  )
```

Suppose you want to append variables but only for observations you observed in the first instance. In this case, we must examine which countries are listed in first data frame that also appear in the second one. The semi_join() function returns observations of the first data frame which also appear in the second one.

```
# Semi join
semi_join(df1, df2, by = "country")

#> # A tibble: 2 x 2
#>    country   gdp
#>    <chr>   <dbl>
#> 1 Germany  3.85
```

```
#> 2 UK          2.67
```

Since the data sets are messy, we certainly do not want to combine them, but now we know which countries of the first data set also appear in the second one. The counterpart to semi_join() is the anti_join() function. It drops observations from the first data set and returns only observations that are not listed in the second one.

```
# Anti join
anti_join(df1, df2, by = "country")
```

```
#> # A tibble: 1 x 2
#>    country   gdp
#>    <chr>     <dbl>
#> 1 China     14.7
```

In a similar sense, set operations from base R such as the intersect() function (intersection) helps us to reveal duplicates as well. The function returns observations that appear in both data sets. Or consider the union() function. Germany and UK are listed in both data set. The union() function combines both data frames and drops the duplicates.

```
# An union combines data frames and drops duplicates
union(df1, df2)
```

```
#> # A tibble: 4 x 2
#>    country   gdp
#>    <chr>     <dbl>
#> 1 China     14.7
#> 2 Germany   3.85
#> 3 UK        2.67
#> 4 Brazil    1.44
```

Keep in mind, the discussed mechanics to combine data are not hard to apply but we can create a real mess if we combine data that is not well prepared. Inspect carefully the unique identifier variable and generate some robustness checks before you go on and analyze the data. In a similar sense, we need to deal with missing values.

5.2 Missing data

What should we do with missing or implausible values? Suppose you conducted a survey and ask people to rate their life satisfaction on a scale from one (very unhappy) to eleven (very happy). As the next console shows, I have created a vector (x) and purposefully inserted missing values. We already saw that base R functions – such as mean() – return NA. The mean of a vector with missing values is itself a missing value. R does not even return an error message.

```
# NAs in summary functions
x <- c(1, 2, NA, 4, 5, 99)
mean(x)
```

```
#> [1] NA
```

R checks if an element of the vector is numeric and we imitate this behavior with the is.na() function. It checks for missing values and returns a logical vector for each element of a vector.

```
# is.na checks if a value is NA
is.na(x)
```

```
#> [1] FALSE FALSE  TRUE FALSE FALSE FALSE
```

To use such a function in the case of missing values, we set the na.rm option to TRUE. The option removes missing values before the function is executed, but is it wise to do so?

```
# na.rm removes NA
mean(x, na.rm = TRUE)
```

```
#> [1] 22.2
```

I included a second missing values indicator (99) in the example. It demonstrates, in a non-technical fashion, why we not only need to deal with missing but also with implausible values. As outlined, x has values from one to eleven. So, I included a blunder, and we estimate a distorted mean if we do not exclude the implausible value. We may declare 99 as a missing value, which solves the problem for the moment.

```
# Shall we include na.rm?
x[x == 99] <- NA
mean(x, na.rm = TRUE)
```

```
#> [1] 3
```

The `na.rm` option gets rid of missing values, but for obvious reasons the mean will remain distorted for as long as we do not acknowledge if and how many missing (and implausible) values we observe. Are there any missing values indicators that we are not aware of? How shall we deal with them? Some advice: Get to know your data – including in terms of missing and implausible values. After cleaning the data and identifying which variables are crucial for the analysis, examine how many observations have missing or implausible values. I included a large missing value on purpose. Therefore, it may seem artificial to say that missing values may have a strong impact on analysis results. It might also appear that identifying implausible values is not a difficult task, but this is only halfway true if you are familiar with the data and the measurement of the examined variables. So, explore the data. You could even run a preliminary analysis if you are aware that further robustness checks are needed to ensure that missing values will not change the results. Perceive first results as preliminary, since missing values and other problems (e.g., due to data preparation steps) may change the results substantially.

It is okay if you do not realize that there is a missing value problem in the first step. However, ignoring missing values may seriously distort results, and dropping missing values may lead to scientific misconduct and data falsification. I can only give a very brief introduction and show you why you need to learn more about missing values. In principle, we have to clarify two questions: How many missing values do we observe? And why are they missing? The first question is easier to answer, and we will use R in the next subsection for this task, but before we dive into this, the *mechanisms of missing values* may shed light on the question of why the values are missing.

5.2.1 The mechanisms of missing values

The pioneer work goes back to Rubin (1987) and Little & Rubin (1987), respectively. The authors developed a theoretical approach and estimation techniques to deal with missing values. They outlined under which circumstances it is feasible to estimate a plausible value to replace the missing value. Today, we apply *multiple imputation* techniques which means that we estimate several plausible values for a missing value to reflect the uncertainty of the measurement. Multiple imputation techniques are an advanced statistical procedure and I will not explain such a complex topic in Practice R. There are several textbooks that introduce the problem of missing values and how to apply multiple imputation techniques (e.g., see Allison, 2001; Enders, 2010). Yet, we

138 — 5 Prepare data

still need to establish why we cannot ignore missing (and implausible) values, and the mechanisms of missing values let us assess the seriousness.

Rubin and Little distinguish three different missing data mechanisms: Missing completely at random (MCAR) implies that the probability of a missing value does not depend on any other observation, regardless of whether it was observed or not. If the probability of a missing value depends on other observed variables, but not on the missing value of the variable itself, the values are missing at random (MAR). Ultimately, an observation is missing not at random (MNAR) if the probability of observing a missing value depends on the value of the unobserved variable itself (as well as on other observed variables).

Rubin's typology can be tricky to comprehend. Let me illustrate the mechanisms with the help of simulated data. With simulated data we are able to generate data and missing values on purpose. Creating such data makes it easy to examine the mechanisms of missing values and the consequences in terms of data analysis. Suppose we ask people about their income and their highest educational degree in a survey. To simulate data, we need to make assumptions on how the income variable is distributed (e.g., mean, dispersion). Regardless of which assumptions we make, I simulated an income variable and I created an extra income variable for each missing value mechanism based on the income variable. The rubin_simdata shows the result.

```
# Summary of the simulated data
head(rubin_simdata)
```

```
#> # A tibble: 6 x 5
#>    income income_mcar income_nmar income_mar education
#>     <dbl>       <dbl>       <dbl>      <dbl>     <dbl>
#> 1   2924.       2924.       2924.      2924.      9.85
#> 2   2755.       2755.       2755.         NA      6.45
#> 3   2526.       2526.       2526.      2526.      9.19
#> 4   3559.       3559.       3559.      3559.     10.6
#> 5   2657.       2657.       2657.      2657.     11.6
#> # ... with 1 more row
```

Thus, the variable income_mcar has the same observations as income, but I deleted 15 percent of the observations randomly. For this reason, we know that the missing values of income_mcar are missing completely at random. In a similar way, I created income_mnar which takes into consideration that people with a higher income may not reveal this information; and income_mar reflects that other observed variables may explain the missing pattern. In the simulated data, people with a low and a high educational background no longer tell us about their income.

Figure 5.6 shows a scatter plot for income and education for each missing mechanism; I used two different colors to highlight which observations would have a missing value. In this example, missing completely at random means that the reason why we do not observe the income of a person does not depend on the income of the person itself; or any other variables that we did (not) observe. As Figure 5.6 (A) highlights, some observations with a higher or a lower income are missing, but there is no systematic pattern, since I randomly dropped observations.

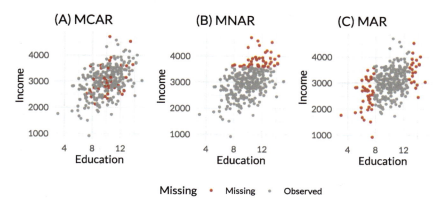

Fig. 5.6: The mechanisms of missing values

Maybe people with a high (or low) income do not want to share this information; maybe because they do not trust us to keep this information safe. In this case, the missing values are missing not at random because the income level determines whether we observe the outcome. As Figure 5.6 (B) shows, we observe more missing values when the income increases, meaning we would underestimate the income of the sample. Ultimately, missing at random means that the missingness depends on other observed variables, but not on the income of a person itself. In accordance with the simulated data, people with a high and low educational background do not reveal their income and Figure 5.6 (C) shows a clear cut-off point due to the simulation.

Often, we have doubts about the nature of the missing values. The patterns of missing data determine how we can handle the problem from a statistical point of view. This is also the reason why you may encounter different missing values indicators. Suppose you are examining whether job satisfaction explains why people move house. Some people may not return the survey on purpose, but maybe the questionnaire cannot be delivered because the respondent has found a new job and moved to another city. Say their e-mail address is no longer valid, resulting in invitations being returned to sender. Such information is crucial if we try to reconsider how we deal with missing values, because it can be related to the research topic and affects the data quality. Say we did not observe a lot of people who moved. We may conclude that job satisfaction

140 —— 5 Prepare data

has only a small effect on peoples' decision to move if those who were unhappy with their jobs already moved before we had the chance to ask them. Dealing with missing values is a hard topic and information on why values are missing is crucial to deciding how to deal with them.

In the next subsection, we shall pretend that we can exclude those missing values without any consequence to our analysis – at least to learn how to deal with missing values with R. This is a heroic assumption, and I will outline a few more words about a systematic data loss at the end. First, we will use R to explore missing values, learn how to replace them in order to run the analysis and robustness checks (e.g., with and without implausible values), before we try to identify patterns of missing values.

5.2.2 Explore missing values

First of all, how can we estimate how many missing values we observe? Say we have observed five persons, and we inspect the following variables with missing values. As the next output shows, some variables do not contain any information. We have no information for age_child2, while the number of missing values for all other variable lies somewhere in between.

```
#Tiny data with NAs
df <- tribble(
  ~person, ~country, ~age, ~children, ~age_child2,    ~sex,
     1L,     "US",    NA,      NA,          NA,    "Male",
     2L,     "US",    33,       1,          NA,      "NA",
     3L,     "US",   999,       1,          NA,  "Female",
     4L,     "US",    27,       1,          NA,    "Male",
     5L,     "US",    51,      NA,          NA,        NA
)
```

We may use the is.na() function in combination with other functions to examine whether missing data is a minor problem or a big issue. Apply the sum() function to count how many missing values a variable has; or use the which() function to find out at which position the information is not available.

```
# How many missing value has the variable sex?
sum(is.na(df$sex))
```

```
#> [1] 1
```

```
# At which position?
which(is.na(df$sex))
```

```
#> [1] 5
```

The variable sex seems to have only one missing value and the which() function tells us that the information is missing for person 5. Again, I included some errors to illustrate that data can be messy. The information about person 5 is missing, but the NA is coded as a string, which is why R does not recognize it. The same applies if a different missing indicator is used. For instance, we observed 999 as the third person's age, which is obviously wrong. Before we deal with such mistakes, let us first stick to the regular missing values indicators.

We can apply different functions to estimate the number of missing values, but the naniar package provides lots of functions and graphs to explore missing values (see Tierney et al., 2021). First, there is no need to count missing values manually since the n_miss() function does the same job. It returns the number of missing values of a vector (or a data set). Furthermore, the n_complete() function is its counterpart and returns the number of complete values.

```
# naniar provides functions and graphs to explore missing values
library(naniar)
```

```
# n_miss counts number of missings
n_miss(df)
```

```
#> [1] 9
```

```
# n_complete counts complete cases
n_complete(df)
```

```
#> [1] 21
```

Besides the counting function, the naniar package comes with many graphs to explore missing values. For example, the vis_miss() function visualizes missing values. It displays the number of missing values for each variable graphically for an entire data set.

```
# How many missings has the data?
vis_miss(df)
```

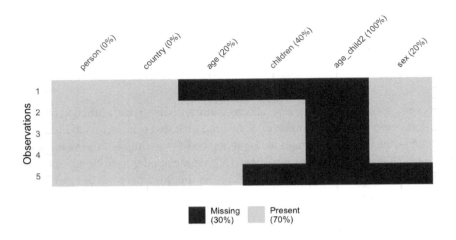

Consider the data frame with the missing values one more time. We still need to replace implausible values and get rid of constant columns.

```
# Inspect the data frame one more time
df
```

```
#> # A tibble: 5 x 6
#>   person country   age children age_child2 sex
#>    <int> <chr>   <dbl>    <dbl> <lgl>      <chr>
#> 1      1 US         NA       NA NA         Male
#> 2      2 US         33        1 NA         NA
#> 3      3 US        999        1 NA         Female
#> 4      4 US         27        1 NA         Male
#> 5      5 US         51       NA NA         <NA>
```

Some of you might be wondering why a data set should contain an entire column (age_child2) with missing values. You may encounter such data if you use process-generated data and the empty column may only be a placeholder. This might happen even if the data is generated by humans. The variable has the name age_child2 which suggests the use of a filter question where all the participants who have fewer than two children do not respond to this question. It has no consequences if we delete a column with missing values, since we lose no information. The same applies if a column contains a constant, such as country. In both instances, we can get rid of them.

In Chapter 4, we used the select() function from dplyr. We can turn around the procedure and exclude variables as well. We may select all variables except certain ones, such as age_child2 or more, if you combine (c()) them. In addition, add a minus sign (-) and you select everything but the variable(s). Drop everything but `age_child2` and get rid of a constant column vector.

```r
# Select all variables, except -x
df |>
  select(-c(age_child2, country))
```

```
#> # A tibble: 5 x 4
#>   person   age children sex
#>    <int> <dbl>    <dbl> <chr>
#> 1      1    NA       NA Male
#> 2      2    33        1 NA
#> 3      3   999        1 Female
#> 4      4    27        1 Male
#> 5      5    51       NA <NA>
```

Sometimes missing values reflect the absence of the measurement. Consider the `children` variable, which indicates how many children a person has. In this case a missing value might imply a missing value or zero kids. For the latter case the `coalesce()` function is useful as it replaces non-missing elements.

```r
# coalesce replaces NAs
children <- c(1, 4, NA, 2, NA)
coalesce(children, 0)
```

```
#> [1] 1 4 0 2 0
```

We may further restrict the analysis sample with the `drop_na()` function from the `tidyr` package. In Chapter 4 we learned that, we could exclude all missing values of one variable or exclude missing values from all variables if we leave the `drop_na()` function empty.

```r
# Drop (all) NAs
library(tidyr)
df |>
  select(-c(age_child2, country)) |>
  drop_na()
```

```
#> # A tibble: 3 x 4
#>   person   age children sex
#>    <int> <dbl>    <dbl> <chr>
```

```
#> 1        2    33       1 NA
#> 2        3   999       1 Female
#> 3        4    27       1 Male
```

As the output shows, we still need to replace the character string for person two and the alternative missing values indicator. Depending on the source of the data, there might be several missing value indicators to address different missing value patterns. We can convert values to NA with the na_if() function, as the next console illustrates.

```
# na_if takes care of alternative missing values
x <- c(1, 999, 5, 7, 999)
dplyr::na_if(x, 999)
```

```
#> [1]  1 NA  5  7 NA
```

However, what shall we do with the NA in a string? For example, use the replace() function. As the next console shows, I first mutate the data and I replace 999 with NA. The same trick works for the sex variable to replace the string with NA.

```
# Replace values
df <- df |>
  select(-c(age_child2, country)) |>
  mutate(
    age = replace(age, age == "999", NA),
    sex = replace(sex, sex == "NA", NA)
  )
df
```

```
#> # A tibble: 5 x 4
#>    person   age children sex
#>     <int> <dbl>    <dbl> <chr>
#> 1       1    NA       NA Male
#> 2       2    33        1 <NA>
#> 3       3    NA        1 Female
#> 4       4    27        1 Male
#> 5       5    51       NA <NA>
```

What shall we do if we cannot guarantee that implausible values are false? Excluding implausible values may have strong implications on the estimation results. So, we need to check whether excluding such observations have consequences for the analysis.

Create an indicator to account for implausible values and run an analysis twice to compare your results with and without implausible values.

The `tidyr` package comes with the corresponding `replace_na()` function which lets us replace NAs. For example, replace missing values of `sex` with a separate text string (e.g., Not available) and include them in the analysis. This makes it possible to compare the results with and without those observations.

```
# Replace NAs
df |> replace_na(list(sex = "Not available"))
```

```
#> # A tibble: 5 x 4
#>    person   age children sex
#>     <int> <dbl>    <dbl> <chr>
#> 1       1    NA       NA Male
#> 2       2    33        1 Not available
#> 3       3    NA        1 Female
#> 4       4    27        1 Male
#> 5       5    51       NA Not available
```

Or consider the `age` variable one more time. We could create a new variable (`age_missing`) that indicates if the information is missing with the help of the `if_else()` and the `is.na()` function. By creating an additional variable, we are able to run the analysis twice and compare our results with and without implausible values (see Chapter 6).

```
# Replace NAs with if_else
df |>
  replace_na(list(sex = "Not available")) |>
  mutate(age_missing = if_else(is.na(age), "Missing", "Not-missing"))
```

```
#> # A tibble: 5 x 5
#>    person   age children sex           age_missing
#>     <int> <dbl>    <dbl> <chr>         <chr>
#> 1       1    NA       NA Male          Missing
#> 2       2    33        1 Not available Not-missing
#> 3       3    NA        1 Female        Missing
#> 4       4    27        1 Male          Not-missing
#> 5       5    51       NA Not available Not-missing
```

There are no consequences if we drop an entire column with missing values or with a constant. We need to clean the data, but we do not lose any information if we delete

5.2.3 Identifying missing patterns

As the mechanisms of missing values highlight, we do not need to worry about the consequences of missing values if we know that the missings are completely at random. How likely is this the case? And what should we do with doubts about the nature of missingness? There might be a systematic missing value pattern and we must examine if there are any missing patterns visible. Unfortunately, we cannot examine if the loss of data is missing not at random (MNAR), because we did not observe the missing values of the variable itself. However, we can inspect missing patterns between variables to see if missing values depend on the outcome of another variable.

Suppose you create a scatter plot. If one of the variables has a missing value, R (automatically) excludes those missing values when creating a scatter plot. Logically, we cannot display what we do not observe. However, the `naniar` package offers several graphical procedures to explore missing data patterns, and the `geom_miss_point()` function provides a simple solution to explore variables with missing values. The function replaces a missing value with a value ten percent below the minimum value of the observed variable. When we use the scatter plot one more time, missing values are now included, and we can examine if there are any systematic patterns.

Figure 5.7 shows two scatter plots based on the simulated data about missing values (`rubin_simdata`). As outlined, I simulated data and deleted observation to illustrate the missing mechanisms. As Figure 5.7 (A) highlights, a regular scatter plot excludes missing values; the `naniar` package makes those observations visible (Figure 5.7 B), even if we do not know how much income the observed participants would make. However, we clearly see that the observed missing values do not depend on educational attainment, in accordance with the simulated data for the missing completely at random mechanism.

The `naniar` package provides more graphs to identify missing patterns. Inspect the package vignette for more ideas on how to explore missing values.[1] Dealing with missing values is a hard topic, but at least, we made first steps to assess the problem and we are now aware that a systematic loss of data may have severe consequences.

We focused on typical data manipulation steps in Chapter 4, but I skipped essential functions from the `forcats` package which help us to manipulate categorical data. Creating new variables is often the last step before we apply a first analysis and the `forcats` package is a good supplement for our `dplyr` skills.

---

1 The functions of the `naniar` package are easy to apply, but they use the `ggplot2` package to create graphs, which we will cover in Chapter 7 and for this reason the book includes the graph only.

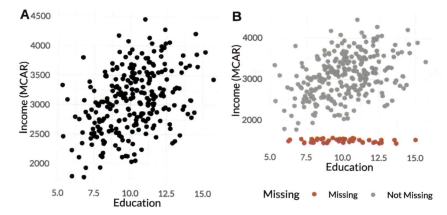

Fig. 5.7: The naniar package

5.3 Categorical variables

In the social sciences, we often work with categorical variables and we started to examine factor variables in Chapter 3. Several independent variables may be saved as factor variables and are, most likely, not prepared for our purpose. Till now, we did not work systematically on our skills to manipulate factor variables. The forcats package offers many functions to manipulate categorical variables (fct_*) and this section introduces the package (Wickham, 2022a). It includes a sample of categorical variables from the General Social Survey (gss_cat), which we use to explore the package's functions, but we stick to two variables. Suppose we need to run separate analyses for people who are (not) married (marital) and differentiate between different religions (relig) as robustness checks.

```
# forcats == for categorical variables
library(forcats)

df <- gss_cat |>
  select(marital, relig)

head(df)

#> # A tibble: 6 x 2
#>   marital       relig
#>   <fct>         <fct>
#> 1 Never married Protestant
#> 2 Divorced      Protestant
```

```
#> 3 Widowed        Protestant
#> 4 Never married Orthodox-christian
#> 5 Divorced       None
#> # ... with 1 more row
```

Both are factor variables and `fct_count()` returns how often each level appears.

```
# Count levels
fct_count(df$marital)
```

```
#> # A tibble: 6 x 2
#>   f                 n
#>   <fct>         <int>
#> 1 No answer        17
#> 2 Never married  5416
#> 3 Separated       743
#> 4 Divorced       3383
#> 5 Widowed        1807
#> # ... with 1 more row
```

The order of the factor variable might be arbitrary, but sometimes a new order is useful to inspect the data or to make a visualization. Change the order of the levels manually with the `fct_relevel()` function. As the next console illustrates, the two levels (`Married`, `Never married`) now come first and we can count again to make sure that no errors are introduced.

```
# Relevel manually
f <- fct_relevel(
  df$marital,
  c("Married", "Never married")
)
fct_count(f)
```

```
#> # A tibble: 6 x 2
#>   f                  n
#>   <fct>          <int>
#> 1 Married        10117
#> 2 Never married   5416
#> 3 No answer         17
#> 4 Separated        743
#> 5 Divorced        3383
```

```
#> # ... with 1 more row
```

Suppose we need to create a binary variable that indicates if a person is (not) married. We have already work with the `recode()` function from `dplyr`. The `forcats` package also includes the `fct_recode()` function, which does the same. We recode all values to `Not married` to create a binary indicator; and may set the level `No answer` to NA.

```
# Recode levels
f <- fct_recode(df$marital,
  "NA" = "No answer",
  `Not married` = "Never married",
  `Not married` = "Separated",
  `Not married` = "Divorced",
  `Not married` = "Widowed"
)

fct_count(f)
```

```
#> # A tibble: 3 x 2
#>   f               n
#>   <fct>       <int>
#> 1 NA             17
#> 2 Not married 11349
#> 3 Married     10117
```

The code works, but look how often I repeated myself to create such a binary indicator. A lot of levels make a manual recode approach nasty; we may introduce errors, and it takes a lot of time. How can we improve this step? Or consider the religion (`relig`) variable. The variable has sixteen unique levels as the `fct_unique()` function reveals. We certainly need a better approach in this case.

```
# Unique levels
fct_unique(df$relig)
```

```
#>  [1] No answer            Don't know       Inter-nondenominational
#>  [4] Native american      Christian        Orthodox-christian
#>  [7] Moslem/islam         Other eastern    Hinduism
#> [10] Buddhism             Other            None
#> [13] Jewish               Catholic         Protestant
#> [16] Not applicable
#> 16 Levels: No answer Don't know Inter-nondenominational ... Not applicable
```

150 —— 5 Prepare data

How should we recode such variables? Collapse a factor variable if we are only interested in certain levels or a binary variable that indicates if someone is (not) religious. The same applies to marital. The fct_collapse() function collapses several levels to one, for example, all people who are not married (anymore).

```
# Collapse levels
f <- fct_collapse(df$marital,
  `Not married` = c(
    "Never married",
    "Separated",
    "Divorced",
    "Widowed"
  )
)
fct_count(f)

#> # A tibble: 3 x 2
#>   f                 n
#>   <fct>         <int>
#> 1 No answer        17
#> 2 Not married   11349
#> 3 Married       10117
```

A similar but different approach offers the fct_other() function. It comes with the keep option and we can specify which levels to keep.

```
# Keep selected levels and others
f <- fct_other(df$marital,
  keep = c("Married", "No answer")
)

fct_count(f)

#> # A tibble: 3 x 2
#>   f             n
#>   <fct>     <int>
#> 1 No answer    17
#> 2 Married   10117
#> 3 Other     11349
```

How many levels of a factor shall we consider in the analysis? Certainly, we cannot answer such a question without any detail about the hypothesis, but we certainly need to consider the largest groups and levels. The `fct_infreq()` function counts levels and returns them ordered. As the next console shows, I added the `head()` function to adjust the number of returned levels.

```
# Sort in frequency
f <- fct_infreq(df$relig)
fct_count(f) |> head(n = 6)
```

```
#> # A tibble: 6 x 2
#>   f               n
#>   <fct>       <int>
#> 1 Protestant  10846
#> 2 Catholic     5124
#> 3 None         3523
#> 4 Christian     689
#> 5 Jewish        388
#> # ... with 1 more row
```

Suppose we want to differentiate between the five largest groups. Again, we may use `recode()` or one of the other discussed functions, but in such cases the `fct_lump()` function is helpful. It lumps together the largest levels and adds the remaining levels to the category other. As an additional step, I used `fct_infreq()` to make sure I did not make any mistakes.

```
# Lump together
f <- fct_lump(df$relig, n = 5)
f <- fct_infreq(f)
fct_count(f)
```

```
#> # A tibble: 6 x 2
#>   f               n
#>   <fct>       <int>
#> 1 Protestant  10846
#> 2 Catholic     5124
#> 3 None         3523
#> 4 Other         913
#> 5 Christian     689
#> # ... with 1 more row
```

The `forcats` package provides more functions to combine factors, change the order, or to add levels of a factor variable. I introduced the package to prepare you for the data preparation step. Consider the package documentation, vignette, and its cheat sheet for more information.

Ultimately, the info box about the `copycat` package outlines, why you already have code snippets for `dplyr`, `forcats`, and other packages of the `tidyverse` at your disposal before I give a short summary of this chapter.

ⓘ The `copycat` package

The `copycat` package is not an R package that lives on CRAN, it is a package that I created for myself and for the students in my classes. Getting fluent in a (programming) language takes some time and we all forget how code works if we do not apply our knowledge on a regular basis. The `copycat` package was created for this purpose. It is a small package to copy, paste, and manage code snippets. The package comes with code snippets (minimal examples) that run with implemented data. Thus, `copycat` was built as a personal package, but it may help (new) R users to manage code snippets.

It returns code snippets for the core `tidyverse` packages based on code from the cheat sheets (the `CopyCatCode` data frame). So, if you cannot remember how the `fct_count()` function works, just let `copycat` search for the corresponding code snippet. The package comes with a graphical interface which lets you pick a package in the viewer, choose a function and then it inserts the code snippet in your R script by clicking on the button. You find the `copycat` addin in the RStudio addins menu after the package is installed. Alternatively, use the `copycat()` function, it searches for the function name, copies the code and save it to your clipboard, as the next console illustrate.

```
# Explore copycat addin
library(copycat)
# copycat::copycat_addin()

# Or copy code snippets from CopyCatCode
copycat("fct_count")
#> [1] "Copied that: fct_count(gss_cat$race)"
```

You may also use `copycat` for your own code snippets if you are not happy with the examples that the packages provides. The packages has more functions to copy code, which are described in the vignette of the package. Remember, `copycat` is living only on my Github account, use the `install_github` function from the `devtools` package should you want to give it a try.

```
#Install CopyCat from GitHub:
devtools::install_github("edgar-treischl/CopyCat")
```

Summary

Data preparation is the most important step before we can analyze data and is therefore crucial to the entire research cycle. This step is time consuming since we need to consider how the data is imported, how the information is coded, and how the data needs to be prepared for the analysis. Take all the time you need for this step as you may draw wrong conclusions if errors are introduced. Moreover, don't expect a linear process, because you will switch back and forth between the typical steps of applied research. Suppose you started to prepare and analyze data. At a certain point you realize that an important variable is missing. You go back, prepare the variable and rerun the analysis, but now you might get weird results. If you made a mistake, you need circle back to the preparation step again. I guess you get my point why the process is not linear.

Since we work with different files, different types of data, and apply different kind of analysis, writing about data preparation is also not an easy task. Keep in mind that this chapter tried to give you an overview about typical steps and pitfalls when it comes to data preparation, and that I did not focus on a file format. Remember, RStudio provides cool features to import data and there are specific packages for this task. The `readxl` package helps you with Excel files or consider the haven package for a variety of other formats such as SPSS, Stata, or SAS. Check out the documentation of the corresponding packages if you run into an error.

6 Analyze data

How large is the effect of school education on income? Does life satisfaction increase income? Or how large is the difference in income between men and women (gender pay gap)? There are many statistical procedures to analyze data, but a linear regression analysis is the workhorse of the social sciences and we may use the latter to examine the effect on a continuous outcome. This chapter introduces the method briefly, shows typical steps to develop a linear regression model, and focuses on graphical procedures.

- Section 6.1 introduces the main idea of a linear regression analysis in a non-technical manner. Many students in the social sciences can apply a linear regression analysis, or at least got the theoretical underpinning in a statistics class. This gives us room to focus on the implementation in R and I introduce the topic only briefly in the first section. To be crystal clear, you will not learn much in the first section if you already have profound knowledge about linear regression analysis. We tackle the following questions: (1) What is the main idea of a linear regression analysis? (2) How are the coefficients of a linear regression interpreted? (3) What is R^2?
- Section 6.2 recaptures the main functions to run a regression analysis. We focus on typical steps to develop and compare regression models. We start simple with a bivariate regression model which we improve gradually. We start to control for variables that may distort the estimate of the main effect; we discuss which kind of variable should (not) be included in the model; we explore how we can compare several models (and their performance) efficiently; and we examine further improvements (e.g., interaction effects, non-linear effects).
- In Section 6.3, we focus on graphical procedures. We concentrate on visualizations for regression assumptions and regression results. A linear regression relies on several assumptions and the last section outlines why graphics in particular are important. I summarize the assumptions of a linear regression and we inspect different graphical approaches (and statistical tests) to check for violations. Finally, we learn how to visualize regression coefficients with dot-and-whisker plots in detail.

```
# The setup of Chapter 6
library(broom)
library(dotwhisker)
library(dplyr)
library(estimatr)
library(effectsize)
library(forcats)
library(ggeffects)
library(HistData)
library(huxtable)
```

https://doi.org/10.1515/9783110704976-006

```
library(interactions)
library(jtools)
library(lmtest)
library(tidyr)
library(palmerpenguins)
library(performance)
library(PracticeR)
library(see)
```

6.1 Linear regression analysis

Suppose your friends are expecting a baby. They are extremely curious what the baby
may look like. Will the baby resemble the father, the mother, or both? One thing seems
to be sure: since they are both tall, they assume that their baby will also be tall, maybe
even taller than they are. Are they right? What is the relationship between parents' and
child's heights?

If you are familiar with the *regression to the mean* phenomenon, you may come to
a different conclusion. Tall (small) parents will most likely have tall (small) children,
but they will not be taller (smaller) than their parents, otherwise humans would one
day become either giants or dwarfs. Sir Francis Galton (1822-1911) described this phenomenon as regression to the mean and it illustrates that to regress implies to trace
back: A dependent variable is traced back to one (or more) independent variable(s).
I use this example to illustrate the main idea of a regression analysis. We predict the
effect of a binary or a continuous variable x (here, parents' height) on a continuous
outcome y (here, child's height).

Install and load the HistData package (Friendly, 2021). It provides several historical
data sets, including the data Galton collected to examine the effect of parents' on child's
height. The Galton data contains the height of 928 children in inches (child) and the
mid-parental height (parent; average of father and mother).

```
# The HistData package gives you access to the Galton data
head(Galton)
```

```
#>    parent child
#> 1   70.5  61.7
#> 2   68.5  61.7
#> 3   65.5  61.7
#> 4   64.5  61.7
#> 5   64.0  61.7
#> 6   67.5  62.2
```

Why do we apply a linear regression analysis? We examine if there is a linear association between x and y and we fit a line in accordance with the observed data. I created several scatter plots that examine if x and y are related and they illustrate the main idea of a linear regression with the Galton data.[1] As Figure 6.1 (A) shows, it looks like parents' height is related to their offspring's height, since smaller (larger) parents on average have smaller (larger) kids.

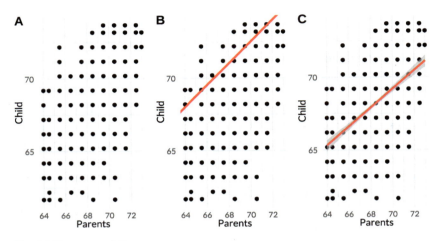

Fig. 6.1: Linear association

With the help of a regression analysis, we try to find a line that describes the association between the observed variables. As Figure 6.1 (B) shows, I added a line manually. I guessed where the line intersects the y-axis (*intercept*) and how steep or flat the line goes (*slope*). If you have no idea which intercept and slope to pick, you may come up with some random guesses, just as I did, but the line does not fit the data. Most observations are beneath the line and the distance between single observations and the line is not equally distributed. Consequently, we make a systematic error if we apply such a model to predict a child's height. By using a model, we want to describe the association that fits well for all observations. Figure 6.1 (C) shows the line when fitted with a linear regression analysis. A regression analysis estimates the effect of x on y by tracing the regression line that summarizes the observed points, and we are able to predict – on average – how many units a child's height increases if the parents' height is increased by one unit.

---

[1] This section shows graphs to illustrate the basic concepts of a linear regression analysis, but not the code to make the graphs. All figures are made with the ggplot2 package (see Chapter 7).

To understand a linear regression analysis, we need to get in touch with its components. We assume that the child's height (y) can be explained as a linear function of three components:

$$y = \beta_0 + \beta_1 x_1 + \epsilon_i$$

β_0 notes where the line intersects the y-axis (intercept); β_1 captures the slope and determines to steepness of the association. Ultimately, we predict the outcome, but not without mistakes, which reflects the error term ϵ_i or the *residual* of the regression analysis (e.g., other variables also explain the outcome).

To estimate a linear regression with R, we run the `lm()` function with the dependent and one (or several) independent variable(s), separated with the tilde (~) operator. As the next console shows, a child's height increases on average by 0.6463 (β_1) inches if the parents' height goes up by one unit.

```
# The lm function
model <- lm(child ~ parent, data = Galton)
model

#>
#> Call:
#> lm(formula = child ~ parent, data = Galton)
#>
#> Coefficients:
#> (Intercept)        parent
#>     23.9415        0.6463
```

By applying a model, we can predict the average increase – or decrease in the case of a negative association – of y with the help of the intercept and the slope. Suppose the parents are 68 inches tall. To make a prediction, take the intercept, multiply β_1 with parents' height, and build the sum.

```
# How tall will a child be on average if the parents are 68 inches?
23.9415 + 68 * 0.6463

#> [1] 67.8899
```

Calculating predictions manually clarifies how a regression analysis works, but the `predict()` function is more comfortable. The function applies our `model` and predicts the outcome for new observations (`new_data`).

```r
# Generate example data
new_data <- data.frame(parent = c(55, 68, 75))
# Apply the model with predict
predict(model, new_data)

#>        1        2        3
#> 59.48751 67.88929 72.41332
```

My random guesses to find the slope and the intercept did not lead to a satisfying solution, but how does a regression analysis find the estimated parameters? This question points to the estimation technique and scrutinizes how well a model describes the relationship (model accuracy).

6.1.1 Estimation technique

Essentially, we fit a straight line into a cloud of data by running a regression analysis. This depiction may help to visualize the technique. Unfortunately, the data cloud becomes a pane if we add a second independent variable. In such cases we need to search a pane in a three-dimensional space that fits the data. We may further extend the model and examine the effect of *n* independent variables in an *n-dimensional* space. Even if we stick to a bivariate analysis, how does a linear regression find the best solution for a given data set?

A linear regression applies an ordinary least square (OLS) estimation. Imagine the scatter plot from the beginning. Sometimes the prediction is larger than the observed value and lies above the regression line. Sometimes a prediction is smaller than the observed value and falls under the line. Obviously, we want to minimize the error and get the best prediction based on the observed values. The OLS estimator picks parameters by minimizing the *sum of the squared error*. This point may become clearer if one sees the steps needed to calculate the slope manually.

To calculate the slope, we divide the covariance (cov) of *x* and *y* by the variance of *x* (variance_x). As the last two lines of the next console illustrate, the variance of *x* is the sum of the squared error from the mean. A linear regression minimizes the sum of the squared error, because otherwise positive and negative error would cancel each other out. Moreover, a larger error should have more weight on the estimator since we make a larger mistake. The next console summarizes the steps to calculate the slope manually.

```r
# Calculate the slope manually
Galton |>
  summarise(
```

```
    mean_x = mean(parent),
    mean_y = mean(child),
    cov = sum((parent - mean_x) * (child - mean_y)),
    variance_x = sum((parent - mean_x)^2),
    slope = cov / variance_x
  )
```

```
#>     mean_x    mean_y      cov variance_x     slope
#> 1 68.30819 68.08847 1913.898   2961.358 0.6462906
```

Speaking about the error, how well does the model explain the outcome? Formally expressed, what's the accuracy of the model?

6.1.2 Model accuracy

The summary() function provides more information about the model, which includes information about the model accuracy. Compared to the output of the lm function, summary() returns the standard error, t-values, and the probability to assess the statistical significance for each regression coefficient.

```
# The summary function gives more information about the model
summary(model)
```

```
#>
#> Call:
#> lm(formula = child ~ parent, data = Galton)
#>
#> Residuals:
#>     Min      1Q  Median      3Q     Max
#> -7.8050 -1.3661  0.0487  1.6339  5.9264
#>
#> Coefficients:
#>             Estimate Std. Error t value Pr(>|t|)
#> (Intercept) 23.94153    2.81088   8.517   <2e-16 ***
#> parent       0.64629    0.04114  15.711   <2e-16 ***
#> ---
#> Signif. codes:  0 '***' 0.001 '**' 0.01 '*' 0.05 '.' 0.1 ' ' 1
#>
#> Residual standard error: 2.239 on 926 degrees of freedom
#> Multiple R-squared:  0.2105, Adjusted R-squared:  0.2096
```

```
#> F-statistic: 246.8 on 1 and 926 DF,  p-value: < 2.2e-16
```

In order to assess the error, R returns R^2 in the penultimate line of the last output. R^2 is an indicator of the accuracy of the model. It ranges from 0 to 1 and conveys the proportion of the variance from the outcome that can be explained with the independent variable. In our case, we can explain approximately 21 percent of the observed variance.

To understand R^2, let us think about the estimation technique and the variance we observe. Figure 6.2 illustrates that we minimize the error to fit the line and gives us an idea how large the error might be. What would a regression line look like if x could not explain the outcome at all? The line would be flat and the distance between each observed value to its predicted value is the maximum variance and error we can make. Figure 6.2 (A) highlights this point. The plot does not show a regression line, it displays a constant line (the mean of y as the best guess). If we imagine a flat line, we can literally see the total variance, highlighted with red lines.

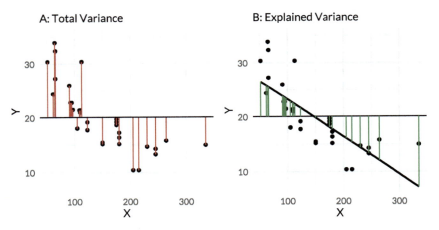

Fig. 6.2: Explained and unexplained variance

To assess the accuracy of the model, we split the variance into an explained and an unexplained part. Figure 6.2 (B) shows the explained variance – it is the green area between a flat line from Figure 6.2 (A) and the regression line that we actually fit. The green area marks the part of the variance that we can explain with the regression analysis. Since we know the total and the explained variance, R^2 brings them into proportion and tells us how much of the variance of y can be explained by x.

We may use further characteristics of the parents to predict the child's height, especially if we want to increase the accuracy. Add further independent variables by using the plus (+) sign and R provides the beta coefficient for all independent variables. Each additional independent variable increases the chance that the prediction is getting better. Since the explained variance increases by chance, the adjusted R^2

takes the number of independent variables into account and penalizes models with a larger number of independent variables. Therefore, use the adjusted R^2 in case of a multivariate analysis, which makes it possible to compare nested models.

How large is large in terms of R^2? Did we observe a small, medium, or large effect? In Chapter 3, we used the effectsize package to interpret the effect size (Ben-Shachar et al., 2022) and we got in touch with the rules by Cohen (1988). The package does the same for R^2. The summary function returns several indicators about the regression, including R^2 (r.squared). As the next console shows, assign the results of the summary() function (e.g., sum_model) and use the interpret_r2() function to assess the effect.

```
# Get summary
sum_model <- summary(model)


# Interpret R2
effectsize::interpret_r2(sum_model$r.squared,
  rules = "cohen1988"
)


#> [1] "moderate"
#> (Rules: cohen1988)
```

This section outlined the main idea of a linear regression with a classical example, but in order to apply a model, we need to reconsider how we develop and improve a model. Which variable should (not) be included to predict an outcome? And which assumptions does the model make and are they – eventually – violated?

I started this chapter by claiming that a linear regression can be used to examine a linear effect, which is why we explored the variables with scatter plots. Graphical procedures are very valuable to assess the regression assumptions, since the relations between the variables must not be linear. We will get in touch with a variety of graphical procedures in the last section of this chapter, but a prominent example illustrates this point. Francis Anscombe (1973) has provided simulated data that underline why we should use graphical procedures to examine effects. Each of his data sets contain two variables (x and y) with eleven observations only. He created four data sets and each data set is (almost) identical in terms of statistical measures (e.g., mean, correlation), but we can see a very different picture if we examine them. Figure 6.3 shows *Anscombe's quartet*: he generated a scatter plot for each case (Data I-IV).

Each graph emphasizes how one or several observation(s) may impact the results of a linear regression analysis and the relationship between the observed variables is different in each case. In the first case, we actually see a linear relationship between x and y. However, a relationship between two variables must not be linear and there is a non-linear relationship in the second case. In the third case, an outlier distorts the analysis, while the analysis of the last illustration is strongly affected by one observation. All other observations are stacked upon each other and there is clearly no linear pattern.

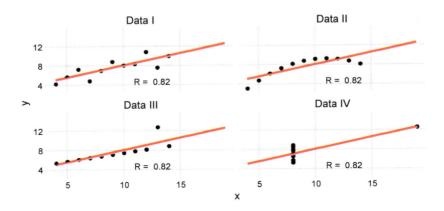

Fig. 6.3: Anscombe's quartet

In the next two sections we increase our skills to develop a linear model and we use different approaches to examine the assumptions of a linear regression. I tried to express all technical terms and concepts, at least briefly, but the next sections might be harder to follow if you have never heard about linear regression analysis, especially with regard to the assumptions of a linear regression analysis. Consider reading first Wolf & Best (2014) or Young (2017) to get a broader understanding about linear regression analysis and its assumptions in general terms, or James et al. (2013) for *An Introduction to Statistical Learning with Applications in R*.

6.2 Develop a linear regression model

We now focus on typical steps to elaborate and improve a model. We use the penguins data from the palmerpenguins package as an example analysis. We examine if we can predict the body mass (body_mass_g) of the penguins, considering their sex, species, and other variables. Doing so, we apply the following steps:
- We *start simple*: we run a bivariate model to estimate an effect of x on y. Next, we run a multivariate analysis to illustrate that we may not identify the true effect of x on y when we do not control for confounding variable(s). The latter is known as *omitted variable bias*. A third variable z may affect x and y and the effect might even be spurious if z is a common cause for x and y. For this reason, we need to control for further confounding variable(s).

- Confounding implies that we need to *think about causality* to elaborate a model. Has *x* an effect on *y* or is it the other way around? Knowledge about the causal structure is key when analyzing data and I can only introduce the core idea that is necessary to elaborate a model. This point underlines that we need to think about which variables should (not) be included in the model.
- Typically, we *develop models step by step*. Start with a simple model, control for variables which may distort the results, and then inspect how the results change. We apply the same logic to improve a model. For example, maybe there is an interaction effect between two independent variables. Regardless of what we do, develop, compare, and improve models step by step to see the consequences of your choices.
- Assess the *performance* of model(s). Creating models step by step implies that we need to compare their predictive performance gradually.
- Ultimately, I highlight *next steps* to further improve the model. For example, check for non-linear effects or maybe we need to transform the outcome. The last steps are not a comprehensive list and model development is a huge topic, but learning how to estimate a non-linear effect and other data transformation steps are not very complicated, use your base R skills or other package from the R community to further improve the model.

6.2.1 Start simple

Before we apply a linear regression model, we must prepare the data and examine the variables. For this reason I use the penguins data, because we do not need to prepare much to predict the body mass (body_mass_g) of a penguin. The variable is numerical and the next console shows a summary of the examined variables.

```
# The penguins
library(palmerpenguins)

varlist <- c("body_mass_g", "species", "sex", "bill_length_mm")

penguins |>
  select(all_of(varlist)) |>
  summary()

#>    body_mass_g         species        sex       bill_length_mm
#>  Min.   :2700    Adelie   :152    female:165    Min.   :32.10
#>  1st Qu.:3550    Chinstrap: 68    male  :168    1st Qu.:39.23
#>  Median :4050    Gentoo   :124    NA's  : 11    Median :44.45
#>  Mean   :4202                                   Mean   :43.92
```

```
#>   3rd Qu.:4750            3rd Qu.:48.50
#>   Max.   :6300            Max.   :59.60
#>   NA's   :2               NA's   :2
```

Let us estimate the effect of `species` on `body_mass_g`; the former is a factor variable with three levels. In order to include a non-numerical variable in the analysis, we may start with a dummy variable. The `if_else()` function lets us create a variable that indicates a certain level or group (e.g., `Adelie`).

```
# Create a dummy
penguins_df <- penguins |>
  mutate(species_bin = if_else(species ==
    "Adelie", "Adelie", "Others"))
```

Make sure that the data preparation steps don't contain any mistakes. Inspect the entire data frame or use a function such as `fct_count()` to examine if we still observe the right number of observations after the data preparation steps.

```
# Check the data preparation steps
fct_count(penguins_df$species_bin)
```

```
#> # A tibble: 2 x 2
#>   f          n
#>   <fct>  <int>
#> 1 Adelie   152
#> 2 Others   192
```

As outlined in the last section, the `lm()` function runs a linear regression, and the `summary()` function returns a summary of a model.

```
# The first model
m1 <- lm(body_mass_g ~ species_bin, data = penguins_df)
summary(m1)
```

```
#>
#> Call:
#> lm(formula = body_mass_g ~ species_bin, data = penguins_df)
#>
#> Residuals:
#>      Min      1Q   Median      3Q     Max
#> -1897.91 -486.09    24.34  452.09 1702.09
```

```
#>
#> Coefficients:
#>                    Estimate Std. Error t value Pr(>|t|)
#> (Intercept)         3700.66      54.31   68.14   <2e-16 ***
#> species_binOthers    897.24      72.67   12.35   <2e-16 ***
#> ---
#> Signif. codes:  0 '***' 0.001 '**' 0.01 '*' 0.05 '.' 0.1 ' ' 1
#>
#> Residual standard error: 667.3 on 340 degrees of freedom
#>   (2 observations deleted due to missingness)
#> Multiple R-squared:  0.3096, Adjusted R-squared:  0.3075
#> F-statistic: 152.4 on 1 and 340 DF,  p-value: < 2.2e-16
```

Compared to Adelie, other species have on average significantly more (897.24 gram) body mass. I created the dummy variable to highlight that we are allowed to include a numerical or a binary variable as dependent variables in the analysis. However, species is a factor variable and there was no need to create the dummy variable in the first place. R creates a dummy variable for each category of a factor and omits one level from the equation if we include it in the analysis. In our case, R omits the first level (Adelie) if we include species instead of the binary indicator. We need to interpret the coefficients compared to the omitted reference group.

```
# Factor variables can be included
lm(body_mass_g ~ species, data = penguins)
```

```
#>
#> Call:
#> lm(formula = body_mass_g ~ species, data = penguins)
#>
#> Coefficients:
#>       (Intercept)  speciesChinstrap      speciesGentoo
#>           3700.66             32.43            1375.35
```

We need to pick the reference group based on theoretical assumptions and the relevel() function helps us with this task. Specified by the ref option, relevel rearranges the data and moves the groups. For example, lets takes the second group (Chinstrap) as reference group.

```
# Relevel the reference group
penguins$species <- relevel(penguins$species, ref = 2)
```

```
# Run model again
lm(body_mass_g ~ species, data = penguins)
```

```
#>
#> Call:
#> lm(formula = body_mass_g ~ species, data = penguins)
#>
#> Coefficients:
#>   (Intercept)   speciesAdelie   speciesGentoo
#>       3733.09          -32.43         1342.93
```

Regardless of which reference group you pick, suppose you apply an analysis but the effect is not statistically significant. Does this mean that that there is no effect between x and y? I can only emphasize to examine the effect size instead of focusing on statistical significance only, because in some instances you will work with large data and even very small effects may become significant due to large sample size and a high *statistical power*. Conversely, you may not find a significant effect due the lower statistical power, even if an effect is large. This may sound abstract, so keep in mind that statistical significance depends on the effect size, the sample size, and further characteristics of the analysis. The next info box about *power analysis* and the pwr package gives you more information how the discussed parameters determine if it's likely to find a significant effect (Champely, 2020).

ℹ Power analysis

Run a power analysis to estimate the *sample size* with a high statistical power to find a significant effect; or estimate the *statistical power* for a given sample size with R. The power of a statistical test is defined as 1 minus the Type II error probability. If you are not familiar with sampling, this definition is hard to understand. Say we have a statistical power of 0.8, which implies a probability of 80 percent that we correctly reject the null hypothesis in cases where there is no effect between x and y. Many researchers perceive a statistical power of 0.8 as sufficient.

The statistical power depends on the number of observations, but also on the strength of the effect. If an effect is small, we need a larger sample size to detect an effect with a sufficient certainty. However, a small sample might be large enough if the effect is large. A power analysis helps us to understand the relationship between sample size, effect size, and statistical power. Figure 6.4 visualizes the result of a power analysis and displays the power depending on the sample size for four different effect sizes. In the case of a small effect ($r = 0.1$), 300 observations are not sufficient to achieve a high statistical power. In the case of a large effect ($r = 0.5$), a small sample of 28 observations has a high statistical power. How do I know the exact number?

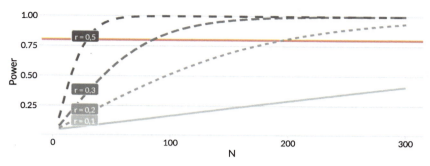

Fig. 6.4: Power analysis

The pwr package provides different functions to estimate the sample size or the statistical power for different analysis techniques (e.g., correlation). In order to do so, we must make assumptions about the effect size (r) and the statistical power to detect the effect. Moreover, we must specify a significance level (e.g., 95 percent) and decide which type of hypothesis testing we apply. The pwr.r.test() returns the number of participants for a large effect of (r = 0.5) with sufficient power, as the console illustrates.

```
#Use the pwr package to run a power analysis
pwr::pwr.r.test(r=0.5, power=0.8, n=NULL, sig.level=0.05, alternative = "two.sided")

#>      approximate correlation power calculation (arctangh transformation)
#>
#>              n = 28.24841
#>              r = 0.5
#>      sig.level = 0.05
#>          power = 0.8
#>    alternative = two.sided
```

Moreover, we need to examine if maybe a third variable is responsible for the effect, especially since we work with observational data. The effect between *x* and *y* could be spurious and other variables might be the reason why we observe a significant effect.

It is important to identify variables that may distort the analysis and it is up to you to elaborate on which one. Let's control for penguin's sex, the variable is a factor variable with two levels. We create a multivariate analysis and add further independent variables with the plus (+) sign. As the next console shows, I add both independent variables and save the model as m2.

```
# Control for confounding variables
m2 <- lm(body_mass_g ~ species + sex, data = penguins)
summary(m2)
```

```
#>
#> Call:
#> lm(formula = body_mass_g ~ species + sex, data = penguins)
#>
#> Residuals:
#>     Min      1Q  Median      3Q     Max
#> -816.87 -217.80  -16.87  227.61  882.20
#>
#> Coefficients:
#>                Estimate Std. Error t value Pr(>|t|)
#> (Intercept)     3399.31      42.13  80.680   <2e-16 ***
#> speciesAdelie    -26.92      46.48  -0.579    0.563
#> speciesGentoo   1350.93      48.13  28.067   <2e-16 ***
#> sexmale          667.56      34.70  19.236   <2e-16 ***
#> ---
#> Signif. codes:  0 '***' 0.001 '**' 0.01 '*' 0.05 '.' 0.1 ' ' 1
#>
#> Residual standard error: 316.6 on 329 degrees of freedom
#>   (11 observations deleted due to missingness)
#> Multiple R-squared:  0.8468, Adjusted R-squared:  0.8454
#> F-statistic: 606.1 on 3 and 329 DF,  p-value: < 2.2e-16
```

Maybe my intuition was not too bad since Adelie is no longer significant, but I only included the variable to illustrate that we need to control for other variables in the case of observational data. If we control for a third variable z, we can estimate the effect of x on y independently from z. However, do we need to control for sex? We need to think about the causal relationship of the examined variables to answer the question whether a variable should (not) be included to estimate the effect.

6.2.2 Think about causality

We applied a linear regression analysis with observational data. We only examined if the variables are correlated, but we do not know if x causes y. In case of cross-sectional data, we cannot even say what comes first. Maybe y is a cause for x. There are several reasons why knowledge about the causal relationship between the observed variables is crucial, even if we work with observational data.

Of course, the analysis of this chapter is just an illustration, and even if we assume that the data has no flaws and we made no mistakes, some of the conclusion might be premature. Instead of the penguins, suppose we examined the effect of happiness on income. We believe that married people create more income and are happier, which is why we control for the marital status. However, higher income could also increase the chance that somebody is married and we cannot assess what came first with cross sectional data. Irrespective of the hypothesis, is the martial status a *confounder* or a *collider* variable? We need to think about causality to build a better model and elaborate a deeper understanding of why x and y are related.

The *Simpson's paradox* helps us to clarify this point. The next plot shows two scatter plots that illustrate the described scenario with simulated data. Figure 6.5 (A) displays the overall effect of income on happiness, while Figure 6.5 (B) displays the same scatter plot but now male and female observations are highlighted with color. As Figure 6.5 (A) shows, there is a positive linear trend, however, we may come to opposite conclusions if we run an analysis for each sex. How is it possible that we observe a positive overall effect, but an opposing negative effect when separating female and male participants? The Simpson's paradox outlines that we may observe a positive or a negative effect, but the effect can be reversed for a subgroup. Which finding should we trust? To find an answer to such questions, we need profound knowledge about the causal relationship of the discussed variables.

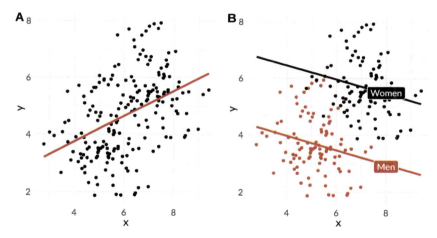

Fig. 6.5: Simpson's paradox

The data for Figure 6.5 was simulated, but the paradox is not fake. It is possible to observe a positive or negative effect which vanishes or is reversed if we stratify the data (based on a third variable). Hence, the estimation of the effect of x on y could be distorted if we ignore the clustered data. I picked the variable sex on purpose, since variables such as income or happiness cannot affect a person's sex. In such an instance we should stratify the data first and calculate the effect separately for each group before we calculate the overall effect. In this example, sex is a confounding variable which we must include as a control variable.

However, a variable could also be a *collider* or a *mediator*. Practice R does not focus on causality, since the latter is an advanced methodological topic. The causality and correlation info box provides a brief summary, and I can only underline that causality is crucial for everyone who works with data. Read Firebaugh (2008) for an intuitive introduction; Imbens & Rubin (2015) to learn more about statistical methods to study causal relationships; and Pearl & Mackenzie (2019) to climb up the "ladder of causation". Knowledge about causality does not help us to learn R, which is why the info box about causality is the only resource in this book.

---

i **Causality and correlation**

Students in the social sciences learn two rules about causality and correlation. As Firebaugh outlines: "No causation without correlation", but unfortunately "correlation does not prove causation" (see Firebaugh 2008: p. 121). In other words, a correlation does not imply that there is causal link from x to y. Two variables may share a common cause, which is the reason why we observe a significant correlation.

The latter is known as *spurious correlation* and quantitative textbooks discuss many examples. Why are the number of churches and bars associated? Do religious people open bars? Or the other way around: Do bar visitors become religious? Both variables share a common cause, larger cities have more bars and more churches. If we control for the size of the city, the number of bars and churches should no longer be significantly correlated in case of a spurious correlation.

The social science often works with observational data and therefore has a long tradition to control for potential confounders. Since more knowledge about causality emerged in the social sciences, perspectives have changed. Today, we are warned that causality may result in an *overcontrol bias* that distorts estimation results. The latter underlines the need for strategies to examine the causal relationship between variables, instead of focusing on confounding variables only. From a causal inference perspective, we need to take *mediator* and *collider* variables into consideration.

A mediator variable represents a causal mechanism between two variables. A mediator channels an effect, we may discover an explanation why x and y are associated when we include a mediator in a multivariate analysis. Unfortunately, you will not get an unbiased estimator for the effect of x on y if we control for the variable since it (partly) explains the effect. The situation is different for a collider: both, x and y affect the collider variable, but not the other way around. If we add a collider in a model, we may create an association between x and y that otherwise would not exist. To put it simply, we induce an association between x and y via the collider and, consequently, draw wrong conclusions. Mediator and collider variables underline that we must not control for all kinds of third variables. It is not necessary to control a mediator and we must not include a collider in the model.

There is too much more to learn about causality to fit into one info box. The purpose of this book is about learning R. Hence, I do not make any assumption or claims about the causal structure in this book. Causality does not matter much in terms of learning R. However, it matters a great deal for a data analysis and you should keep the research design and limitations of the data in mind.

In summary, we need theoretical claims about the underlying causal structure. A correlation coefficient does not reveal if x is a cause of y. We cannot assess the causal structure without knowledge about the topic and a sound research design to identify causal effects. At least, we must observe the examined variables more than once to distinguish what came first – the cause or its effect. We started already to compare models as we examined how potential confounder variables affect the results. The next section illustrates the need to develop models step by step.

6.2.3 Develop models step by step

Up to this point, we have estimated two models: The first model (m1) included only one independent variable, while the second model (m2) took control variables into consideration. This is the typical procedure to develop and improve a model. Comparing the output of two (or more) models is tricky. Nobody wants to scroll up and down to see how the parameters of two models have changed. The huxtable package creates tables and we learn more about this topic in Chapter 8. The package can also generate a table comparing models. Compare multiple models with the huxreg() function (Hugh-Jones, 2022).

```
# Compare models
m1 <- lm(body_mass_g ~ species, data = penguins)
m2 <- lm(body_mass_g ~ species + sex, data = penguins)

# But use huxreg to compare them!
huxtable::huxreg(m1, m2)

#> ================================================================
#>                          (1)               (2)
#>                       ---------------------------------
#> (Intercept)           3733.088 ***      3399.311 ***
#>                        (56.059)          (42.133)
#> speciesAdelie          -32.426           -26.924
#>                        (67.512)          (46.483)
#> speciesGentoo         1342.928 ***      1350.934 ***
#>                        (69.857)          (48.132)
#> sexmale                                  667.555 ***
#>                                          (34.704)
#>                       ---------------------------------
#> N                      342               333
#> R2                       0.670             0.847
#> logLik               -2582.337         -2387.797
#> AIC                   5172.673          4785.594
#>                       ---------------------------------
#>
#>
#> Column names: names, model1, model2
```

Visualizations are crucial in terms of applied data analysis and they are the second most important tool to develop and compare models. Visualizations helps us to focus on the bigger picture instead of comparing the raw numbers of each coefficient. Do we see any substantial difference if we compare them graphically? Visualizations help us greatly to understand what is going on when we analyze data.

The jtools package provides convenient functions to visualize regression results with *dot-and-whisker plots* (Long, 2022) which we can use right from the start. The latter displays a regression coefficient with a dot and the confidence intervals with whiskers. To visualize the result of a model, insert one or several models into the plot_summs() function, as the next console highlights.

```
# jtools returns a dot-and-whisker plot
jtools::plot_summs(m1, m2)
```

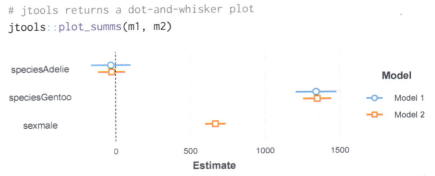

Such dot-and-whisker plots make it easier to compare models and to focus on the bigger picture. We see how the coefficients change when we compare models, control for variables, and we see confidence intervals change or overlap. In the last subsection, we learn how to improve this plot (e.g., get rid of the ugly variable names). Before we elaborate on such minor details, there is still plenty of room to improve the model.

We should at least learn how interaction effects are implemented within R. Suppose we examine if two independent variables interact with each other and the main effect of x on y may depend on the value of a third variable (interaction effect). For example, maybe sex interacts with species or bill_length_mm. Irrespective of the hypothesis, include an interaction effect with an asterisk (*). Both variables – species and sex – are factor variables, but of course we could also estimate an interaction between a nominal or ordinal variable and a numerical outcome, or an interaction between two numerical outcomes. To illustrate this point, I estimated two models and I included two interactions, the interaction between species and sex and between bill_length_mm and sex.

```
# Interaction of two categorical variables
m3 <- lm(body_mass_g ~ species * sex, data = penguins)
# Interaction between a categorical and a numerical variable
m3a <- lm(body_mass_g ~ bill_length_mm * sex, data = penguins)
```

```r
summary(m3)
```

```
#>
#> Call:
#> lm(formula = body_mass_g ~ species * sex, data = penguins)
#>
#> Residuals:
#>     Min      1Q  Median      3Q     Max
#> -827.21 -213.97   11.03  206.51  861.03
#>
#> Coefficients:
#>                       Estimate Std. Error t value Pr(>|t|)
#> (Intercept)            3527.21      53.06  66.474  < 2e-16 ***
#> speciesAdelie          -158.37      64.24  -2.465  0.01420 *
#> speciesGentoo          1152.54      66.83  17.246  < 2e-16 ***
#> sexmale                 411.76      75.04   5.487 8.19e-08 ***
#> speciesAdelie:sexmale   262.89      90.85   2.894  0.00406 **
#> speciesGentoo:sexmale   393.33      94.08   4.181 3.73e-05 ***
#> ---
#> Signif. codes:  0 '***' 0.001 '**' 0.01 '*' 0.05 '.' 0.1 ' ' 1
#>
#> Residual standard error: 309.4 on 327 degrees of freedom
#>   (11 observations deleted due to missingness)
#> Multiple R-squared:  0.8546, Adjusted R-squared:  0.8524
#> F-statistic: 384.3 on 5 and 327 DF,  p-value: < 2.2e-16
```

There is a significant effect between species and sex, but is it a large effect? Inspecting interaction effects visually offers often a clearer picture how the variables are related. Visualize the interaction effects with the interactions package (Long, 2021), as the next console highlights. The cat_plot() visualizes an interaction effect between categorical variables; the interact_plot() does essentially the same for the interaction with a numerical variable.

```r
library(interactions)

# Left: cat_plot for categorical predictors
cat_plot(m3,
  pred = species, modx = sex,
  point.shape = TRUE, vary.lty = FALSE
)
```

```
# Right: Interaction plot
interact_plot(m3a,
  pred = bill_length_mm, modx = sex,
  interval = TRUE, plot.points = FALSE
)
```

The `cat_plot()` function displays point estimates and confidence intervals for each group, which help us to see if and how large the difference between the groups is. We can see that there is a significant interaction effect between `sex` and `species` since the confidence intervals do not overlap, and the effect seems quite substantial for `Gentoo`. The `interact_plot()` returns a line plot with confidence bands and shows us the interaction between the categorical and the numerical outcome.

6.2.4 Performance

We estimate models step by step. To improve a model, you may include an interaction effect, but was it worth in terms of performance? There are several performance indicators to examine the model fit. Load the `performance` package, to get a convenient function to estimate the performance. The `r2()` function makes it easy to retrieve R^2, all it needs is the model name (Lüdecke, Makowski, Ben-Shachar, Patil, Waggoner, et al., 2022).

```
# Compare model performance, for example:
m1 <- lm(body_mass_g ~ species, data = penguins)
m2 <- lm(body_mass_g ~ species + sex, data = penguins)

# R2
```

```
library(performance)
r2(m1)


#> # R2 for Linear Regression
#>          R2: 0.670
#>    adj. R2: 0.668
```

Are you aware that R^2 is not the only performance indicator? Depending on the model, inspect AIC, BIC, and further indicators with the help of the compare_performance() function from the performance package. Use the metrics option to get the most common performance indicators, all that are available, or only those that are of interest, as the next console illustrates.

```
# Compare performance
compare_performance(m1, m2,
  metrics = c("AIC", "BIC", "R2_adj")
)


#> # Comparison of Model Performance Indices
#>
#> Name | Model |  AIC (weights) |  BIC (weights) | R2 (adj.)
#> ------------------------------------------------------------
#> m1   |    lm | 5172.7 (<.001) | 5188.0 (<.001) |    0.668
#> m2   |    lm | 4785.6 (>.999) | 4804.6 (>.999) |    0.845
#>
#> Warning:
#> When comparing models, please note that probably not all models were
#> fit from same data.
```

The function makes it convenient to compare several models and specifications, and it even provides a rank option to find the model with the best fit. Did you see that the performance package returned a warning that not all models were fit from the same data. My console shows this warning because m2 includes sex which has missing values. We tried to elaborate models step by step, but we did not prepare the data to run the analysis. I neglected this topic to focus on the analysis step. To compare models implies that we need to compare them on fair grounds. We need to make sure that the same observations are used for all models before we compare them.

Moreover, we need to examine what influence missing and implausible values have on our estimation results (see Chapter 5). In order to run a model with the same sample, create a filter condition or, as the next code shows, use the drop_na() function and re-estimate and re-evaluate the models before the data loss takes place. To this end, we can compare nested models that rely on the same observations.

```
# Drop observations that will be dropped in later steps
penguins <- penguins |>
  tidyr::drop_na(sex)

# Rerun the model
m1 <- lm(body_mass_g ~ species, data = penguins)
```

The more indicators (and models) we take into consideration, the trickier it gets to compare. The compare_performance() function helps us to inspect the model performance graphically.[2] It returns a radar plot from the see package that depicts all performance indicators of each model (Lüdecke, Makowski, Patil, et al., 2022). Even though a graphical approach also has its limitations with regard to the number of models, assign the results of the compare_performance() function and plot it. As the radar plot shows, the second model outperforms the first model.

```
# Radar plot
library(see)
result <- compare_performance(m1, m2)
plot(result)
```

Comparison of Model Indices

---

[2] In cases when you need to apply any additional steps with the performance parameters, the glance() function from the broom package returns performance indicators as a tidy data frame (Robinson et al., 2022).

6.2.5 Next development steps

To develop models includes more steps than I will outline in depth, especially if you apply a linear regression model with data set that was not created for teaching purposes. For example, consider non-linear effects. In the tutorial of this chapter we use the gss2016 data and examine the relationship between life satisfaction and income. A third variable such as age may have an effect on x and y, but the linear trend may diminish as people get older. At a certain point in life, people's life satisfaction lowers because of, for example, physical health problems. This may lead to a misspecification of the model if there is a non-linear age effect that we did not consider (see Chapter 6.3 for graphical approaches). You can generate a squared age variable and including it in the model.

```
# Make a squared age variable
gss2016$age_sqr <- gss2016$age^2
```

Or consider income. An income variable is often skewed, and we transform the variable to improve the model fit. The transformer() function from PracticeR transforms a numerical variable, applies several transformations (e.g., log()), and returns a histogram for each transformation. The latter may help to examine which transformation may lead to be a better fit.

```
# Transform a numerical outcome
PracticeR::transformer(gss2016$income)
```

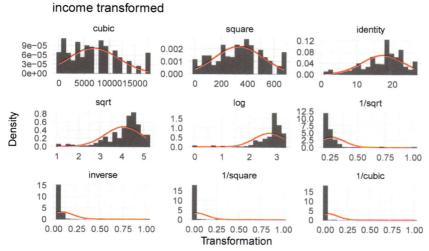

In the case of income, a logarithm is often used to transform the variable, which changes the interpretation but not how we estimate the model. The same applies to polynomial terms or to other improvements. Thus, develop the model step by step and compare your results.

Finally, one last word about regression tables. Do not transfer (regression) results manually. In Chapter 8, we learn how to create documents and (regression) tables with R. However, the `jtools` package might be the right choice if you need to export a regression table right away. Consider the next console and table 6.1; it summarizes the results from a model. The `export_summs()` function from the `jtools` package creates this table and it only needs the results of a model. In addition, I added a list with variable names instead of using the original text labels.

```
# Model
model <- lm(body_mass_g ~ sex, data = penguins)

# Create a list with text labels
library(jtools)
coef_names <- c(
  "Intercept" = "(Intercept)",
  "Male" = "sexmale"
)

# Create a table
export_summs(model, coefs = coef_names)
```

Tab. 6.1

	Model 1
Intercept	3862.27 ***
	(56.83)
Male	683.41 ***
	(80.01)
N	333
R2	0.18

*** $p < 0.001$; ** $p < 0.01$; * $p < 0.05$.

The `jtools` package returns the table via the console, but it lets us export the table also as a Word document. Add the two options `to.file` and `file.name` to the `export_summs` function. Moreover, `jtools` package provides further options to adjust the regression table. For example, the `scale` option provides standardized coefficients and `error_format` may include the confidence interval or other measures into the document.

```
# Export the table, but learn how to make a report (and tables) with R!
export_summs(model,
  scale = FALSE, coefs = coef_names,
  error_format = "{statistic})",
  to.file = "docx", file.name = "test.docx"
)
```

Keep in mind, in Chapter 8 we will focus on documents and tables in detail, but the `jtools` package might be the right choice if you need to export a single regression table only. Instead of talking about tables, the next section highlights visualization techniques.

6.3 Visualization techniques

In Chapter 7, we learn in detail how to visualize research findings. In this subsection we begin with two types of visualization for regression analysis. I discuss graphs (and statistical tests) to examine the assumptions of a linear regression first. Furthermore, I have already underlined the importance of graphs in comparing and developing models and we got in touch with dot-and-whisker plots. The second section elaborates on these skills and shows how we can improve such plots to communicate research results.

6.3.1 Regression assumptions

Graphs are very helpful to examine the assumptions of a linear regression. *Anscombe's quartet* made that clear but there is another prominent example that underlines this point. Consider Figure 6.6. Do you have any idea what the graphs depict? Scatter plots with random noise? Is it just a coincidence that the data looks like a star, a circle, or a dinosaur? The data was simulated by Matejka & Fitzmaurice (2017) to highlight why visualization are important when it comes to data analysis. They show that algorithms are able to generate any kind of distribution and before we run any analysis, we should at least visually inspect each variable. Each simulated data set is (almost) identical in terms of statistical measures (e.g. correlation coefficient), but the data can be generated in any shape, even as a *datasaurus*. The datasauRus package provides the data if you want to inspect it (Davies et al., 2022).

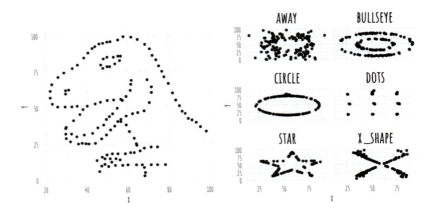

Fig. 6.6: The Datasaurus

R has several built-in diagnostic plots to inspect the assumptions quickly. To inspect them, run and save the results of a model first. Next, use the plot() function and insert the model, it returns the built-in diagnostic plots one after the other. For example, inspect the residuals vs fitted plot to examine if there is a non-linear relationship between the independent variables and the outcome. Or consider the scale-location plot, it depicts standardized residuals, and you can check if the model violates the *homoscedasticity* assumption.

This section will focus on graphs and statistical tests to examine the assumptions of a linear regression and further concerns which are not an assumption but may distort the estimation results (e.g., multicollinearity, outliers, and influential cases), based on the following example model.

```
# Example model
model <- lm(body_mass_g ~ bill_length_mm + sex, data = penguins)
```

We use several packages to check the assumptions of a linear regression, especially the performance package. It has integrated many functions and plots to explore the assumptions. In addition, the lmtest package provides several statistical tests to examine the assumptions; and the estimatr package lets us apply (cluster) robust standard errors.

The performance package

Overall, the `performance` package provides a good first orientation because it has several check functions (with visualizations) to inspect the assumptions of a linear regression. Use the `check_model()` function for a quick overview about potential violations: it returns six diagnostic plots and it even helps with the interpretation of each graph.

```
# Get a quick overview
x <- check_model(model)
plot(x)
```

Figure 6.7 displays the result of the `check_model()` function. Moreover, the package provides functions (and plots) to address the assumptions individually. For example, use the package to examine *outliers (influential cases)*, *multicollinearity*, and *linearity* assumption. In terms of outliers and influential cases, we need to understand how single observation affect a linear regression. Thus, we need to understand what *leverage* and *influence* mean. An observation has a high leverage if it has an extreme value on an independent variable and in consequence may have a substantial effect on the estimation results. Furthermore, an observation is said to be influential if its removal changes the regression coefficients significantly. There are several statistical measures to identify outliers and influential cases. A lot of students have heard of Cook's distance (or Cook's D), which combines information of the residual and leverage to identify outliers and influential cases (Cook, 1977). The higher the value of Cook's D, the higher the influence, and we may check each observation that exceeds a certain threshold (as a convention: 4/n). R has the corresponding function to calculate Cook's D.

```
# Identify outliers with Cook's D
cookD_model <- cooks.distance(model)
cookD_model[1:3]
```

```
#>          1          2          3
#> 0.0008550359 0.0001002037 0.0012814026
```

However, Cook's D is not the only measure to identify influential observations. I will not introduce further measures, because the `performance` package includes Cook's D and other statistics to identify outliers. As outlined in the help file of the `performance` package, the `check_outliers()` function: "locates influential observations (...) via several distance and/or clustering methods" (Lüdecke, Makowski, Ben-Shachar, Patil, Waggoner, et al., 2022). You can get all or explicitly pick a certain measure – such as Cook's D – with the `method` option.

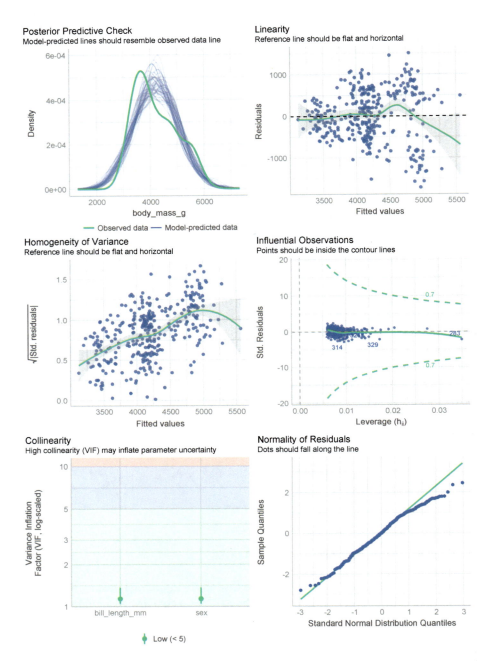

Fig. 6.7: Regression diagnostics overview

```
# Search for influential observations
check_outliers(model)
```

```
#> OK: No outliers detected.
#> - Based on the following method and threshold: cook (0.79).
#> - For variable: (Whole model)
```

The check_* functions return visualizations of the result when we assign the result of the function and plot it. The package even includes instructions on how to interpret the results. As the check_outliers plot indicates, outliers and influential observations will show up outside the contour line.

```
# Plot influential observations
x <- check_outliers(model)
plot(x)
```

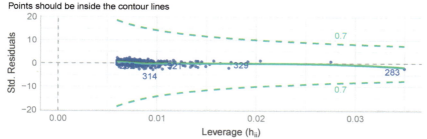

The package also helps us to address the multicollinearity assumption: The latter expresses that two (or more) variables are a linear combination of one another. Inspect the *variance inflation factor (VIF)* and the *tolerance* (1/VIF) to examine multicollinearity. Both express whether a variable might be a linear combination of each other. Again, the performance package helps us with this task because the check_collinearity() function returns them. The package documentations outlines even a rule of thumb to interpret: "A VIF less than 5 indicates a low correlation of that predictor with other predictors. A value between 5 and 10 indicates a moderate correlation, while VIF values larger than 10 are a sign for high, not tolerable correlation of model predictors" (see Lüdecke, Makowski, Ben-Shachar, Patil, Waggoner, et al., 2022).

```
# VIF values
check_collinearity(model)
```

```
#> # Check for Multicollinearity
#>
```

```
#> Low Correlation
#> 
#>           Term  VIF  VIF 95% CI Increased SE Tolerance Tolerance 95% CI
#> bill_length_mm 1.13 [1.05, 1.36]         1.07      0.88     [0.73, 0.95]
#>            sex 1.13 [1.05, 1.36]         1.07      0.88     [0.73, 0.95]
```

Next, we use the performance and ggeffects package to examine the linearity assumption. A linear regression assumes a linear relationship between *x* and *y*, but we fit a straight line even if the relationship is not linear. Thus, we should use a scatter plot to examine the variables before you even apply an analysis. Certainly, a scatter plot may reveal whether the relationship is (not) linear in a bivariate analysis.

What shall we do in the case of a multivariate analysis? Inspect the residuals vs fitted plot (Figure 6.7: Linearity or the built-in diagnostic plots) to examine if there is a non-linear relationship between the independent variables and the outcome. The residuals should spread around a horizontal line if variables are associated in a linear fashion.

A slightly different approach is offered by the ggeffects package (Lüdecke, 2022). It inserts the residuals in a scatter plot instead of the observed values. The next plot illustrates this point with simulated data from the ggeffects package. The left plot shows a regular scatter plot, and we may not realize that there is a non-linear trend. The right plot includes the residuals and an extra line to display the functional form of the residuals.

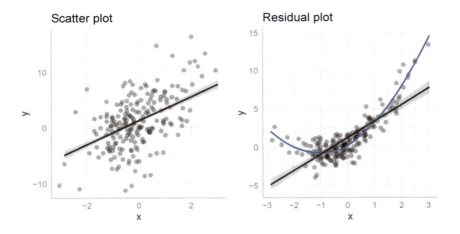

Keep in mind that I used simulated data for the last graph since it includes a non-linear trend on purpose. Inspect the documentation if you want to use the ggeffects package and consider to transform the variables if you come across a non-linear effect.

Ultimately, we explore how the lmtest and the estimatr package help us to address the *homoscedasticity* and the *independence of error* assumption.

The lmtest and the estimatr package

We can make an error if we predict the outcome, but is the error systematic? We assume that the variance of the error is constant (homoscedastic), but the assumption is violated if the variance of the error is *heteroscedastic*. We may make a larger or smaller mistake depending on the observed value of x. If the variance of the error is constant, we should not see a clear pattern. The next plot depicts the standardized residuals against the fitted values, as the check_heteroscedasticity() function returns.

```
# check_heteroscedasticity
x <- check_heteroscedasticity(model)
plot(x)
```

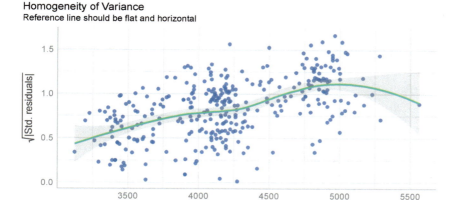

In cases of equal variance, we should see a horizontal line and points should spread without a distinct pattern. In the case of the penguins data, we need to examine both in more detail since the assumptions are clearly violated. If the picture is not that clear, use a statistical test. The lmtest package provides several tests to examine the assumptions of linear regression models (Hothorn et al., 2022). For example, the Breusch & Pagan (1979) test assumes as null hypothesis that the variance of the error is homoscedastic, which we must reject. The check_heteroscedasticity() also calls the Breusch & Pagan test and helps us with the interpretation, as the next console illustrates.

```
# Breusch & Pagan test (1979)
lmtest::bptest(model)
```

```
#>
```

```
#>  studentized Breusch-Pagan test
#>
#> data:  model
#> BP = 88.775, df = 2, p-value < 2.2e-16
```

```
# check_heteroscedasticity
check_heteroscedasticity(model)
```

```
#> Warning: Heteroscedasticity (non-constant error variance) detected
#> (p < .001).
```

What shall we do in case of a heteroscedastic error? To transform the variables may help and you can use robust standard errors to take into consideration that the error is non-constant. The `lm_robust()` function from the `estimatr` package provides different types of standard errors (for example, the `stata` equivalent `HC1`), but further options are available (Blair et al., 2022).

```
# Robust standard errors
library(estimatr)
robust_model <- lm_robust(body_mass_g ~ bill_length_mm + sex,
  data = penguins,
  se_type = "stata"
)
```

Both packages also help us to address the independence of error assumption: we assume that the error of one observation does not depend on the error of another observation. Suppose we compare children from different classes. All children from one class are exposed to the same conditions. Thus, observations from children of the same class are more similar than observations from children of different classes. In consequence, the error is not independent and observations from different classes build a cluster. We may even have a second cluster if we compare different schools and classes.

In such a case we need a robust regression (`lm_robust()`), but this time we need to specify a cluster variable. In the case of the `penguins`, all penguins of the same `island` are exposed to the same conditions and may be considered as a cluster.

```
# Cluster robust
cluster_model <- lm_robust(flipper_length_mm ~ bill_length_mm + sex,
  data = penguins,
  clusters = island
)
```

A second reason why the independence of an error assumption might be violated is auto-correlation. Suppose you measure the skills of children several times. It is likely, that the error of the first measurement is correlated with the second measurement since the same child was tested. In the case of time-series data, use the Durbin-Watson test (dwtest) to check for correlated residuals.

```
# Run a Durbin-Watson test in case of auto-correlation
lmtest::dwtest(model)
```

Further assumptions

A linear regression relies on further assumption which I will not outline in detail, since the performance package includes them. For example, a linear regression assumes that the error is normally distributed and there are several tests and graphical procedures. The check_normality() function uses the shapiro.test to examine if the standardized residuals are normally distributed, and the function also visualizes the results. Consider transforming the examined variables if the normality assumption is violated.

```
# check_normality
check_normality(model)
```

Ultimately, you should be aware that a linear regression relies on even more assumptions. Unfortunately, they are harder to address, especially in terms of applying R. For example, we need to assume that the model includes all relevant variables. In order to decide which variable is (not) relevant to explain the outcome, theoretical assumptions and knowledge about the causal structure of the examined variables is needed. Think about omitted variables that are of high relevance to explain the outcome; or maybe we have included irrelevant control variables that do not change the bigger picture at all? Thus, theoretical assumptions and knowledge about the causal structure should guide your way to addressing this assumption. The same applies to measurement error: we cannot prove that there is no measurement error, which underlines the importance of robustness checks. For example, we may exclude extreme but plausible cases which may induce measurement error. Unfortunately, this does not solve the problem in general terms but it increases the confidence if the results are not affected. Instead of talking about regression assumptions, the next section focuses on skills to visualize and communicate regression results.

6.3.2 Visualize regression results

Visualizations are an important tool to communicate the results of an analysis. As outlined, the jtools package provides convenient functions to visualize regression

188 —— 6 Analyze data

results with dot-and-whisker plots. To create a dot-and-whisker plot, just insert a model object into the `plot_summs()` function, as the first plot on the left side highlights. In addition, `plot_summs()` can also return a plot for several models, as illustrated in the second plot on the right. Moreover, the `plot_summs()` function comes with several handy options. For example, the `scale` option returns standardized coefficients, the `model.names` option allows us to give descriptive names for each model; and, as the next console shows, we can get rid of ugly text strings (e.g., `bill_length_mm`) by providing coefficient (`coefs`) names.

```
# Two example models
m1 <- lm(flipper_length_mm ~ bill_length_mm,
  data = penguins
)
m2 <- lm(flipper_length_mm ~ bill_length_mm + sex,
  data = penguins
)

# Left: plot_summs from jtools returns a dot-and-whisker
plot_summs(m1)

# Right: add coefficient labels
plot_summs(m1, m2, coefs = c(
  "Bill length" = "bill_length_mm",
  "Male" = "sexmale"
))
```

You may not realize it, but the `jtools` package makes it convenient to visualize regression results. The package only needs the model, it picks colors and inserts a vertical reference line in the plot. The `jtools` package is an excellent start to visualize regression results, especially to compare and develop models.

Let us inspect how we create dot-and-whisker plots with the `dotwhisker` package, which gives us even more possibilities to visualize and communicate regression results (Solt & Hu, 2021). In order to make a dot-and-whisker plot, we need a data frame with the name of the variables, the estimates of the analysis, and the standard errors. In other words, tabular or tidy data, as the corresponding function from the broom package illustrates (Robinson et al., 2022).

```r
# broom::tidy returns a tidy data of your model
broom::tidy(m1, conf.int = TRUE)
```

```
#> # A tibble: 2 x 7
#>   term       estim~1 std.e~2 stati~3  p.value conf.~4 conf.~5
#>   <chr>        <dbl>   <dbl>   <dbl>    <dbl>   <dbl>   <dbl>
#> 1 (Interce~   127.     4.67    27.2  3.65e-87  118.    136.
#> 2 bill_len~     1.69   0.105   16.0  1.74e-43    1.48    1.90
#> # ... with abbreviated variable names 1: estimate,
#> #   2: std.error, 3: statistic, 4: conf.low, 5: conf.high
```

Just like jtools, the dotwhisker package includes this step and creates a dot-and-whisker plot with the dwplot() function. Creating a simple version works essentially the same way; refer to the model to display the regression estimates. The function returns only the dot and the whisker of the coefficient, without a vertical reference line. You can add one with the vline option and adjust its position (xintercept); color and linetype. As the next console underlines, the dotwhisker package is more complex as the first approach but is also more flexible.

```r
library(dotwhisker)
# Left: the dwplot
dwplot(m1)

# Right: add a reference line
dwplot(m1, vline = geom_vline(
  xintercept = 0,
  color = "black"
))
```

To compare models, we must include them as a list in the dwplot() function. Furthermore, model_order lets you adjust the order of the displayed models.

```
# Include several models as list
dwplot(list(m1, m2))

# Sort/resort models via model_order
dwplot(list(m1, m2),
  model_order = c("Model 2", "Model 1")
)
```

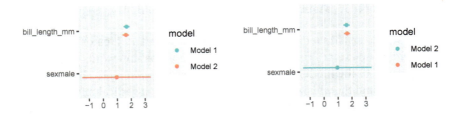

In a similar way, order the variables manually with the option vars_order, starting from the top to the bottom of the graph. Or, provide a descriptive text label for the predictors (relabel_predictors).

```
# Results are displayed on the next page:
# Sort variables
dwplot(m2,
  vars_order = c("sexmale", "bill_length_mm")
)

# Relabel variables
dwplot(m2) |>
  relabel_predictors(c(
    bill_length_mm = "Bill length",
    sexmale = "Male penguins"
))
```

The dotwhisker package provides more options which I cannot discuss in detail, inspect the package vignette for more information. Irrespective of the options, let us presume that we have combined some of them to create a fully customized plot. The next console

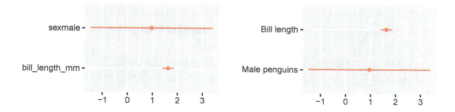

shows the code to create such a graph. Please, don't get intimidated by the code. There is no need to inspect each line of code, just take a look at the final plot.

```
#The final plot
dwplot(list(m1, m2),
       dot_args = list(size = 2),
       vline = geom_vline(xintercept = 0,
                          colour = "black",
                          linetype = 2),
       model_order = c("Model 1", "Model 2")) |>
  relabel_predictors(c(bill_length_mm = "Bill length",
                       sexmale = "Male penguins"))+
  ggtitle("Results")+
  theme_minimal(base_size = 12)+
  xlab("Effect on body mass") +
  ylab("Coefficient") +
  theme(plot.title = element_text(face = "bold"),
        legend.title = element_blank()) +
  scale_color_viridis_d(option = "plasma")
```

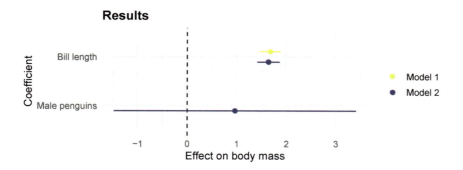

Now, you really understand why packages such as jtools make our life easier. Maybe you cannot believe it, but creating such a customized plot can be worth the trouble, since you can adjust all aspects to your needs. That is the reason why I introduced both approaches in this section, although we prefer the simpler solution when we develop models.

Can you do me a favor and examine how I added the title in the last plot? I used `ggtitle()` from the ggplot2 package. In the next chapter we will learn how to visualize research findings from the ground with ggplot2. Regardless of which approach you apply, the `jtools` and the `dotwhisker` packages actually return a ggplot2 object. This implies that everything you will learn in the next chapter will also work for plots that are made with `jtools`, `dotwhisker`, and other packages that rely on ggplot2 to create graphs.

Summary

This chapter introduced the main principles to apply a linear regression analysis. We estimated the effect of one (or several) independent variable(s) on a continuous outcome. Keep in mind that building a model takes time and experience. For this reason, we started simple and I tried to underline the need to improve the model step by step. We compare how the results change if we control for confounding variables or if we transform the outcome. Many students in the social sciences know – at least in theory – how a linear regression works, which is why I decided to focus on practical steps and how they are applied with R. In consequence, I did not explain many concepts in detail. Even though I concentrated on the practice steps, I could have spent much more time talking about different specifications (e.g., log-linear model) or further advanced topics and improvements (e.g. splines). I guess it's up to you to discover these topics, but with R you have an excellent companion to analyze data. For example, consider reading Gelman et al. (2020) to learn more about *Regression and Other Stories*.

```
# E-book: Regression and other stories
PracticeR::show_link("regression")
```

Finally, Chapter 12 introduces the nuts and bolts of logistic regression, since the latter is also often part of the standard curriculum in the social sciences.

7 Visualize research findings

The first steps to prepare and to analyze data are behind us and it is time to visualize the results. Maybe you did not expect an entire chapter about visualizations, but they are the most powerful tool to communicate central insights of the analysis. A good visualization makes it easier for your audience to grasp and even memorize results. Unfortunately, a graph may not clearly communicate the results or leave room for interpretation, which is why some people may have a hard time to understand it. Visualize your research findings, but try to draw a coherent and clear picture of it.

A graph should transport the main insight or finding. To illustrate this point, Figure 7.1 shows an updated version of the hockey stick graph (Mann et al., 1999).[1] It depicts the temperature anomaly with a line plot and shows that the temperature rises like a hockey stick in the late 20th century. The hockey stick graph was one of the first graphs to scrutinize climate change. Suppose you don't know anything about climate change. Would you believe that we face a serious problem because the temperature rises like a hockey stick? How we assess research findings also depends on prior knowledge, but some people lack that knowledge, and in consequence may doubt climate change. This is one of the reasons why we are supposed to make visualizations, but also why we must question ourselves, did we make the graph's message obvious (enough)?

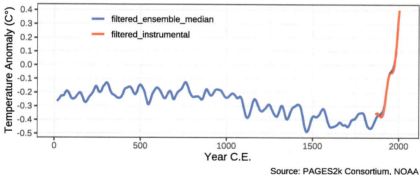

Fig. 7.1: Global common era temperature reconstruction

Don't get me wrong, I am not saying that the hockey stick graph is not well suited for its purpose. The question is how can we improve our work and make it easier for

---

[1] The graph was made with the help of the `hockeystick` package (Cortina, 2022). The package provides data and many graphs about climate change.

https://doi.org/10.1515/9783110704976-007

the audience to understand the main message? Do we have the data, the technical equipment, and the visualization skills to convince our peers and to make the broader public understand that global warming is a pressing issue?

In this chapter I introduce the `ggplot2` package and we lay the foundation to create high-quality graphs to communicate key research insights (Wickham, Chang, et al., 2022). The package offers many possibilities to visualize data and implements a theoretical framework – the grammar of graphics – which outlines how graphs are composed. Regardless whether we talk about a dot plot, a bar graph, or a pie chart, we can create many different graphs with `ggplot2`, and knowledge about the grammar of graphics lets us adjust all aspects of a graph; in principle we could even invent a new one! This sounds complicated and to be honest with you, such an endeavor would result in a long and complicated code. That is not a bad thing. Let me explain.

The `ggplot2` package has well-established default options and you may not bother with tiny details of a graph if you are happy with it. Of course, you can make some adjustments, like adding a title, but we do not need to customize the entire graph if we are happy with the default version. The `ggplot2` package is not complicated as long as we create standard graphs (e.g., bar graph, etc.). Profound knowledge about the underlying framework is not necessary to make our first graph.

- In Section 7.1, we focus on the basics of data visualization. We apply steps which are typical for almost all (scientific) graphs. We learn how to make labels, adjust the legend, and pick some colors. Such steps are easy to apply, but they are essential to communicate clearly. I hope that this first section proves that you can adjust a default version quickly for your needs.
- To understand how `ggplot2` works, we get in touch with the grammar of graphics in Section 7.2. I introduce several terms that refer to the individual components of a graph. We concentrate on the grammar of graphics to get a deeper understanding of `ggplot2`. We create one specific plot in the first section, but by the end of the second section you will be able to create many graphs. Please, don't get me wrong. I don't say that you will be able to create a high quality graph in no time. That would be a lie and I am not a teaching wizard! However, you will be able to create many different graphs as we will lay the foundation to apply the grammar of graphics.
- In Section 7.3, we explore packages that extend the possibilities of `ggplot2`. There are too many `ggplot2` extensions to discuss them all in detail. Some packages help you to create text boxes for annotations, some improve how we can combine several graphs into one, and some support us to make advanced graphs such as maps, animations, and other fancy things. Thus, this section is like a picture book showing you potential next steps to visualize research findings. Now that the scope it set, let us dive into the basics.

The `ggplot2` package is included in the `tidyverse` package. Furthermore, you need the following packages:

```
#Libraries for section 7.1
library(ggplot2)
library(ggthemes)
library(palmerpenguins)
library(PracticeR)
library(RColorBrewer)
library(showtext)
```

7.1 The basics of ggplot2

Let us make a scatter plot to examine the association between the body mass (body_mass_g) and the bill length (bill_length_mm) with the penguins data from the palmerpenguins package. Figure 7.2 shows two different versions of the same scatter plot. Figure 7.2 (A) shows the default version of a scatter plot made with ggplot2, while Figure 7.2 (B) displays an improved version. We will learn all necessary steps to improve the default version in this section.

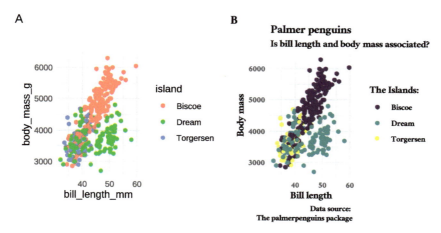

Fig. 7.2: Scatter plot example

We start with the minimal code to create a scatter plot and we adjust it step by step: (1) We focus on the main ggplot() function. Next, I outline the steps to change the appearance of the graph: (2) We learn how to adjust the labels (axes, title, etc.), (3) the theme, (4) the font type, (5) the colors, (6) the legend, and (7) we will export a graph. Certainly, this is a less-than-ideal recipe to make a graph, but you need to apply the discussed steps anyway.

7.1.1 The ggplot() function

Each time you make a graph with ggplot2, use the ggplot() function, you insert a data frame, and specify which variables to visualize. Include the latter in the aes() (*aesthetic*) function which maps variables to graphical objects (*geoms*). In a minimal version, I insert bill_length_mm as x and body_mass_g as y variable in the aes() function. In the case of a scatter plot, ggplot() takes the observed values and displays them with points in a coordinate system. However, the data will not be displayed if we use the ggplot()function only. We must add a geometrical object (geom_*) with a layer.

The next console returns three graphs to illustrate this point. The first graph on the left side shows only that the graphical interface is opened. The aes() function adds a default coordinate system and the variables, but without any visual representation of the data. Add a second layer with a plus (+) sign and the geom_point() to create a scatter plot, as the third plot on the right side highlights.

```
#Left plot: The ggplot function
ggplot(data = penguins)

#Center: The aes function
ggplot(data = penguins, aes(x = bill_length_mm, y = body_mass_g))

#Right plot: Add layers with a + sign!
ggplot(data = penguins, aes(x = bill_length_mm, y = body_mass_g))+
   geom_point()
```

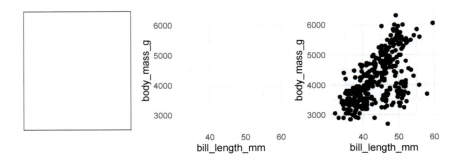

So, we need to specify how to depict the data and we then add (+) a geom as an additional *layer*. Each graph starts with the ggplot() function, and we adjust all sorts of graphical aspects with layers. We can add the labels of the axis, modify the legend, or change the colors with an additional layer. The layers are the reason why ggplot2 is powerful. By the end of this chapter, we will be more familiar with layers, but irrespective if we add a label for a bar graph or a scatter plot, the code to add the labels is often identical. You cannot add a layer that exists only for a certain graph, but you can recycle a lot of code by changing the data, the variables, and the geom. Wait till the end of this chapter if this seems obscure.

Before you go on and you try it on your own, let me give some advice. Take care that each layer is added with a plus (+) sign at the end of the line; and that each new layer starts on a new line. I can't say how often I stared at a code and wondered why R did not return a graph. In most instances I forgot to add a plus sign for a new layer or I deleted a layer and forgot to delete the plus sign. R expects us to deliver a layer if the code ends with a plus sign and waits patiently until it gets one. At some point this might be the reason why nothing happens if you run code. The console prints a plus sign if R expects to get another layer and you may use the <ESC> button to abort the call.

The next console shows the minimal code for the scatter plot one more time. We use it as a starting point to examine how a layer changes the appearance of a graph. As the next console displays, we can skip the data argument and I inserted the name of the data frame only. The same applies to x and y within the aes() function. You may skip these arguments, since it makes the code a bit more elegant.

```
#The minimal code
ggplot(penguins, aes(bill_length_mm, body_mass_g))+
    geom_point()
```

Talking about elegance, let's get rid of the ugly axes labels (e.g., variable names spelled in snake case).

7.1.2 Labels

Give the axes proper text labels. It helps to communicate the graph's message clearly. Variable names are often not optimal and do not have the same aim as text labels. Variable names should be concise and are often saved in small letters, which looks odd in a graph. Labels give us the possibility of providing more information about the variables, because even a very_long variable name may lead to confusion.

The steps to add a label are easy and there is little to explain. As the next code highlights, add a label for the x-axis (xlab()) and the y-axis (ylab()). If the graph needs a title, use the ggtitle() function.

```
#Provide precise labels for the axis and a title
ggplot(penguins, aes(x = bill_length_mm, y = body_mass_g))+
    geom_point()+
```

```
xlab("Bill length")+
ylab("Body mass")+
ggtitle("Palmer penguins")
```

Depending on the purpose of the graph, it could be useful to provide a title, a caption, and other annotations to help the audience understand the main message. Such texts may not be necessary if you, for example, describe your work in detail at a conference. But what happens if you share the slides of the presentation? Someone inspects the work and you will not be there to explain it. Thus, descriptive texts may help to transport the message.

A smooth alternative for all those text labels offers the labs() function. You can modify the axis labels, provide a title, subtitle, tag, and caption with the labs() function. Such steps seem trivial, but compare the scatter plot with the default version. The audience now gets a chance to understand what is going on.

```
#Combine all texts with the labs function
ggplot(penguins, aes(x = bill_length_mm, y = body_mass_g))+
  geom_point()+
  labs(title = "Palmer penguins",
       subtitle = "Is bill length and body mass associated?",
       tag = "Fig. 1",
       x = "Bill length",
       y = "Body mass",
       caption = "Data source: The palmerpenguins package")
```

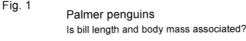

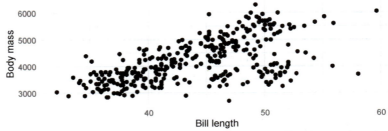

Did you run the code on your computer? Did you realize that my graphs look slightly different than yours? There is a simple explanation: I picked a different default theme for this book.

7.1.3 Themes

We can adjust all graphical aspects that determines the graphical appearance with ggplot2. Before we focus on the nitty-gritty details, let us first explore the theme_* functions, which are predefined rules to style a graph. Themes are very useful since they change the appearance with just one line of code. The ggplot2 package includes several themes. For example, add the theme_minimal() or the theme_gray() as a layer. The theme_minimal() should look familiar, since graphs in this book are made with this theme, the theme_gray() is the default ggplot2 theme. Regardless of the choice, not all themes work for all purposes. To get a first overview about the implemented themes, Figure 7.3 shows six standard themes from the corresponding theme_* functions.

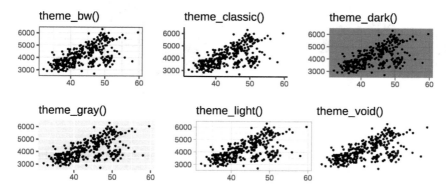

Fig. 7.3: Standard themes

We may add theme_minimal() as a layer or set a favorite theme permanently with the theme_set() function.

```
#Set a different default theme, for example:
theme_set(theme_minimal())
```

If you didn't like the standard themes, give the ggthemes extension package a shot (Arnold, 2021). It provides several themes, among them The Economist, an Excel, and a Stata theme. Give it a try by adding the corresponding theme function.

```
#The ggthemes package provides more themes
library(ggthemes)

#Left: Stata style
ggplot(penguins, aes(x = bill_length_mm, y = body_mass_g))+
  geom_point()+
  theme_stata()

#Right: Excel "style"
ggplot(penguins, aes(x = bill_length_mm, y = body_mass_g))+
  geom_point()+
  theme_excel()
```

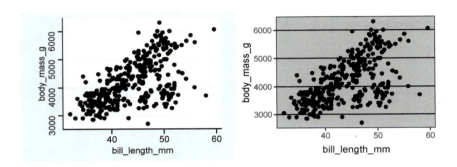

The ggplot2 package gives us full control to customize a graph and this also applies to the theme() function, regardless of which predefined theme you apply. For example, the next console shows how to modify two different theme elements by adjusting the theme() layer. I changed the color and the angle of the axis text. Furthermore, I increased the text size of the title, and the text is bold in the second plot on the right. Customizing a theme is complicated, since we can change a lot of elements. In consequence, the theme() function may become quite complicated, as the next console illustrates.

```
#Left: Adjust the axis.text
ggplot(penguins, aes(x = bill_length_mm, y = body_mass_g))+
  geom_point()+
  theme(axis.text = element_text(color="gray", angle=45))

#Right: Change how the plot.title is displayed
ggplot(penguins, aes(x = bill_length_mm, y = body_mass_g))+
```

```
geom_point()+
ggtitle("Title")+
theme(plot.title = element_text(size=16, face="bold"))
```

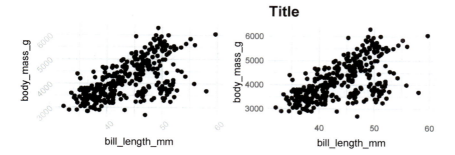

There are too many theme() options and parameters that determine how a graph is plotted to discuss all of them. Run ?theme if you are searching for something specific; R returns a list of all theme elements, or use Google to find out how to change a theme aspect. This might be too overwhelming in the beginning and it is probably for the best if we stick to the predefined themes for now; just keep in mind that a plot can be fully customized.[2]

The same applies to fonts. We could change the font type and the font size of the title, subtitle, and the caption separately, but that's not a useful workaround. Let's see if we can find a better solution in the next subsection since the right font size depends on the font type anyway.

7.1.4 Fonts

Suppose you want to use a fancy font type to transport the graph's main message. The showtext package offers a convenient way to work with font types (Qiu, 2022). Do you know which font types are installed on your computer? And where they live? Font files are saved in a system directory (e.g., C:\Windows\Fonts), but wait a minute before you hunt them down, because showtext helps you with this task. The font_paths() function shows the directories where the package searches for font types and you have access to all listed fonts.

---

[2] You may even create your own theme function when you have more experience with ggplot2. This sounds quite complicated, but in principle we copy a predefined theme and change only specific aspects.

```r
#font_paths shows you where your font types live
font_paths()


#> [1] "/Library/Fonts"
#> [2] "/System/Library/Fonts"
#> [3] "/System/Library/Fonts/Supplemental"
#> [4] "/Users/edgartreischl/Library/Fonts"
```

Wait just a moment longer before you visit these directories. The font_files() function returns all font types of this directory. As the next console shows, I assigned the result of the font_files() function and I printed a subset, but only to create a smaller output for this book. The font_files() function returns the file and the family name for all font files that showtext has found.

```r
#font_files returns the path, file, and family name of fonts
df <- font_files()
df[1:5, 1:3]


#>                    path                            file            family
#> 1         /Library/Fonts             Arial Unicode.ttf Arial Unicode MS
#> 2 /System/Library/Fonts Apple Braille Outline 6 Dot.ttf    Apple Braille
#> 3 /System/Library/Fonts Apple Braille Outline 8 Dot.ttf    Apple Braille
#> 4 /System/Library/Fonts Apple Braille Pinpoint 6 Dot.ttf   Apple Braille
#> 5 /System/Library/Fonts Apple Braille Pinpoint 8 Dot.ttf   Apple Braille
```

Now that we know the file and family name of the installed fonts, how does it work? Add a font type by proving its name (or the path to the file). Next, we run the showtext_auto() function which lets us render the text of the graph with showtext. Finally, we need to refer to the imported font type. For example, change the font type with base_family within the theme function. As the next console highlights, I used the American Typewriter font for the first plot on the left side.

```r
library(showtext)
#Add a font
font_add(family = "American Typewriter",
         regular = "AmericanTypewriter.ttc")


showtext_auto()

#Include the font within the theme, as the left plot shows:
ggplot(penguins, aes(x = bill_length_mm, y = body_mass_g))+
```

```
geom_point()+
ggtitle("Font: American Typewriter")+
theme_minimal(base_family = "American Typewriter")
```

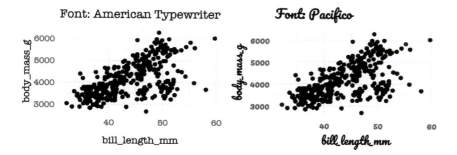

On the right side, I used Pacifico as the font type. Working with font type is hard work, especially if the font type is not installed. We must rerun the entire script to find its path and the name of the font. What happens if we do not know which font type fits best for our purpose? We rerun our script more than once before we are happy with the results. Fortunately, we need not install a font type locally, as the second plot demonstrates. The Pacifico font comes from Google Fonts, and I did not install it locally. The Google platform stores a lot of font types, and we get access with the font_add_google() function. It downloads the file and makes the font temporary available. The steps to use fonts from Google are pretty much the same as before:

```
#Add a font from Google: https://fonts.google.com/
font_add_google("Pacifico")

ggplot(penguins, aes(x = bill_length_mm, y = body_mass_g))+
  geom_point()+
  ggtitle("Font: Pacifico")+
  theme_minimal(base_size = 12, base_family = "Pacifico")+
  theme(plot.title = element_text(size=14))
```

Examine the theme_minimal() function of the last code. The base_family option inserts the new font type. The option base_size works in a similar way for the font size. The choice for a font size depends on the font type. If it is clear which font type it should be, just insert the base_size argument in the predefined theme() function, which sets a reasonable base size for all regular texts of the graph. Even if we use the base_size

7.1.5 Colors

The R community is very colorful and so is R. It includes 657 different predefined colors. Inspect them with the `colors()` function.

```
#colors() returns implemented colors
colors()[1:4]
```

```
#> [1] "white"        "aliceblue"     "antiquewhite"  "antiquewhite1"
```

Colors are harder to handle because there are so many possibilities and it depends on your goals. Do you want to pick colors to make the graph look nice or do you want to convey information with the colors? And for which kind of graph? Do you want to color the circles of a scatter plot or fill a geometrical object?

As long as a color is not used to convey information, it is not difficult to adjust colors. For example, add the `color` and the `fill` argument inside the geom function. The `fill` option lets us fill a geom and the `color` option modifies the border of a geom. The next console shows how we adjust colors for a bar graph and a scatter plot. The left plot shows a bar graph (`geom_bar()`) with white bars and a black border. The right plot adjusts the color for a scatter plot.

```
#Left: Bar plot with colors
ggplot(penguins, aes(x = species))+
  geom_bar(fill = "white", color = "black")
```

```
#Right: Scatter plot with colors
ggplot(penguins, aes(x = bill_length_mm, y = body_mass_g))+
  geom_point(fill = "red", color = "black", shape = 21)
```

Examine the code for the second plot. The `fill` option fills a geometrical object, but the default symbol of a `geom_point()` cannot be filled. In order to use the `fill` aesthetic, we must use a shape that can be filled. For this reason, I used a different shape in the `geom_point()` function. Keep in mind that you can only use the `fill` option if there is something that can be filled. This applies to other aesthetics as well, such as line types. Changing the shape makes it necessary to know which shapes are available and what their corresponding numbers are. There is no need to remember which number refers to which shape, because I included a graph in the `PracticeR` package that depicts the available shapes. Run the `show_shapetypes()` function and it returns a graph that shows the shapes, as Figure 7.4 displays.

```
#Which shape shall it be?
PracticeR::show_shapetypes()
```

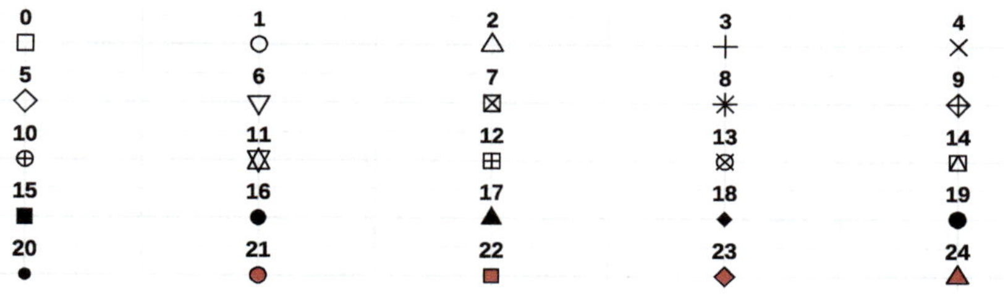

Fig. 7.4: Shape types in R

By the way, I created a similar graph for the line types. You get different types of lines using their corresponding number. The next console shows only the code, but `show_linetypes()` function returns the line types (and the corresponding numbers) as a graph.

```
#Line types
PracticeR::show_linetypes()
```

Insert `fill` or `color` inside the `geom()` function, but should you want to convey information, use them inside the `aes()` function. In the next section, we learn more about the underlying theory, but it will help us to understand how `ggplot2` works if we discover a bit more about *aesthetic mappings*.

Each geom has specific aesthetics to map data. As a first step, we define which variable is mapped as x and y, and we may use further aesthetics such as `color`, `shape`, or `fill` to map information. See what happens if we insert the `color` argument inside

206 —— 7 Visualize research findings

the `aes()` function. For example, use the categorical variable `island` to color the points of the scatter plot, to accentuate between the islands the penguins are coming from. In addition, the second plot includes the `shape` argument, which gives each island its own color and shape.

```
#Left: Add color aesthetic
ggplot(penguins, aes(x = bill_length_mm, y = body_mass_g,
                     color = island))+
  geom_point()
```

```
#Right: Add shape aesthetic
ggplot(penguins, aes(x = bill_length_mm, y = body_mass_g,
                     color = island ,
                     shape = island))+
  geom_point()
```

Maybe you are less enthusiastic about this plot than I am. Think of it! First, we modified only the appearance of a graph, but now we depict information with colors and shapes. One aesthetic is enough to show where our penguins live, but the last plot illustrates that aesthetics can be combined.

How can we adjust colors to map information? As before, we could include the colors inside the `geom_()`, but this is not an efficient way to work with colors. There are several `scale_` functions which determine how geometric objects are scaled. There is a scale function for the axis, for the position of geometrical objects, but also for the colors. To apply a `scale_` function, we need to consider for which aesthetic mapping we want to change the color. This sounds abstract and we elaborate more on these skills in the next section. For now, it suffices to understand that the `scale_fill_manual()` lets you manually fill objects, while `scale_color_manual()` works with the `color` aesthetic. Comparing a bar graph with a scatter plot underlines this point.

```
#Left: scale_fill_manual
ggplot(penguins, aes(x = species, fill = island))+
  geom_bar()+
  scale_fill_manual(values = c("red", "blue", "lightblue"))


#Create a color palette with color names or hexadecimal code
my_palette <- c("#e63946", "#457b9d", "#a8dadc")

#Right: scale_color_manual
ggplot(penguins, aes(x = bill_length_mm, y = body_mass_g,
                     color = island))+
  geom_point()+
  scale_color_manual(values = my_palette)
```

The last output illustrates, we have to provide a color for each group (island) if we adjust the colors manually, otherwise ggplot2 grumbles. We can also make a color palette, as the second plot showed. The ggplot2 package even understands hexadecimal color codes. This might be useful if you need very specific colors and there are plenty of websites to create color palettes with hexadecimal codes. A color is defined by three successive hexadecimal numbers. Each hexadecimal number represents one color of the red, green, and blue (RGB) color space.

Picking colors is tedious work. Fortunately, ggplot2 and further R packages provide color palettes. For example, ColorBrewer (https://colorbrewer2.org) provides several color palettes and is a website to check if the palette is colorblind or photocopy safe. Figure 7.5 shows a selection of color palettes and ggplot2 includes all palettes from the Colorbrewer package (Neuwirth, 2022). Keep in mind that there is no need to remember the names of all the palettes, because Figure 7.5 is made with the RColorBrewer package. The display.brewer.all() function returns all color and Figure 7.5 shows the sequential ones.

```
#The display.brewer.all function shows palettes from ColorBrewer
RColorBrewer::display.brewer.all()
```

Fig. 7.5: ColorBrewer palettes

To use a color palette is not complicated, but which one should you pick? This chapter does not introduce color theory, but we should be aware of the effect that different types of color palettes have. Pick a *sequential* set of colors (e.g., Blues) to display a numerical or ordered variable, a *qualitative* palette (e.g., Set1) in case of a categorical variable; or use a *diverging* color palette (e.g., RdBu) if the variable has a center. Once you have made your choice, add the scale_fill_brewer() (or scale_color_brewer for color) layer with the palette name, as the next code shows.

```
#scale_color_brewer
ggplot(penguins, aes(x = bill_length_mm,
                    y = body_mass_g,
                    color = island))+
  geom_point()+
  scale_color_brewer(palette = "Set1")
```

The `ggplot2` package even includes the viridis color scales from the `viridis` package, which are created to increase the readability, especially to reduce the chance that color-blind people won't be able to distinguish between colors (Garnier, 2021). The package contains eight color palettes with `viridis` as default, but maybe an alternative (e.g., `magma`, `plasma`, `mako`) suits you better. Use one of the `scale_color_viridis_*` functions to apply them. For example, for a discreet or continuous variable. Moreover, did you realize that the text labels of the last bar graph overlap? The `coord_flip()` function flips the coordinates of the bar graph, which fixes the overlap of the text labels.

```
#Left: scale_fill_viridis_d and coord_flip
ggplot(penguins, aes(x = species,
                     fill = island))+
  geom_bar() +
  coord_flip()+
  scale_fill_viridis_d(option = "viridis")+
```

```
#Right: scale_color_viridis_c
ggplot(penguins, aes(x = bill_length_mm, y = body_mass_g,
                     color = bill_length_mm))+
  geom_point()+
  scale_color_viridis_c(option = "mako")
```

There are a lot of colors and possibilities to consider and maybe it is hard to believe, but I tried to cut down this subsection to the most important color facts. I will not mention colors anymore, but the next info box about the `paletteer` package gives further hints about how to use colors palettes (Hvitfeldt, 2021), for example, from the `rtist` (Okal, 2020) or the `tayloRswift` package (Stephenson, 2021).

The `paletteer` package

There are a lot of packages that provide color palettes. For example, the `rtist` package provides several color palettes based on famous paintings such as the *The Great Wave off Kanagawa* (Hokusai), *The Night Watch* (Rembrandt), or *The Scream* (Munch). The `rtist_help()` function returns all available color palettes from the `rtist` package. Or who is your favorite music artist? Miley Cyrus, Rihanna, or Taylor Swift? I am kidding, but the `tayloRswift` package provides color palettes based on Taylor Swift album covers. Irrespective of your musical taste, the `paletteer` package gives us access to palettes from several packages and we can include them directly in our code.

For example, let us use the `munch` palette from `rtist` and the `lover` palette from the `tayloRswift` package. In case of a discreet color palette, the `paletteer_d()` function returns the following hexadecimal values:

```
#paletteer_d returns discreet color palette
paletteer::paletteer_d("tayloRswift::lover")


#> #B8396BFF #FFD1D7FF #FFF5CCFF #76BAE0FF #B28F81FF #54483EFF
```

The package also comes with corresponding `scale()` functions. Refer to palletes name like a function (via ::) within the `scale_fill_paletteer_d()` function in case of a discreet color palette. The next console illustrates the code to use the `paletteer` package and two example scatter plots.

```
#The paletteer package gives you access to several palettes
library(paletteer)
ggplot(penguins, aes(body_mass_g, flipper_length_mm, color = island))+
  geom_point()+
  scale_color_paletteer_d("rtist::munch")+
  ggtitle("rtist::munch")
```

Did you realize that `ggplot2` automatically adds a legend if we add an additional variable in the `aes()` function? Learning some basic on how `ggplot2` handles legends is the last step to finalize the scatter plot.

7.1.6 Legend

A legend is important to understand the graph, but it can be painful to make manual adjustments and find the right position. Change its position (legend.position) inside the theme() function. As default, the legend is displayed on the right side, but the legend can also be displayed on the left, top, or bottom of the graph. Moreover, insert none to discard the legend.

```
#Left: Discard the legend
ggplot(penguins, aes(x = bill_length_mm, y = body_mass_g,
                     color = island))+
  geom_point()+
  theme(legend.position = "none")

#Right: Display the legend on the right, left, top, or bottom
ggplot(penguins, aes(x = bill_length_mm, y = body_mass_g,
                     color = island))+
  geom_point()+
  theme(legend.position = "bottom")
```

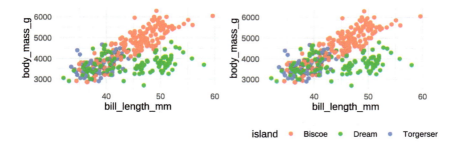

Depending on the data and the type of graph, it may take some time to find the best position. It is also possible to adjust the legend's position manually by proving coordinates. Give it a try if all predefined positions don't suit.

There remains only one step to reproduce the graph from the beginning, we need to adjust the title and labels of a legend. Look at the last examples, island is printed in lower case and depending on a variable name; we may get ugly text labels for the legend. We can refer to the scale_color_discrete function to create a nice text label for the title name and all labels. Or in a similar approach, remove the entire legend title by changing legend.title to element_blank(), as the second plot on the left side shows.

```
#Left: Adjust the legend title and labels
ggplot(penguins, aes(x = bill_length_mm, y = body_mass_g,
                     color = island))+
  geom_point()+
  scale_color_discrete(
    name = "The Island:",
    labels = c("A", "B", "C"))

#Right: Remove the legend title
ggplot(penguins, aes(x = bill_length_mm, y = body_mass_g,
                     color = island))+
  geom_point()+
  theme(legend.title = element_blank())
```

Certainly, playing around with the legend and similar changes are minor issues, but such adjustments are often needed to finalize a graph. At least, you are now able to remove the legend or adjust the text labels. Next we learn how to export a graph.

7.1.7 Export

We discussed all aspects that are necessary to reproduce Figure 7.2 (B). We learned many small steps on the last pages. The good news is, almost all steps can be applied regardless if you create a scatter plot or another visualization. We may change the geom to create a different graph, but a lot of the code can be recycled.

Let us combine all steps and assign our graph as an object (scatter_plot) in order to export it. We have come quite far, the entire code looks impressive:

```r
#the penguins scatter plot
scatter_plot <- ggplot(penguins, aes(x = bill_length_mm,
                                      y = body_mass_g,
                                      color = island))+
  geom_point()+
  theme_minimal(base_size = 12, base_family = "Ramaraja")+
  labs(tag = "Fig. X",
       title = "Palmer penguins",
       subtitle = "Is bill length and body mass associated?",
       x = "Bill length",
       y = "Body mass",
       caption = "Data source: \nThe palmerpenguins package",
       color = "The Islands:")+
  theme(plot.title = element_text(size = 14))+
  scale_color_viridis_d(option = "viridis")
```

Before we learn how to export the graph, let me say a few words about that code. I tried to convince you that it is not necessary to memorize code in Chapter 4. Knowledge about ggplot2 boosts your visualization skills but such a new framework can be overwhelming. Create a snippet for a ggplot or build a template for the next graph that includes most of the typical steps. Maybe the code to customize a plot is still too complicated and too long to remember, especially if a graph is for internal use only.

Irrespective of the reasons, you have ggplot2 at your disposal and you need not even remember most of the discussed code from this chapter to create a basic graph, because the esquisse package has a ggplot2 builder (Meyer & Perrier, 2022). It provides a graphical interface (addin) to make ggplot2 graphs and lets us apply the discussed steps without code. Just pick variables and insert labels, or adjust your legend, all from the interface. As the esquisse info box outlines, the ggplot2 builder creates the plot and, more important, it returns the code to create a graph.

The esquisse package   **i**

The esquisse package helps us to create a graph even if we have little knowledge about ggplot2. The latter provides a graphical interface for RStudio to explore data with ggplot2, as Figure 7.6 shows. The addin opens a new window and you can pick data and variable(s) to create a graph. Variables are displayed at the top of the window; drag them into the corresponding field to create the plot.

Such a tool is awesome if you have little experience working with ggplot2. It is true that you need not remember one line of code to create a basic version of the graph. There is a code button on the right side bottom of the window that returns the code. The next time you restart R, the code is already at your fingertips, more importantly, the graph can be reproduced.

214 — 7 Visualize research findings

Fig. 7.6: The esquisse addin

Of course, our knowledge about `ggplot2` lays the foundation to understand how graphs are made and how we can improve it beyond the possibilities of the `ggplot2` builder. Thus, do not take it personally that I waited until the end of this section to introduce the `esquisse` package. We got a first impression how `ggplot2` works and of course we are free to use such tools as long as we can reproduce our work.

Let us now explore how we export a graph. There are several ways, but RStudio makes this task convenient. Figure 7.7 shows RStudio's plots pane and there is an export button (highlighted in red) in the middle of the pane. Press the button and export a graph as an image or as a PDF file. After you have pressed the button, the *Save Plot as Image* window appears with several options to export an image: the format (e.g., .png file), the export directory, and the file name.

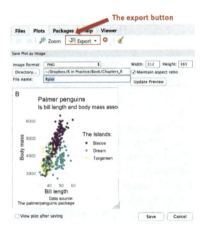

Fig. 7.7: The Export menu

You are probably familiar with image files, but have you ever heard about vector graphs? Vector graphs create images directly from geometric shapes which leads, in a nutshell, to a scalable high-quality file. You can test if an image is a vector graph by zooming in without seeing pixels or distorted graphical elements. If possible, export a graph as a vector graph (e.g., .svg) or save your work as PDF file, because elements in a PDF file are embedded as vectors graph. Some software does not work (well) with vector graphs and sometimes there is no necessity for it. In such instances, an image file is just fine.

Using the export button is a piece of cake, but maybe you need to export several graphs in a row and we can do so by running the ggsave() function. The function export the last plotted graph if you do not provide the object name. Furthermore, it comes with several arguments to adjust the export, as the next console highlights for our scatter_plot. The file option determines the output format (e.g., .png); export the graph in a specific size with the width and the height option (e.g, here A5); ultimately, dpi controls the plot resolution with 300 dots per inches as default.

```
#The ggsave function exports a plot
ggsave(scatter_plot,
       file = "output_file.png",
       width = 210,
       height = 148,
       units = "mm",
       dpi = 300)
```

In this section we explored ggplot2. We applied different styles and adjusted several aspects of a scatter plot. To understand how ggplot2 works, we have to step back and ask, from a theoretical point of view, what most visualizations have in common. How are graphs composed, regardless whether we are talking about a scatter plot, a bar graph, or a pie chart? To this end, we need to apply the grammar of graphics.

7.2 The applied grammar of graphics

The *grammar of graphics* provides a theoretical foundation and outlines the essential components of a graph (Wilkinson, 2005). The term might sound odd, but think about the grammar as a visualization language that describes individual components of a graph. As we know, graphs use geometrical objects to depict data and the grammar of graphics gives us the language - geoms - to talk about it. In this section, we get in touch with five general aspects from the grammar of graphics:

1. Geoms: Are geometrical objects to depict data (e.g., the dots)
2. Statistical transformation: Each visualization rests upon statistical transformations (e.g., a regression line)

3. Mapping aesthetics: The aesthetic properties determine how the information is displayed (e.g., shape and color)
4. Facets: Split a graph in several sub-graphs (e.g., one for each group) with facets
5. Coordinate system: A graph is embedded in a coordinate system (e.g., the Cartesian coordinate system)

Wickham (2016) developed `ggplot2` which implements the principles of the grammar of graphics with layers. The latter implies that we add layers to the `ggplot()` function that defines individual aspects of each graph. The layered grammar of graphics framework allows us to change all aspects of a graph and all graphs are based on the same framework or grammatical style. I already tried to outline this, but this is the reason why `ggplot2` is such a powerful tool. It allows us to adjust core elements separately.

In this section we examine, for example, how the gross domestic product (GDP) and life expectancy are related with the `gapminder` data (Bryan, 2017). However, we do not focus on the nitty gritty details of one specific plot, but examine how `ggplot2` applies the grammar of graphics. As the next console shows, the `gapminder` data starts with six observations for Afghanistan from 1952 up to 1977. Moreover, the next console shows all packages for this section.

```
#The setup for section 7.2 #####
library(dplyr)
library(ggbeeswarm)
library(ggforce)
library(ggplot2)
library(palmerpenguins)
library(patchwork)
#The gapminder data
library(gapminder)
head(gapminder)
```

```
#> # A tibble: 6 x 6
#>   country     continent year lifeExp      pop gdpPercap
#>   <fct>       <fct>     <int>  <dbl>    <int>     <dbl>
#> 1 Afghanistan Asia       1952   28.8  8425333      779.
#> 2 Afghanistan Asia       1957   30.3  9240934      821.
#> 3 Afghanistan Asia       1962   32.0 10267083      853.
#> 4 Afghanistan Asia       1967   34.0 11537966      836.
#> 5 Afghanistan Asia       1972   36.1 13079460      740.
#> # ... with 1 more row
```

We cannot include all observations of all years in one static plot. For this reason, I restricted the data (gapminder_07) to the latest observation period (2007); I excluded observations from Oceania, since the number of countries is limited. Furthermore, I create a new variable for the population size (population) and for GDP (gdp) to increase the readability of the graphs. The new population variable measures the population in millions; gdp per thousand dollar.

```
#Create a smaller data frame
gapminder_07 <- gapminder |>
  filter (year == 2007 & continent != "Oceania") |>
  mutate(population = pop/1000000,
         gdp = gdpPercap/1000)
```

In the last section we created a scatter plot, and our minimal example included three components. We gave ggplot() a data frame, decided which variables to map within the aesthetics function, and we chose a geom to map the data. Let's use the minimal example to examine how gdp and lifeExp (life expectancy) are related.

```
#Minimal code for a scatter plot
ggplot(gapminder_07, aes(x = gdp, y = lifeExp)) +
  geom_point()
```

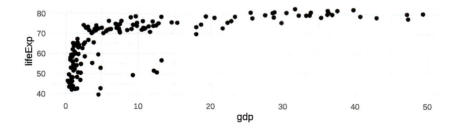

The main conclusion is not surprising: People in richer countries have access to health care, can afford medical treatments, and higher income makes it easier to follow up on activities with life-prolonging effects. For such reasons, GDP is positively associated with life expectancy in many countries. Nevertheless, the minimal code skips a lot of aspects. For example, where are the color and the coordinate system coming from? We know that ggplot2 picks the default option if we use the minimal code. In the next subsections we explore how ggplot2 implements the grammar of graphics step by step.

In conclusion, we use this smaller data frame to get in touch with the grammar of graphics and we inspect, geoms to visualize numerical outcomes, the statistical transformation that runs in the background, mapping aesthetics and positional adjustments, facets, and why each visualization is embedded in a coordinate system. To this end, you will be able to decompose the ggplot() function and it underlines that each geom offers unique possibilities and limitations to visualize data.

7.2.1 Geoms

The decision to start with a scatter plot was arbitrary. We could have used a different visual representation to depict the same data. In the grammar of graphics language, we assigned a geometrical object to the values. The ggplot2 package includes many geoms. We can use the minimal code from the last graph and create an entirely different graph when we pick a different geom.

Before we analyze the relationship of two variables, we should examine the distribution of each variable, maybe with a histogram. The corresponding geom is called geom_histogram() and I am convinced that you know how to adjust the minimal code to make a histogram for lifeExp. Or maybe you want to create a density plot. We need only change the corresponding geom, as the next console illustrates.

```
#Left: The geom_histogram
ggplot(gapminder_07, aes(x = lifeExp)) +
  geom_histogram()

#Right: The geom_density
ggplot(gapminder_07, aes(x = lifeExp)) +
  geom_density()
```

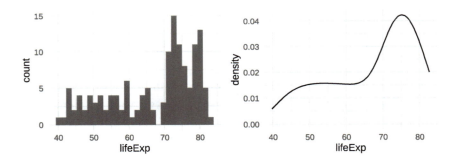

There are more options to depict continuous variables and Figure 7.8 shows four other geoms that we may use to visualize the distribution of lifeExp. Each geom depicts the data based on different aesthetic mappings. Thus, each geom has default options, such as the shape, the size of shape (points), or the type of a line. All those graphs have in common that they map the data in a coordinate system, and we need only provide the data, specify which variables to display, and pick a geom to visualize the data.

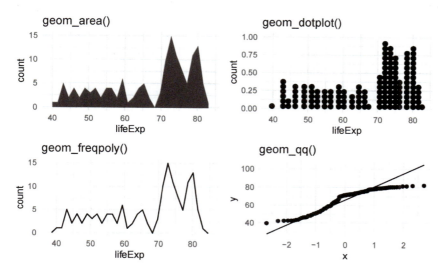

Fig. 7.8: Geoms for continuous variables

Different geoms have strengths and weaknesses in visualizing data. For example, a bar graph does a good job in depicting an outcome for a discreet variable, but what if we want to explore a time trend? A line plot does a better job in this case. Keep the main message of the graph in mind to pick the geom. You need to figure out what the graph should display and which geom best suits this purpose. Once you have figured it out, you may focus on typical aspects to make the visualization, but in the beginning it's all about the geom. Note also that not every graph relies on a unique geom: we need to think about the geometrical object that builds a graph. For example, the scatter plot:

```
#Does geom_scatter exist?
ggplot(gapminder_07, aes(x = gdp, y = lifeExp)) +
  geom_scatter()
```

```
#> Error in geom_scatter(): could not find function "geom_scatter"
```

A geom_scatter does not exist. To inspect how the variables are related, a scatter plot displays the values of *x* and *y* with points (geom_point()). Moreover, we need to combine two geoms to summarize the relationship of the examined variables (e.g., to add a line) by applying the geom_smooth() function and by examining its statistical transformation.

7.2.2 Statistical transformation

Statistical transformation is an essential step to visualize data. Consider the steps to create a simple bar graph: we count the number of observations for each continent and display them with bars.

```
#The data transformation step ...
gapminder_07 |> count(continent)

#> # A tibble: 4 x 2
#>   continent    n
#> 1 Africa      52
#> 2 Americas   25
#> 3 Asia        33
#> 4 Europe      30

#And the bar graph
ggplot(gapminder_07, aes(x = continent)) +
  geom_bar()
```

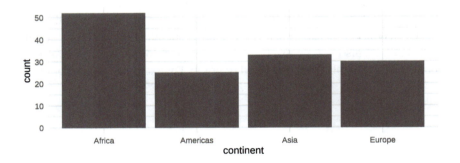

We see the numbers right in front of us, which makes it easier to understand what the visualization displays. A lot of people have such a procedure in mind when they talk about a visualization. A graph may only display raw numbers, but the data transformation steps are vital for the visualization process. We cannot neglect this point any longer.

Do you realize that we do not need the last data preparation step in order to make the graph? We did not visualize the counting, ggplot2 counted as we made the bar graph. If we want to depict the counted numbers, we must use geom_col() function. There are two ways to generate a bar graph, and the main difference comes from the statistical transformation. A geom_col does not apply any transformation, it uses the statistics option (stat = "identity") as a default and displays the values as they are, while geom_bar() creates a counting variable. This is not trivial, because such a variable does not exist in the data. By default, geom_bar() creates an internal counting variable in order to display the numbers. We can inspect this process if we write down the statistical transformation that geom_bar() applies to generate the counting variable (after_stat()):

```
#geom_bar fills in the counting!
ggplot(gapminder_07) +
  geom_bar(aes(x=continent, y = after_stat(count)))
```

Keep the statistical transformation of a graph in mind if you start to create visualizations. Creating such a bar graph seems trivial, but other graphs include sophisticated statistical transformations. If you don't provide any information about the statistical transformation, ggplot2 picks a default, but sometimes we don't get what we need. Suppose you use a scatter plot to examine if there is a linear association between GDP and life expectancy. Is a linear function appropriate to describe the association between the variables? We may examine the relationship by adding a geom_smooth().

```
#Minimal example for a scatter plot with geom_smooth
ggplot(gapminder_07, aes(x = gdp, y = lifeExp)) +
  geom_point() +
  geom_smooth()
```

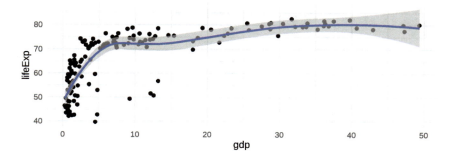

There is clearly a non-linear trend, especially for countries with lower GDP. A linear function seems not to be appropriate to describe the relationship between *x* and *y*. Different statistical transformation can be used to generate a graph and the last scatter plot did not include a regression line. We used the geom_smooth() function without any adjustments and as default, it applies the LOESS function to describe the association – a locally estimated scatter plot smoothing (Cleveland, 1979) – it fits the line locally based on the observed cases. The latter results in a smooth regression line to describe the association between the variables, but is not the result of a linear regression.

In Chapter 6, we learned that fitting a straight line is not a good idea in case of a non-linear association. As Anscombe's Quartet underlined, the assumptions of a linear regression analysis are violated if *x* and *y* are not associated in a linear fashion. How do we include a linear fit and a quadratic term in the scatter plot? To add a regression line and confidence bands, insert the linear (lm) method inside the geom. Moreover, we need to insert a formula to depict mathematical functions such as a polynomial term (e.g., y ~ poly(x, 2). The next console shows two plots. The left plot displays the scatter plot with a linear regression line. The second plot highlights that we can add a quadratic term (or other mathematical functions) to describe the association.

```
#Left: Linear fit
ggplot(gapminder_07, aes(x = gdp, y = lifeExp)) +
  geom_point() +
  geom_smooth(method = "lm", formula = y ~ x)

#Right: A quadratic term
ggplot(gapminder_07, aes(x = gdp, y = lifeExp)) +
  geom_point() +
  geom_smooth(method="lm", formula = y ~ poly(x, 2))
```

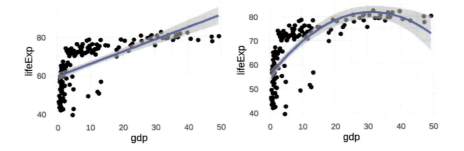

In a nutshell, a graph is often more than just a simple visual representation of raw numbers and rests upon statistical transformations. The default option might be a good start, but the LOESS function does not lead to the same results as a linear fit.

7.2.3 Mapping aesthetics

We pick a geom to visualize data. This decision affects the appearances of a graph and not all geoms work with all aesthetics. We cannot change the line type if the geom does not include one. So, how do we change the aesthetic mappings and, in terms of visualization, why should we care? Which mapping aesthetics can we apply if we use a geom_point()? As the R documentation outlines, we can adjust several aesthetics, among them, *alpha (opacity), color, fill, shape, size,* and *stroke.*

Let us recall that we talked about aesthetic mappings in the last section. We started from a purely data-driven perspective and elaborated that we can use colors in a graph, for instance, to distinguish between two groups. The gapminder includes life expectancy for different countries and continents. We can include the latter to see if the association differs between continents. As we know, we could map information with different colors or use different shapes for each continent. Use color palettes or adjust the color manually. As the next console shows, I pick the colors manually and insert them in the scale_color_manual() function. I used only two different colors to highlight observations from Africa compared to other continents. We could do the same and pick shapes manually if the default shapes are not well suited to distinguish between groups.

```
#Left: Map with color
ggplot(gapminder_07, aes(x = gdp, y = lifeExp,
                         color = continent)) +
  geom_point()+
  scale_color_manual(values = c("red", "gray", "gray", "gray"))

#Right: Map with shapes
ggplot(gapminder_07, aes(x = gdp, y = lifeExp,
                         shape = continent)) +
  geom_point()+
  scale_shape_manual(values = c(0, 2, 3, 14))
```

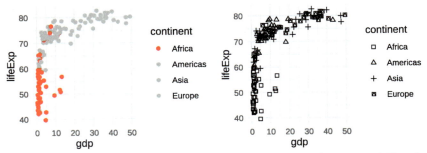

Sometimes it is not enough to pick distinct shapes or colors, especially when there are too many groups, or if geometric objects overlap. That's where the opacity (`alpha`) comes into play. Add `alpha` inside a `geom` (the opacity of the geom is set to 1 as default) or use it as an aesthetic.

```
#Left: Alpha
ggplot(gapminder_07, aes(x = gdp, y = lifeExp,
                         color = continent)) +
  geom_point(alpha = .5)
#Right: Map with alpha
ggplot(gapminder_07, aes(x = gdp, y = lifeExp,
                         alpha = continent)) +
  geom_point()
```

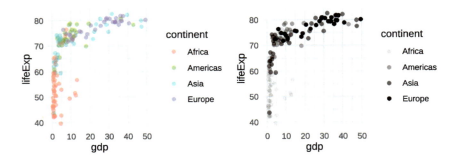

The last example used a discrete variable to map information, but of course we can use a numerical variable as well. Maybe the association between GDP and life expectancy differs in terms of population size. Increase the size of the point with the size aesthetic, as the next plot on the left side shows. If we include the `color` and the `size` aesthetics, it becomes clearer how the `gapminder` bubble chart is made (see Chapter 1).

```
#Left: Include color
ggplot(gapminder_07, aes(x = gdp, y = lifeExp,
                         color = continent)) +
  geom_point()
```

```
#Right: Include color and size
ggplot(gapminder_07, aes(x = gdp, y = lifeExp,
                         color = continent,
                         size = population)) +
  geom_point()
```

Keep in mind that the more aesthetics we add, the more information is displayed and maybe the graph becomes too complex. What is your audience's domain knowledge? Does the graph clearly communicate its message? We will catch up on this point in the facets section where we learn to split the graph in several subplots to reduce the complexity. Before we jump to facets, we briefly inspect positional adjustment of a geom function.

Positional adjustments

Positional adjustments are the fine-tuning to draw geoms. In the case of a scatter plot, we can prevent the over-plotting of single dots by adding position_jitter() to the geom_point() function. The jitter adds a little bit of random noise to prevent over-plotting. Let us inspect how this works by creating a simple dot plot that depicts life expectancy for each continent.

The next console shows three plots and strategies to prevent over-plotting. As the first plot on the left side shows, I tried to reduce the size of each point, but this does not help much to avoid over-plotting. To add some random noise, I used the position_jitter() function, as the second plot in the center shows. Of course, there are limitation to reduce over-plotting and in this example it becomes hard to differentiate which observations belongs to which continent. A beeswarm plot (from the `ggbeeswarm` package, see Chapter 7.3) helps to reduce such over-plotting by adding vertical noise, as the third plot on the right sight illustrates (Clarke & Sherrill-Mix, 2017). Moreover I use the `stat_summary()` function to plot the median to further improve the graph.

```
#Left: A dot plot
ggplot(gapminder_07, aes(x = continent, y = lifeExp)) +
  geom_point(size = 1)
```

```
#Center: Add position_jitter
ggplot(gapminder_07, aes(x = continent, y = lifeExp)) +
  geom_point(size = 1, position=position_jitter())
```

```
#Right: A ggbeeswarm plot
ggplot(gapminder_07, aes(x = continent, y = lifeExp)) +
  geom_beeswarm(size = 1, cex = 3)+
  stat_summary(fun = "median", color = "red",
               size = 1, geom = "point")
```

Thus, a geom has specific positional adjustments which further determine how graphical objects are displayed. Let me give you a second example. Consider a bar graph. If we do not provide any positional adjustment, `ggplot2` returns a stacked bar graph and each category is displayed on top of each other. However, each bar is displayed side by side if we add `dodge` as `position`. Or consider the `fill` position, it creates relative proportions and standardize each bar, which makes it easier to compare groups. Unfortunately, the `gapminder` data has only factor variables with many levels (e.g., `country`), which makes it harder to examine this behavior. For this reason, I use to the `penguins` data from the `palmerpenguins` to illustrate this point.

```
#Left: Position stack is the default
ggplot(penguins, aes(x = species, fill = island))+
```

```
  geom_bar(position = "stack")

#Right: Position fill
ggplot(penguins, aes(x = species, fill = island))+
  geom_bar(position = "fill")
```

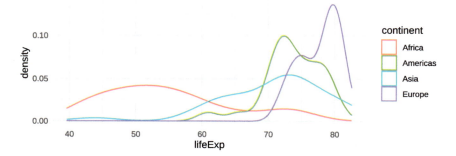

Instead of speaking about the fine-tuning, facets substantially help to communicate complex data.

7.2.4 Facets

We may transport the graph's message with colors, shapes or any other aesthetics, but there are clear limitations with respect to human perception and the complexity of a graph. Consider the next console. I created a density plot but I should split the graph into smaller sub-graphs. I played around with colors for each continent, but the lines overlap and we are having a hard time to compare the distribution for each continent. Sub-graphs make it easier to compare the density of each continent.

```
#A messy density plot - how could we improve it?
ggplot(gapminder_07, aes(x = lifeExp, color=continent)) +
  geom_density()
```

Thus, we split the last graph into four subplots. For example, we can create a plot with four columns for each included continent if we add cols = vars(continent) in the facet_grid() function.

```
#Split a graph with facet_grid
ggplot(gapminder_07, aes(x = lifeExp)) +
  geom_density()+
  facet_grid(cols = vars(continent))
```

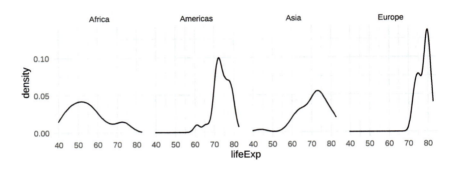

It becomes much easier to see how life expectancy is distributed in each continent if we compare the last plot with the sub-plots. In general terms, we add facet_grid() as a layer and provide a discrete variable for a horizontal *split by columns* or a vertical *split by rows*. The next output compares both splits.

```
#Left: Split by columns (on the vertical axis)
ggplot(gapminder_07, aes(x = lifeExp)) +
  geom_density()+
  ggtitle("A: facet_grid(cols = vars(x))")+
  facet_grid(cols = vars(continent))

#Right: Split by rows (on the horizontal)
ggplot(gapminder_07, aes(x = lifeExp)) +
  geom_density()+
  ggtitle("B: facet_grid(rows = vars(x))")+
  facet_grid(rows = vars(continent))
```

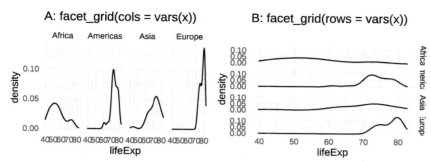

A split by columns is better suited here. Look at the distribution of Africa in the right split by rows plot, we hardly see any differences if we compare the distributions. This example shows us that we must decide how to depict information based on both theoretical and practical grounds. Due to the orientation of the page and the number of groups, a split by columns provides a better picture in this case since it compresses the distribution vertically.

Many people use a shortcut: for a split by rows, add `facet_grid(x ~ .)`; or add `facet_grid(. ~ x)` for a split by columns. Did you realize that I inserted a period (.) in the shortcut? It is a placeholder for a second variable to split. For example, let's split the graph by two different years and for each continent. I restricted the data to the last observations period so this will not work without some extra effort to prepare the data. As the next console shows, I used a filter to get the first and the last observation. Next, I split the graph to display life expectancy for each year and continent with `facet_grid()`.

```
#Split by facet_grid(row . column)
gapminder |>
  filter (year == 1952 | year == 2007) |>
  filter (continent != "Oceania") |>
  ggplot(aes(x = lifeExp)) +
  geom_density()+
  facet_grid(year ~ continent)
```

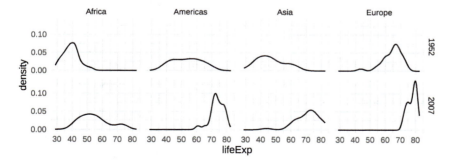

Facets can also be placed or wrapped next to each other using the facet_wrap() function instead of splitting the plot into grids. Defined by the number of rows and columns, facet_grid() builds a matrix of panels in which the graphs are built. As the package authors outline in the documentation: "It is most useful when you have two discrete variables, and all combinations of the variables exist in the data" (Wickham, Chang, et al., 2022). Thus, facet_wrap() is more efficient in terms of space and is the right choice if the variable has many levels. The steps to apply a facet_wrap() are the same. Facets can be wrapped horizontally or vertically. However, we must tell R the number of the columns (ncol) or the number of rows (nrow) to determine how many subplots are included.

The gapminder data comes with a long observational period. Let's explore how life expectancy developed over time, for example, in Europe. I claimed that we cannot create one static graph considering all those time periods. Obviously, I was wrong. The facet_wrap() function helps to visualize a time trend and we see how the distribution is changing from one year to another.

```
#Vertical facet, but wrapped
gapminder |>
  filter (continent == "Europe") |>
  ggplot(aes(x = lifeExp)) +
  geom_density()+
  facet_wrap(year ~ ., nrow = 2)
```

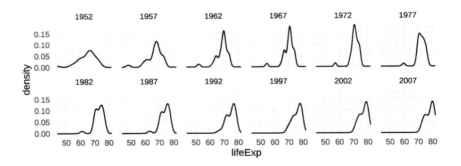

For a fair comparison of sub-plots, fixed coordinates are important and ggplots applies the same scale to each sub-plot. Sometimes it might be useful to provide different scales for different groups, especially if we explore the data. For this reason, scales can be set free for x-axis (free_x), y-axis (free_y) or for both within the facet function. Please keep in mind that the audience will wonder why the scales differ if you do not explicitly outline it. It may look like fraud or as a huge mistake if you fail to explain why the scales differ.

Almost all figures in this chapter contained two or more graphs, which makes it easier to compare different versions of a graph. However, they are not made with a facet, since they often display different versions of a graph. The patchwork package makes it possible to combine plots and the corresponding info box outlines more details (Pedersen, 2022b).

The patchwork package   **i**

The patchwork package helps you to combine and create customized graphs. Suppose you have generated several graphs and saved them as objects (p1, p2, and p3). To illustrate how the package lets us combine graphs, I created three different graphs and assigned them to objects, but it does not matter which graphs we combine.

```
#Create several plots, for example:
p1 <- ggplot(gapminder_07, aes(x = gdp, y = lifeExp)) +
  geom_point() +
  ggtitle("p1")
```

Add a graph and put each graph next to each other with the plus (+) operator. Moreover, the package also provides the pack operator (|) which puts each plot beside each other; while the stack operator (/) builds a pile to stack them. As the next console highlights, we can combine them to create customized graphs.

```
#Combine graphs
library(patchwork)
p1 + (p2 / p3)
```

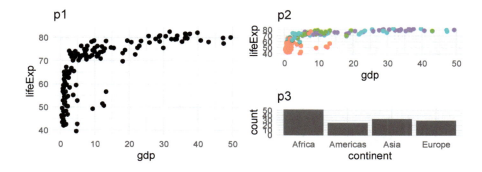

Check out the vignette of the patchwork package. It offers more functions to combine graphs (e.g., annotations) and outlines in detail how the package works.

7.2.5 Coordinate system

A lot of people who are interested in data visualization loathe pie charts. I don't like pie charts too because they do not display proportions well (see pie charts info box in Chapter 3). The funny thing is, we create a pie chart to learn more about the coordinate system. For the sake of illustration, let's say that we counted fruits.

```
#Fake data for a pie chart ...
data <- tribble(
  ~fruits,    ~Percentage,
  "Apples",    50.0,
  "Bananas",   30.0,
  "Cherries", 20.0
)
```

The next console shows two plots. First, I make a bar graph to display the `fruits` variable. This time, we must adjust our minimal code since the observations sum up to 100 percent, which is why I added the `width` option in the `geom_col` function. Furthermore, I plot the number of observed fruits (as y) and I use the `fill` aesthetic to highlight the categories. As the plot on the left side shows, we get a bar plot and you may wonder what the latter has to do with a pie chart. See what happens if we add the `coord_polar()` function (polar coordinate system) to the second plot on the right side. We get a bull's eye chart, it looks like a dartboard and the inner circle is called the bull's eye.

```
#Left: A bar plot
ggplot(data, aes(x = "", y = Percentage, fill = fruits))+
  geom_col(width = 1)

#Right: The bull's-eye chart
ggplot(data, aes(x = "", y = Percentage, fill = fruits))+
  geom_col(width = 1) +
  coord_polar()
```

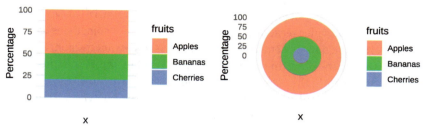

As default, the ggplot2 package uses the Cartesian (coord_cartesian) coordinate system, but there are other coordinate systems as well. We need the polar coordinate system to make a pie chart and we must determine which variable should be used to map the slices of the pie chart. As the next console shows, I add theta inside the coord_polar() function to create the pie chart; it uses y to map the angle of each slice. As the second plot shows, the polar coordinate system vanishes if we use the theme_void() function to get rid of the axis labels. A typical pie chart without any visible coordinate system appears.

```
#Left: Add theta = "y" to get a pie chart
ggplot(data, aes(x = "", y = Percentage, fill = fruits))+
  geom_col(width = 1, stat = "identity")+
  coord_polar(theta = "y")

#Right: The theme_void "finalizes" the pie chart
ggplot(data, aes(x = "", y = Percentage, fill = fruits))+
  geom_col(width = 1)+
  coord_polar(theta = "y")+
  theme_void()
```

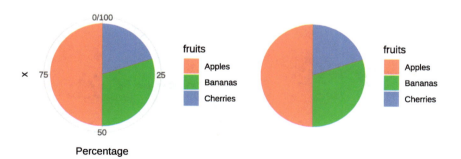

Such pie charts give us the impression that they float in the blank space, but the coordinate system determines how the geom will be displayed. Keep in mind that we can use different coordinate systems or apply transformations to restrict the scale. Most of the time ggplot2() provides reasonable values of the scale, but sometimes we must inspect only a part of the data closer. Thus, what happens if we want to zoom in to see only a selective part of the data? In order to do so, we need to adjust the upper and lower limit of *x* and *y* within the coordinate function.

In the gapminder example, we discovered a non-linear trend between life expectancy and GDP, which is why we want to inspect certain observations closer. Adjust the coordinate system and add xlim inside the coord_cartesian() function. What would happen if we did not know that we are supposed to set xlim only inside the coord_cartesian() function? As the next output highlights, that would be a terrible idea because the xlim() function replaces observation outside the limit with NA. The plot is generated after this step and excluding cases distorts the graph. Look how both graphs differ if we apply the limit wrong (left side) or correct (right side).

```
#Left plot: Never use xlim outside of the coordinate system!
ggplot(gapminder_07, aes(x = gdpPercap, y = lifeExp)) +
  geom_point() +
  geom_smooth(method = "lm", formula = y ~ x)+
  xlim(c(0, 10000))+
  ggtitle("xlim")

#Right plot
ggplot(gapminder_07, aes(x = gdpPercap, y = lifeExp)) +
  geom_point() +
  geom_smooth(method = "lm", formula = y ~ x)+
  coord_cartesian(xlim = c(0, 10000))+
  ggtitle("coord_cartesian(xlim)")
```

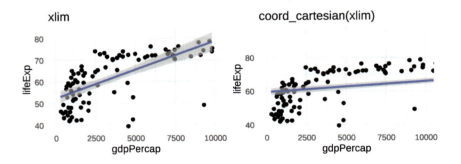

If we make a scatter plot with restricted data, it almost looks like there is a linear trend. The observed countries may not scatter perfectly around the regression line, but we may not discover the non-linear trend and consequently come to a wrong conclusion. Remember, use the lim function only within the coord_cartesian() function, otherwise the data gets restricted and you may create a bogus.

The x-axis now starts at the new minimum and has a new maximum value. Apparently we could do the same with y (ylim); but please be cautious and make sure that everybody knows that the data is restricted, otherwise it gives the impression that you have manipulated it to build your case. Instead, apply the facet_zoom() function from the ggforce package which is an extension for ggplot2 (Pedersen, 2022a). As the next console highlights, it shows the reader graphically that we have zoomed in and only display a smaller subset of the data. The overall plot is displayed above.

```
#Zoooom in with ...
library(ggforce)

ggplot(gapminder_07, aes(x = gdpPercap, y = lifeExp,
                        color = continent))+
  geom_point()+
  facet_zoom(xlim = c(0, 10000))
```

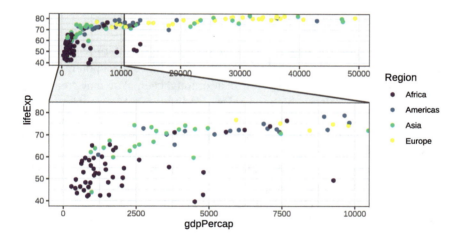

Next, we explore further ggplot2 extensions and potential next steps.

7.3 Extensions of ggplot2

The last section focused on the grammar of graphics, which emphasized why `ggplot2` is such a successful package. The acquired knowledge helps you to visualize research findings and the package provides many ways to visualize data. Keep in mind that every visualization was invented for a specific purpose and each visualization has limitations in how efficiently it can communicate findings. For example, a box plot displays the summary of a distribution, but it does not depict the data. Visualizing data goes hand in hand with a reduction of information. In consequence, we may miss some important patterns if we don't dig deep enough. Or some graphs are not well suited to transport the message.

Against this background it is good to know that there are many additional packages to visualize data. This section introduces packages that extend the possibilities of `ggplot2`, but there are too many extensions to discuss them all here. Some packages change the way we handle text (`ggtext`, see Wilke, 2020); some give us the tools to apply statistical methods (`survminer` for survival analysis, see Kassambara et al., 2021); and others let us create animated graphs (`gganimate`, see Pedersen & Robinson, 2022). Visit the package website to get a broad overview of the possibilities.

```
#The ggplot2 website
#https://exts.ggplot2.tidyverse.org/
```

Due to the large number of extensions, this section does not provide an all-encompassing overview. Instead, it is like a picture book that shows potential next steps. I concentrated on packages providing an additional geom. You may create any kind of visualization regardless whether a corresponding `ggplot2` extension exists. Most of the time you will find a lot of helpful resources online even if a specific graph is not implemented as a `ggplot2` extension. However, it is very convenient if a package provides an extension, since we can build on the acquired knowledge.

Thus, this section cannot fully appreciate the hard work many authors have put in, but it gives a first impression in three steps: (1) I describe each visualization. (2) I show you an example for each graph. (3) Each subsection ends with a minimal code example to create such a graph with implemented data. The code for the minimal examples is included in the `PracticeR` package.

By relying on implemented data, you get a first impression how these packages work without the hassle of running many data preparation steps. Of course, the fine-tuning will take more time and effort. I hope the minimal examples make it easier to discover the possibilities of visualizing data with R. Now, sit back and get inspired by the many `ggplot2` authors and extensions.

Alluvial

Alluvial charts are awesome to highlight the flow of a process or how proportions develop over time. As the example plot shows, I used the titanic data which indicates who survived the sinking of the Titanic. The alluvial chart depicts how the three socio-demographic variables (sex, age, class) are related in terms of survival. As the plot shows, most persons who did not survive were male, adults, and crew members.

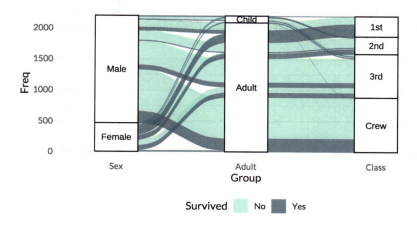

Create an alluvial plot with the ggalluvial package (see Brunson & Read, 2020). The geom_stratum() returns boxes that display the frequency of each group level and the geom_alluvium draws the flow from one level to another. The package vignette also outlines how to create an alluvial chart.

```
#Minimal code example #####
library(ggplot2)
library(ggalluvial)
#A wide data format
titanic_wide_format <- data.frame(Titanic)

ggplot(data = titanic_wide_format,
       aes(axis1 = Class, axis2 = Sex, axis3 = Age, y = Freq)) +
  geom_alluvium(aes(fill = Survived)) +
  geom_stratum()
```

Beeswarm plots

A beeswarm plot is a categorical scatter plot that shows the distribution of a numerical variable, shaped for each category (Clarke & Sherrill-Mix, 2017). Just like a scatter plot, a beeswarm plot displays single observations with points. Unfortunately, sometimes there are too many observations to display, and in consequence, points are no longer visible. Beeswarm plots help to reduce such over-plotting by adding vertical noise.

For example, the following plot depicts the age of Titanic passengers, compared for those who did (not) survive and single points are colored by passenger's sex. What do you say, how old were people who did (not) survive? Did more men or women perish?

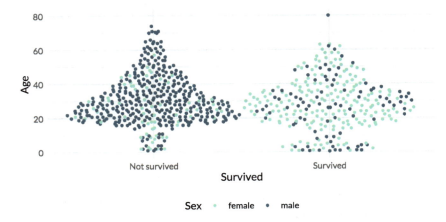

The ggbeeswarm package includes geom_quasirandom() which adds quasi-random noise to each observation as a default method, even though it has several methods to reduce over-plotting (e.g., pseudorandom, smiley).

```
#Minimal code example #####
library(titanic)
library(ggbeeswarm)

ggplot(titanic_train, aes(Survived, Age,
                          color = Sex)) +
  geom_quasirandom(method = "quasirandom")
```

Choropleth maps

Create a choropleth map with `ggplot2`. The latter displays a geographical area (or region) and, for example, fills the shape of the area. The next plot displays the number of arrests in the US. It takes time and effort to create a choropleth map, but the result is worth the trouble.

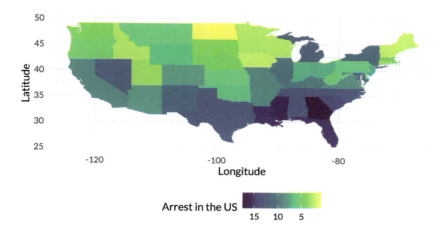

In addition, the `ggmap` package helps to create maps (Kahle et al., 2022; Kahle & Wickham, 2013), because we need to draw the shape of each area (e.g., country shape) first. The shape must be displayed by its longitude and latitude before we can fill the area or display numbers that describe the area. The minimal code does not need any additional package and shows an example from the `ggplot2` cheat sheet. If the corresponding geographical areas can be matched with the data, `geom_map()` draws the map and fills each area with the observed value.

```
#Minimal code example #####
#Source: This example comes from the ggplot2 cheat sheet!
map <- map_data("state")
data <- data.frame(murder = USArrests$Murder,
                   state = tolower(rownames(USArrests)))

ggplot(data, aes(fill = murder))+
  geom_map(aes(map_id = state), map = map)+
  expand_limits(x = map$long, y = map$lat)
```

Dumbbell and lollipop charts

The ggplot2 package lets you build a graph from scratch, but creating a visualization is hard work. The ggcharts package is for the lazy cats and gives access to a lot of common charts (Neitmann, 2020). The package has implemented those graphs with its own functions, and we don't have to create each step on our own. Furthermore, the package returns ggplot2 objects, which implies that you can apply your ggplot2 knowledge as well.

For example, create a dumbbell or a lollipop chart. I used the former to examine how life expectancy increased between 1952 and 2007 based on the gapminder data. The example shows the top 10 European countries with the highest increase in life expectancy.

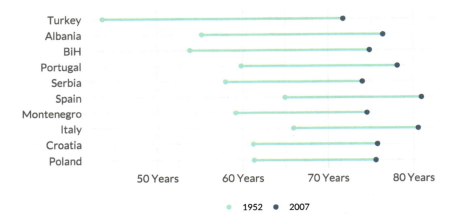

```
#Minimal code example #####
library(ggcharts)
data("popeurope")

dumbbell_chart(popeurope,
               x = country,
               y1 = pop1952, y2 = pop2007,
               top_n = 10)
```

Hexbin map

Build a hexbin map with `ggplot2`. It displays hexagons as shapes. Actually, this graph is as an Easter egg since we do not need any additional package to make this plot. There are a lot of great extensions for `ggplot2`, but you can create many graphs with `ggplot2` alone and we did not explore all geoms. For example, the `geom_polygon()` function creates the hexbin map and here it shows US unemployment rates.

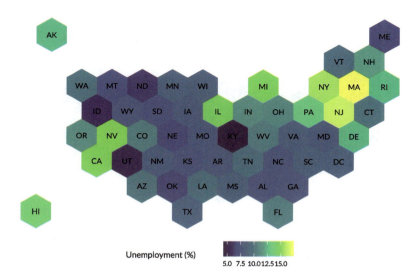

The graph is inspired by r-graph-gallery.com website. It shows a great variety of (`ggplot2`) visualization, provides a lot of resources to create plots, and has articles that discuss the limitations of graphs as well. Have you ever seen a radar, a stream, or a sunburst chart? Visit the website and learn how to make them.

```
#Minimal code example #####
#There are many graphs (and code) to explore on:
#www.r-graph-gallery.com
```

Mosaic plots

Mosaic (or spine) plots are very powerful when visualizing descriptive results, and we created one with base R in Chapter 3. However, mosaic plots are also implemented in ggplot2. The ggmosaic() package provides the corresponding geom (Jeppson et al., 2021). The illustration uses the titanic data and depicts the effect of passenger's sex on survival. Obviously, more women than men survived the accident.

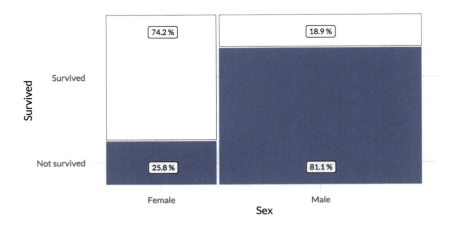

As the minimal code illustrates, the geom_mosaic comes with a product() function to estimate frequencies for each category and fills each box accordingly.

```
#Minimal code example #####
library(ggmosaic)

ggplot(data = titanic) +
  geom_mosaic(aes(x = product(Sex),
                  fill = Survived))
```

Ridge plots

Compare the distribution of a numeric variable with a ridge plot (Wilke, 2021). In the example, I used the gapminder data to inspect how life expectancy differs between continents in 2007. As the plots shows, Europe has the highest, while Africa had the lowest life expectancy. The distribution is much wider in Africa compared to other continents.

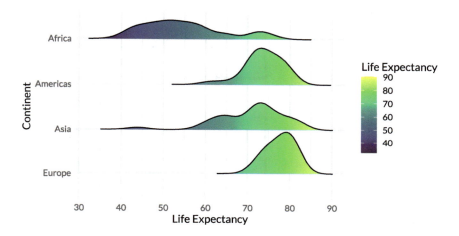

The ggridges package comes with data and a lot of illustrative examples provided by Claus Wilke, the author of the package. As the code from the vignette illustrates, explore how the weather (temperature) develops within a year.

```
#Minimal code example #####
library(ggridges)

#Minimal code by Claus Wilke:
ggplot(lincoln_weather, aes(x = `Mean Temperature [F]`, y = Month,
                            fill = stat(x))) +
  geom_density_ridges_gradient(scale = 3,
                               rel_min_height = 0.01) +
  scale_fill_viridis_c(name = "Temp. [F]",
                       option = "C")
```

244 —— 7 Visualize research findings

Treemaps

You can visualize hierarchical data with a treemap, because the area of the rectangle is chosen proportionally to the size of each cluster. Before he was banned, Donald Trump was a huge fan of Twitter and Axios collected and categorized his tweets. Some tweets were about *the media*, *democrats*, and the grand old party (*GOP*), with further subgroups within each category. I used this data and the treemapify package to make a treemap (Wilkins, 2021). Mr. Trump tweeted a lot about "the media" and the "Democrats" in 2019.

The data of the last plot is not available, but you can use the gapminder data to explore how treemapify works.

```
#Minimal code example #####
library(treemapify)
library(gapminder)

data <- gapminder::gapminder |>
  dplyr::filter(year == 2007 & continent == "Europe")

ggplot(data, aes(area = gdpPercap,
                 fill = lifeExp,
                 label = country)) +
  geom_treemap() +
  geom_treemap_text(color = "white",
                    grow = TRUE)
```

Waffle charts

Do not make a pie, make a waffle. Waffle charts depict a whole (or part of the whole), and it gives the audience visual clues to assess the size of each group, especially if each square represents exactly one percentage point. The example plot illustrates the "leaky pipeline" in academic careers. Did you know that after each transition step in higher education (e.g., graduation, Ph.D.), more men than women remain in the system? The sex ratios become more and more skewed till the end of the academic pathway. I used a waffle chart to illustrate the leaky pipeline for Germany in 2020.

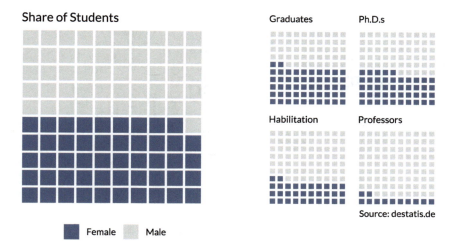

The `waffle` package makes it easy to create waffle charts (Rudis & Gandy, 2017). It only needs a numerical input to create the chart and the function returns a `ggplot2` object.

```
#Minimal code example #####
library(waffle)
parts <- c(66, 22, 12)

waffle(parts, rows = 10)
```

Word clouds

Use a word cloud to depict the result of a text analysis. A word cloud displays, for example, the frequency of words by its font size. The plot shows the word cloud of a children's book that I made with the ggwordcloud package (Le Pennec & Slowikowski, 2022). Do you know which one? A white rabbit and the queen of hearts play a big role in this book.

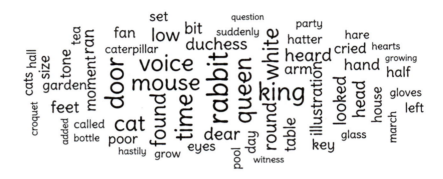

Creating a word cloud is not rocket since, but working with text is a complicated topic in the beginning. Fortunately, there is no need to learn text mining first, the ggwordcloud package includes data to make word clouds. Consider reading *Text Mining with R* by Silge & Robinson (2017) to learn more about text mining.

```
#Text Mining with R:
#PracticeR::show_link("text_mining")

#Minimal code example by Erwan Le Pennec
library(ggwordcloud)
#set a seed (starting point)
set.seed(123)

ggplot(love_words_small, aes(label = word,
                             size = speakers)) +
  geom_text_wordcloud() +
  scale_size_area(max_size = 30)
```

Summary

The ggplot2 package provides fantastic opportunities to visualize research findings. Unfortunately, all of its possibilities can be overwhelming. Keep in mind that the package implements the principles of the grammar of graphics with layers and that we created a scatter plot without much knowledge about ggplot2 in the first section. The latter illustrates that we do not need to remember all details to create a plot, but that we have the possibilities to create a plot that fulfills all of our requirements. Thus, use base R or the minimal code to make a graph that will not last long, for example to explore data. In all other instances, the gglot2 package provides everything you need to adjust the graph for specific needs.

Practice R gives an introduction, but of course there is much more to learn about ggplot2. Consider reading *R Graphics Cookbook* by Chang (2012), it provides a lot of details on how to make and improve graphs. If you are not interested in specific graphs but want to learn more about the package itself, read *ggplot2: Elegant Graphics for Data Analysis* by Wickham (2016).

```
#R Graphics Cookbook
show_link("r_graphics")

#ggplot2: elegant graphics
show_link("ggplot2")
```

There are also plenty of excellent books about data visualization that are worth to consider. For example, *Fundamentals of Data Visualization: A Primer on Making Informative and Compelling Figures* by Wilke (2019) or *Data Visualization: A Practical Introduction* by Healy (2019).

```
#Fundamentals of Data Visualization
show_link("fundamentals_dataviz")

#Data Visualization
show_link("dataviz")
```

8 Communicate research findings

Did you prepare the data? Did you run all analysis steps and visualize the results? Then it is time to write down the research findings. But is it time to close R and switch to a text program like Word? We can write a document, a report, or even a book with R and the rmarkdown package (Allaire, Xie, McPherson, et al., 2022). The document will not look like an R script; it will look like any other text document with tables and graphs. Actually, you are holding the result of an rmarkdown document in your hands.

Please don't get me wrong, I am not saying that you should never use Word again. There is no reason to use R if the document does not contain any content from R. However, if you write down the empirical results of your thesis, or if the document contains more than one plot made with R, consider writing at least the results section in one piece with rmarkdown. There are several good reasons why we should consider R for this task. Most importantly, we reduce the chance of generating errors if we eliminate the need to transfer results.

Furthermore, we increase our capacity to reproduce the results when we skip manual steps. Let me outline this thought. Suppose you are describing the mtcars data. Say the mean average of the mpg variable is 20.09 with a standard deviation of 6.03. I cannot remember how many times I checked a document to make sure that the inserted values are correct. I am sure that the numbers of this document are correct, because I used inline code in the rmarkdown file of this chapter, as the following console highlights.

```
#inline code:
`r mean(mtcars$mpg)`
```

If you insert such code in an rmarkdown document, R runs the function while the document is being created and inserts the values. Of course, you may connect a Word document with Excel, but your R skills are integrated into one document with rmarkdown. If the data gets an update, there is no need to check whether the values are still correct. The same applies, for example, for tables with regression results or any other calculation you made with R. Everything will be reproduced if you rerun the rmarkdown document.

I am not claiming that I have never transferred research result from a statistics software to Word, but consider all the wasted time: I formatted the text, updated tables, and, foremost, I tried to be very cautious not to make a mistake, which slowed down my efficiency. With rmarkdown, all the magic happens in a single document, which helps us to focus on the writing part. Do me and your future self a favor: Do not transfer research results manually.

Besides the discussed advantages, is learning rmarkdown really worth the trouble? From my point of view, there are at least two additional advantages. First, you can convert an rmarkdown document into many formats, for example, into a PDF file or

https://doi.org/10.1515/9783110704976-008

a Word document, with just the click of a button. Or say your findings need to be accessible on a website, then just create an HTML file.

Second, knowledge about rmarkdown lays the foundation to make books, presentations, and websites, just to mention potential next steps. In this chapter, we learn how rmarkdown works and we get in touch with Markdown, a markup language to format text. Learning a new language sounds crazy, but Markdown is easy to apply, and we use it only to format text. Knowledge about rmarkdown and Markdown will boost your skills, because there are packages that rely on (or work in similar ways as) rmarkdown. Instead of creating a PDF, we use other packages and Markdown to create (online) books, presentations, or even interactive documents. Thus, rmarkdown is an excellent starting point and I hope that I cleared all possible doubts.

- In Section 8.1, we focus on the basics of rmarkdown. We explore a simple template and we will clarify the main purpose of each individual component of an rmarkdown file.
- In Section 8.2, we extend our knowledge and we talk about the basics to create documents from scratch. We format text with Markdown; we explore the magic behind rmarkdown and learn why it is possible to create different documents from an rmarkdown file; and finally we will see how R handles our code.
- In Section 8.3, we start to create a template for a scientific document. For this purpose the PracticeR package includes a template which we will rebuild step by step. We focus on aspects that are typical for a scientific document (e.g., abstract, citations, etc.) and we learn how to integrate research findings that are made in R.

```
# The Setup for Chapter 8 #####
library(dplyr)
library(flextable)
library(HoRM)
library(huxtable)
library(jtools)
library(PracticeR)
library(stargazer)
library(summarytools)
library(tibble)
```

8.1 The basics of rmarkdown

The first steps to create an rmarkdown (.Rmd) document are easy, because RStudio provides a template that includes everything we need. Go to the toolbar and click on *File*; choose *New File* and pick *R Markdown*. As Figure 8.1 shows, a window appears and asks you to insert a document title, the author's name, and to pick a *default output format*. Give the document at least a title and choose the HTML output option. You can change the format of the output later, but the first steps are easier to apply if we make it an HTML file. The latter will be created on the fly and the viewer pane shows a preview of it.

Figure 8.1 also highlights that RStudio has further templates. Several R packages provide templates to create documents, and I have included two templates in the `PracticeR` package. A minimal template just like the one RStudio provides if you create a new file; and a template for Section 8.3.[1] Thus, create a new file, but keep in mind that you have the discussed steps already at your disposal if you pick the template from the `PracticeR` package (via *From Template*). I will outline more about templates in the next section.

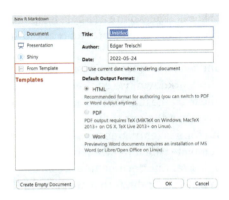

Fig. 8.1: Create a new R Markdown document

Create a new file. After you clicked on the OK button, RStudio opens an `rmarkdown` template which contains R code and text. Figure 8.2 shows a screenshot of the template with some annotations to help you to get going. RStudio itself gives us a hint about what we are supposed to do with the template. They write on line twelve: "When you click the *Knit* button a document will be generated that includes both content as well as the output of any embedded R code chunks within the document." What the heck, the *Knit* button? Chunks? We will clarify this new vocabulary in a minute, but first, look at Figure 8.2. I tried to outline these steps. RStudio converts the `Rmd` template into an HTML file if you click on the *Knit* button. RStudio asks you first to save the file if you click on the button for the first time. The HTML file appears in the viewer pane after you have saved the file and knit the document.

Scroll down in the viewer to examine what the template contains and compare it with the `Rmd` file. The viewer pane shows the rendered output of the `Rmd` file, just as any

---

[1] The minimal `PracticeR` template is identical with the RStudio template. Use the former if the RStudio template should be updated in the near future and does no longer match with the described steps.

browser displays such an HTML file. The template contains a title, a header, R code is displayed in boxes, and the template includes a plot as well. If you think the viewer is too small to inspect the output, click on the built-in *Open in a new window* symbol in the viewer. It opens the browser and shows the document.

Fig. 8.2: Render a document

Thus, we create a document that is based on the Rmd file. The document includes R code, output from the console, and text. When we knit a document, R sends the content of the Rmd file to knitr (Xie, 2022b), a package that provides the engine to execute the file. To put it simply, knitr weaves the content of the document together. I will outline in more detail what happens in the next section, but for now it is enough to understand that knitr combines text, R code, and output from the console in the document.

Before we dive deeper into the topic, let us focus on the structure of the template. In principle, each Rmd file consists of three different parts: a meta section, text formatted in Markdown, and R code chunks. Figure 8.3 shows where to find these parts and I outline the purpose of each part step by step.

First, each Rmd file contains a meta section or a header which starts and ends with three dashes (---). The meta section defines the document type and applies the global settings for the entire document by means of *fields*. To make your life a little bit more complicated, the fields of the meta section are written in yet another markup language. The name is not a joke: the language really was originally called yet another markup language (YAML). I outline more about the YAML header in Section 8.3, when we start to create a template. As the next console shows, the header of the template includes fields for the document title, the name of the author, and the date. Moreover, we define which output the file creates, in our case an HTML document (html_document).

```
#The YAML header/meta section
---
title: "Title"
```

```
author: "Edgar Treischl"
date: "9 2 2022"
output: html_document
---
```

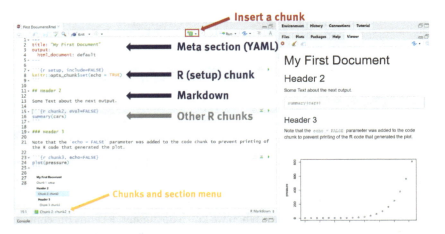

Fig. 8.3: The structure of an R Markdown document

Second, the template includes text, and we use Markdown to format it. To get a first idea on how Markdown works, look at the HTML file and compare it with the code. We will learn more about Markdown in the next section, but the template gives us some clues. For example, the document includes two hashtags (##) which will be translated as a second header. Markdown is a simple markup language and RStudio makes it comfortable to work with Markdown. So, don't be afraid about it.

Finally, the template contains different types of R chunks which we need to inspect in more detail. The first is called the setup chunk and the template also includes regular R chunks – one that displays code, and another one that makes the graph. Regardless of whether we talk about the setup or a regular R chunk, each starts with three backticks; which open the r chunk and another three backticks to close it, everything in between will be treated as R code:

```
#R code chunk example:
```{r }
mean(x)
```
```

It sounds tedious to create code chunks. And where are those backticks on the keyboard? As Figure 8.3 highlights, RStudio has an *Insert new code chunk button* and there is also a shortcut to include an empty code chunk. Hover with your mouse over the button and wait until RStudio reveals its secret.

Chunks may have a *label* and we can adjust how the code is handled with *chunk options*. Put both inside the braces, as the next output illustrates.

```
#Chunk label and chunk options
```{r chunk-label, chunk-option}
#Don't forget comments for your chunks!
mean(x)
```
```

Consider the `setup` chunk to learn more about chunk options. The setup chunk has a similar task as the header of the document, but this time to set up R. Compared to regular chunks, the setup chunk is used to run code that is not important for readers. For example, we include global settings that define how the code and the output are displayed, or we load libraries that run in the background. For this reason, the `setup` chunk is not included in the document and the chunk option `include` is set to `FALSE`. Chunk options can also be put inside a chunk if the line starts with a hashtag and a vertical bar (#|), as the next console highlights.

```
#Put chunk label and options inside via: #|
```{r}
#| my-chunk, include = FALSE
```
```

You can set options globally for the complete document or for each chunk individually. Inside the R `setup` chunk, we set the global chunk options, even though the template includes only one chunk option (`opts_chunk`) at the moment:

```
# the setup chunk: all code will be printed by default
knitr::opts_chunk$set(echo = TRUE)
```

The latter calls the `knitr` package and sets the chunk option `echo` globally to `TRUE`. This implies that the R code of all chunks will be displayed in the document. If you set the option to `FALSE`, no code appears in your document. Well, as long as we choose not to change the option in an individual chunk. Maybe this all sounds abstract; we explore more details about chunk options in the next section. For now, keep in mind that they determine how R handles code and the output of the console.

In contrast to options, the meaning of chunk labels is easier to grasp. Suppose you have a long document with many chunks, just give them unique names and you can inspect chunks in a small menu in the left corner of the code pane, as Figure 8.3 shows. If you click on a chunk (or a section), you will jump to this point in the document.

If you insert chunks via the button, you may realize that R is not the only programming language we can include in the document. I cannot outline much about these possibilities in Practice R, but the next info box underlines that we can integrate further engines and run, for example, Python with the `reticulate` package (Ushey et al., 2022).

ⓘ The `reticulate` package

You can run a `rmarkdown` document with different engines. For example, the `reticulate` provides an interface to work with *Python* from RStudio. Python is a general-purpose programming language and the use of Python is widespread within the data science community. This info box cannot introduce Python, however, it shows that the `reticulate` package embeds Python in RStudio.

You need to install Python and the `reticulate` package, before you are able to embed Python in active R session, run Python scripts, or embed Python code and its output in an `rmarkdown` document. The package sends the code to Python and integrates the result in the `rmarkdown` document. The next code demonstrates this point and underlines how effective your R skills already are. I import some Python libraries, load example data (`mpg`) and make a visualization. Irrespective of the data and the graph, the code to create the graph should be very familiar. I used the `plotnine` library which is an implementation of the grammar of graphics in Python.

```python
#Import libraries and make a plot
from plotnine.data import mpg
from plotnine import ggplot, aes, geom_bar
ggplot(mpg) + aes(x="class") + geom_bar()
```

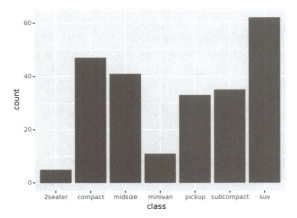

That's amazing, even if you have never worked with Python you can apply your `ggplot2` skills. But never mind about Python, the important point is that there are more engines to run code from RStudio and the `reticulate` package provides an interface for Python. Inspect the package documentation for more information how to combine Python and R.

Now that you are familiar with the structure of an rmarkdown file, let us focus on the basics of creating a document.

8.2 Create a document

To write documents with rmarkdown, we first learn the basics of Markdown. Next, we talk about Pandoc which helps us to understand how the document is created. Ultimately, we talk about the most import chunk options that determine how R handles code and output.

8.2.1 Markdown

The next console shows three examples to illustrate how Markdown works. We use the latter to format text and to structure the document. A document is structured with hashtags (#). One hashtag creates the first header (the title) of a document. If we provide two hashtags, we create a second header, and so on. To format text is also straightforward. If we provide two asterisks (**) before and after one or several words, the word becomes **bold**. A word or sentence is displayed in *italic* letters if we use one asterisk at the beginning and the end. Moreover, the next console also shows how to make a list with indented dashes (-). Overall, that's not very complicated, don't you think?

```
# A Markdown example

# Header 1

Make a text **bold** or *italic*

## Header 2

Make a list:

- Item 1
- Item 2
  - subitem
```

This gives you a first idea about Markdown and why I will not discuss the latter in detail. I do not spend much time on Markdown because RStudio includes a *visual markdown editing mode*, which makes a lesson about text formats almost redundant. As Figure 8.4

highlights, the visual markdown editing mode starts by clicking the *Visual* button on the top left side of the code pane (and you can switch back to the source code). If you don't see the editing mode, you are working with an older version of RStudio. Go and install the latest version.

Fig. 8.4: The visual markdown editing mode

Similar to a Word document, the editing mode applies the WYSIWYG (what you see is what you get) principle, it shows the text outline, and it comes with a menu to format text. As Figure 8.5 shows, structure the document with headings, make a word bold, or insert a picture just by clicking on the symbol. This is a great feature since it allows us to focus on our main task of creating a document.

Fig. 8.5: Menu of the visual markdown editing mode

Like this, you can use Markdown without the need for detailed knowledge. Give it a try. Click inside your document, start the visual markdown editing mode, and insert a table or a picture. If you have finished, switch back to the source editor and check how the script has changed. RStudio inserted the Markdown code. As the next console illustrates, I used the visual markdown editing mode to make a table. Each column of a table is separated with a vertical bar (|) in Markdown. Creating tables in Markdown is bothersome, but the visual markdown editing mode did the job for me.

```
#A table in Markdown
| Col1 | Col2 | Col3 |
|------|------|------|
|      |      |      |
|      |      |      |
|      |      |      |
```

I could spend a lot of time showing you how Markdown works. The alternative is that you work it out by yourself. I may sound like a villain in a James Bond movie, but what strategy do you believe will have the strongest impact on your skills? Use RStudio's visual markdown editor to learn more about how to format text, how to include a picture, or how to insert a footnote. Moreover, consider the rmarkdown website and the cheat sheet, it shows also how to write with Markdown.

```
# The rmarkdown website
# https://rmarkdown.rstudio.com/
```

Instead of formatting text, we must clarify what happens after we have fed the document with text, graphs, or other content. How do we get an HTML file if we knit the document, and why is it possible to create a PDF or a Word document from the same Rmd file? The short answer: Pandoc.

8.2.2 Pandoc

With Pandoc running in the background, it is possible to create different files from a single rmarkdown file. Pandoc makes it possible to convert files from one markup language format – such as Markdown – into another one. For this reason, we may insert HTML code in the rmarkdown file. As long as we create an HTML file, the HTML code will be translated just as a browser does it if we visit a website. With Pandoc we are able convert a file to HTML, Word, and other formats.

For example, click on the arrow next to the knit button and choose Word as output. RStudio renders the document and adds the code to create the Word file. As the next console shows, RStudio adds the default word_document to the output field.

```
#Render the file as word_document
---
output:
  word_document: default
---
```

The latter comes with one restriction: Microsoft Word (or OpenOffice) is needed for a Word document and LaTeX is needed to convert the document into a PDF file. In a nutshell, LaTeX is a typesetting language designed to produce high-quality text documents. You may need to learn LaTeX if you write a book, and some journals also ask you to submit your article as a LaTeX file. You can learn more about LaTeX and Pandoc in the info box about file conversion.

File conversion:

The rmarkdown package uses Pandoc to convert files into different formats. This makes it possible to insert HTML code if we create an HTML or use LaTeX code in the case of a PDF file. Let's see how this works based on a minimal example for each language. Inspect the following Markdown code:

```
# Header 1
## Header 2
**bold** and *italic* text
```

As we know, we format headings with hashtags (#) in Markdown, but we could use the HTML code as well. For instance, the code <h1>Title</h1> displays the same first heading as # Title. The second header translates to <h2>Header 2</h2> in HTML. The following code shows the output of how the Markdown code is translated into HTML.

```
<h1>Header 1</h1>
<h2>Header 2</h2>
<b>bold</b> and <i>italic</i> text
```

Markdown makes it easy to format code and we can include HTML code if the output is an HTML file. Do you have any idea why we cannot insert HTML code when we create a PDF file? We use LaTeX to create a PDF file and, to put it plainly: LaTeX does not speak HTML. We must, therefore, provide the corresponding LaTeX code if we generate a PDF. For instance, we can make a text bold with \textbf{bold} or italic with \emph{italic}. Basic knowledge about HTML or LaTeX is helpful to customize a document, but it might not be necessary, depending on your goal. Some basics to format texts are not that difficult, neither in HTML nor in LaTeX. Just keep in mind that LaTeX does not speak HTML, nor will a web browser speak LaTeX – only Pandoc knows them all. We may thus add HTML or LaTeX code where needed. Pandoc inspects the document for the corresponding code and converts a # Header 1 into <h1>Header 1</h1> if we create a HTML or into \section{Header 1} in the case of a PDF file. The next console shows the minimal example in LaTeX.

```
\section{Header 1}
\subsection{Header 2}
\textbf{bold} and \emph{italic} text
```

Learning LaTeX is hard, and much more complicated than Markdown. Learning LaTeX is not worth the trouble if you need a document only to show the results of an analysis. In this case, let rmarkdown do the hard work for you. You will, however, need to install a LaTeX distribution in some instances before you can create PDF files. A distribution should be installed automatically, but you should know that the `tinytex` package runs in the background and provides a LaTeX distribution (Xie, 2022c). If you run into an error, install the package first. After the installation is done, install the LaTeX distribution via the `install_tinytex()` function:

```r
# Install a latex distribution
tinytex::install_tinytex()
```

Next we examine how chunk options determine how our R code will be handled.

8.2.3 Chunk options

Up until this point, we have inspected the R `setup` chunk and we saw how to exclude an entire chunk by setting the chunk option `include` to `FALSE`. Which further chunk options exist? For example:

- Echo is responsible if code will be displayed. Set `echo` to `FALSE` and code will not be displayed, but evaluated and executed.
- Eval determines if code will be evaluated. The results of a chunk will not show up in the document if `eval` is set to `FALSE`, but the code will be displayed in the document.
- The R chunks return messages and warnings from the console. Such information are useful while we create a document, but may look odd in a final version of the document. Messages and warnings will not be displayed if the options `message` and `warning` are set to `FALSE`.

Remember, we can include global chunk options in the R setup chunk and define how R knits the document. We don't have to check that each chunk is correctly knitted if we consider how R should knit the document by default. Of course, there is always the possibility to switch back and adjust chunks individually should the default option not fit. In a research document, we probably want to evaluate all chunks, but our reader might not be interested in the R code, the warnings, and the messages from the console, which is why I set them to `FALSE`, as the next console illustrates.

```r
# Example setup
knitr::opts_chunk$set(
  eval = TRUE,
  echo = FALSE,
  warning = FALSE,
```

```
  message = FALSE
)
```

The rmarkdown package makes it easy to include a graph: just insert the code in an R chunk. If you want to display only the results (graph), set the chunk option eval to TRUE and echo to FALSE. Further chunk options that determine how graphs will be displayed are also worth discussing:

- Adjust the *height* and the *width* of a graph with the corresponding chunk options. The default options are fig.width = 6.5 and fig.height = 4.5. Depending on the content and the output format, you may want to increase (decrease) the size of a graph.
- By the way, adjusting your graph size with fig.width and fig.height has no effect on *image files* that are included in your document. Consider the out.width chunk to adjust the size of the file. Alternatively, insert the file in your rmarkdown file and use the visual editor to modify the appearance. You can adjust several options and attributes with a double click on the picture in the visual markdown editing mode, including the width, height, and the caption.
- Regardless whether a graph is included from a file or from code chunk, a caption is always a good idea to refer to. The chunk option fig.cap inserts a capture.
- Create a folder for all images. The chunk option fig.path will save all image files that are created from a chunk in a given folder.

Consider to include such parameters in the setup chunk. Moreover, give a chunk that creates a graph a chunk label and the image file will get the same name as the corresponding chunk label. The next console summarizes the discussed chunk options.

```
# Improved example setup
knitr::opts_chunk$set(
  # further options ...
  fig.width = 7,
  fig.height = 5,
  fig.path = "images/"
)
```

All these options are not an all-encompassing list. Have a look at the rmarkdown website and the cheat sheet for further information about chunk options. Moreover, the opts_chunk$get() function returns a list of chunk options, which is why I skip the output of the next console.

```
# opts_chunk$get() returns chunk options and defaults
str(knitr::opts_chunk$get())
```

I have one last chunk option for the future heavy user: You can include a cache in the R setup chunk. R checks whether the result of a chunk has already been evaluated and the chunk will only be evaluated the first time the document is rendered or when you change it. Thus, a cache may save time in rendering the document, but take care that all chunks are up to date before submitting your work. By using a cache, one chunk may depend now on another chunk and we need to address this problem (with the dependson option, see Wickham & Grolemund, 2016, p. 432). Before you go on and adjust the setup chunk, let's explore the PracticeR template because it includes the discussed chunk options and creates a template for a scientific report.

8.3 Create a template

Suppose we make a template for a thesis, a paper, or any other scientific document. What should the template contain? A scientific document needs at least a cover page with a title, author name, and an abstract. Depending on the scope of the work, we may want to include a table of contents and we should also set up a bibliography to automatically insert citations and references. Again, this not an all-encompassing list, but it gives us a reasonable start to learn a few things about the meta section, because that's where we define the output.

In the next step, we include elements that are typical for a research report and we explore how to manage citations with R. Moreover, we learn how to make tables in R and integrate them in the document.

8.3.1 Meta section

Let's inspect the meta section of the minimal template from the beginning. The meta section determines how the file will be structured. It contains information about the title, the author, the date, and the output field. Those are YAML commands and, depending on the template, you may add such fields to the meta section (see e.g., ?pdf_document to inspect the options for PDF files).

```
#The YAML header of the minimal template
---
title: "Template Title"
author: "Author Name"
date: 'Last update: 2023-01-24'
```

```
output: pdf_document
---
```

In this section I will show you step by step how we can change the minimal template and adjust it for our purposes. Thus, this section outlines how the PracticeR template is built step by step. Create a new file from templates, pick the PracticeR template, and save the file in a new folder. The template includes the following steps.

First, we manage the output of the document. If you change the output in your own document, add a colon (:) after the document type (pdf_document:). Be careful, indentation is important for YAML code. Make sure that all sub-fields that determine the output are indented to the top field (output). The next console shows the meta section of the PracticeR template, I add several fields to structure the document as a first step:

- I included a table of contents (toc) and the toc_depth field defines how many headings are listed.
- By default, sections are not listed with numbers, but you can print them with the number_sections field.
- The highlight field determines which style is used to print the code. I use the style kate in this book, but feel free to use the default or another style (e.g., tango, monochrome, or the espresso style, see Xie (2022a), p. 79).
- Moreover, I included a preamble LaTeX file (preamble.tex) that will be executed before the body of the main text (before_body). You find the LaTeX file in the same directory as the document after you created it – it includes a placeholder for contact details and inserts a new page before the main text starts. The next console shows the YAML code:

```
#First step: Adjusted the output
output:
  pdf_document:
    toc: yes
    toc_depth: '2'
    number_sections: yes
    highlight: kate
    includes:
      before_body: "preamble.tex"
---
```

In a second step, I add an abstract with the corresponding field; I include a bibliography file (MyBib.bib); and I change how citations are styled by pointing to a Citation Style Language (csl) file (apa.csl). In terms of citations, R use the files and display citations in accordance with the citations of the text.

```
#Second step
abstract: A very short abstract.
bibliography: MyBib.bib
csl: apa.csl
---
```

Including those fields in the meta section is not complicated, but maybe you have no idea how to manage citations or what a bibliography file is. Before I show you how to include citations in the text, the info box about citation management software outlines in a nutshell how such software work.

Citation management software:　　　　　　　　　　　　　　　　　　　　　　　　**i**

Have you ever used Zotero, Citavi, or any other software to manage references? If the answer is no, stop reading and download Zotero (www.zotero.org), an open-source software to manage your references. With the help of a citation management software, you can import references and refer to them in a text document. Thus, there is no need to manually make references, use a citation management software.

Such software tools let you collect citations (e.g., with the browser) and export the references as a bibliography (.bib) file, which contains the information of all references of a bibliography. Consider the next console, it illustrates the content of a bibliography file with the information about a book from Little & Rubin (1987). If we refer to little_1987 in the text, the following book will be cited:

```
#A bib file (.bib) example:

@book{little_1987,
    address = {New York},
    title = {Statistical {Analysis} with {Missing} {Data}},
    publisher = {Wiley},
    author = {Little, Roderick J. A. and Rubin, Donald B.},
    year = {1987},
}
```

We use such files to refer to authors and publications and a list with all cited publications will show up at the end of the document automatically. Moreover, citations management systems can also be used to determine the citation style. Suppose you plan to publish your work in a specific journal. The Zotero Style Repository offers a lot of csl files to style citations. If you are lucky and you find one for the journal, you get the desired citation style without any effort. Or, think of different academic disciplines and departments that prefer different citations styles. You can download many csl files from the Zotero Style Repository. Put the name of the csl file in the directory and citations will be printed accordingly. If you do not provide a csl file, rmarkdown applies the Chicago author-date style by default.

In order to include publications in the document, R needs the bibliography file and we need to refer to the reference name with the at (@) sign. In the visual mode, you may access and manage your references also via the citation menu (Insert > Citation).

Depending on your citation style, you may use one of the following options to refer to a publication:
- Refer directly to a publication with an in-text citation, such as Little & Rubin (1987), by using the at sign and the reference name in the document. For example: `@little_1987`.
- If several authors are cited, such as (Enders, 2010; Little & Rubin, 1987), put them into brackets and separate each reference with a semicolon: `[@enders_2010; @little_1987]`.
- Page numbers and additional text, such as (e.g., see Little & Rubin, 1987, p. 1), can also be included in the brackets: `[e.g., see @little_1987, p. 1]`.

Of course, there are more structural aspects of a scientific document that are worth discussing. You have three options if you are not happy how the template looks so far. First, and due to the PDF output, you could learn more about LaTeX. This sounds like bad advice; maybe I should have refrained from telling you that LaTeX is complicated to learn. Nonetheless, you may consider learning a few things in LaTeX should you work with PDFs on a regular basis. LaTeX is not complicated if you just want to change some minor aspects of a document. For example, consider the `preamble` file of the `PracticeR` template. I insert a cover page with help of the LaTeX code `\newpage`. It will insert a new page and puts the remaining text on the next page.

A second option goes in a similar direction, but with a completely different drift. Was it necessary to create our own template? The `rticles` and several other R packages provide `rmarkdown` templates. The former provides templates for Elsevier, Springer, or the PLOS journals (Allaire, Xie, Dervieux, et al., 2022). Of course, you can use such templates as well.

If you are still not sure whether writing a document in R is a good idea, then this last option might sway you over. Suppose you already have a Word template with fancy style rules. This Word document may serve as a template from which you can create a new Word document with R. The `rmarkdown` package extracts the style of a Word template and knits the document accordingly. Save the template in your working directory and refer to it in the meta section. Add the `reference_docx` field and point to the Word template. Even though you work with a Word document, the analysis is reproducible and the document can get an update.

```
#reference_docx uses your docx as reference to format the output
---
title: "My Template"
output:
  word_document:
    reference_docx: Template.docx
---
```

Ultimately, we learn how to make tables with R. This will boost your work efficiency, because then you will be able to generate all content of a scientific document (text, graphs, and tables) from a single and reproducible file.

8.3.2 Tables

What would you say, which James Bond actor is the best? And which one drank the most martinis, or who had the most love affairs? Was it Daniel Craig, Richard Moore, or Pierce Brosnan? The question probably came as a surprise to you, but if making a table sounds boring, then let's at least fool around with the data. The HoRM package includes data about the Bond movies (Young, 2021). As always, install and load the package before you run the steps on your computer. As the next console shows, it will be easier for us if we generate a table with a selection of the variables from the JamesBond data only. I selected the movie title, the name of the Bond actor, the number of (romantic) conquests, the number of martinis, the number of killings, and the average movie rating. Remember, the help function provides more information about the data.

```r
library(HoRM)
library(dplyr)
data("JamesBond")

# Select variables from JamesBond
bond_data <- select(JamesBond,
  Movie, Bond, Conquests, Martinis,
  Killings = "Kills_Bond",
  Rating = "Avg_User_IMDB"
)
```

Let's say we want to create a summary table that show which of the Bond actors is the most popular, deadly, or successful. We use our dplyr knowledge to group the data by each Bond actor and make a summary for all numeric variables. Apparently, Pierce Brosnan was the most brutal James Bond actor, while Daniel Craig got the best ratings and also drank the most martinis.

```r
# Group by each Bond, give me the mean of each variable
bond_data |>
  group_by(Bond) |>
  summarise(across(where(is.numeric), ~ round(mean(.x), 2)))

#> # A tibble: 6 x 5
```

```
#>    Bond            Conquests Martinis Killings Rating
#>    <fct>               <dbl>    <dbl>    <dbl>  <dbl>
#> 1 Daniel Craig         2.25     2.75     20.8    7.3
#> 2 George Lazenby       3        1         5      6.8
#> 3 Pierce Brosnan       2.5      1.25     33.8    6.47
#> 4 Roger Moore          2.71     0.29     12.9    6.61
#> 5 Sean Connery         2.67     0.67     12      7.2
#> # ... with 1 more row
```

How can we make a table from this output? Are we supposed to create a table like we do in Word? Decide how many columns and rows the table has and apply some styles to format the table? Since we write this document in Markdown, we could do the same and insert a table in Markdown. But what happens if the data gets an update? If we create tables manually, then we must update the table too and there is always a chance that some mistakes happen if you transfer figures manually. Of course, this does not happen if we skip manual steps and use R to make the tables.

To be honest with you, creating good tables is a complex topic and I could have written an entire chapter about tables. This is especially the case because there are different packages specialized on tables for each output format. For this reason, we will not learn how to make tables in general terms; we will only make a table for summary statistics, and one for analysis results (e.g., a linear regression). Both tables are essential for a report and make a good start to see how R helps us to create reproducible results.

Summary statistics

I often use the `stargazer` package to create a table for summary statics since I work with PDF files most of the time (Hlavac, 2022). The package is very easy to apply: use the `stargazer()` function, the name of the data, and the `type` of output.

```
# Stargazer returns a table for summary statistics
library(stargazer)
stargazer(bond_data, type = "text")
```

```
#>
#> ========================================
#> Statistic N   Mean   St. Dev.  Min    Max
#> ----------------------------------------
#> Conquests 24 2.542   0.779      1      4
#> Martinis  24 1.083   1.316      0      6
#> Killings  24 17.000  11.348     1      47
#> Rating    24 6.858   0.517    6.000  7.900
#> ----------------------------------------
```

As the last console shows, it returns the summary statistics as text, but also the LaTeX or HTML code if you change the type option. As always, the package has more options to tweak and improve the table. Add a title, round the number of digits, or determine which summary statistics (summary.stat) are returned. Table 8.1 was created with the following code and we must set the results chunk option and to asis. By adjusting the chunk option, the result of the console is interpreted *as it is* (see Chapter 10.2 for more information).

```
# Some options to improve the table
stargazer(bond_data,
  type = "latex",
  digits = 2,
  title = "Summary statistics",
  summary.stat = c("sd", "min", "max", "n")
)
```

Tab. 8.1: Summary statistics

Statistic	St. Dev.	Min	Max	N
Conquests	0.78	1	4	24
Martinis	1.32	0	6	24
Killings	11.35	1	47	24
Rating	0.52	6.00	7.90	24

Unfortunately, the package has no reproducible solution for Word. For this reason, we examine the flextable package, which helps us to generate tables for PDF, HTML, and Word (Gohel & Skintzos, 2022).

To make a table with summary statistics, we must first calculate each statistic for each variable that we use in the analysis. Our R skills would definitely profit from this data preparation step, since we have to bring them together in a tidy format. In this chapter we will not focus on data management steps, since I want to convince you that making tables in R is the last essential step to communicate research results efficiently. Instead, let us recall what we learned in Chapter 3. Several packages – such as summarytools (Comtois, 2022) – provide convenient functions to describe data. We learned that descr() does the heavy lifting for us and calculates the summary statistics. All we must do is provide the corresponding stats options and decide which one we want to report. In addition, if we set the transpose option to TRUE the output almost looks like a summary statistics table.

```
#Calculate summary stats
library(summarytools)
table <- descr(bond_data,
               stats = c("n.valid", "min", "mean", "max", "sd"),
               transpose = TRUE)

table <- as.data.frame(table)
table

#>            N.Valid Min      Mean  Max    Std.Dev
#> Conquests      24   1  2.541667  4.0  0.7790276
#> Killings       24   1 17.000000 47.0 11.3482425
#> Martinis       24   0  1.083333  6.0  1.3160107
#> Rating         24   6  6.858333  7.9  0.5174492
```

There are only two more things we need to take care of. First, we may want to round the numbers; and our variable names are included as row names, so we must put them in their own column with the `rownames_to_column()` function from the `tibble` package.

```
# Round results and add rowname to the data
table <- table |>
  round(digits = 2) |>
  tibble::rownames_to_column(var = "Variable")

table

#>      Variable N.Valid Min  Mean  Max Std.Dev
#> 1   Conquests      24   1  2.54  4.0    0.78
#> 2    Killings      24   1 17.00 47.0   11.35
#> 3    Martinis      24   0  1.08  6.0    1.32
#> 4      Rating      24   6  6.86  7.9    0.52
```

Look what happens if we add exactly one line of code to our data preparation step for the Bond movies. We add the `flextable()` function and it returns a table:

```
# Make a flextable
table |>
  flextable::flextable()
```

Variable	N.Valid	Min	Mean	Max	Std.Dev
Conquests	24	1	2.54	4.0	0.78
Killings	24	1	17.00	47.0	11.35
Martinis	24	0	1.08	6.0	1.32
Rating	24	6	6.86	7.9	0.52

The `flextable()` package gives you a lot of options to create tables with R. The package provides features to export tables and will also help to create tables for a multivariate analysis. Just to give you some impression of how the package works, inspect what happens if you add a theme (e.g., `theme_vanilla()`) and I used the `autofit()` function for the last table. The `theme_vanilla` makes the header bold and the `autofit()` function adjusts the width of the table.

Such steps seem straight forward, but creating a table from the ground up is a complicated task. If we make such basic tables, there is not much that we must learn. However, we should put more effort into our tables if we want to create something special or customized. For example, you could add a picture of each James Bond, or even include a graph that describes the examined variables in the table. However, this is not the purpose of this chapter, instead we need to acknowledge the importance of the topic. If the data gets an update, if you include (exclude) variables from the analysis, or if you change anything that affects the results, the table gets an update after you knit the document again.

Multivariate analysis

Let's run a linear regression and summarize the results. The workflow to create a table for a different kind of analysis technique is the same, regardless of whether we report the results of a linear regression, logistic regression, or another analysis technique. Depending on the statistical procedure, we must adjust certain aspects of the table, but these are merely minor adjustments.

Let us estimate if the rating for a Bond movie depends on any of the examined variables. A Bond movie should be entertaining and, in consequence, people may give better ratings if a movie is full of action. The same applies to the number of drinks or love affairs. The number of martinis, conquests, and killings may explain the movie's rating, even though these are quick-and-dirty assumptions.

We use the `huxtable` package to create regression tables (Hugh-Jones, 2022). We already used the package to compare models, and we can translate the results of the `huxtable` package into a `flextable`. The `huxtable` package provides several nice features to adjust our regression tables and we can also use it to create tables for PDF, Word, or HTML files. As the next output shows, I estimate two example models (`m1` and m2) to make the table. The huxreg function returns the models via the console or as a table if we include the code in an R chunk.

```
# Two example models
m1 <- lm(Rating ~ Conquests, data = bond_data)
m2 <- lm(Rating ~ Conquests + Martinis, data = bond_data)
```

```
# Show my models via huxreg()
library(huxtable)
huxreg(m1, m2, error_pos = "right")
```

Tab. 8.3

	(1)		(2)	
(Intercept)	6.814 ***	(0.376)	6.675 ***	(0.471)
Conquests	0.017	(0.142)	0.052	(0.159)
Martinis			0.048	(0.094)
N	24		24	
R2	0.001		0.013	
logLik	-17.723		-17.577	
AIC	41.447		43.154	

*** p < 0.001; ** p < 0.01; * p < 0.05.

We get a regression table, just like we have seen before – but think of it! The book in your hands is a PDF file, which implies that the huxreg function returns the LaTeX code to create the table. Thus, the huxtable package figured out that I knit my document as a PDF, but you can also create an HTML file, or a Word document.

Depending on the purpose, you may want to tweak some options to improve the table. First, let us create a list of all models (modelfits) and give each element of the list a name. In doing so, our model names will be included as labels in the header of the table.

```
# create a list with models and labels
modelfits <- list(
```

```
  "Model 1" = m1,
  "Model 2" = m2
)
```

In addition, we may improve the table with respect to:
- Coefficients: Sometimes, a lot of variables are included, and we may split the table in two – one for the body of the document and another one for the appendix. The option `omit_coefs` omits variables from the table.
- Statistics: Maybe it is not necessary to show the entire list of all default `statistics`. Adjust the list of statistics and, as the next console highlights, we can give each statistic a proper text label for the table.
- Round numbers: Round the report results with `number_format`; the reader will thank you.
- Note: The next code also adds a `note` to provide more information about the model, the variables, and other important information.

```
# The improved table (see Tab. 8.4):
huxreg(modelfits,
  omit_coefs = "(Intercept)",
  statistics = c(`Number of observations` = "nobs", `R²` = "r.squared"),
  number_format = 2,
  note = "Note: Some important notes."
)
```

Tab. 8.4

	Model 1	Model 2
Conquests	0.02	0.05
	(0.14)	(0.16)
Martinis		0.05
		(0.09)
Number of observations	24	24
R^2	0.00	0.01

Note: Some important notes.

The huxreg function comes with many possibilities to adjust a regression table. I cannot discuss all of them in detail. Maybe you want to replace the crude names of certain variables with text labels, or maybe you want to change the significance levels and display significant coefficients in bold. That's all possible. Go on and inspect the huxreg vignette which provides more options and improvements for the (regression) table.

```
# The huxreg vignette shows more options how to adjust the table
vignette("huxreg", package = "huxtable")
```

Creating tables for research results might be quite complicated in the beginning, but it boosts your skills and increases your work efficiency. Keep in mind that we can make a flextable from a huxtable by adding the as_flextable() function. This might not be necessary, but it highlights that you can make further adjustments with the flextable package. The flextable package also provides a convenient way if you want to export your work only. As the next console illustrates, export the table as a Word, PowerPoint, or HTML file.

```
# Export, for example as .html, .pptx, or Word (docx) file:
flextable::save_as_docx(table, path = "./table.docx")
```

Let me give you one last advice how to handle long code chunks. Suppose your document contains a long code chunk, for example, for a ggplot2 graph to visualize the regression results. It is not convenient to have all that code within your document, even if the code is not displayed in the document. Put the source() function in your setup chunk and point to the .R script that generates the graph; or any other results from R that should be available but not displayed in the document.

For example, the code to visualize the regression results of the last analysis does not live in the Rmd file of this chapter. Instead, I put it in a separate script called regression_results.R and I make the results of that script available via the source() function.

```
# Use source to run R script in the background
source("regression_results.R")
```

In this file, I created and saved the plot (as regression_plot). If I insert the object name in an R chunk, it returns the graph. Apparently, none of the examined variables has an effect on the James Bond movie ratings, but the code that creates this graph is not included in the Rmd file of this chapter; I only need to call the object once more.

```
# The result of the regression_results script
regression_plot
```

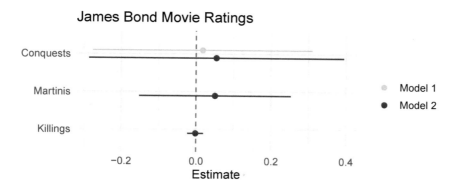

One last word on how life becomes trickier with LaTeX. It could be that you first need to install the corresponding LaTeX packages. They should be installed on the fly and the discussed R packages included them in the LaTeX file. The huxtable package offers two useful functions that you may consider if you run into an error. The report_latex_dependencies() function returns packages that are needed to create the table, and you can even install LaTeX packages via the install_latex_dependencies() function, as the next console summarizes.

```
# Use report_latex_dependencies to inspect the LaTeX packages
huxtable::report_latex_dependencies()
# The install_latex_dependencies function installs them via R
huxtable::install_latex_dependencies()
```

Summary

This chapter introduced the rmarkdown package and I wrote this chapter to underline that we do not need to manually transfer results. When we write a document with rmarkdown there will be no need to worry how the analysis results come into the text document. We reduce potential sources of manual errors, and we can make updates of our analysis by just rendering the document again. Writing a document with rmarkdown is not difficult, but creating a document in a way that suits your needs might be a demanding task. We worked on a template for this reason, but I cannot discuss all rmarkdown features. Check out the rmarkdown website, it shows a lot of next steps and a gallery with examples.

I cannot close this chapter without mentioning some of the possibilities which are at your disposal. As outlined in the introduction, your rmarkdown skills are the foundation to create books with bookdown, (Xie, 2022a), websites with rmarkdown or distill (Dervieux et al., 2022), and presentations with xaringan (Xie, 2022d). Chapter 12 covers some of those opportunities, but there are more packages out there. For example, create a resume with vitae (O'Hara-Wild & Hyndman, 2022) or a scientific poster with posterdown (Thorne, 2019).

I outlined also a few basics about HTML, LaTeX, Markdown, and YAML. I focused on the output and I tried to avoid going into too much detail on how they work, especially where LaTeX is concerned. Depending on the preferred output, it is useful to learn more about those languages. Nevertheless, I did not want to elaborate too much, since we can make a report with limited knowledge about those languages. If you need more help with rmarkdown, visit the bookdown website. It lists many books about R, among them *R Markdown Cookbook* by Xie et al. (2020) or *bookdown: Authoring Books and Technical Documents with R Markdown* by Xie (2016) which show in detail how documents are made with R.

```
# The bookdown website:
show_link("bookdown_website")

# Bookdown
show_link("bookdown")

# R Markdown Cookbook:
show_link("rmarkdown_cookbook")
```

Part III: **Beyond the basics**

9 GitHub

Git is a version control system for code and *GitHub* is an host (website) for Git-based projects. Think of Git/GitHub as some sort of cloud system to manage code. Git/GitHub has a technical background and was developed for programmers, but there are several reasons why such a version control system is valuable for applied research, even if you already work with a cloud service. Most importantly, GitHub helps us to increase the reproducibility of our work and it traces the change of code. On GitHub, each project gets its own *repository*, which is essentially a folder that contains all project files. A repository can be private – which means that it is only visible for yourself – or you can share it by making it public. People may reuse your code and hopefully reproduce your results, even if they do not have their own GitHub account.

GitHub keeps track of our code. Suppose we work on a project and we tried to improve the code, but we made a mistake. GitHub marks changes to the code and each time we make an update of a project we are forced to explain – in a few words – what happened to the code. A version control system lets us travel back in time to find out where a possible error occurred. Figure 9.1 illustrates this feature with code from the PracticeR package. I changed the source code of the package and GitHub marks code in red that has been changed and at the same time displays the new version in green.

Fig. 9.1: GitHub code changes

GitHub is not made to handle large data sets or text documents; it does not keep track of each word. For example, look at line 1 of Figure 9.1. I changed only one word in a text field of the package, but GitHub marks the entire block. Other systems are better suited to track changes in text documents and files (e.g., Google Docs), but GitHub is made to keep track of code.

In a similar vein, the steps of applied empirical research do not necessarily proceed in a sequential manner. Say you analyze data, but the next day you realize that an important control variable is missing. You go back, prepare the data and run the analysis again. Unfortunately, you made a mistake in the data preparation step. Again, you circle back, and you will probably create a new version each time you improve the

https://doi.org/10.1515/9783110704976-009

analysis substantially. In the final project stage, the folder contains a lot of files and you will probably end up with several final versions (e.g., `data_prep_final_v4`). But do you know what happened in-between? Can you remember what you have changed a week, a month, a year ago? We may add comments to explain what happens in each new version. However, GitHub makes it possible to see the changes and forces us to explain what happened to the code.

Unfortunately, Git(Hub) is full of jargon and hard to learn in the beginning. For this reason, this chapter introduces Git/GitHub briefly and in a non-technical fashion:

- Section 9.1 highlights additional advantages of GitHub to further push your motivation. We start to elaborate on the technical terms and processes of working with GitHub.
- Section 9.2 guides you through the installation process. I ask you to create a GitHub account and install Git.
- Section 9.3 outlines in detail how to work with GitHub and RStudio: we create a repository and connect RStudio with your GitHub account. We get in touch with the RStudio Git pane to apply the basics steps.

There is so much more we could learn when working with GitHub, but this chapter only highlights that the principle steps to work with GitHub and RStudio are not rocket science. As a last step, we inspect how GitHub makes it possible to travel back in time and we talk about problems and conflicts that we possibly need to resolve.

```
# Chapter 9 needs the following packages:
library(devtools)
library(gitcreds)
library(gh)
library(PracticeR)
library(usethis)
```

9.1 The Git(Hub) basics

Git(Hub) is a large struggle in the beginning:[1] It takes time to setup and to acquire the experience working with GitHub; it is full of jargon which makes it hard to learn; and even if you managed the setup, at some point you will face problems that I did not mention. Learning GitHub is hard, but definitely worth the trouble. Before we dive into the jargon, let me try to convince you that GitHub is worth the trouble with three additional features that a typical cloud system (e.g. Dropbox) probably cannot deliver: (1) GitHub facilitates cooperation. (2) Code on GitHub is accessible everywhere. (3)

---

1 As outlined, Git and GitHub are two different things, but I will only use the two terms in a differentiated way where it is necessary (e.g., Git code, the GitHub website).

GitHub has additional features beyond code managing, such as running apps, hosting websites, and automating building steps.

GitHub facilitates cooperation by allowing people to simultaneously work on a project. Of course, team members could send files around, but this often results in chaos with different file versions in several mails, each containing part of the changes. Or suppose the files live somewhere in the cloud. Why has someone else opened the file, exactly when we start to work on the project? GitHub allow us to create a *branch*, making it possible that each team member can work on the project. The changes can then be combined (merged) after the work is done. GitHub even tries to match branches automatically and shows conflicts between versions that need to be solved.

Code on GitHub is accessible everywhere. For example, consider the gapminder_plot() function. As the next console illustrates, it returns the bubble chart for the gapminder data that I introduced in Chapter 1.

```
# Show me the gapminder plot
gapminder_plot()
```

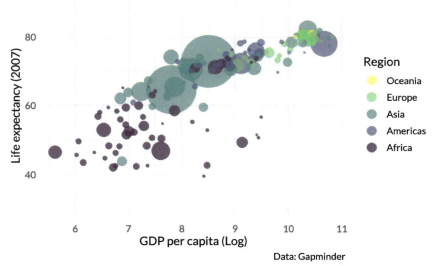

The graph is created automatically when I render this document, but the code to create the graph is not included here. The book is built with rmarkdown (see Chapter 8), and the setup chunk of this chapter includes the url_source() function from the devtools package (Wickham, Hester, Chang, et al., 2022). The code to create the plot is saved on my GitHub account and the function collects and runs the code to create the plot. Irrespective where you are and which computer you use, code that lives on GitHub can be retrieved via the source_url() function. On GitHub, you can also inspect the raw (text) version of the code which the source_url() function collects.

```
# source_url runs code from GitHub
script <- "./raw.githubusercontent.com/username/file.R"
devtools::source_url(script)
```

GitHub has more advantages that I can outline. You can run apps, host websites, and GitHub even allows us to automate building steps. Let me outline this last point in more detail. Suppose you are working for an NGO which conducts a large survey on a regular base. You are responsible to prepare the data, run some analysis, and make a report. More specifically, you are supposed to do so each time the data gets a new release. In Chapter 10, we will learn how to automate this process with R, but GitHub also helps with this task. With GitHub Actions, we can run a workflow and automate a work process. GitHub Action is event-driven, which means that we can implement a workflow that runs each time a specific event has occurred. For example, we can create a workflow that is triggered each time our files get an update and - depending on our workflow – they can trigger specific jobs. In our case we let GitHub Actions run an R script and rebuild the report automatically each time the event occurred.

Thus, GitHub has more to offer then this chapter could possibly show, and I hope that these advantages motivate you to get in touch with GitHub. Before we install and work with GitHub, let us clarify some of the technical jargon.

You already know that files live in a repository, actually there are two different kinds of repositories if your computer is connected with GitHub: A *local repository* on your computer and a *remote repository* on GitHub. If a repository is public, you can inspect it in your browser to get a first idea about GitHub. For example, visit the PracticeR package repository. This is not very exciting, but it outlines that the repository contains all files that are necessary to build the package and you cannot visit my local repository.

```
# Inspect a GitHub repository. For example:
show_link("pr_github")
```

In order to track changes, we send files to GitHub or get files from a remote repository. In the GitHub universe, we *push* code from a local repository to GitHub; while *pull* turns it around and we retrieve code from GitHub. Suppose we worked on a project and we changed our code. We save the files, but this will not change the remote GitHub repository. The changes will only show up if we intentionally push the new version to GitHub. Or imagine you are working with a colleague who made some substantial improvements. You need to pull the latest version of the remote repository before you start to contribute to this project.

Before we push files, we have to *commit* changes. Commits are actually the part where version control comes into play. Without version control, we save the document and everything that has been changed is gone. A commit tracks changes of the code and should be done consciously. Therefore, GitHub asks you to stage files and add a *commit message*. Don't worry, we need not write a novel, but the commit message should help us to understand what changed. Suppose you add a new histogram in a project, the commit message, `"Add histogram"` might be enough to understand which part of the code has been changed. In addition, GitHub gives each commit a unique label – a *secure hash algorithm* (SHA, e.g., `992bb07`) – which makes it possible to restore a repository to a certain point in time. So, keep in mind, we *stage* files by adding a *commit message*, before we *push* it to GitHub.

There is no need to make a commit every time the code changes. It all depends on the project and your sense of security. Just save your files as you would do without using GitHub. Changes appear in the GitHub repository only after you pushed the code to GitHub. GitHub has more jargon that I will not outline in detail, but you should at least know what *branches*, *forks*, *issues*, and *pull requests* are:

- Branches are an extra project line to safely develop and integrate a new feature. Suppose you want to add a feature to the project, but you are unsure if it works and the branch gives you the room to try something new. If the feature is a success, branches can be merged, but if the new feature was a failure, the main branch remains unaffected.
- Forks are interconnected repositories, for example, to examine a repository from someone else.
- Issues encompass a list of all code issues (e.g., to report a bug) of a repository. GitHub enforces cooperation between programmers and by default gives all repositories an issue page.
- Pull requests also aim to increase cooperation. Suppose you found a bug in an R package, a pull request makes it possible to copy the file of the R package, develop a solution and get in touch with the author. Pull requests facilitate this process because the author sees which commits have been made and files can be merged if the author agrees on the solution.

In conclusion, GitHub is somewhat complicated, but the discussed advantages may outweigh the initial struggle. Moreover, this paragraph only introduced the GitHub jargon, and we inspect the main steps in detail in the next section.

9.2 Install Git

Go to GitHub and create a free GitHub account. Pick a username that clearly states your name as this makes it easier for people to find your profile and work.

```
# Create a GitHub account
# https://github.com/
```

Next, install Git on your computer. Go to the website, download and install Git.

```
# Install Git on:
# https://git-scm.com/downloads
```

Git has no interface to work with, but we can check if Git runs by using the command line. RStudio has integrated the shell or – depending on your operating system – the terminal. Go to the R console in RStudio. The pane has several tabs, including the shell. Or use the toolbar (Tools > Shell) to open a new shell window. You can check if Git has been installed by inserting the Git code git --version. If Git runs, it returns the installed version.

```
#Which git version is running?
git --version
```

```
#> git version 2.30.0
```

In principle, Git is made to run via the shell. Learning Git code is an additional effort and we will use RStudio and certain R packages for the most important steps, especially to make the introduction as smooth as possible. I nevertheless provide both approaches since some Git code basics may have a larger impact in case you run into an error.

Before we can work with GitHub, you must introduce yourself by giving Git your name and email address. Make sure that you use the same name and email address as your GitHub account. If you are still in the shell, you can introduce yourself with the following Git code:

```
#Introduce yourself: name and email
git config --global user.name "User Name"
git config --global user.email "email@address.com"
```

To check if the last step worked, ask Git to list the global settings. In my case, the shell returns my email address, my username, and further cryptic global settings.

```
#List global settings
git config --global --list
```

```
#> user.email=edgar.treischl@MyProviderName.com
#> user.name=edgar-treischl
#> filter.lfs.clean=git-lfs clean -- %f
#> filter.lfs.smudge=git-lfs smudge -- %f
```

```
#> filter.lfs.process=git-lfs filter-process
#> filter.lfs.required=true
```

With respect to R, the gh package (Bryan & Wickham, 2022) and the usethis package (Wickham, Bryan, et al., 2022) have functions to configure and work with GitHub. For example, the use_git_config() function lets you introduce yourself with R, instead of using the shell.

```
# Introduce yourself with R
library(usethis)
use_git_config(
  user.name = "Jane Doe",
  user.email = "jane@example.org"
)
```

The same applies to further Git commands. For example, the next console illustrates the Git code to add a new file, to commit a message, and to push it to a repository. The next code only illustrates the principle.

```
#How to push code via the shell:
#Add a new_file
git add new_file.txt
#Add commit message
git commit --message "I finally add new_file"
#And puuuush....
git push
```

You may use the shell to add a file, make a commit, and push, but Git clients include those features. There are several Git clients available to interact with GitHub (e.g., GitHub Desktop, GitKraken). Instead of focusing on Git commands, let us explore the advantages of a Git client. In the next section we explore how RStudio has integrated Git in detail, but the GitHub Desktop (or other clients) might be an option to consider if you need to manage your files outside of RStudio. GitHub Desktop is free of charge and Figure 9.2 shows a screenshot of it.

A Git client provides many functions to work with GitHub. I'd say the most important one is that it gives us a graphical interface which makes it more convenient to work with GitHub, especially in the beginning. For example, GitHub Desktop automatically checks the version of a file and it shows graphically if you can push or pull code. The RStudio Git pane has those functions integrated, but you may want to download an additional client when you work with GitHub on a regular basis. In the beginning it might not be necessary to use an additional client, but keep in mind that several Git clients exist. Instead of exploring additional features of GitHub Desktop, we connect RStudio with your GitHub account in the next step and I show in detail how they work together.

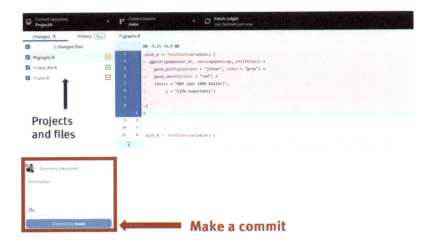

Fig. 9.2: GitHub Desktop

9.3 GitHub and RStudio

Let's connect RStudio with your GitHub account. There are several ways, but I will show you only how a *personal access token* (PAT) works, since this is a convenient way to establish the connection. Instead of a password, a token (long text string) will be used to connect your account.

Go to the GitHub website and sign in. The usethis package will show you where you can create a PAT, but first you need to sign in for this purpose. Next, switch back to RStudio and run the create_github_token() function. It opens the GitHub website and shows you the page where the token can be created.

```
# Go to the GitHub website to create a token:
# https://github.com/settings/tokens
usethis::create_github_token()
```

Essentially, the function points you to the *Developer settings* of your GitHub account; there we are able to create a PAT. The function also picks some recommended scopes to create a PAT. For example, it inserts a note that describes the purpose of the PAT. These options are not very important in the beginning; stick to the default values and create the PAT. Scroll down the page, create the PAT, and most importantly, copy your token.

After you have copied the token, run the `gitcreds_set()` function from the gitcreds package (Csárdi, 2022). The function will ask for the token and connect RStudio with your GitHub account.

```r
# Give RStudio your token
gitcreds::gitcreds_set()
```

Now check if RStudio is connected with your account. The `gh_whoami()` function shows who you are on GitHub.

```r
# Check who you are
gh::gh_whoami()
```

```
#> {
#>    "name": "Edgar Treischl",
#>    "login": "edgar-treischl",
#>    "html_url": "https://github.com/edgar-treischl",
#>    "scopes": "gist, repo, user, workflow",
#>    "token": "ghp_...w0sd"
#> }
```

To show you how GitHub and RStudio work together, you need to create a repository. The repository is for illustration purposes only, so don't be afraid to make mistakes. I will show you later how you can delete it. Go to the GitHub website and make a new repository via the navigation bar, or you can go the repositories tab on your GitHub profile. Figure 9.3 highlights the necessary steps to create a new repository.

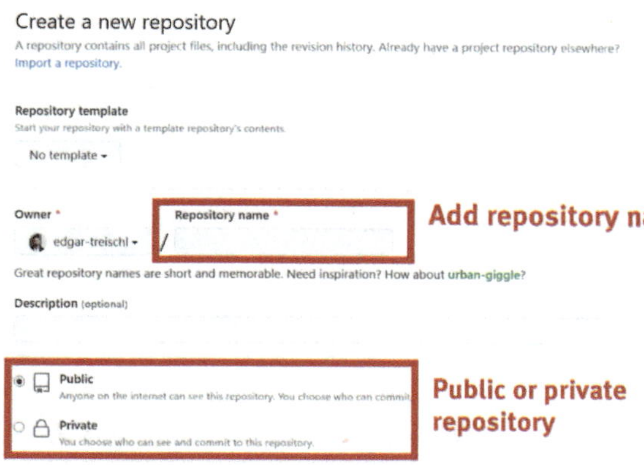

Fig. 9.3: Create a GitHub repository

The repository needs a name and we need to decide whether it shall be a public or a private repository. Create a test repository and make it public. Furthermore, GitHub asks about your opinion on several repository files:
- README file: You may initialize the repository with a README file. This gives visitors an idea what the repository contains.
- License file: You may determine under which license the work is published (e.g., creative commons license).
- gitignore file: Lists files that are not supposed to be upload to GitHub. They remain locally available, but will not show up on GitHub.

You can ignore these files and pick the default settings. They are not important for the first steps. Next, we *clone the repository* – I use this term explicitly, because it's a vital part in the GitHub universe. It implies that we copy all files from the GitHub repository and create the same folder as a local repository.

There are several ways to clone the repository. After you created your repository, GitHub displays a page with *Quick setup* instructions. Figure 9.4 shows a screen shot of this step. If you have installed GitHub Desktop, you can also use the *Setup in Desktop* button on the left side to get a local copy. Moreover, the website shows the HTTPS and SSH path to your repository. Press the copy button on the GitHub website and copy the HTTPS link.

Fig. 9.4: GitHub quick setup

We can clone a repository from the shell and the following console shows the corresponding Git code. However, RStudio's project wizard has integrated this step in a convenient way and you don't need code to clone a repository.

```
#Clone a repository from the shell
git clone https://link_to_your_project.git
```

Instead of using the shell, create a new project, pick the option *Version control*, and choose GitHub. After those steps, the project wizard opens a window in which we can insert the copied repository path, as Figure 9.5 shows for a test repository. RStudio will build the project directory name from the URL. Moreover, you should pick a directory where all your GitHub repositories will be saved before you create the project.

Fig. 9.5: Clone repository

The steps to clone a repository from GitHub can also be achieved with the usethis package (Wickham, Bryan, et al., 2022). The create_from_github() function needs the HTTPS link and a destination directory (destdir) where the repository will be saved. It will copy the files from GitHub and will create a local repository.

```
# Clone a repository with R
usethis::create_from_github(
  "https://github.com/username/repository.git",
  destdir = "~/local/path/repo/"
)
```

Once RStudio has created the project and cloned the repository, the Git pane should be visible. A restart may do the trick if the Git pane does not show up immediately as one of the RStudio panes. Alternatively, go the RStudio settings and enable version control manually, restart RStudio and open your project again.

As Figure 9.6 illustrates, RStudio integrates the most important functions to work with GitHub and I used a test repository to outline them. Use the pane to make a *Commit*, *Push* and *Pull* code, or inspect code *Differences* or the *History* of the repository. The Git pane shows you, based on colored symbols, which files in your local repository have been changed: *Modified* files (e.g., graphs.R) are marked in blue; *Deleted* files are marked in red (e.g., model.R); new files (e.g., test_file.R) are marked in yellow with a question mark, because GitHub has no history about this file. After you stage them, they are marked green and are displayed as *Added* files (e.g., new_model.R) and finally *Renamed* files are marked in purple (e.g., analysis_v77.R).

Files:	
Modified	R/graphs.R
Deleted	R/model.R
Added	R/new_model.R
Untracked	R/test_file.R
Renamed	R/analysis_v77.R -> R/analysis_final.R

Fig. 9.6: Git pane

Let's check if we can push code to GitHub. Create a new R scripts, and save it in your local repository. For now, it isn't important what the file contains; just create one to test if you can push code to GitHub. After you have created the file, go to the GitHub pane and press the commit button to see the review window. The window shows all changes between the local and the remote repository.

As Figure 9.7 depicts, we need four steps to push code to GitHub: (1) Set a check mark and stage files. As illustrated, you need to stage all files if you have worked on a real project. Press <Ctrl/Cmd> + <A> to select all files and stage them. (2) Insert a descriptive commit message. As a best practice, consider the changes you made. Here I just insert a few words to test if I can add a test file. (3) Click the *Commit* button to add the commit message. And finally, (4) push it to GitHub.

Fig. 9.7: Push with the Git pane

After we committed and pushed the code, RStudio opens a window that shows what actually happens in the background. The next console illustrates what the window may look like. It displays the path to Git, the commit message, the SHA, and – in my case – it tells us that one file has been changed. Those messages may seem cryptic in the beginning, but as long as you don't get an error message everything seems to have worked.

```
#> >>> C:/././././././Git/bin/git.exe commit -F
#> >>> C:/././././././git-commit-message-45b8696c483e.txt
#> [main 241afad] Changed X
#>
#>  1 file changed, 1 insertion(+), 1 deletion(-)
```

After you committed and pushed the code, go back to the GitHub website and inspect your repository. If everything worked, the changes should now be included in the remote repository. GitHub displays the commit message next to your username and also the time of your last push.

We created this repository only for illustration purposes. If you do not want to keep it, go to the main repository site and examine the settings. Scroll down the general settings page and you will find the possibility to change or delete a repository. Be cautious: There is no recycle bin on GitHub and you will permanently delete a repository. Moreover, keep in mind that the local repository remains untouched if you delete it on GitHub.

There is much more to learn when it comes to GitHub, at least let me outline how typical code merging conflicts can be solved and how to undo mistakes.

9.3.1 Conflicts

GitHub lets you work with other people on the same project, and you will need to pull code if someone else has changed the repository since the last time you worked on the project. Thus, pulling code from the repository should be the first step when you work on a shared project. GitHub retrieves the code and merges it with your local repository. Unfortunately, sometimes GitHub cannot merge files automatically, leading to a merging conflict. A conflict may even occur between your local and the remote repository if competing changes have been made. GitHub will throw an error message when it cannot merge two (or more) files, and we cannot push our code.

GitHub inserts conflict markers (<<<<<<<, =======, >>>>>>>) that outlines the conflict between the local and the remote repository. If you are the repository's owner, it will be up to you to decide which version of the code should be used, or how the versions should be combined. Delete the conflict markers and the code that creates the conflict.

Such merge conflicts further illustrate that there is always the chance that you will run into an error and that you cannot push or pull certain code. GitHub has a large community, and therefore, you will find many solutions for typical problems on the web. For example, consider the *GitHub Docs* website which has a dedicated page about merge conflicts and gives a broader overview if you run into an error.

290 —— 9 GitHub

```
# GitHub Docs:
# https://docs.github.com/en
```

The git_sitrep() function from the usethis package returns a situation report on your current Git/GitHub status and the latter also reveals hints on what might be the problem. I also ran into an error while I wrote this chapter. As the next console illustrates, I needed to renew my token. For security reasons, tokens are only valid for a limited time.

```
# Get a situation report on your current Git/GitHub status
usethis::git_sitrep()
#> * GitHub user: 'edgar-treischl'
#> * Token scopes: 'gist, repo, workflow'
#> x Token lacks recommended scopes:
#>   - 'user:email': needed to read user's email addresses
#>   Consider re-creating your PAT with the missing scopes.
#>   `create_GitHub_token()` defaults to the recommended scopes.
#> x Can't retrieve registered email addresses from GitHub.
#>   Consider re-creating your PAT with the 'user' or at least 'user:email'
```

9.3.2 Undo mistakes

GitHub keeps track of code and makes it possible to travel back in time. As we saw, GitHub marks code differences, which is the main distinction to other version control systems. Each time you make a commit and push, GitHub takes a snapshot of the repository. We did not yet change much, but once you start working with GitHub on a regular basis, you can inspect changes between the local and the remote repository in the differences (diff) window of the git pane. In the same sense, git status returns the actual status and git diff returns differences between your local and the remote repository.

```
#Inspect status and differences
git status
git diff
```

Furthermore, go to the Git pane and press the *History* button. RStudio has integrated the commit history and shows changes, as Figure 9.8 highlights. All commits are shown in the header, and you can inspect what happened to the code if you choose a commit from that list. It shows the subject, the author, the date, and the SHA of the commit.

RStudio shows a link to the file on the right side. This makes it convenient to travel back in time. Just click *View file* to revisit the code at that particular point in time. In addition, you may also use the secure hash algorithm to reset your repository, but be cautious, because you may loose information. It's certainly good to know that such possibilities exist, but it remains safer to inspect an old file than to make a (hard) reset.

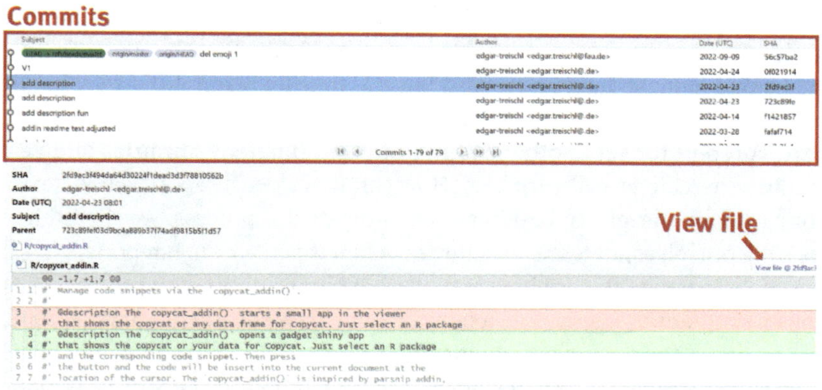

Fig. 9.8: Track changes of code

Summary

This chapter gave a brief and non-technical introduction to GitHub, especially to emphasize that GitHub is a valuable tool for applied (social science) research. GitHub helps us to increase the reproducibility of our research, it facilitates cooperation by allowing people to simultaneously work on a project, and GitHub keeps track of code changes.

This chapter does not intend to give you a comprehensive overview of all GitHub functions, instead the aim is humbler for a good reason. Consider *Pro Git* by Chacon & Straub (2014) if you want to increase your Git skills.

```
# Pro Git
show_link("pro-git")
```

The book explains everything you need to know about Git in a mere 519 pages, which is why I did not even try to give you a comprehensive overview in this chapter. Instead, I emphasized the advantages of GitHub. I tried to make the entry into the GitHub world as informal as possible and I outlined the workaround with RStudio. Keep in mind that you don't need to become a GitHub expert in order to get the advantages of a version control system.

10 Automate work

Suppose somebody asks you to analyze how life expectancy has developed in Belgium and you should summarize the results in a report. The data includes many countries, so you apply a filter and create tables and graphs specifically for the report. The next day, you get asked to make the same report, but this time for Spain. No big deal, right? You make a copy of the document, adjust the filter, and change the text. But what comes next? A report for yet another country or year? Different countries and years are placeholders of categorical variables. How can we create a report that is flexible enough for each group level? And how can we automate this process. We should try to avoid repeating ourselves, in terms of code and when we create such reports.

In this chapter, you will learn how to make a dynamic report with rmarkdown. We will create a document that serves as a template to create several documents on the fly. For this purpose, the document includes a parameter (e.g., country name), which makes it possible to recreate the same document for a different country, year, or any other parameter as needed. All we must do is change the parameter and recreate the document.

Talking about dynamic documents sounds like I try to encourage you to be lazy, but there is a good reason why I introduce this topic. There are better ways to use your limited time and resources. Changing a few lines of code is fine, but creating the same document repeatedly is a waste of time. A dynamic report not only reduces the workload, the work also becomes less error-prone when we automate the creation steps. Thus, the main objective of this chapter is to create a dynamic report, learn more about automation, and avoiding the need to repeat ourselves.

- In Section 10.1, we create a dynamic document and learn how to automate the process. Based on an example analysis with the palmerpenguins, we learn how to include parameters and update the document. Furthermore, there is a lot of room for improvements when many documents are created. Our time is too precious to manually render each document or give each file a unique name. Let R do the work for you.
- In Section 10.2, we create text for the document. Say the report contains a description of the data and a few sentences that outline the main findings for each country. Unfortunately, R cannot write the entire text, but there are several packages that help us to automatically describe the data or the report's statistical findings.
- In Section 10.3, we use R to send reports via email. After we have finished the document, we may send it to another person. If we can automate creating the documents, why should we now manually send it? There is no need for a copy and paste approach. Even if we are not supposed to send the reports via email, we gain further insights in functional programming in this last step.

https://doi.org/10.1515/9783110704976-010

As always, the `PracticeR` package gives you access to the source code, but in this chapter we develop functions to create documents; and we improve them step by step. For this reason, I created a GitHub repository (`penguins_report`) with a clean, final version of the code. The files contain all steps to create and send documents automatically. Thus, the repository may help in case you run into any error. Download the files from my GitHub account or use the `create_from_github()` function from the `usethis` package to clone the repository. In addition, the next console shows also the packages for Chapter 10.

```r
# Get the link to the repository
penguins_report <- PracticeR::show_link("penguins_report",
  browse = FALSE
)
```

```r
# Clone the GitHub repository of this chapter:
usethis::create_from_github(penguins_report,
  destdir = "~/path/to/your/local/folder/"
)
```

```r
# Setup of Chapter 10 #####
library(beepr)
library(blastula)
library(correlation)
library(dplyr)
library(effectsize)
library(flextable)
library(ggplot2)
library(glue)
library(here)
library(palmerpenguins)
library(purrr)
library(PracticeR)
library(report)
library(tibble)
library(tidyr)
```

10.1 Reports

To create a dynamic report, we first need an example analysis. In this chapter I use the `penguins` data from the `palmerpenguins` package to illustrate how to automate a report, but the focus does not lie on the data or the analysis (Horst et al., 2022). The `penguins` data has observations for three different years, as the `distinct()` function and the next console reveals (Wickham, François, et al., 2022). Let's pretend that the report includes several tables and graphs based on the `penguins` data, but for the report we need observations from the `year` 2007 only.

```
# How many distinct years has the penguins data?
dplyr::distinct(penguins, year)
```

```
#> # A tibble: 3 x 1
#>     year
#>    <int>
#> 1   2007
#> 2   2008
#> 3   2009
```

Consider the next console. It displays the code to create a scatter plot and examines how `bill_length_mm` and `body_mass_g` are related. Irrespective of the variables and steps to prepare the data, we use a `filter()` to restrict the data for a specific year and we create a scatter plot with the `ggplot2` package.

```
# An example scatter plot
penguins |>
    filter(year == 2007) |> # here comes the filter
    ggplot(aes(bill_length_mm, body_mass_g, color = species)) +
    geom_point() +
    ggtitle("2007")
```

In the next section we make a dynamic document based on this code snippet. The `rmarkdown` package lets us define parameters (e.g., `year`) and makes it possible to create a document for each level of the parameter with the same template. Our code remains almost untouched; we only change the parameters.

10.1.1 Parameters

The next console shows the meta section (YAML) of a corresponding `rmarkdown` document. If we include the parameters (`params`) field, it allows us to render a document with different values of the parameter. Do not forget the indentation if you try this on your own.

```
---
title: "Dynamic Reports"
author: "Edgar"
output: pdf_document
params:
  year: 2007
---
```

By including `params` in the meta section, we can define and then refer to default values in the document. Actually, I inserted the same `params` fields in the `rmarkdown` document of this chapter of the book. Look what `params$year` returns if I insert it in the console. It returns the value of the `params`. If I change the default value in the YAML to `2008`, `params$year` will return `2008`.

```
# The default value of params$year is:
params$year
```

```
#> [1] 2007
```

Examine the code for the scatter plot from the beginning again. If we insert `params$year` inside the `filter()` function, we are able to refer to `params$year` to create the plot. Moreover, I included the parameter in the `ggtitle()` function, which makes it a bit easier to check which group level is used. The rest of the code remains the same.

```
# Insert a parameter to filter the data
penguins |>
  filter(year == params$year) |> # insert the params
  ggplot(aes(bill_length_mm, body_mass_g, color = species)) +
  geom_point() +
  ggtitle(params$year)
```

Suppose the report contains several graphs. To create the report for a different year (value), we need to change the default value of the `params` in the YAML and then render the document again. All graphs get an update and we must not change the code in the rest of the document.

We can create dynamic tables as well. Suppose we want to make a table that displays the body mass for each species. Insert the `params` in the data preparation step and the table will get an update when we change the `year`. First, I create the output for a table that includes the `params` field; and as second step, `flextable()` returns the output as a table.

```r
# Create output of the table
df <- penguins |>
  filter(year == params$year) |>
  group_by(species) |>
  drop_na() |>
  summarise(`body mass` = round(mean(body_mass_g), 1))

# Create a table
df |> flextable()
```

species	body mass
Adelie	3714.2
Chinstrap	3694.2
Gentoo	5100.0

Use your time to improve the document, not for creating the same document over and over again. For example, create dynamic tables for your purpose with the `flextable` package (Gohel & Skintzos, 2022). Since we reduce the effort by automating the reporting process, we may spend more time to create tables or other content that improves the final document. As the next console shows, I created a table that shows several plots for each species. It is just an example to underline that the `flextable`, the `reactable` (Lin, 2022) and other R packages to create tables offer much more possibilities to make and improve tables. The next example is made with the `kableExtra` package (Zhu, 2021).

```r
# Do some fancy stuff instead of boring repetitions
# This code may not work ;)
df |> fancy_stuff()
```

Species	Mean	Boxplot	Histogram	Lineplot
Adelie	3706.16			
Chinstrap	3733.09			
Gentoo	5092.44			

Notice, we can include a data set and variable names as parameter in the YAML:

```
---
params:
  year: 2007
  data: penguins
  x: body_mass_g
  y: flipper_length_mm
---
```

Technically it is not necessary, but we are able to run the document with a different data frame if we include the name of the data. Consider the `get()` function. It returns the data insert by the `data` parameter.

```
# Get returns the values of the object
df <- get(params$data)
glimpse(df)
```

```
#> Rows: 344
#> Columns: 8
#> $ species           <fct> Adelie, Adelie, Adelie, Adelie, ~
#> $ island            <fct> Torgersen, Torgersen, Torgersen,~
#> $ bill_length_mm    <dbl> 39.1, 39.5, 40.3, NA, 36.7, 39.3~
#> $ bill_depth_mm     <dbl> 18.7, 17.4, 18.0, NA, 19.3, 20.6~
#> $ flipper_length_mm <int> 181, 186, 195, NA, 193, 190, 181~
#> $ body_mass_g       <int> 3750, 3800, 3250, NA, 3450, 3650~
#> $ sex               <fct> male, female, female, NA, female~
#> $ year              <int> 2007, 2007, 2007, 2007, 2007, 20~
```

A parameter only returns the default value. Keep that in mind when you include independent and dependent variables as parameters. For example, I included the `body_mass_g` and the `flipper_length_mm` (as x and y parameter) variables in the document of this chapter. Parameters return their default values and consequently text strings in case of variable names. This is the reason why we cannot apply a function such as cor(), since it needs a numerical input.

```r
# Keep in mind what a param returns
class(params$x)
```

```r
#> [1] "character"
```

```r
# The cor function needs a numerical input
cor(params$x, params$y)
#> Error in cor(params$x, params$y) : 'x' must be numeric
```

Hence, we need a different approach when we include variable names instead of levels. For example, the correlation package lets us pick variables as text stings (Makowski, Wiernik, et al., 2022).

```r
# The correlation function let us select variable as strings
cor_xy <- penguins |>
  correlation(select = params$x, select2 = params$y)

cor_xy
```

```r
#> # Correlation Matrix (pearson-method)
#>
#> Parameter1       |  Parameter2 |    r |        95% CI |t(340) |        p
#> -----------------------------------------------------------------------
#> flipper_length_mm | body_mass_g | 0.87 | [0.84, 0.89] | 32.72 |< .001***
```

```r
#> p-value adjustment method: Holm (1979)
#> Observations: 342
```

Or consider the aes_string() function from the ggplot2 package. It lets us work with text strings instead of variables. Insert the params in the function to render a scatter plot for the examined variables.

```r
#Insert params via the aes_string function
ggplot(penguins, aes_string(x = params$x,
                            y = params$y)) +
  geom_point()
```

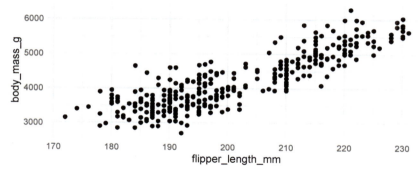

Finally, suppose we wanted to run a (linear) model with parameters. We need to create a formula (f) with the params, but since they return text strings, we need the as.formula() function. The latter converts the text stings as a formula. As the next console outlines, we first create text strings with the help of the paste() function before we can apply the formula. The paste() function combines strings and separates them with a blank space as default, the collapse option collapses two or more strings to one, while the sep option let us determine how the strings are separated.

```
# The as.formula function understands the input as a formula
f <- as.formula(
  paste(params$y,
    paste(c(params$x, params$z), collapse = " + "),
    sep = " ~ "
  )
)
print(f)

#> body_mass_g ~ flipper_length_mm + bill_length_mm
```

The object f is only the formula for the model, but we can insert it in the lm() function to run a model with those parameters. Now, even the model gets an update when we pick different parameters.

```
# Run the model with params
model <- lm(f, data = penguins)
model

#>
#> Call:
#> lm(formula = f, data = penguins)
#>
```

```
#> Coefficients:
#>     (Intercept)   flipper_length_mm      bill_length_mm
#>       -5736.897              48.145               6.047
```

The discussed approach still includes a lot of repetitive work, especially if many documents are needed. For example, we must give each document a unique name when we render it manually. A boring task, but a good example to further explore how we can automation such steps.

10.1.2 Automate the report

RStudio has integrated an interactive user interface to knit a document with parameters. Click on the arrow next to the *Knit* button, pick *Knit with parameters* and a menu shows up that lets you enter values before the document is rendered. Figure 10.1 shows a screenshot of the interface.

Fig. 10.1: Interactive interface to knit documents

If we tweak the YAML in the template, we are even able to include predefined choices for a drop-down menu to pick values. The next console shows the code that makes the interactive user interface a bit more user friendly. You can give each params a text label, a default value, define an input selector, and predefined choices become available in the drop-down menu.

```
params:
  data: penguins
  year:
    label: "Year"
    value: 2007
    input: select
    choices: [2007, 2008, 2009]
```

This is a pretty cool feature to create one document, but it illustrates that many manual steps are needed to create several documents on the fly. In order to automate a report, we need to change the default value(s) in the meta section, but there is no need to touch the document or the menu. Use the `render()` function from `rmarkdown` to create a new document and include the values of the `params` as a list. The `render` function needs an Rmd file (here a template) and values for the included `params`.

```
# rmarkdown::render knits/renders the document
rmarkdown::render(
  "template.Rmd",
  params = list(year = 2007)
)
```

To further automate this process, we may adjust several options. First, add the `clean` option in the case of PDF files (`pdf_document`). As outlined in Chapter 8, Pandoc runs in the background and creates several Markdown and LaTeX files. Set the `clean` option to `TRUE` and all files that are only necessary to create the output will be discarded after the PDF file is rendered. Furthermore, we should give each document a unique name with the `output_file` option. It expects a text string (e.g., `report`) as file name:

```
# The clean and output_file option
rmarkdown::render(
  "template.Rmd",
  "pdf_document",
  clean = TRUE,
  output_file = "report",
  params = list(year = 2007)
)
```

If we create a document for each year, all documents should have a distinct name that we can include as a vector in the `render()` function. As long as we create a small number of reports, we could make a vector manually. However, recall that the `pull()` function pulls a vector and we can combine it with the `distinct()` function. We get a vector with each distinct year to build unique file names.

```
# Create a vector with unique years
years <- distinct(penguins, year) |>
  pull(year)

years
```

```
#> [1] 2007 2008 2009
```

Next, we create a second vector with the file names. We need a string that starts with the distinct name of each group, the document name (e.g., _report), and the file extension. As the following example outlines, we may use the paste0() function to create a file name for each year:[1]

```
# The paste function pastes strings together
paste0(years, "_report.pdf")
```

```
#> [1] "2007_report.pdf" "2008_report.pdf" "2009_report.pdf"
```

We insert paste0() into the render() function; when we now render the reports in the same order as the vector, each document will get an unique name.

```
# This code does not yet work, but give the output_file a unique label
rmarkdown::render(
  "template.Rmd",
  "pdf_document",
  output_file = paste0(year, "_report.pdf"),
  clean = TRUE,
  params = list(year = year)
)
```

Unfortunately, the code of the last console is not yet working, since we still need to define for which year the document should be created. In the last code, year is a placeholder to create the output_file and in the params list. Create a function (e.g., render_report) to make the report for a certain year and include the discussed steps. The function needs only a year as input, it searches for the template in the working directory, and renders the document for a specific year.

```
# Create a function to render the report
render_report <- function(year) {
  rmarkdown::render(
    "template.Rmd",
    "pdf_document",
    output_file = paste0(year, "_report.pdf"),
    clean = TRUE,
```

---

1 The paste() and the paste0() function do essentially the same, but the latter without inserting a separator.

```r
    params = list(year = year)
  )
}
```

In terms of work efficiency, we should save all reports and templates in corresponding folders. The here package is useful in this situation (Müller, 2020). With the help of the latter, we can determine where our template lives or where our reports should be saved without the hassle of having to adjust the working directory manually. The here() function returns the working directory.

```r
# here helps you to set the directory
here::here()
```

```r
#> [1] "/Users/Edgar/Practice R/Chapters/10_Automation"
```

Now we can build a relative file path to refer to the template and to save the rendered documents in a specific folder. The next time we start over, we can build a report even for a different project as long as the folders exist. Suppose all reports shall be saved in a folder called report_files. Insert the name inside the here() function to build a relative path.

```r
# Create relative file paths
here("report_files")
```

```r
#> [1] "/Users/Edgar/Practice R/Chapters/10_Automation/report_files"
```

It doesn't matter anymore in which project folder the script is stored, the code runs smoothly as long as the corresponding folder exists in the project. As the next console shows, I included the here() function within the setwd() function twice. First, I adjust the working directory to search for the template.Rmd in the Rmds folder. After the report is rendered, the report will be saved in the report_files folder as the output directory (output_dir).

```r
# Render the document for each continent
render_report <- function(year) {
  setwd(here("Rmds")) # here is the template
  rmarkdown::render(
    "template.Rmd", "pdf_document",
    output_file = paste0(year, "_report.pdf"),
    output_dir = here::here("report_files"), # here will be the result
```

```r
    clean = TRUE,
    params = list(year = year)
  )
}
```

A function helps us a lot in making reports, but depending on the number of reports, the code is quite repetitive. Shall we run the `render_report()` function several times to create all documents? This is bothersome and repetitive, since we must call the function for each year. There are different approaches to render several documents in a row, including a very simple solution I have yet to introduce. A *for loop* lets us create the documents for all years. Loops iterate and repeat code several times for each element. Consider the next console: The loop prints each element i of the sequence from 1 to 3.

```r
# For loops: Loop through a task
for (i in 1:3) {
  print(i)
}
```

```r
#> [1] 1
#> [1] 2
#> [1] 3
```

We can use this principle to render several documents. Remember, we already have a vector with distinct values (`years`) and we use this to render the document for each year. More specifically, we apply the `render_report()` function for each `year` in `years`.

```r
# Apply render_report for each year
for (year in years) {
  render_report(year)
}
```

Depending on the number of reports, the loop takes some time. If you do not want to wait until R has finished this job (or other time consuming tasks), consider the `beepr` package (Bååth, 2018). The `beep()` function plays a sound as soon as the job is done.

```r
#The beepr package informs you if the job is done:
for(year in years) {
  render_report(year)
};beepr::beep("ping") #pinnnng ;)
```

Loops are fine if there is only one parameter involved, but what shall we do if we create a document for different years and countries? We may loop through two variables, but such nested loops become ugly and hard to read. In Section 10.3, we will learn how to avoid such loops and apply a function several times.

Before we move on, can you still remember what we have done in Chapter 2? We created a simple `mean` function to illustrate how functions works. Look where you are standing now, you created a function to achieve a specific goal. Maybe you did not realize it, but you could further improve the function and create an R package that makes your functions available. Imagine, you start R and could load your own package. Package development is a bit trickier, but it might be worth the trouble. The next section introduces automated texts for the report, but consider reading first the next info box. It outlines in detail why you should at least think about an R package to make your work easily accessible.

R Package Development   **i**

An info box about package development probably comes as a surprise. This book only introduces R and even though R packages extend the possibilities, developing them can be complicated. At the same time, an R package can also be perceived as the ultimate goal to automate work processes. Suppose you created several functions in order to create and send the report and all functions live in an R script in your project folder. If you stick them all together in an R package with some effort in terms of package development, other people and your future-self get access to those functions.

An R package might be a good idea even if you don't plan to share your code. The creation an R package forces us to consider how to make our work reusable and reproducible. It lets us think about what the code should achieve even if we change some of the current working parameters. Thus, don't think of giant R packages (e.g., `ggplot2 dplyr`) when it comes to package development. An R package may only contain functions that you apply on a regular basis, tailored to your specific needs and suited for your repetitive tasks.

For example, consider the `PracticeR` package again. The latter lives only on my GitHub account and I decided against publishing it on CRAN since it only accompanies the book. Keeping it on my GitHub account gives me the freedom to update it each time the R landscape changes or when I find an error. I introduced GitHub in Chapter 9, not only for this purpose, but because you can do the same for your own package and give people access to your code.

This info box does not try to introduce package development; however, it tries to convince you that package development is not as complicated as it may seem, especially not if you don't have any intentions to publish it (on CRAN). RStudio and several packages provide an excellent infrastructure to create a package. Consider reading *R Packages: Organize, Test, Document and Share Your Code* by Hadely Wickham (2015). The book outlines in ample detail how to make your work reproducible and reusable.

```
#R Packages:
show_link("r_packages")
```

10.2 Text

Maybe you did not expect a section about automated text, because the creation of text seems complicated. True, R cannot write the document, but we are able to create fragments of text with the `report` package. The latter returns texts to describe objects, for example, text for the descriptive statistics or the parameters of a model (Makowski, Lüdecke, et al., 2022). In a similar way, the `effectsize` package interprets effects and we may use it to build our own report functions (Ben-Shachar et al., 2022).

Let's start with a few simple sentences to show you how text from the console can be included in the `rmarkdown` document. Suppose we describe the `species` variable of the `penguins` data, and we want report how often a species appears. We could combine insights from the last section and use `params` in order to create texts, but it is not necessary to understand how it works.

For this reason, I assigned an object (`param_specie`) instead of using parameters. The code also becomes clearer if we see the assigned value of a parameter in the output. In order to create a sentence, we need to count how often a species like `Adelie` appears.

```r
# Calculate the number for params$species: Adelie
param_specie <- "Adelie"
number <- penguins |>
  filter(species == param_specie) |>
  summarise(number = n()) |>
  pull(number)

number

#> [1] 152
```

Next, we combine the text, the parameter (`param_specie`), and the `number`. Like the `paste()` function, the `glue` package has convenient functions to paste strings (Hester & Bryan, 2022). As the next console shows, just glue a string together. Refer to objects (or a parameter) within braces (`{}`) and build a sentence.

```r
# Glue them together
glue::glue("- We observed {param_specie} {number} times.")

#> - We observed Adelie 152 times.
```

How can we include the output of the (last) console in a document? The `results` chunk option lets us determine how the results are handled in an `rmarkdown` document. Add the chunk option and set it to `asis`. By adjusting the chunk option, the result of the console is interpreted *as it is*.

```
```{r, results='asis'}
#Glue them together with the chunk-option: results = 'asis'
glue("- We observed {param_specie} {number} times.")
```
```

The `glue` function returns a character vector which will be rendered as text in the document if we adjust the `results` option. Thus, the next time you render the document for a different species, the text will update automatically. The next console shows how the last console will be interpreted if the `results` option is set to `asis`.

```
# Glue them together with the chunk-option: results = 'asis'
glue("- We observed {param_specie} {number} times.")
```

—   We observed Adelie 152 times.

We may build longer sentences or include different statistics, but the principle to build such static sentences remains the same. Maybe this feels like a machine is talking to you. We could improve the sentences and pick some affirmative or negative words randomly for more variation. Such a procedure can be a good start to automate text for a report, but it would take a lot of time and effort to create customized solutions, especially when we know that R packages are available to generate standard texts automatically. The following subsection highlights functions from the `report` and the `effectsize` packages to create automated texts that describe data, effects, and models.

10.2.1 Describe data

Add a description of the data if the document contains an empirical analysis. Our readers need information about the data and examined variables before the empirical findings are presented. The `report()` function helps us with this task. It uses all variables, counts levels, and estimates statistics to describe the data. Use the `report()` function in combination with the `summary()` function, which returns a (shorter) summary text.

```
# Describe the data
report::report(penguins) |>
  summary()
```

```
#>The data contains 344 observations of the following 8 variables:
#>
```

```
#>- species: 3 levels, namely Adelie (n = 152), Chinstrap (n = 68) ...
#>- island: 3 levels, namely Biscoe (n = 168), Dream (n = 124) and ...
#>- bill_length_mm: Mean = 43.92, SD = 5.46, range: [32.10, 59.60],...
#>- bill_depth_mm: Mean = 17.15, SD = 1.97, range: [13.10, 21.50], ...
#>- flipper_length_mm: Mean = 200.92, SD = 14.06, range: [172, 231]...
#>- body_mass_g: Mean = 4201.75, SD = 801.95, range: [2700, 6300], ...
#>- sex: 2 levels, namely female (n = 165), male (n = 168) and ...
#>- year: Mean = 2008.03, SD = 0.82, range: [2007, 2009]
```

In addition, the report_participants() function returns typical information about the characteristics of a sample, such as age, sex, or education. The penguins data does not include most of these variables, but the report package provides a code snippet to create a data frame that illustrates the function. In a nutshell, the report_participants() function only needs the corresponding column names.

```
# Create a small data frame
df <- data.frame(
  "Age" = c(22, 23, 54, 21, 8, 42),
  "Sex" = c("F", "F", "M", "M", "M", "F"),
  "Education" = c(
    "Bachelor", "PhD", "Highschool",
    "Highschool", "Bachelor", "Bachelor"
  )
)
```

```
# Describe the participants
report_participants(df,
  age = "Age",
  sex = "Sex",
  education = "Education"
)
```

```
#> [1] "6 participants (Mean age = 28.3, SD = 16.6, range: [8, 54];
#> Sex: 50.0% females, 50.0% males, 0.0% other; Education: Bachelor,
#> 50.00%; Highschool, 33.33%; PhD, 16.67%)"
```

Of course, we may apply our R skills to further tweak these sentences to our purpose, but compared to the simple sentences from the start, the report package conveniently generates descriptive texts about the data. However, we did not purposefully build these sentences manually to learn how it works, but to describe effects.

10.2.2 Describe effects

Suppose we examine the association of two variables, and we make an automated report for a lot of countries. Certainly, the examined effect depends on the observed countries. For this reason, we want to create scatter plots that depict the variables and describe the effect with a sentence. For example, Figure 10.2 shows a scatter plot which displays the effect of bill length (bill_length_mm) on body mass (body_mass_g). I included a text box with the interpretation of the effect, it includes the effect size, direction, and the correlation coefficient. How can we build such sentences? And if we automate our document, how do we get an update of the text? First, I estimate the correlation (corr_estimate) with the correlation package.

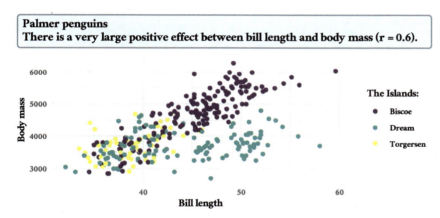

Fig. 10.2: An automated scatter plot

```
# Calculate the correlation between param X and Y
x <- "bill_length_mm"
y <- "body_mass_g"

corr_estimate <- penguins |>
  correlation(select = x, select2 = y)

corr_estimate$r

#> [1] 0.5951098
```

Next, we use the effectsize package to get an interpretation of the effect. The interpret_r() function returns the effect size for the correlation.

310 —— 10 Automate work

```r
# The interpret_r function interprets the effect
effect <- interpret_r(corr_estimate$r, rules = "cohen1988")
effect

#> [1] "large"
#> (Rules: cohen1988)
```

After we have estimated the correlation, extract the coefficient, round it, and save the results (r_xy). To build the sentence with these values, combine the objects and the text with glue().

```r
# Round() the calculation for the text
r_xy <- round(corr_estimate$r, 2)

# Glue() them together
cor_sentence <- glue("There is a {effect} effect between {x} and {y}.
                      (r = {r_xy}).")

cor_sentence

#> There is a large effect between bill_length_mm and body_mass_g.
#> (r = 0.6).
```

To get more variation, we may determine if the effect is positive or negative. As the next console shows, I assign a string (direction) as a placeholder. Next, if() checks if the estimated correlation is smaller than zero and replaces the string if the condition is fulfilled.

```r
# Check if effect is positive/negative
direction <- "positive"

if (r_xy < 0) {
  direction <- "negative"
}
```

Now we can combine all steps and build a function (report_correlation) that returns the sentence. The function needs data and two numerical variables to run.

```r
# Bring all steps together:
report_correlation <- function(data, x, y) {
  corr_estimate <- data |>
```

```
  correlation(select = x, select2 = y)
r_xy <- interpret_r(corr_estimate$r)
r_round <- round(corr_estimate$r, 2)

direction <- "positive"

if (r_round < 0) {
  direction <- "negative"
}

cor_sentence <- glue("There is a {r_xy} {direction} effect
                      between {x} and {y} (r = {r_round}).")
return(cor_sentence)
}
```

We should use a different data set to test whether the function works. Built-in data sets are clean and made for teaching purposes, and therefore not the best choice to test a function, but we can try our first report function with it anyway.

```
# Does the function work?
report_correlation(
  data = iris,
  x = "Sepal.Length",
  y = "Sepal.Width"
)
```

```
#> There is a small negative effect between Sepal.Length and Sepal.Width
#> (r = -0.12).
```

The correlation package returns more information than Pearson's r. Feel free to include t-statistics, confidence intervals (CI), or the number of observations in your function.

```
# t-statistic
corr_estimate$t
```

```
#> [1] 13.6544
```

```
# Confidence intervals: CI_low and CI_high
corr_estimate$CI_low
```

```
#> [1] 0.522004
```

```
# Number of observations
corr_estimate$n_Obs
```

```
#> [1] 342
```

10.2.3 Describe models

Finally, we can use the `report` package to describe different types of models. Consider a linear regression `model` as an example.

```
# An example model
model <- lm(body_mass_g ~ flipper_length_mm, data = penguins)
```

The `report_model()` function returns a description of the estimated model and the `report_performance()` function does the same for the performance of the model.

```
# What kind of model do we have?
report_model(model)
```

```
#> linear model (estimated using OLS) to predict body_mass_g with
#> flipper_length_mm (formula: body_mass_g ~ flipper_length_mm)
```

```
# What about the performance?
report_performance(model)
```

```
#> The model explains a statistically significant and substantial
#> proportion of variance (R2 = 0.76, F(1, 340) = 1070.74, p < .001,
#> adj. R2 = 0.76)
```

The report package offers more functions: use it to report findings of a general linear model (e.g., logistic regression), mixed models, or just for a t-test. For example, the `t.test()` function runs a one and two sample t-test and the `report` package returns an interpretation.

```
# Report package returns reports for several procedures
# t-test:
penguins_ttest <- t.test(penguins$body_mass_g ~ penguins$sex)
report(penguins_ttest)
```

```
#> Effect sizes were labelled following Cohen's (1988) recommendations.
#>
#> The Welch Two Sample t-test testing the difference of penguins$body_mass_g
#> by penguins$sex (mean in group female = 3862.27; male = 4545.68)
#> suggests that the effect is negative, statistically significant, and
#> large (difference = -683.41, 95% CI [-840.58, -526.25], t(323.90) = -8.55,
#> p < .001; Cohen's d = -0.94, 95% CI [-1.16, -0.71])
```

Of course, it takes more time and effort to finalize the report, but the discussed functions help us to provide text. What shall we do if we have rendered all files? If you normally send the reports via email, consider using R to send them automatically.

10.3 Emails

There are several packages to send emails with R, but the blastula package even makes it possible to create HTML formatted emails (Iannone & Cheng, 2020). None of your (future) receivers will question that you did not use a regular email software.

To work with blastula, we need to compose an email first. As the next console shows, the corresponding compose_email() function expects you to deliver the content, i.e. the body of the mail. The blastula package creates an HTML version of the email and shows a preview in the viewer pane when you call the object (email) once more. Figure 10.3 shows a screenshot of an email.

```
# Create/Compose a (first) mail
email <- blastula::compose_email(
  body = "Hello,
  I just wanted to give you an update of our work.
  Cheers, Edgar"
)

email
```

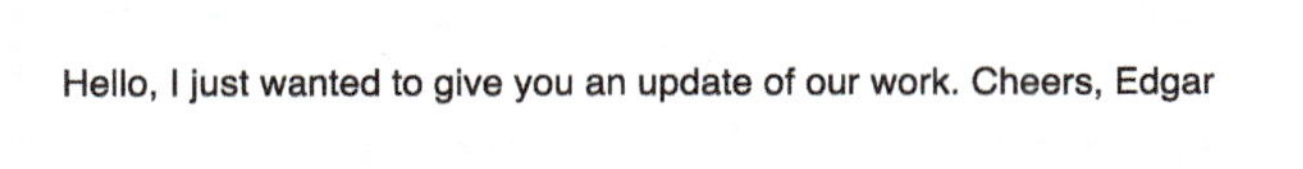

Hello, I just wanted to give you an update of our work. Cheers, Edgar

Fig. 10.3: Preview of an email

Of course, this is only a test email. We first need to learn how to send an email before we can improve the content. In order to send emails, you need to provide the *credentials* for your SMTP (simple mail transfer protocol). Email software use the latter to connect with the mail server and to authorize the request. The package provides a convenient solution if you are using a Gmail account. As the next console illustrates, use the `create_smtp_creds_key()` function and insert your email address. The function stores the credentials in the system key value and returns a prompt that asks for your password.

```
# For a gmail user only
# create_smtp_creds_key creates a system key-value

create_smtp_creds_key(
  id = "gmail",
  user = "user_name@gmail.com",
  provider = "gmail"
)
```

If you use a different email provider, you will have to provide more details for your email account. The `create_smtp_creds_file()` function creates a JSON credential file in your working directory with the necessary information to connect with the SMTP server. It contains information about the email account (e.g., `username`), the host (e.g., `host`, `port`), and the transfer protocol that is used to send emails (e.g., `use_ssl`). Use Google and search for your account details. All providers have a webpage with instructions and specifics.

```
# Create a smtp credentials file
create_smtp_creds_file(
  file = "my_mail_creds",
  user = "user_name@gmail.com",
  host = "smtp.gmail.com",
  port = 465,
  use_ssl = TRUE
)
```

Do keep in mind that the credential contains sensitive information. Creating a credential file is the most convenient way to explore how the process works, but you definitely do not want to share such a file. Moreover, you may provide the information whenever you send an email, but I'd stick to the first approach since it is more convenient to show you how it works.

After the credential key is set or a credential file is available, we are ready for a first trial. Send the composed `email` with the `smtp_send()` function; insert to whom the email needs to be sent and `from` which address it is coming. Furthermore, insert a `subject` and the name of your `credentials` file (here `my_mail_creds`). The email will be sent via the `smtp_send()` function and the console informs you if it was a success.

```
# Send the email with smtp_send
email |>
  smtp_send(
    to = "john.doe@test.com",
    from = "edgar.doe@test.com",
    subject = "Update on X",
    credentials = creds_file("my_mail_creds")
  )
```

Next, we improve the email. We insert a plot in the email and include a report as an attachment.

10.3.1 Improve the email

We started with a simple version of the email, but including a graph and an attachment is far from complicated. We will start with a graph in the body of the email. The `blastula` package comes with the `add_ggplot()` function and lets us add a `ggplot2` graph to the email. As the next console illustrates, create a `plot`, add it with `add_ggplot()` function which creates an HTML version of the plot, and save the result as an object (`mail_plot`).

```
# Create any plot, for example:
plot <- penguins |>
  ggplot(aes(bill_length_mm, body_mass_g)) +
  geom_point()

# Create a plot for the mail
mail_plot <- blastula::add_ggplot(plot_object = plot)
```

To include the plot or another object in the email, refer to the object with braces (`{}`) inside the body of the email. Create a new object for the body text (`body_text`) and insert the `mail_plot`. Additionally, we can refer to other objects as well to make the template more flexible. For example, I add a name as a placeholder for the email `recipient` which will be included inside the `body_text`.

```
# Who gets the email
recipient <- "Mr. Smith"
```

```r
# The improved email:
body_text <-
  md(glue(
    "
## Dear {recipient},

I just wanted to send you an update of my work, see the corresponding
graph (and file in the attachment).

{mail_plot}

Best regards,
Edgar
"
  ))
```

Did you see the md() function inside the body_text? It interprets the input as Markdown (see Chapter 8) and Figure 10.4 shows the result of the body_text and the new email. The font type of the header is larger and in bold because I included Markdown to format the text. In order to see the new email, rerun the compose_email() function and refer to the body_text.

```r
# Compose the email again
email <- compose_email(body = body_text)
email
```

Finally, we can add a file as an attachment. As the next console highlights, the add_attachment() function includes an attachment before we send the email. The function needs the name of the file that will be attached from the working directory.

```r
# add_attachment before the file is send
email |>
  add_attachment(file = "report.pdf") |> ## add attachment
  smtp_send(
    to = "jane.doe@test.com",
    from = "edgar.doe@test.com",
    subject = "Update on X",
    credentials = creds_file("mail_creds")
  )
```

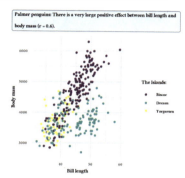

Fig. 10.4: Preview of an improved email

Now that we have a basic understanding of how to send files, let's automate the process and send several reports automatically.

10.3.2 Automate emails

Essentially, we need two things to send emails automatically: the email address and the report for each recipient. First, create a function to send the emails (send_mails) which includes all previously discussed steps. The function needs the mail address and the name of the report that will be sent as an attachment.

```
# Make a function
send_mails <- function(mail, report) {
  email |>
    add_attachment(file = report) |>
    smtp_send(
      to = mail,
      from = "edgar.doe@test.com",
      subject = paste0("Update on ", report),
      credentials = creds_file("mail_creds")
    )
}
```

By creating a function, we are able to send an email in a convenient way since we only need to provide a mail address and the report name. However, sending email after email is bothersome, how can we automate this process? First, we need data that contains both variables, the `mail` address and the corresponding `report`. Consider the following example data.

```
# Example data
df <- tibble::tribble(
  ~emails, ~report,
  "oliver.brown@aol.com", "2007_report.pdf",
  "emma.davies@aol.com", "2008_report.pdf",
  "elizabeth.jones@aol.com", "2009_report.pdf"
)
```

Suppose we are unfortunate and we do not have such a data frame. Of course, we know the emails addresses and which report each person gets; so we can generate a data frame. If all reports are saved in one folder, use the `list.files()` function to create a vector with each file name and then combine it with the corresponding email addresses. For example, the `report_files` folder on my GitHub repository contains reports for each year (like we made in this chapter) and `list.files()` lists them.

```
# List all files of a directory
list.files(
  path = "~/Documents/GitHub/penguins_report/report_files",
  pattern = ".pdf",
  full.names = FALSE
)
```

```
#> [1] "2007_report.pdf" "2008_report.pdf" "2009_report.pdf"
```

We can now combine both variables and create a data frame, but be cautious how the variables are sorted and combined. Consider reading Chapter 5 if you have no idea how to combine (merge) data sets. For now, I assume that we have prepared data to send the emails.

We created several reports with a `for` loop and we may use a similar approach to send emails. Unfortunately, a loop is complicated when we use two variables instead of one (vector). Say we use a loop to apply the `send_mails()` function and we need to insert the correct `email` and the corresponding `report` file. We need to loop over each `row`, from the first until the last row, plus subset the data to fill in the function. As the next console highlights, even if we only print the emails and the report names to check if the loops works, creating such a loop is quite complicated.

```
# A for loop is getting complicated ...
for (row in 1:nrow(df)) {
```

```
    name <- df$emails[row]
    report_name <- df$report[row]
    report <- paste("Send", report_name, "to:", name)
    print(report)
}
```

```
#> [1] "Send 2007_report.pdf to: oliver.brown@aol.com"
#> [1] "Send 2008_report.pdf to: emma.davies@aol.com"
#> [1] "Send 2009_report.pdf to: elizabeth.jones@aol.com"
```

The purr package improves R's capacities of functional programming and provides an efficient solution to automate this process (Henry & Wickham, 2022). Thanks to the purrr package, the code of the for loop will be reduced to exactly one line. Before we apply it to send several emails, let us inspect how purrr works with an analysis example that underlines how we can reduce our workload if we learn more about functional programming.

Suppose you apply a linear regression analysis, and you need to compare the results of two groups. For example, is the effect of an examined independent variable larger for male or female penguins? As the next console shows, we start to examine male penguins. We use the lm() function and apply a filter to run a regression for male penguins.

```
# Estimate a model for male penguins
male_penguins <- penguins %>%
  filter(sex == "male") %>%
  lm(body_mass_g ~ bill_length_mm, data = .)
```

Never mind about the example, but what is the next step? We save the results of the model, we copy the code, change the filter to female, and rerun the model to compare them. That is a lot of steps just to compare the performance of two models. The purrr package reduces the number of steps by running a function several times and it makes the code less clunky. Take a look at the next console. First, we split() the data by .sex, then we apply the map() function from purrr to apply the lm() function for each split.

```
#Apply a map function
penguins %>%
  split(.$sex) %>%
  map(~ lm(body_mass_g ~ bill_length_mm, data = .))
```

```
#> $female
```

```
#>
#> Call:
#> lm(formula = body_mass_g ~ bill_length_mm, data = .)
#>
#> Coefficients:
#>    (Intercept)  bill_length_mm
#>         537.75           78.97
#>
#>
#> $male
#>
#> Call:
#> lm(formula = body_mass_g ~ bill_length_mm, data = .)
#>
#> Coefficients:
#>    (Intercept)  bill_length_mm
#>        1337.32           69.97
```

The function returns a list that contains the regression results for female and male observations. In general terms, the map() function applies a function (such as lm() or a formula) to a list (or a vector) and returns a list, the map2() applies a function to two lists (or vectors) and returns a list; while pmap() can be used for parallel, multiple inputs.

Applying a function several times is not restricted to the lm() function. If we want to know if the examined variable has a larger effect on female (male) penguins, we need to apply the summary() function and extract R^2 from the result. See what happens if we use the pipe and apply the map() function to extract R^2 of each model.

```
# Run a model, apply a summary, and get R² for each model
penguins %>%
  split(.$sex) %>%
  map(~ lm(body_mass_g ~ bill_length_mm, data = .)) %>%
  map(summary) %>%
  map_dbl("r.squared")


#>    female      male
#> 0.3379035 0.2273012
```

This is amazing, especially if we compare the purrr approach with the previously described steps without any functional programming. Consider the purrr website to learn more about it, since we have only seen the tip of the purrr iceberg here. For example, maybe the function should return a different output. There are several variants of map_ functions that return different outputs, as the `map_dbl()` of the last console illustrates. The `map_dbl()` function returns a double vector instead of a list. Or consider the `map_dfc()` function that returns a data frame.

Thus, use `purrr` to send one specific report to one specific recipient. The `map2()` function iterates over two vectors and applies the function. It takes each element of both inputs (`mail_adresses` and `reports`) and applies it to the `send_mails` function.

```
# map2 takes two inputs and applies a function
map2(mail_adresses, reports, send_mails)
```

Introducing `purrr` on the last pages of this chapter is certainly not ideal. However, you should at least know a basic example of `purrr` and where to find more resources if you start to automate, iterate, and `purrr` on a regular basis.

```
# Visit the purrr website:
# https://purrr.tidyverse.org/
```

Ultimately, suppose you need to create a weekly report. Do you want to run the code each weak manually? A computer will not forget the task and saves us a lot of time. The cronR package will give you a lot of spare time, because it helps us to run an R script automatically and on schedule (Wijffels, 2022). The last info box gives a few hints how the package works.

The cronR package　　　　　　　　　　　　　　　　　　　　　　　　　　　　　　　**i**

Cron lets you execute processes (or code) at a certain time on Unix-based operating systems (or alternatively use a task scheduler for Windows). The cronR package comes with a convenient addin, as Figure 10.5 shows. Select the R script and pick a time for the Cron job to run. The cronR package waits until the launch time and runs the script automatically. Keep in mind that this approach is only working if your computer is not switched off, but a cloud-based implementation (e.g., via GitHub Actions) of the Cron job lifts that restriction.

After you scheduled the Cron job, you might wonder how you can know for sure that the job was done without any errors? GitHub Actions informs you if the job fails, but you can establish a similar process if the script runs on your computer. For example, the tryCatch() function catches all warnings and errors of the script and saves them. After the Cron Job is done, send them via email to your account. By automating this last step, you will get an update about the job status, if all ran smoothly, you can focus on your non-repetitive work.

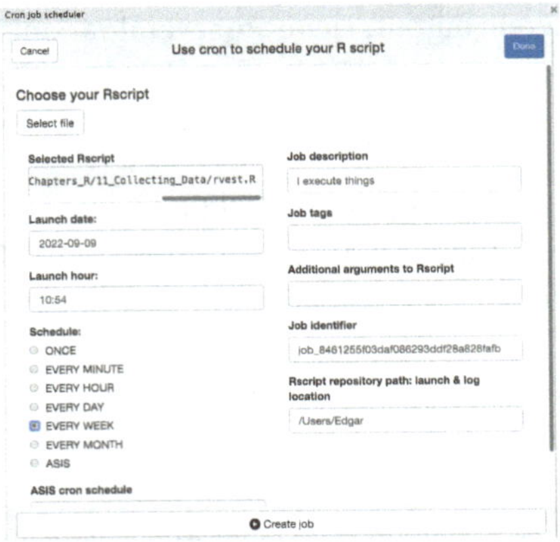

Fig. 10.5: The cronR package

Summary

This chapter introduced dynamic reports as an illustration of how to automate your work. Keep in mind that we are not supposed to repeat ourselves in terms of code; I tried to highlight this principle in this chapter. We started with a basic analysis and then learned how to include params in the meta section of the document. Parameters are a powerful tool to automate various steps when creating a document. The same principles applied as we created text and emails. In the latter case, we saw how packages such as report or effectsize help us to automatically add text in the document, and we also learned to write our own report functions. In terms of emails, we made first steps in functional programming to automate the sending of emails.

All of these examples illustrate there are a lot of manual steps involved, even when we use the right tools. It also reminds us that we should elaborate strategies to reduce redundant steps which gives us the chance to focus on the important ones. Consider reading the third part of *R for Data Science* by Wickham & Grolemund (2016) or *Hands-On Programming with R* by Grolemund (2014) if you want to learn more about programming.

```
# R for Data Science
show_link("r4ds")

# Hands-On Programming
show_link("hands_on_R")
```

Consider a dynamic report even if there are only a limited number of documents needed, since the approach is less error-prone once the template is set up. Of course, making a template takes more time and effort than creating the second report from the first one. However, it also gives you the opportunity to revisit the code, find errors, and fix them. Thus, instead of repeating yourself, make the report and then use it as a draft for a dynamic report.

11 Collect data

Suppose you run an analysis and you need to control the gross domestic product (GDP) of each country, but the data does not contain that specific variable. You search for additional data sources and the OECD website lists the GDP of the examined countries. How can we extract information from an external resource – such as a website – and combine it with the data we have on hand? Use R to collect data from a PDF file, a website (web scraping), or from a web server using an application programming interface (so called APIs). In this chapter, we lay the groundwork and I show you how each approach works.

Introducing three different approaches to collect data seems like sheer madness. Why not focus on one of these topics and explain it in a bit more detail? Consider web scraping, what information shall we collect from which website? The main principle to collect data from a website is always the same, regardless of whether we scrape a simple or a complex one. However, if we extract information from a complex website, we need to talk about many step in detail, but the approach may only work for this particular website. The same applies to PDFs and APIs: a reliable solution needs to consider how the information is structured in a specific PDF document. And each API works essentially the same way, but how we exchange data depends on the application. Thus, this chapter raises awareness that it is possible to collect data from different external resources and focuses on the bigger picture.

- In Section 11.1, we extract data from a PDF report. This seems old-fashioned, but it isn't an unrealistic showcase. Many PDF reports are published without giving access to the data. Irrespective if we extract information from a PDF file or a website, we need to know how R handles text strings and unstructured data. For this reason, we learn how to extract data from a PDF, because the knowledge about string manipulation is helpful in other areas as well.
- In Section 11.2, we explore how web scraping works. First, we build a foundation and I introduce HTML (Hyper Text Markup Language). Next, we explore and extract data from an example website to learn the main principles. Web scraping is a demanding task. To further improve our skills, we will see how specific HTML elements (attributes) help us to extract information.
- In Section 11.3, learn more about the theoretical background of APIs. There are many R packages to retrieve data from APIs (e.g., from social media platforms), but ultimately we will develop an approach that let us retrieve data from an API without a specialized package. We learn how we can make a request from a server to retrieve data. By doing so, we extend our knowledge how APIs and corresponding packages that let us retrieve data from an API work.

https://doi.org/10.1515/9783110704976-011

```
# Set the engine for Chapter 11 #####
library(DemografixeR)
library(dplyr)
library(gapminder)
library(httr)
library(pdftools)
library(purrr)
library(PracticeR)
library(rvest)
library(stringr)
library(stringi)
library(tibble)
library(tidyr)
```

11.1 PDF files

In order to extract information from a PDF file, we need to increase our skills on how to work with strings first. R imports the content of a PDF file as character strings and, thus, as unstructured data. We therefore need to learn how to manipulate these to extract the desired information. To this end, this section introduces regular expressions (regex) and the `stringr` package (Wickham, 2022c), before we extract a table from a PDF file.

11.1.1 Regular expressions

Suppose we have imported a PDF file as plain text, as the following `strings` underline. Each string contains the name and birth year of a person. String manipulation and regular expressions help us extract this information.

```
# Example strings
library(stringr)
strings <- c(
  "Tom. 2000",
  "Olivia: 99"
)
```

The `stringr` package provides functions to manipulate strings. For example, the `str_extract()` function extracts a search string – a `pattern` – and returns a vector that indicates which strings it includes. Or suppose we want to extract only observations that include a certain pattern, such as a name. This is a job for `str_subset()`, which returns the elements of a vector that matches the pattern.

```
# The search pattern
pattern <- "Tom"

# Extract a string
str_extract(strings, pattern)


#> [1] "Tom" NA

# Subset a string
str_subset(strings, pattern)


#> [1] "Tom. 2000"
```

Thus, we subset or extract a pattern from strings, but what exactly do we mean by a *pattern*? A pattern can be anything that is typical for the examined strings. In our example, each string starts with the name of the person, a punctuation, and digits.

We build a pattern based on regular expressions, a language to describe the patterns of the examined strings. For example, the *match character* for any word character is \w (non-word characters: \W); and the match character for digits is \d (non-digits: \D). If we insert them as a search string with two back slashes (\\), we retrieve the first character or digit.

```
# Extract a string with regular expressions
str_extract(strings, "\\w")


#> [1] "T" "O"

str_extract(strings, "\\d")


#> [1] "2" "9"
```

To extract the digits of the years, we need a regex that returns all digits. Unfortunately, we cannot insert \d four times, because the approach is not flexible enough, as the next console shows.

```
# Search for four digits
str_extract(strings, "\\d\\d\\d\\d")


#> [1] "2000" NA
```

Not all numbers consist of four digits, which is why we get NA in the second case. Apparently, I did not describe the pattern precisely enough, because the string consists of one or more digits. Insert a plus sign (+) to indicate if the string has *one or more* digits.

```r
# A + indicate if a character appears one or more times
str_extract(strings, "\\d+")
```

```r
#> [1] "2000" "99"
```

The plus sign is a metacharacter used to build patterns. The next console shows further metacharacters based on simple strings to illustrate their function.

```r
# Does a character appear? A ? matches a character 0 or 1 times
x <- c("Haïti", "Haiti", "Honduras")
str_extract(x, "Ha\\ï?i?ti")
```

```r
#> [1] "Haïti" "Haiti" NA
```

```r
# How often does it appear? A * matches a character 0 or more times
x <- c("9", "99", "981")
str_extract(x, "9\\d*")
```

```r
#> [1] "9"   "99"  "981"
```

```r
# A . matches any single character, e.g., to extract the usernames
x <- c("edgar-doe@test.com", "jane.doe@test.com")
str_extract(x, "\\w+.\\w+")
```

```r
#> [1] "edgar-doe" "jane.doe"
```

Metacharacters help us to describe a pattern, but why do we need two back slashes for a regex? Consider the strings from a shoppinglist. It lists products in a formatted manner, but the raw string seems weird. The writeLines() function lets us examine how R handles (raw) strings.

```r
# How R handles strings
shoppinglist <- "Cheese,
                Fish/Chips,
```

```
                    Strawberries"
writeLines(shoppinglist)


#> Cheese,
#>                  Fish/Chips,
#>                  Strawberries
```

Why are the strings not outlined? The shoppinglist contains special characters that we cannot see. The string has a new line for each product, and I used <TAB> to outline them. Both are special characters, and we need to escape them with a back slash (\) to restore the meaning of the characters. For example, we may insert \n for a new line, or \t for <TAB>.

```
# shoppinglist contains new lines (\n)
shoppinglist <- "Cheese\nFish/Chips\nStrawberries"
writeLines(shoppinglist)


#> Cheese
#> Fish/Chips
#> Strawberries
```

Thus, we escape special characters in R, but a regular expression applies exactly the same logic. For this reason, we need to include two back slashes (\\) to work with them. As the next console demonstrates, a period (.) is a metacharacter that matches any single character (without \n); and we need to escape it (\\.) when we want to match a period, otherwise we use the metacharacter to extract the strings.

```
# Print the strings once more
strings


#> [1] "Tom. 2000"  "Olivia: 99"


# Escape to identify strings with a period
str_extract(strings, "\\w+\\.")


#> [1] "Tom." NA


# Otherwise, a . is a meta character
str_extract(strings, "\\w+.")
```

```
#> [1] "Tom."     "Olivia:"
```

Regular expressions are a real struggle and hard to apply, especially if we do not use them on a regular basis. The following examples will further illustrate how regexes work and why it often takes several steps to build them. You not only need to make sure that the regex matches all intended patterns, but also that only the intended cases are returned. The str_view_all() function and an example string help us with this task. As Figure 11.1 depicts, the function displays the strings in the viewer and marks which characters are matched by the regex. I insert the search string (aeiou) as a *character class* ([]) to match vocals. Irrespective of the search pattern, use the str_view_all() function and example strings to test your regex.

```
# The str_view_all function shows matched strings
# [aeiou] is a character class for lower vocals
str_view_all(strings, "[aeiou]")
```

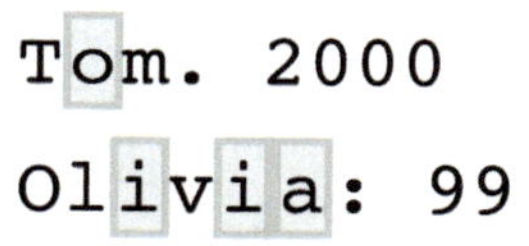

```
Tom. 2000
Olivia: 99
```

Fig. 11.1: Preview regular expressions

A character class is also a metacharacter to build patterns. Instead of writing each character, character classes ([]) help us to identify strings and the stringr package includes several. For example, we can extract numbers with the [:digit:] and letters with the [:alpha:] class.

```
# [:alpha:] == letters
str_extract(strings, "[:alpha:]+")
```

```
#> [1] "Tom"    "Olivia"
```

```
# [:digit:] == digits
str_extract(strings, "[:digit:]+")
```

```
#> [1] "2000" "99"
```

There are more character classes: extract `lower` and `upper` case letters, the punctuation (`punct`), or the combination of letters and numbers (`alnum`). The next console illustrates each of them with a simple `string`.

```
# Example string
string <- c("abc", "ABC", "123", ",?()")

# Lowercase
str_extract(string, "[:lower:]+")

#> [1] "abc" NA    NA    NA

# Uppercase
str_extract(string, "[:upper:]+")

#> [1] NA    "ABC" NA    NA

# Letters and numbers
str_extract(string, "[:alnum:]+")

#> [1] "abc" "ABC" "123" NA

# Punctuation
str_extract(string, "[:punct:]+")

#> [1] NA    NA    NA    ",?()"
```

Let us build a more realistic scenario and learn step by step how to create a regex. Suppose the `strings` are sentences that include the exact birth dates that we need to extract.

```
strings <- c(
  "Tom is born on 29 May 2000.",
  "Olivia has her birthday on 19 August 1999."
)
```

Let's start with the date. In order to extract the date, we may use *ranges* as a character class and *quantifiers*. Each date starts with digits, the name of the month, and the year. The digits are within the range of zero and nine. Ranges work the same way as predefined character classes (e.g., `[:digit:]`), so it is a question of what you prefer. For example, extract the first digit.

```r
# Create a range with -
str_extract(strings, "[0-9]")
```

```
#> [1] "2" "1"
```

```r
# Or use character classes
str_extract(strings, "[:digit:]")
```

```
#> [1] "2" "1"
```

More importantly, the day contains *one* or *two* digits, and we quantify such patterns with braces (`{}`). To this end we can determine how often each character appears.

```r
# Use a quantifier {}: exactly 1 (or n) times
str_extract(strings, "[0-9]{1}")
```

```
#> [1] "2" "1"
```

```r
# 1 (n) or more times
str_extract(strings, "[0-9]{1,}")
```

```
#> [1] "29" "19"
```

```r
# Between n (1) and m (2)
str_extract(strings, "[0-9]{1,2}")
```

```
#> [1] "29" "19"
```

Thus, quantifiers help us to describe the pattern precisely, but keep in mind that outliers may break the rules and we may introduce an error if the extracted string is not within the quantified range. Next, the word for the month. Each month starts with a capitalized letter (`[A-Z]`) and has one or more lowercase letters (`[a-z]+`).

```r
# Regex are case sensitive: [A-Z] for upper, [a-z] for lowercase
str_extract(strings, "[0-9]{1,2} [A-Z][a-z]+")
```

```
#> [1] "29 May"    "19 August"
```

Finally, we need to add a regex for the year, which has at least two digits and we save the result as dates.

```
# Extract and save the dates:
dates <- str_extract(strings, "[0-9]{1,2} [A-Z][a-z]+ [0-9]{2,}")
dates

#> [1] "29 May 2000"    "19 August 1999"
```

Now that we have the dates, we still need to extract the days, the month, and the year with *anchors*. The circumflex (ˆ) indicates the start of a string, while the dollar sign ($) points the end of the string.

```
# Start of a string: ^
str_extract(dates, "^[0-9]+")

#> [1] "29" "19"
```

```
# End of a string: $
str_extract(dates, "[0-9]+$")

#> [1] "2000" "1999"
```

We apply similar steps to extract the name of each person and the month; then we put all steps together to create a data frame.

```
# Further ado
day <- str_extract(dates, "^[0-9]+")
year <- str_extract(dates, "[0-9]+$")
month <- str_extract(dates, "[A-Z][a-z]+")
name <- str_extract(strings, "^[A-Z][a-z]+")

df <- data.frame(name, day, month, year)
df

#>      name day  month year
#> 1     Tom  29    May 2000
#> 2 Olivia  19 August 1999
```

Regular expressions are hard to apply, but we need a basic understanding about them to work with strings. Be patient with yourself if your regex is not working immediately, all people struggle to apply them. The good news is, the `stringr` package helps us to work with strings. The next subsection does not include regular expressions, since they make the code harder to read. Instead, we focus on the main functions of the `stringr` package.

11.1.2 The stringr package

The `stringr` package has a lot of functions to handle strings efficiently (Wickham, 2022c). For example, the last steps to split the `dates` were not really necessary if we knew how the package could *join and split* strings. The `str_split_fixed()` function splits strings when we adjust the number of words that are included (n) and the `pattern` how to split them (e.g., blank space).

```r
# str_split_fixed splits the string
dates |>
  str_split_fixed(pattern = " ", n = 3)
```

```
#>      [,1] [,2]     [,3]
#> [1,] "29" "May"    "2000"
#> [2,] "19" "August" "1999"
```

The `str_c()` function does the exact opposite; it joins strings of two or more vectors.

```r
# Example strings
days_str <- c("29", "19")
month_str <- c("May", "August")
years_str <- c("2000", "1999")

# str_c combines strings (sep adds an string separator)
str_c(days_str, month_str, years_str, sep = " ")
```

```
#> [1] "29 May 2000"    "19 August 1999"
```

The `stringr` package has two example data sets (`fruit` and `sentences`) and we do not need to generate example strings to see how `stringr` works.

```r
# Some fruits?
head(fruit)
```

```
#> [1] "apple"     "apricot"    "avocado"    "banana"     "bell pepper"
```

```
#> [6] "bilberry"
```

```
# Or sentences:
head(sentences)
```

```
#> [1] "The birch canoe slid on the smooth planks."
#> [2] "Glue the sheet to the dark blue background."
#> [3] "It's easy to tell the depth of a well."
#> [4] "These days a chicken leg is a rare dish."
#> [5] "Rice is often served in round bowls."
#> [6] "The juice of lemons makes fine punch."
```

Both data sets may help you to explore and apply the functions of the stringr package and we use a shorter vector with fruits to explore how the package lets us *detect*, *mutate*, and *replace* strings. The stringr package has several functions to detect matches. The str_detect() function checks if a string includes a search string (pattern) and returns a Boolean operator as a result. The str_count() function does essentially the same, but it returns a binary indicator. The latter makes it possible to count how often the pattern appears.

```
# Example fruits
fruits <- c("apple", "banana", "pear", "pineapple")
```

```
# Detect a search pattern
str_detect(fruits, "apple")
```

```
#> [1]   TRUE FALSE FALSE   TRUE
```

```
# How often appears the search pattern
str_count(fruits, "apple")
```

```
#> [1] 1 0 0 1
```

The str_starts() function checks if a string starts with a pattern, while we locate the position of the search string with str_locate().

```
# Strings that start with a pattern
str_starts(fruits, "apple")
```

```
#> [1]   TRUE FALSE FALSE FALSE
```

```
# And at which location
str_locate(fruits, "apple")
```

```
#>      start end
#> [1,]     1   5
#> [2,]    NA  NA
#> [3,]    NA  NA
#> [4,]     5   9
```

Unstructured data is by definition messy and text often contains character signs that have no value for us (e.g., €). In such cases, we mutate and replace strings. As the next console shows, the `str_replace()` function replaces a search string (e.g., the letter a) with the new string (e.g., 8), while the `str_replace_all()` function replaces all strings that match.

```
# Replace (all) strings
fruits <- c("banana", "apricot", "apple", "pear")
str_replace(fruits, "a", "8")
```

```
#> [1] "b8nana"  "8pricot" "8pple"   "pe8r"
```

```
str_replace_all(fruits, "a", "8")
```

```
#> [1] "b8n8n8"  "8pricot" "8pple"   "pe8r"
```

As always, the discussed functions are only a selection of the possibilities and the package has more to offer. For example, sometimes we need to count the length of a string (`str_length`) or sort strings (`str_sort`) alphabetically.

```
# Lengths of strings
str_length(fruits)
```

```
#> [1] 6 7 5 4
```

```
# Sort strings
str_sort(fruits, decreasing = FALSE)
```

```
#> [1] "apple"   "apricot" "banana"  "pear"
```

336 —— 11 Collect data

Check out the package website (and the cheat sheet) for more information. If you face a problem that you cannot solve with the stringr package, consider also the stringi package (Gagolewski et al., 2022). As Wickham (2022c) described on the stringr website, the package: "focusses on the most important and commonly used string manipulation functions whereas stringi provides a comprehensive set covering almost anything you can imagine." Next, we extract data (character strings) from a PDF file.

11.1.3 Pdftools

In this section, we use the pdftools package to extract data from a PDF file (Ooms, 2022). As a showcase, we extract unemployment rates from the OECD Labour Force Statistics report (2021, p. 36). The PracticeR package includes the file and the extracted (raw) data of the PDF file, so you don't need to download the PDF file to apply the discussed steps. As the next console shows, the data contains unemployment rates (as a percentage of the labor force) between 2011 and 2020.

```
# The unemployment data
head(PracticeR::unemployment)
```

```
#> # A tibble: 6 x 11
#>    Country    `2011` `2012` `2013` `2014` `2015` `2016` `2017`
#>    <chr>       <dbl>  <dbl>  <dbl>  <dbl>  <dbl>  <dbl>  <dbl>
#> 1 Australia    5.1    5.2    5.7    6.1    6.1    5.7    5.6
#> 2 Austria      4.6    4.9    5.3    5.6    5.7    6      5.5
#> 3 Belgium      7.1    7.5    8.4    8.5    8.5    7.8    7.1
#> 4 Canada       7.6    7.3    7.1    6.9    6.9    7.1    6.4
#> 5 Chile        7.1    6.5    6.1    6.5    6.3    6.7    7
#> # ... with 1 more row, and 3 more variables: `2018` <dbl>,
#> #    `2019` <dbl>, `2020` <dbl>
```

By extracting this table, you may realize that the steps depend on the PDF file and its structure. Different steps are necessary to extract data for a different PDF file. For this reason, I put the emphasis on regular expressions and the stringr package in this chapter, which built the foundation to extract data irrespective from which PDF file.

In a similar vein, this section will underline that importing a PDF as text is a piece of cake, but it is difficult to work with unstructured data and it may take a lot of steps before we get a clean data set. Is it worth extracting data from a PDF file? This certainly depends on the complexity of the task. Suppose you have a large and consistent PDF file where each table has the same format: then you will be able to extract all tables in a jiffy. Unfortunately, the code breaks if each table has a different format and other irregularities. In this case you may wish to consider other options as well.

In order to extract information from a PDF file, we may download it and save it in the working directory. However, I included the file (oecd_table) in the files folder of the PracticeR package, which means that the file is already on your computer. The system.file() function returns the path to the file.

```
# System.file returns the path of system files
oecd_table <- system.file("files", "oecd_table.pdf",
  package = "PracticeR"
)
```

Next, use the pdf_text() function from the pdftools package to extract information from the file. The function scans the document and extracts the content as plain text.

```
# Read the content of a pdf file via pdf_text
raw_text <- pdftools::pdf_text(oecd_table)
```

I already applied this step and the PracticeR package includes also the raw text (unemployment_raw) of this table. Inspect the raw data in the console. The pdf_text() extracts all texts as strings, and depending on the PDF file, the output of the console can be very long, which is why I do not print it in this book.

Before I can inspect the content in the console, I use the str_split() function to split the string after each new line (\n). The function returns a list, which is why I apply the as_vector() function from purrr to create a vector. Now, if I use the head() function, the console shows the first six lines of the text.

```
# str_split splits the raw text after each new line
text <- str_split(raw_text, "\n")
text <- as_vector(text)
head(text)
```

```
#> [1] "                              INTERNATIONAL COMPARISONS"
#> [2] ""
#> [3] "              Table 29. Unemployment as a percentage of labour force"
#> [4] "Percentage"
#> [5] "    2011        2012            2013        2014            2015
#> 2016       2017        2018        2019       2020"
#> [6] "Australia                        5.1:        5.2:           5.7:
#> 6.1:           6.1:       5.7:       5.6:       5.3:       5.2:       6.5:"
```

338 —— 11 Collect data

We imported a real mess – the PDF contains blank spaces, punctuation marks, and empty lines. Inspect the PDF file and the raw data before you start to extract the data.[1] For example, consider how values for Belgium and several other countries are saved. As the next console shows, I picked also a messy table because some of the unemployment rates are split into two rows and contain vertical bars (|).

```
# Inspect for irregularities
text[17:18]
```

```
#> [1] "Belgium      7.1:      7.5:      8.4:      8.5:      8.5:      7.8 |\n"
#> [2] "             :7.1:      5.9:      5.4:      5.5 |"
```

For this reason, we need to replace those values from the raw_text and rerun the steps from the last console. Otherwise, those observations will show up in separate rows.

```
# Replace extra lines and |
text <- str_replace_all(raw_text, pattern = "\\|\n", "")
text <- str_replace_all(text, pattern = "\\|", "")

# Rerun first step
text <- str_split(text, "\n")
text <- as_vector(text)
```

Next, we need to identify where the table starts and ends in order to extract the data. The first entry is Australia and the last table entry starts with United States. The str_which() function tells us the positions of those search strings.

```
# str_which returns at which position(s) the string appears
str_which(text, "Australia")
```

```
#> [1] 6
```

```
str_which(text, "United States")
```

```
#> [1] 193
```

Try to find such landmarks to isolate the data from the PDF document, especially if you want to extract several tables. Compare each table to find a pattern to exclude them.

---

1 Inspect the PDF file, for example, with your browser and the browseURL() function.

Most tables in the OECD report contain those countries, which is why the approach also works for a different table in the report. So, let's create an object that indicates the start and the end point of the table. This makes it possible to subset the text.

```
# Use the position to extract the data
start <- str_which(text, "Australia")
end <- str_which(text, "United States")
# Slice the data from the start to the end
text_df <- text[start:end]
head(text_df)
```

```
#> [1] "Australia        5.1:        5.2:        5.7:        6.1:      6.1:
#> [2] ""
#> [3] ""
#> [4] ""
#> [5] ""
#> [6] "Austria          4.6:        4.9:        5.3:        5.6:      5.7:
```

Still a mess! This clearly illustrates why we cannot recycle the code if we extract data from a different PDF file. A different report probably has different landmarks, and we need to identify those patterns to extract the data. In this chapter we extract only one table to illustrate the procedure. In a real application, we may need to extract several tables, illustrating the need to find a pattern that matches for all (or at least most) tables that we want to extract, otherwise the code breaks and a lot of manual steps are necessary.

As the next step, we need to get rid of the colons (:), blank spaces, and the empty lines. Use the str_replace_all() function for colons, trim blank space with the str_trim() function and tell R to keep elements only if they are not (!=) empty.

```
# Discard
text_df <- str_replace_all(text_df, ":", "")
# Trim blank spaces
text_df <- str_trim(text_df)
# Keep everything that is not (!=) empty
text_df <- text_df[text_df != ""]
head(text_df)
```

```
#> [1] "Australia      5.1       5.2        5.7       6.1       6.1
#> [2] "Austria        4.6       4.9        5.3       5.6       5.7
#> [3] "Belgium        7.1       7.5        8.4       8.5       8.5
#> [4] "Canada         7.6       7.3        7.1       6.9       6.9
```

```
#> [5] "Chile            7.1       6.5        6.1        6.5        6.3
#> [6] "Colombia        10.9      10.4        9.7        9.2        9.0
```

To split the strings and to create columns, apply the `str_split_fixed` function. The table from the PDF file has eleven columns and between each string are two or more blank spaces. Additionally, I make a tibble for a nicer output.

```
# Split vector
text_split <- str_split_fixed(text_df, " {2,}", n = 11)
# Create data
df <- tibble::as_tibble(text_split)
head(df)
```

```
#> # A tibble: 6 x 11
#>   V1          V2    V3    V4    V5    V6    V7    V8    V9
#>   <chr>       <chr> <chr> <chr> <chr> <chr> <chr> <chr> <chr>
#> 1 Australia 5.1     5.2   5.7   6.1   6.1   5.7   5.6   5.3
#> 2 Austria   4.6     4.9   5.3   5.6   5.7   6.0   5.5   4.8
#> 3 Belgium   7.1     7.5   8.4   8.5   8.5   7.8   7.1   5.9
#> 4 Canada    7.6     7.3   7.1   6.9   6.9   7.1   6.4   5.9
#> 5 Chile     7.1     6.5   6.1   6.5   6.3   6.7   7.0   7.4
#> # ... with 1 more row, and 2 more variables: V10 <chr>,
#> #   V11 <chr>
```

Now the data looks almost like any other data frame, but it still does not have useful column names. We may extract the string with the variable names, but since the column names are year numbers, we can recreate the sequence, combine it with a string for the first column (`country`), and use the `names()` function to add the column names (`colum_names`).

```
# Create a vector
colum_names <- c("country", seq(2011, 2020, by = 1))
# For the column names
names(df) <- colum_names
head(df)
```

```
#> # A tibble: 6 x 11
#>   country    `2011` `2012` `2013` `2014` `2015` `2016` `2017`
#>   <chr>      <chr>  <chr>  <chr>  <chr>  <chr>  <chr>
#> 1 Australia 5.1     5.2    5.7    6.1    6.1    5.7    5.6
#> 2 Austria   4.6     4.9    5.3    5.6    5.7    6.0    5.5
```

```
#> 3 Belgium   7.1     7.5     8.4     8.5     8.5     7.8     7.1
#> 4 Canada    7.6     7.3     7.1     6.9     6.9     7.1     6.4
#> 5 Chile     7.1     6.5     6.1     6.5     6.3     6.7     7.0
#> # ... with 1 more row, and 3 more variables: `2018` <chr>,
#> #   `2019` <chr>, `2020` <chr>
```

Unfortunately, we're still not finished. We must apply the `str_remove_all` function to remove strings that refer to footnotes. I remove letters (`alpha`) from the `2020` variable.

```
# The strings include footnotes, for example:
str_subset(df$`2020`, "e")
```

```
#> [1] "3.8 e" "4.5 e"
```

```
# Remove footnote signs
df$`2020` <- str_remove_all(df$`2020`, "[:alpha:]")
```

After the data preparation steps, use the `slice_max()` or `slice_min()` function from the `dplyr` package to inspect countries with the highest (lowest) unemployment rates.

```
# Which country has the highest unemployment rates?
df |>
  select(country, `2020`) |>
  slice_min(order_by = `2020`, n = 5)
```

```
#> # A tibble: 5 x 2
#>    country   `2020`
#>    <chr>     <chr>
#> 1 Chile     10.8
#> 2 Turkey    13.1
#> 3 Spain     15.5
#> 4 Colombia  16.1
#> 5 Greece    16.3
```

At first glance this output looks good, but why are the unemployment rates not sorted? We extracted the information from characters and R still treats the unemployment rates as characters. Thus, we need to transform the variable into a numerical vector.

```
# Don't forget that we imported characters from a PDF!
df$`2020` <- as.numeric(df$`2020`)
```

342 — 11 Collect data

```
df |>
  select(country, `2020`) |>
  slice_min(order_by = `2020`, n = 5)
```

```
#> # A tibble: 5 x 2
#>   country         `2020`
#>   <chr>            <dbl>
#> 1 Czech Republic     2.5
#> 2 Japan              2.8
#> 3 Poland             3.2
#> 4 Germany            3.8
#> 5 Netherlands        3.8
```

All the last data preparation steps clearly underline that importing a PDF as text is a piece of cake, but it is difficult to work with unstructured data, at least we need to put some effort in the preparation steps. If you are lucky, the tables will also be available on a website. Not as a download, but embedded in the HTML file that we can scrape.

However, extracting data from a PDF or a web server are not the only options at your disposal to retrieve data. Maybe the data is not stored locally, but in a relational database. *SQL* (Structured Query Language) is a prominent language to work with a relational database and you can connect R to a database as well. Before we learn more about web scraping, the next info box outlines some tips to learn SQL and demonstrates why the dbplyr package may help (Wickham, Girlich, et al., 2022).

11.2 Web scraping

In this section we scrape data from the PracticeR website. We learn how to scrape texts, links, and data to illustrate the principle. To this end, we need to establish some basics about HTML, and we will get in touch with further web-related languages. Before you continue, visit the website to get an idea of what it contains. The discussed steps will be easier to follow if you know what it looks like. Go and visit and the webscraping website from the PracticeR package:

```
# The PR website has a web scraping page:
show_link("webscraping", browse = FALSE)
```

```
#> [1] "https://edgar-treischl.github.io/PracticeR/articles/web_only/
#> webscraping.html"
```

Regardless of the website we scrape, all rely on the same HTML structure.

11.2 Web scraping — 343

SQL and the dbplyr package

i

Suppose the data does not live on a web server, but in an SQL database. Your dplyr knowledge will help you to work with SQL because the dbplyr package works with databases and is a sibling of the dplyr package. The next data preparation step shows an example. I used the mtcars data and created a mean value of mpg for each of the two am group levels.

```
#An example data preparation step
mtcars |>
  group_by(am) |>
  summarise(mpg = mean(mpg, na.rm = TRUE))
```

```
##      am    mpg
## 1     0   17.1
## 2     1   24.4
```

Use the dbplyr package to translate this data preparation step into SQL – the package even returns the SQL code. First, we need to establish an example SQL connection to see how dbplyr translates the code into SQL but that is not the important point here (see Chapter 12 for more information).

```
#Establish a connection
library(DBI)
con <- dbConnect(RSQLite::SQLite(), dbname = ":memory:")
dbWriteTable(con, "mtcars", mtcars)
mtcars_sql <- tbl(con, "mtcars")
```

In the next console I assign the data preparation steps from the beginning (data_prep) and the show_query() function translates the steps to SQL code. Thus, the dbplyr package translates your code and skills into SQL which may offer new opportunities to retrieve data.

```
#Save the data preparation steps as an object
library(dbplyr)
data_prep <- mtcars_sql |>
  group_by(am) |>
  summarise(mpg = mean(mpg, na.rm = TRUE))
```

```
#Inspect the SQL query for the last data preparation step
data_prep |> show_query()
```

```
## <SQL>
## SELECT `am`, AVG(`mpg`) AS `mpg`
## FROM `mtcars`
## GROUP BY `am`
```

11.2.1 HTML

Consider the next console, it shows the minimal code of a website. Each HTML file starts with an `<html>` and ends with an `</html>` *tag*. HTML tags may have children and include further tags. The `<html>` tag includes the `<head>` and a `<body>` tag. Each HTML element has an *opening tag* (e.g., `<body>`), optional *attributes* (e.g., `id`), and a *closing tag* (e.g., `</body>`). Everything between the opening and a closing tag belongs to the tag.

The `<head>` is not important to scrape data, because it includes information about the website and not its content; it usually includes the language of the website, the `<title>`, or an external `<script>` that is loaded when we visit the website. The actual content of the document – headings, texts, and pictures – can be found inside the `<body>` tag, which is why we need to inspect the latter more closely.

```html
<!-- I am an HTML comment -->
<!-- A basic website -->
<html>
<html lang="en">
  <head>
    <meta charset="utf-8">
    <title>Title</title>
    <link rel="stylesheet" href="style.css">
    <script src="script.js"></script>
  </head>
  <!-- page content -->
  <body>
    <h1>Webscraping</h1>
      <p>This is an <b>example</b> text.</p>
  </body>
</html>
```

Consider the `<h1>` tag in the body; it creates the first header and text between the opening and the closing tag (`Webscraping`) is interpreted as the first header. Elements like `<h1>` are called *block tags*, because they form the overall structure of the document. Further examples are text *paragraphs* `<p>`; as well as *ordered* (`<ol>`) and *unordered* (`<ul>`) lists. In addition, there are also *inline tags*. Consider the paragraph (`<p>`) tag after the first heading. The word `example` is enclosed by a bold (`<b>`) inline tag. The browser will display the word `example` in bold letters.

A browser can show the HTML source code and modern browsers include developer tools to examine the code of a website (e.g., via the right-click context menu). The latter mode makes it convenient to explore the source code. Figure 11.2 shows a screenshot from Firefox's developer mode for the `PracticeR` website. On the left side, the website is shown; on the right side the source code is displayed. If you select an element of the source code, the developer mode highlights the corresponding elements of the website that the source code creates. As Figure 11.2 illustrates, I search for the code that creates the table header and the developer mode selects the result of the HTML code. This basic understanding of HTML should be enough to scrape a simple website.

Fig. 11.2: Firefox's developer mode

11.2.2 Websites

To scrape a website, install and load the rvest package (Wickham, 2022c). Create an object (pr_site) with the address of the website and use the read_html() function to read the content of the website.

```
# Get the website address
library(rvest)
pr_site <- show_link("webscraping", browse = FALSE)

# read_html reads the website
pr_html <- read_html(pr_site)
```

The read_html() function scrapes the website and saves the content as an extensible markup language (XML) object. XML is a language to exchange data used in many web-based applications. The next console shows a minimal XML file with information about R books. XML files are built upon nodes, and in this example each book is inside the catalog node. We need to extract such nodes to get access to the information of the HTML file. The basics of HTML already pay off, since all information about the books is listed with an opening and closing tag, and the code should look pretty familiar.

```
<?xml version="1.0"?>
<catalog>
   <book id="book1">
      <author>Wickham, Hadley</author>
```

```
        <title>Mastering Shiny</title>
        <genre>Shiny</genre>
    </book>

    <book id="book2">
        <author>Hvitfeldt, Emil; Silge, Julia</author>
        <title>Supervised Machine Learning for Text Analysis in R</title>
        <genre>Machine learning</genre>
    </book>
</catalog>
```

How do we work with XML files? The rvest package lets us examine the document without much XML knowledge, but it remains helpful to know that we get an XML file should we start to scrape more complex websites. Let's keep it simple to illustrate the principle. Inspect the nodes of the HTML file with the html_node() function; we may even include all of its children with the pipe and the html_children() function. Say we want to inspect the body node and all children of the website.

```
# Body node with all children
pr_html |>
  html_node("body") |>
  html_children()
```

```
#> {xml_nodeset (3)}
#> [1] <a href="#main" class="visually-hidden-focusable">Skip to contents<...
#> [2] <nav class="navbar fixed-top navbar-light navbar-expand-lg bg-light...
#> [3] <div class="container template-article">\n\n\n\n<script src="webscr...
```

The function extracts the code of the body and all of its children, and returns them as a list. If we do not need the entire node, we can just extract single elements with the html_elements() function. For example, we extract the heading (h1) and the paragraphs (p).

```
# Extract elements h1
pr_html |> html_elements("h1")
```

```
#> {xml_nodeset (1)}
#> [1] <h1>Webscraping</h1>
```

```
# Extract elements p
pr_html |> html_elements("p")
```

```
#> {xml_nodeset (5)}
#> [1] <p>Welcome to the example website to learn web scraping with R.
#> On this website you find content such as links and tables.</p>
#> [2] <p></p>
#> [3] <p>Developed by <a href="https://www.edgar-treischl.de/"
#> class="external-link">Edgar Treischl</a>.</p>
#> [4] <p></p>
#> [5] <p>Site built with <a href="https://pkgdown.r-lib.org/"
#> class="external-link">pkgdown</a> 2.0.6.</p>
```

Data

Consider the next console. It highlights that we can use the `minimal_html()` function to create a minimal html file (object) in R. Creating a minimal file makes it easier to understand the next steps and we can test if our code to scrape data works. Using the `<ul>` tag, I created an unordered list that contains sentences with names and years of age. Irrespective of which kind of information we want to extract, it is complicated to extract if the information is embedded in an unstructured way.

```
# A minimal html website
html <- minimal_html(
  "<body>
  <p>A unordered list:<p>
  <ul>
  <li>Tom is 15 years old.</li>
  <li>Pete is 20 years old.</li>
  <li>Ingrid is 21 years old.</li>
  </ul>"
)
```

Maybe you have a premonition on how to solve this problem. Use `stringr` and your regular expression skills to extract the information. First, we extract the corresponding elements.

```
# Get elements
html |>
  html_elements("li")
```

```
#> {xml_nodeset (3)}
```

```
#> [1] <li>Tom is 15 years old.</li>
#> [2] <li>Pete is 20 years old.</li>
#> [3] <li>Ingrid is 21 years old.</li>
```

If we extract single elements, we extract HTML code. In case of text strings, `html_text2()` discards the HTML code and returns only the character strings.[2]

```
# Get text
txt <- html |>
  html_elements("li") |>
  html_text2()

txt

#> [1] "Tom is 15 years old."    "Pete is 20 years old."
#> [3] "Ingrid is 21 years old."
```

Next, we apply our `stringr` knowledge to extract the desired information.

```
# Extract names
stringr::str_extract(txt, "[A-Z][a-z]+")

#> [1] "Tom"    "Pete"    "Ingrid"
```

```
# Extract age
stringr::str_extract(txt, "[0-9]+")

#> [1] "15" "20" "21"
```

Our life becomes easier if the data is included as table. The next console shows you how a table is structured in HTML. A table is created with the corresponding `<table>` tag. Inside the tag, each *table row* is embedded with a `<tr>` tag. In our case, it includes also a *table header* (`<th>`) and the data is listed inside the *table data* (`<td>`) tag.

```
<!-- The <table> tag -->
<html>
...
```

---

2 There are two `html_text` functions. Similar to the unstructured content of a PDF file, the raw text of a website can be messy. The `html_text()` function returns the raw text, while the `html_text2` discards noise such as blank spaces.

```
<body>
    <table>
  <tr>
    <th>Name</th>
    <th>Age</th>
  </tr>
  <tr>
    <td>Tom</td>
    <td>15</td>
  </tr>
    </table>
  </body>
</html>
```

The structure makes it convenient to extract the data. Use the `html_table()` function to extract a table from the website (`pr_html`). I included the unemployment rates from the OECD Labour Force Statistics report on the website.

```
# Get tables
pr_html |>
  html_element("table") |>
  html_table()
```

```
#> # A tibble: 38 x 11
#>    Country    `2011` `2012` `2013` `2014` `2015` `2016` `2017`
#>    <chr>      <dbl>  <dbl>  <dbl>  <dbl>  <dbl>  <dbl>  <dbl>
#> 1 Australia    5.1    5.2    5.7    6.1    6.1    5.7    5.6
#> 2 Austria      4.6    4.9    5.3    5.6    5.7    6      5.5
#> 3 Belgium      7.1    7.5    8.4    8.5    8.5    7.8    7.1
#> 4 Canada       7.6    7.3    7.1    6.9    6.9    7.1    6.4
#> 5 Chile        7.1    6.5    6.1    6.5    6.3    6.7    7
#> # ... with 33 more rows, and 3 more variables:
#> #   `2018` <dbl>, `2019` <dbl>, `2020` <dbl>
```

Unfortunately, you will not always be so lucky, and the data might not be saved as a table, or the website is large and includes many tables. What shall we do in cases of a large website that contains many tables? HTML *attributes* facilitate how we select specific parts of an HTML file.

An HTML element may have one or several attributes, which provides further information about the element and its behavior. For example, the anchor (<a>) tag creates a hyperlink. The `href` attribute determines the destination of the link, while the `target` attribute determines where the link will be opened (e.g., in a new tab). The next console shows the code of a link to the W3Schools website, which illustrates the <a> tag, and the link gives more information about HTML tags.

```
<!-- The a tag -->
<a href="https://www.w3schools.com" target="_blank">Click here</a>
```

We can extract information for specific attributes with the `html_attr()` function. Suppose we scrape a website, but the information is spread over several sub-pages. For this reason, we need to extract all links from the main page. We can extract these links via the `href` attribute from the <a> tag.

```
# Get elements with attributes
pr_html |>
  html_elements("a") |>
  html_attr("href") |>
  head()
```

```
#> [1] "#main"                              "../../index.html"
#> [3] "../../articles/PracticeR.html"     "../../reference/index.html"
#> [5] "#"                                  "../../articles/web_only/News.html"
```

Attributes help us to extract data, especially if we combine them with knowledge about CSS.

CSS

Cascading style sheets (CSS) are used to separate the formatting of an HTML file from its content. It may seem that CSS has nothing to do with web scraping if we inspect how we can format a website with CSS. Be patient, some knowledge about CSS will substantially increase your skills to select and to scrape data.

Suppose you created a personal website and you want to format several paragraphs (p) in a specific manner. Of course, we could use inline-blocks, but they are not efficient and make the code messy. With CSS, we can apply rules to format the entire website, save the style in an external file, and include the file in the meta section of the website. To apply the styling rules, we refer to the CSS file with the <link> tag in the head. In addition, I insert three paragraphs that we will style with CSS as the next console shows.

```
<!-- All <p> elements should get a text color -->
<head>
<link rel="stylesheet" href="CSS_File.css">
```

```
</head>
<body>
    <h1>My Blog</h1>
        <p>This is my first paragraph.</p>
        <p class="alert">I am an important paragraph.</p>
        <p id="unique">Look, a unicorn.</p>
</body>
```

With the help of CSS, we can refer to all <p> elements of the website and give them a specific text color (or other aspects that determine the appearance). The next console shows the corresponding CSS code.

```
/* All <p> elements get a red text color */
p {
  color: red;
}
```

Instead of changing each paragraph manually, we define the style for all paragraphs in the CSS file. An HTML element may have a class attribute, which makes it possible to give all elements of a certain class the same properties. Suppose we want to display important messages in red. The second paragraph of the example code has the alert class. We can refer to a class property with the CSS class (.) selector and the name of the class attribute.

```
/* Elements with the class (.) = "alert" will be red */
.alert {
  color: red;
}
```

All elements of the class alert are displayed in red, but we can combine both approaches if we want to color only paragraphs in red (p.alert).

```
/* All p elements with the class (.) = "alert" will be red */
p.alert {
  color: red;
}
```

Thus, we may refer to all elements or change only the appearance for certain elements of the class. Ultimately, an HTML element may have a unique id attribute, which makes

352 —— 11 Collect data

it possible to refer to this specific element only. The corresponding CSS selector is a hashtag (#) and the last paragraph included `unique` as `id` attribute.

```
/*Apply rules uniquely with id attributes: */
#unique {
  color: red;
}
```

Irrespective of text properties, CSS selectors help us to pick certain elements of a website because we can apply the same logic. For example, we may select elements of a certain class attribute (e.g. `.table`). In our case, it at least reveals that the Practice R website has two tables. Unfortunately, they share the same class.

```
# Get class via .
pr_html |> html_elements(".table")
```

```
{xml_nodeset (2)}
[1] <table class="table" id="table1">\n<colgroup...
[2] <table class="table" id="table2" style="text-align:left; font-si...
```

Here we may use the id attribute to differentiate between the tables, and you can select them with the corresponding selector. Insert a hashtag (#) and the id attribute in the `html_elements()` function to inspect the second table.

```
# Get id attribute via #
pr_html |>
  html_elements("#table2") |>
  html_table()
```

```
#>                    State    Capital Population GDP..in.billions.
#> 1 Baden-Württemberg Stuttgart 11,069,533               461
#> 2            Bavaria    Munich 13,076,721               550
#> 3             Berlin    Berlin  3,644,826               125
#> 4        Brandenburg   Potsdam  2,511,917                66
#> 5             Bremen    Bremen    682,986                32
#> 6            Hamburg   Hamburg  1,841,179               110
```

In a nutshell, the principles of web scraping are not complicated, but it can become quite complex depending on how a website is built, and also on your prior experience working with HTML, XML, and CSS. This section gave you a first impression, even if it only tries to convince you that scraping might be worth considering, although it is demanding. One last tip: you can also install a selector gadget (browser addin). It allows you to manually pick elements of the website and it shows information about an HTML element (e.g., attribute name) graphically. Such tools make it easier to extract specific elements and the rvest website outlines how a selector gadget works in more detail.

```
# The rvest website
# https://rvest.tidyverse.org/
```

Before you start web scraping, also check if the website has an API, because that is the most convenient way to retrieve data. If the website has one, check if there is an R package that offers you an interface to work with the API. The next section provides more information how APIs work.

11.3 APIs

An application programming interface (API) connects technical interfaces with each other. Say your smartphone synchronizes with your computer; they exchange information via an API that runs on a server and hosts the data. This sound unrelated in terms of data analysis, but when an API is available we can connect R to the server and retrieve the data.

Working with APIs can be intimidating, depending on the API and your prior experience. Most of the time you will need to identify yourself to the API before you can make a request to get the data. We thus need to know how an API communicates and we need to prepare the retrieved data before we can process it. To see how APIs work, let us stick to a simple API that does not require authentication.

The DemografixeR package (Brenninkmeijer, 2020) gives access to the Genderize API. The API predicts a person's sex based on a first name. All we need to retrieve the data from the API is a vector with names and the genderize() function. The DemografixeR package sends the names to the genderize.io API, fetches the results from the algorithm that runs on their server, and returns the prediction.

```
# The genderize API
library(DemografixeR)
names <- c("Edgar", "James", "Veronica", "Marta", "Fritz")
genderize(names, simplify = FALSE)

#>      name   type gender probability  count
#> 1   Edgar gender   male        0.99  16632
#> 2   James gender   male        0.99 117309
```

```
#> 3 Veronica gender female      0.99  47316
#> 4    Marta gender female      0.98 184145
#> 5    Fritz gender   male      0.95   3715
```

Never mind about the algorithm. The important point is that the DemografixeR package provides an interface to retrieve the data from the API. How does the package retrieve the information? In many cases, an API returns a JavaScript Object Notation (JSON) file. You can inspect how it works with your browser. The next console shows the web address that let us send a first name to the genderize.io API and the prediction for the name is displayed in the browser. We need to include the information that is send to the API within the web address (?name=). The next console shows the result for my name.

```
# Inspect the API via the browser:
# https://api.genderize.io/?name=edgar
# My browser returns:
```

```
{"name":"edgar","gender":"male","probability":0.99,"count":16632}
```

How we interact with an API, which parameters it needs to return data depends on the application, but the principle is identical for each API. We send parameters to a web server to get the results. For this reason, it is important to inspect the API's documentation.

Understanding the main idea of APIs is straightforward, but how do we retrieve data and what shall we do if there is no package that lets us interact with an API? Packages for APIs make a request to a server, retrieve data, and return the result in the console. With a little effort and the httr package (Wickham, 2022b), you can do that on your own. In the last chapter, I introduced GitHub. GitHub has an API which can be used to get information about GitHub accounts and repositories. More precisely, we will use this API and the httr package to get access to code that lives on GitHub.

Consider the show_script() function from the PracticeR package. If you have an internet connection: the source code of each Practice R chapter does not come from the installed package, it lives on GitHub. The function copies the code and creates a new script. However, if we do not insert any value, it returns an error message that lists all available files from the corresponding GitHub account.

```
# show_script knows which scripts are available
PracticeR::show_script()
```

```
#> Error in `PracticeR::show_script()`:
#> ! Please run `show_script()` with a valid file name as an argument.
#> Valid examples are:'chapter02', 'chapter03', 'chapter04', 'chapter05',
```

```
#> 'chapter06', 'chapter07', 'chapter08', 'chapter09', 'chapter10',
#> 'chapter11', 'chapter12'
```

We don't need an API to generate the chapter names, but we could use the httr package to fetch data from the GitHub account with all available files names of a repository. Interaction with such an API is not rocket science if we know how the httr package works. Let us recreate this function with the GitHub API – a function that returns a vector with available .R files from a GitHub account. First, inspect the GitHub API.

```
# Inspect the GitHub API
# https://api.github.com/
```

Next, we need to create a link to retrieve data from a GitHub repository, but the search query of the GitHub API is quite complicated. I used the API to search within the Practice R (edgar-treischl/Scripts_PracticeR/) repository (repo:). Moreover, I restricted the search query to R files (+extension:R). As Figure 11.3 illustrates, using a browser the API has found several files and returns a long list with information; this includes the name, the path, and further information about the items of the GitHub repository.

```
total_count:          11
incomplete_results:   false
▼ items:
  ▼ 0:
      name:     "chapter08.R"
      path:     "R/chapter08.R"
      sha:      "b585e344f41de97819be1bb2c76a591b6a1a46ac"
    ▼ url:      "https://api.github.com/repositories/458778179/contents/R/chapter08.R
    ▼ git_url:  "https://api.github.com/repositories/458778179/git/blobs/b585e344f41d
    ▼ html_url: "https://github.com/edgar-treischl/Scripts_PracticeR/blob/766cd072150
    ▼ repository:
```

Fig. 11.3: The GitHub API

In order to get access to these API results, we need to create the strings of the web address (git_url). As the next console highlights, I split the URL in four parts: the first part of the GitHub link (gitlink), complemented by the author, the repository name, as well as the extension parameter. Splitting the git_url makes it easier to recycle our work. We can retrieve data for another repository by changing the input.

```
# Build the link for the API
gitlink <- "https://api.github.com/search/code?q=repo:"
author <- "edgar-treischl"
repository <- "Scripts_PracticeR"

# Put them together
```

```r
git_url <- paste0(
  gitlink,
  author, "/",
  repository, "/",
  "+extension:R"
)

git_url
```

```
#> [1] "https://api.github.com/search/code?q=repo:edgar-treischl/
#> Scripts_PracticeR/+extension:R"
```

Next, we need to understand how `httr` and the *request method* works. You make a request if you interact with a server, and there are four common methods to do this: POST, PUT, DELETE, and GET. You may ask to create new information (POST), update existing information (PUT), or delete information (DELETE) from the server. In our case, we want to get (GET) information.

The `httr` package has implemented those functions; we get the same information that the browser returns with the GET() function. As the next console shows, I assign the result of the request as `response`. You may call the `response` object to get some basic information about the retrieved data (date, status, etc.). The GET() function retrieves the same information from the API as Figure 11.3 showed, but now as a JSON file.

```r
# GET a response from the Github API
response <- httr::GET(git_url)
response
```

```
#> Response [https://api.github.com/search/code?q=repo:edgar-treischl/
#> Scripts_PracticeR/+extension:R]
#> Date: 2022-12-01 17:05
#> Status: 200
#> Content-Type: application/json; charset=utf-8
#> Size: 65.6 kB
#> {
#>   "total_count": 11,
#>   "incomplete_results": false,
#>   "items": [
#>     {
#>       "name": "chapter08.R",
#>       "path": "R/chapter08.R",
#>       "sha": "b585e344f41de97819be1bb2c76a591b6a1a46ac",
```

```
#>      "url": "https://api.github.com/repositories/458778179/contents/ ...
#>      "git_url": "https://api.github.com/repositories/458778179/git/  ...
```

JSON is used to exchange the data; essentially, it returns *attribute-value pairs* (e.g.,
"total_count": 11). Do not worry if you are not familiar with JSON, because we can
extract information of the response with the content() function. Depending on the
API and the response, we may however wish to extract it differently. For this reason, we
can determine how the information is extracted with the as option (e.g., as text, as
raw). If possible, the content can be parsed into an R object. In our case, the content
function creates a list (response_parsed) and extracts the information from the JSON
file.

```
# Parse the content
response_parsed <- httr::content(response, as = "parsed")
class(response_parsed)
```

```
#> [1] "list"
```

The next data preparation steps are not that important, since they may depend on the
API. All GitHub files are saved as items in the response_parsed list. We can make a
vector of each item and bind them together with bind_rows() function from the dplyr
package.

```
# Prepare data
parsed_tree <- response_parsed$items
df <- dplyr::bind_rows(parsed_tree)
df
```

```
#> # A tibble: 506 x 8
#>   name        path  sha   url   git_url html_~1 repos~2 score
#>   <chr>       <chr> <chr> <chr> <chr>   <chr>   <named> <dbl>
#> 1 chapter08~ R/ch~ b585~ http~ https:~ https:~ <int>       1
#> 2 chapter08~ R/ch~ b585~ http~ https:~ https:~ <chr>       1
#> 3 chapter08~ R/ch~ b585~ http~ https:~ https:~ <chr>       1
#> 4 chapter08~ R/ch~ b585~ http~ https:~ https:~ <chr>       1
#> 5 chapter08~ R/ch~ b585~ http~ https:~ https:~ <lgl>       1
#> # ... with 501 more rows, and abbreviated variable names
#> #   1: html_url, 2: repository
```

In addition, the GitHub API returns a lot of duplicate names, since it includes all changes made to the listed files. The `stri_unique()` function returns only unique strings, or in our case, unique file names. To create a nicer output, we can sort them as last step.

```
# stringi::stri_unique returns unique strings
git_scripts <- df$name |>
  stringi::stri_unique() |>
  stringr::str_sort()

head(git_scripts)

#> [1] "chapter02.R" "chapter03.R" "chapter04.R" "chapter05.R" "chapter06.R"
#> [6] "chapter07.R"
```

Now you have a list with all available R files of the repository. Thus, we started to create a wrapper function for the GitHub API, which is essentially the same as an API package may offer, even if this is only our first approach. We need to put more effort into the function and, for example, deal with errors and other problems if we develop such a function.

Creating a wrapper function illustrates that you can retrieve data even if there is no dedicated R package. Let's put all the steps together and create a function (`which_gitscripts`). Because I split the link and inserted the repository name as a variable inside the function, we can now use `which_gitscripts()` for other repositories as well.

```
#Create your own wrapper function
which_gitscripts <- function(repository) {
  #Make URL
  author <- "edgar-treischl"
  git_url <- paste0("https://api.github.com/search/code?q=repo:",
                    author, "/",
                    repository, "/",
                    "+extension:R")

  #Get response
  response <- httr::GET(git_url)
  response_parsed <- httr::content(response, as="parsed")
  parsed_tree <- response_parsed$items

  #Prepare response
  df <- dplyr::bind_rows(parsed_tree)
```

11.3 APIs —— **359**

```r
  git_scripts <- df$name
  git_scripts_unique <- stringi::stri_unique(git_scripts)
  listed_script <- stringr::str_sort(git_scripts_unique)
  return(listed_script)
}
```

For example, which files does the `penguins_report` repository contain? You may recognize some of the script names from Chapter 10. I created this GitHub repository to render reports and send mails.

```r
# A test run
which_gitscripts("penguins_report") |> head()
```

```r
#> [1] "01_render_reports.R" "02_send_mails.R"      "utils.R"
```

Keep in mind that the discussed steps are essentially the same regardless of the used API. For example, the Weather API returns a weather forecast.

```r
# The weather API
# https://www.weatherapi.com/
```

Again, we need to learn first how the API works, but the main steps are the same: we create the search query, get the response, and prepare the response in order to process it. However, you need to register to use Weather API. For this reason, we need to include a key inside the `weather_url` and the code will not work on your computer until you have a valid `key`. All the remaining steps are then essentially the same, as the next console demonstrates.

```r
# Create url
weather1 <- "http://api.weatherapi.com/v1/current.json?"
place <- "Munich"
weather2 <- "&aqi=no"

# Insert your KEY
weather_url <- paste0(weather1, key, place, weather2)

# Get response
response <- httr::GET(weather_url)
response_text <- httr::content(response, as = "parsed")
```

360 — 11 Collect data

```
# Prepare response
df <- response_text$current
weather <- as.data.frame(df)
```

I picked `Munich` as a location. So, how's the temperature and the weather condition right now in Munich?

```
# Today is
Sys.Date()
```

```
#> [1] "2023-01-23"
```

```
# The temperature (in celsius)
weather$temp_c
```

```
#> [1] 1
```

```
# And how is the weather?
weather$condition.text
```

```
#> [1] "Overcast"
```

In summary, check out if you can get data from an API and look out for a dedicated R package to collect data before you start on your own. There are many package that provide access to APIs. For example, the `rtweet` package collects Twitter data (Kearney et al., 2022); or `tuber` connects you with the YouTube API (Sood, 2020). Maybe you are lucky and you find one, if not, you can create your own functions to retrieve data. Do not forget that a lot of companies restrict access and sometimes you need an account to retrieve data. That is the reason why I used freely accessible APIs. Inspect the corresponding packages and conditions of the API carefully if you plan to collect data from YouTube, Twitter, or any other API.

To work with APIs may seem quite impressive, but the principles are not complicated. It takes some time and effort to connect to and retrieve information from an API, but it is worth the trouble. With help of the `plumber` package (Schloerke & Allen, 2022), you are even able to create your own API, as the next info box outlines. Probably you do not plan to create an API, but it highlights once more how APIs work and I could not talk about APIs without highlighting such a cool R feature and package.

The plumber package

The plumber package makes it possible to setup an API that can be hosted on a server. One info box is certainly not enough to outline how the package works, but an example may give you a first idea. Suppose the API should return the GDP for a specific country. You created the return_gdp function, which returns the GDP for a country and a given year.

```
#Which country?
return_gdp("Spain")
```

```
#> 28821.
```

The plumber package lets us add API functions by inserting special comments in a script. For example, we create a new API and give it a title (@apiTitle) and a description (@apiDescription):

```
#* @apiTitle Test API
#* @apiDescription Get the GDP
```

Next, we need to specify which parameters or input the API needs (e.g., param country) and what kind of data the API returns. In this example, it returns a value and we apply the post method. Moreover, we need to add the function that the API should apply.

```
#* Returns most recent GDP for a country
#* @param country
#* @post /calculate_gdp
#Insert FUN here
```

After we insert the parameters, the package lets us create an API, which is running on a virtual server. The package shows the API interface in the viewer pane and you can test if it works. As Figure 11.4 highlights, the preview lets us insert a country name and, if we made no mistakes, the API returns the GPD.

Fig. 11.4: The plumber API

Summary

This chapter demonstrates that we can collect data with R. It may take some time and effort to extract data from a PDF, but it might be worth the trouble if we can extract a lot of information. The same applies to web scraping and APIs. Both may appear overwhelming if you have little knowledge about web-based technologies and languages, but I showed you that scraping data is not rocket science. Regardless of the source, you can answer unique research questions when you collect data and then combine it with available data. Consider reading *Automated Data Collection with R* by Munzert et al. (2014) if you want to learn more about the topic.

Before you start to collect data, also keep the `stringr` package in mind. It has many functions to manipulate strings. I introduced the package to extract data from a PDF, but knowledge about strings may also help us to scrape data or work with unstructured data, especially in combination with regular expressions. Don't forget to check out the cheat sheet to get an overview of all functions used to manipulate strings.

```
# Inspect the stringr website
# https://stringr.tidyverse.org/
```

12 Next steps

The last chapter highlights potential next steps. I briefly introduce topics, packages, and frameworks that would otherwise not find a place in this book. The discussion is not complete by itself, since R and in particular the R community offers too many possibilities. The last section underlines that there are many cool packages and features to discover. We explore next steps related to data preparation, analysis, visualization, and reporting.

```
# Setup Chapter 12
library(DBI)
library(dplyr)
library(dbplyr)
library(gapminder)
library(ggplot2)
library(ggrepel)
library(lubridate)
library(margins)
library(parameters)
library(titanic)
library(tibble)
library(shiny)
```

Data preparation

In Practice R, we worked with cross sectional data only and most of the time we manipulated data with the `dplyr` package. We also extended our knowledge about categorical variables and strings with the `forcats` and the `stringr` package. What about other types of data? How can we manipulate longitudinal data? There is so much more to explore when it comes to your next data preparation steps, but the good news is that we did not explore all functions from the introduced packages. Consider the `dplyr` package once more, it provides functions to work with longitudinal data. Suppose you have observed the following three persons in 2019 and 2020.

```
#Example data
df <-  tribble(
  ~person, ~year, ~income,
        1,  2019,    1821,
        1,  2020,    2291,
        2,  2019,    1971,
        2,  2020,    2146,
```

https://doi.org/10.1515/9783110704976-012

```
      3,   2019,   3544,
      3,   2020,   2877
)
```

For example, we may need a *lag* and a *lead* variable in order to work with longitudinal data. A lag variable is lagged in time and has the value from a previous wave, while a lead variable points to the next observational period. Create a lead variable with the `lead()` function; or, as the next console shows, generate a lag variable. In our case, the income in the first wave (2019) is the lag income for the second wave (2020). Group the data by `person` and create a new variable with the `lag()` function.

```
# Create a lag variable
df |>
  group_by(person) |>
  mutate(income_lag = lag(income))

#> # A tibble: 6 x 4
#> # Groups:    person [3]
#>    person  year income income_lag
#>     <dbl> <dbl>  <dbl>      <dbl>
#> 1       1  2019   1821         NA
#> 2       1  2020   2291       1821
#> 3       2  2019   1971         NA
#> 4       2  2020   2146       1971
#> 5       3  2019   3544         NA
#> # ... with 1 more row
```

Of course, this snippet does not prepare you to work with longitudinal data, but it illustrates that a package such as `dplyr` offers many opportunities, and sometimes you are already familiar with the package that provides a solution for a specific task. Remember, many packages come with vignettes and `dplyr` has further functions and vignettes to discover.

Sometimes, you will need other packages (or approaches) to prepare data. For example, we did not work with *time and date* variables, but the `lubridate` package provides functions to manipulate them (Spinu et al., 2022). Consider the `date` variable from the `lakers` basketball data that comes with the package. The variable indicates the date of a basketball game as integers. How can we transform the `date`?

```
# Use lubridate to prepare time and date variables
x <- lakers$date[1]
x
```

```
#> [1] 20081028
```

The ymd() function converts the integers to a date, it saves the date as year, month, and day. Moreover, the year(), the month(), and the day of a month (mday) function extract each piece of information separately:

```
# The ymd() function converts integers to a date
dates <- ymd(x)
dates
```

```
#> [1] "2008-10-28"
```

```
# Still an integer?
class(dates)
```

```
#> [1] "Date"
```

```
# Extract the day of a month
mday(dates)
```

```
#> [1] 28
```

```
# Extract month
month(dates)
```

```
#> [1] 10
```

```
# Extract year
year(dates)
```

```
#> [1] 2008
```

In order to improve our data preparation skills, there are more packages and possibilities to explore. Let me give you one last example: Suppose the data does not live on a hard drive, but in an SQL database. As outlined in Chapter 11, your dplyr knowledge will help you to work with SQL because the dbplyr package works with databases and is a sibling of the dplyr package (Wickham, Girlich, et al., 2022).

To connect R with a database, we need to establish a connection using the dbConnect() function from the DBI package, which provides the database interface (Wickham & Müller, 2022). It needs a driver (drv, e.g., from the odbc or other packages),

366 —— 12 Next steps

database specific arguments (e.g., host name, port number), and authentication details (e.g., user, password). After we connected R, we can make queries (e.g., update, filter data, etc.) and send or retrieve data from the database. The next console illustrates the procedure.

```
# Establish a connection to the database
library(DBI)
con <- DBI::dbConnect(
  drv = odbc::odbc(),
  host = "host",
  port = 3306,
  dbname = "database_name",
  user = "user",
  password = "password"
)
```

Working with a database may seem complicated, especially if you only started to learn SQL. The good news is, the RSQLite package helps you to learn SQL and we must not connect R to a data base for the first steps (Müller et al., 2022). The package relies on SQLite (a lightweight SQL database engine) and lets you make some dry runs on your local memory. Thus, we can test if an SQL code works and improve our skills without establishing a connection. The next console shows an SQL code example. It selects the variable mpg from the mtcars data and limits the output to three lines.

```
#A SQL example:
SELECT mpg FROM mtcars LIMIT 3;
```

In order to test this SQL code, we need to establish a connection as well. Insert the SQLite() function in the dbConnect() function and the memory argument as a database name. As a result, we pretend that we work with a database and use the memory of the local hard drive.

```
# Establish a connection to the local memory
con_myDB <- dbConnect(
  drv = RSQLite::SQLite(),
  dbname = ":memory:"
)
```

Next, we need to feed the local database by creating an example table with the dbWriteTable() function. As the next console highlights, we connect to the database (con_myDB) and create a new table based on the `mtcars` data. To check if we were successful, the `dbListTables()` function returns all tables of the database.

```
# Write a table into the "database"
dbWriteTable(
  conn = con_myDB,
  name = "mtcars",
  value = mtcars
)

# List all tables
dbListTables(con_myDB)

#> [1] "mtcars"
```

Now we can test the SQL code. The `dbGetQuery()` functions sends queries to the database and returns the result via the console.

```
# Get SQL Query
dbGetQuery(con_myDB, "SELECT mpg FROM mtcars LIMIT 3;")

#>    mpg
#> 1 21.0
#> 2 21.0
#> 3 22.8
```

In Practice R, we used data that was not (too) complicated to prepare, but this does not imply that you are not prepared to work with longitudinal data, dates, and you may even connect RStudio to a database. Of course, it will take some time and effort to take such next steps, but I am confident that you will find solutions to prepare the data, even if this book did not cover them.

Data analysis

In Chapter 6, we learned how to run a linear regression analysis. Sometimes, other methods are better suited to analyze the data. Say you examine who has access to public health services. How often do people go to a physician and can we explain disparities between social groups? Regardless of the hypothesis, the outcome is a count variable and we may apply a *Poisson regression* (see Tang et al., 2012).

Suppose the data contains information about patients who are sick. If we have observed the time and measured how long these people are sick, we can examine the survival time given that they have a certain disease. In this case you may apply an *event history analysis* (see Brostrom, 2021). However, if the data does not contain the exact time, but a binary outcome that indicates who has (not) survived, you may run a *logistic regression* (see Best & Wolf, 2014). Never mind if these topics are new, I will not introduce them in the last section, but depending on the outcome, you may want to run a different statistical analysis.

The `tidymodels` package provides a common framework – a series of packages for modeling and machine learning – which we could use to apply different analysis techniques (Kuhn & Wickham, 2022). What does this mean? Let's say an analysis is like a car. Each car comes with one specific engine. What if we could swap the engine or let the car have different driving modes? In terms of a linear regression, you may use the linear engine. What if you were asked to apply a different statistical analysis on another day? If your analysis is embedded in the `tidymodels` package, all you have to do is change the engine to use a different estimation technique. All the rest – how the code works, which estimates the model returns, how the output is formatted – is identical. Such a framework gives us the opportunity to focus on the content and we do not have to learn how the code works for a specific method.

Unfortunately, we need to know at least two different estimation engines to apply the `tidymodels`. For this reason, I show you the nuts and bolts of logistic regression in this section, especially since the latter is also a standard analysis technique in the social science curriculum.

Nuts and bolts of logistic regression

Why do some people smoke? Why do some students get a degree when others fail? In the social sciences we are often interested in examining binary outcomes (0/1) and you may use a logistic regression for this purpose. A logistic regression tries to classify the outcome and the approach was created because the assumptions of a linear regression might be violated in the case of a binary outcome.

The Titanic example is a classic to introduce a logistic regression and the corresponding `titanic` package gives you access to the data. For instance, examine if more women than men survived the Titanic. The outcome `Survived` indicates if a person has survived (1) or not (0).

```
# The Titanic data
library(titanic)

# Select variables, for example:
titanic_df <- titanic::titanic_train |>
  dplyr::select(Survived, Sex)
```

```r
# Inspect
head(titanic_df)
```

```
#>   Survived    Sex
#> 1        0   male
#> 2        1 female
#> 3        1 female
#> 4        1 female
#> 5        0   male
#> 6        0   male
```

Run a logistic regression with the `glm()` function and adjust which generalized model you want to use with the `family` option. Apply a logistic regression with the `logit` option, but you can use other functional forms (such as a `probit` model) as well. The `summary()` function returns the most important information about the model.

```r
# Minimal code to run a logistic regression
logit_model <- glm(Survived ~ Sex,
  family = binomial(link = "logit"),
  data = titanic_df
)
```

```r
# Print a summary
summary(logit_model)
```

```
#>
#> Call:
#> glm(formula = Survived ~ Sex, family = binomial(link = "logit"),
#>     data = titanic_df)
#>
#> Deviance Residuals:
#>     Min       1Q   Median       3Q      Max
#> -1.6462  -0.6471  -0.6471   0.7725   1.8256
#>
#> Coefficients:
#>             Estimate Std. Error z value Pr(>|z|)
#> (Intercept)   1.0566     0.1290   8.191 2.58e-16 ***
#> Sexmale      -2.5137     0.1672 -15.036  < 2e-16 ***
#> ---
#> Signif. codes:  0 '***' 0.001 '**' 0.01 '*' 0.05 '.' 0.1 ' ' 1
```

```
#>
#> (Dispersion parameter for binomial family taken to be 1)
#>
#>     Null deviance: 1186.7  on 890   degrees of freedom
#> Residual deviance:  917.8  on 889   degrees of freedom
#> AIC: 921.8
#>
#> Number of Fisher Scoring iterations: 4
```

Even though it seems a good idea to apply a logistic regression exclusively in terms of a binary outcome, a lot of people also use linear models (linear probability model) to analyze a binary outcome. There are several reason why this is the case, but one reason is that estimates from a logistic regression are tough to interpret.

Consider the `logit_model`. Due to its assumptions, the estimate of the logistic regression is a logarithm of the odds (log-odds) and the `glm()` function returns them. In our case the log-odds indicates a negative effect and fewer men than women survived the Titanic. How can we assess the log-odds? The estimate for male passengers (`Sexmale`) compared to female is –2.51. We can only say that the effect is negative and significant.

A lot of people have a hard time in explaining what this figure means. Instead of the log-odds, we can estimate odds ratios or predicted probabilities. Both are easier to interpret and most studies do not report log odds, but odds ratios or predicted values. An odds ratio is a ratio of two odds and the estimates are interpreted as a multiplicative factor. To examine odds ratios, use the `parameters()` function from the `parameters` package and `exponentiate` the coefficients (Lüdecke, Makowski, Ben-Shachar, Patil, Højsgaard, et al., 2022). As the next console shows, the model indicates that men's odds to survive is reduced by the factor 0.08 compared to the odds of women.

```
#Inspect odds ratios with the parameters package
logit_model|> parameters::parameters(exponentiate = TRUE)
```

```
#> Parameter    | Odds Ratio |   SE |        95% CI |      z |       p
#> -----------------------------------------------------------------------
#> (Intercept) |       2.88 | 0.37 | [2.24, 3.72] |   8.19 | < .001
#> Sex [male]  |       0.08 | 0.01 | [0.06, 0.11] | -15.04 | < .001
```

The `margins` package delivers average marginal effects (AME) and men's chances to survive are on average reduced by 55 percent as the next console shows (Leeper, 2021). As always, the package offer more than I can outline. Inspect the package's vignette if you want to calculate marginal effects at means, marginal effects at representative cases, or for marginal effect plots.

```
# Inspect marginal effects with the margins package
logit_margins <- margins::margins(logit_model)
summary(logit_margins)


#>    factor     AME     SE        z      p   lower   upper
#>   Sexmale -0.5531 0.0296 -18.6975 0.0000 -0.6111 -0.4951
```

In summary, I did not highlight all of the analysis techniques to boast about the possibilities; instead it should illustrate that you can run a Poisson regression, do an event history analysis or apply a logistic regression (and further models) with R. You may even use the `tidymodels` package and swap the engine. Check out the `tidymodels` website since the frameworks encompass several packages and contains more features than I could possibly highlight as a next step.

```
# The tidymodels website
# https://www.tidymodels.org/
```

Visualization

Practice R has a large focus on visualization, because it's my belief that visualizations are of great importance to communicate findings from empirical research. I introduced `ggplot2` and several extensions in Chapter 7, but this does not imply that there is nothing left to explore when it comes to visualization. For example, create interactive visualizations from a `ggplot2` graph with the `ploty` package (Sievert et al., 2022); make animated graphs with `gganimate` (Pedersen & Robinson, 2022); or visualize time-series data with `dygraphs` (Vanderkam et al., 2018).

Furthermore, I only introduced the `ggplot2` extensions that implement geoms, but there are many more packages that increase our visualization skills. For example, the `ggrepel` package provides functions to avoid overlapping text labels (Slowikowski, 2022). The next console shows two scatter plots made with the `gapminder` data. See how the first scatter plot that displays text labels (A) improves when we apply the `geom_text_repel()` function instead of the `geom_text()` function (B). It's fantastic how `ggrepel` improves the scatter plot by replacing one line of code. It substantially reduces the overlapping of the country names.

```
# Gapminder data
gapminder_df <- gapminder |>
  filter(year == "2007" & continent == "Europe")

# Left Plot: geom_text
ggplot(gapminder_df, aes(gdpPercap, lifeExp, label = country)) +
```

```
  geom_point(color = "red") +
  labs(title = "A: geom_text()") +
  geom_text()

# Right plot: geom_text_repel
ggplot(gapminder_df, aes(gdpPercap, lifeExp, label = country)) +
  geom_point(color = "red") +
  labs(title = "B: geom_text_repel()") +
  geom_text_repel()
```

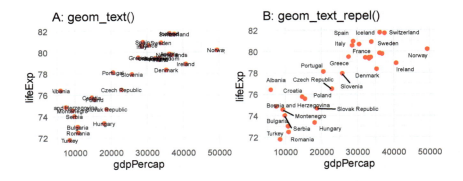

Unfortunately, I did not emphasize enough why text labels are important to communicate the graph's message. Inspect the ggplot2 website to learn more about text labels, and the ggrepel documentation to discover more about the package and its possibilities.

Or consider the shiny package (Chang et al., 2022). In a strict sense, shiny does not belong in this section because it is not a visualization (technique), but shiny makes it possible to create interactive dashboards with visualizations. The package includes several example apps that demonstrate how shiny apps work. Figure 12.1 shows one of these examples. The 01_hello app displays a slider and a histogram. Shiny apps are reactive and let user interact with data. In the app, the user can adjust the number of bins with the slider on the left side. The shiny package reacts and recreates the histogram on the right side, in accordance with the selected number of bins.

The shiny package is awesome and the examples will help you to make the first app. As the next console illustrates, use the runExample() function to explore one of the example apps. And don't forget to check out the website, because the package has more didactic apps to explore.

```
# Inspect example shiny apps: 01_hello, 02_text, etc.
library(shiny)
runExample("01_hello")
```

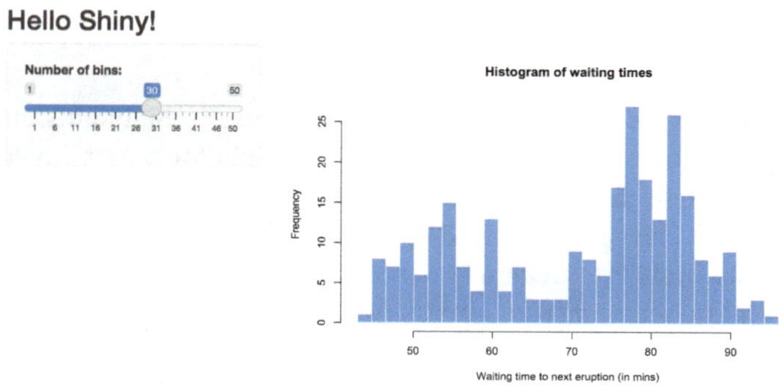

Hello Shiny!

Fig. 12.1: The shiny app

I decided not to introduce shiny in a systematic manner. We focus on typical steps of applied research, and unfortunately, this does not (yet) include dashboards. If you want to learn shiny, the website has plenty of information to start with, apart from the example apps. There are video tutorials and many shows cases. In addition, check out *Mastering Shiny* by Wickham (2021) to learn more about shiny apps.

```
# Mastering Shiny:
PracticeR::show_link("master_shiny")
```

Reporting

Finally, there are also several next steps to consider about reporting. We learned how to create (dynamic) documents with rmarkdown, but maybe your ambition is larger and you are about to write a book. The bookdown package provides a framework to write (e-) books with R (Xie, 2022a).

How about a website? Creating a basic website is easy with rmarkdown and you can see first results after four simple steps. Go the RStudio menu and create a new project for the website, chose the simple R Markdown website as project type, choose a directory for the website files, and render it. The rmarkdown website shows the steps in more detail and provides further information on how to personalize the website.

Quarto might also be a next step to consider. Quarto is an open-source publishing system and a multi-language extension for rmarkdown. Quarto allows you to work with other programming languages (e.g., Python, Julia) and the procedure to render documents is almost identical to rmarkdown. However, Quarto introduces new features and templates to create articles, reports, presentations, and more. Go and this visit the Quarto website for more information.

```
# Quarto website:
# https://quarto.org/
```

Instead of focusing on books, websites, or Quarto, this last subsections highlights the possibility of creating a presentation. More precisely, I will highlight the possibility to create HTML slides with R. Maybe this seems odd, since you expect me to talk about a PowerPoint presentation or at least a PDF instead of an HTML file. Keep in mind that you already have the rmarkdown skills to create a PowerPoint presentation. Moreover, do we really need a PowerPoint presentation if you can show slides in all modern browsers and export the file as a PDF? I am not trying to convince you to abandon PowerPoint or any other Microsoft product (forever). I would never say such a thing. All I am saying is that an HTML presentation gives us an excellent alternative to conventional slides, because we can include all kinds of interactive web applications.

For example, the xaringan package implements remark.js in R, which is a Java Script package to create HTML slides (Xie, 2022d). The package includes a template called the ninja presentation which gives you a comprehensive impression of what xaringan has to offer. The template includes many examples of how to create a present-ation. You may feel a bit overwhelmed if you start to work with this template. It shows you how to highlight R code, how to insert interactive tables, and it even includes a map. Including such fancy things in your presentation is more complicated than creating a simple presentation, but I believe you don't need much time and assistance to create slides with R.

For this reason I created a minimal xaringan template and included it in the PracticeR package as the last goodie. Create a new rmarkdown file from the templates and use the PracticeR slides template. It shows the typical first steps to create a present-ation. For example, it shows that texts are formatted with Markdown, you can insert R code via chunks, and there is a meta section to define the global settings of the document.

It goes without saying that you need to learn a few tricks to create slides. For example, individual slides are separated with a line that contains three dashes (---) and you may add a new slide at the end of the template to see how it works. However, the first slide does not start with three dashes, because the xaringan package automatically creates the title slide from the information of the meta section. Set the seal field in the YAML to false if you want to create your own title slide.

Furthermore, the xaringan package provides many CSS themes and fonts to style slides (or you can create your own style). To apply a theme, change the css field in the

YAML of the template and pick one of the predefined style (or refer to your own CSS file). For example, how about the chocolate, robot, or the metropolis theme? Inspect the minimal template and the package documentation to learn more about the package. There is even an extension package for xaringan, examine the xaringanExtra package if you need extra styles, to embed the picture of a webcam into the slides, or for fancy slide transitions (Aden-Buie & Warkentin, 2022).

If you need a PDF file of your slides, use the chrome_print() function from the pagedown package (Xie et al., 2022). The function converts the HTML file and saves it in your working directory.

```
# chrome_print exports the file as a PDF
pagedown::chrome_print("my_presentation.html")
```

Finally, there is only one thing left to say: At the time this book was written, the CRAN package repository had 18993 available packages stored and thus many potential next steps for you to explore. The last chapter lists all R packages to build this book with the bookdown package (Xie, 2022a).

Session info

```
#Session info of Practice R
sessioninfo::session_info()


#> - Session info ------------------------------------------------------------
#>  setting  value
#>  version  R version 4.1.1 (2021-08-10)
#>  os       macOS Big Sur 10.16
#>  system   x86_64, darwin17.0
#>  ui       X11
#>  language (EN)
#>  collate  en_US.UTF-8
#>  ctype    en_US.UTF-8
#>  tz       Europe/Berlin
#>  date     2023-01-23
#>  pandoc   2.19.2 @ /Applications/RStudio.app/Contents/Resources/app/quarto
#>
#> - Packages ----------------------------------------------------------------
#>  package      * version date (UTC) lib source
#>  assertthat     0.2.1   2019-03-21 [1] CRAN (R 4.1.0)
#>  bookdown       0.31    2022-12-13 [1] CRAN (R 4.1.2)
#>  cli            3.4.1   2022-09-23 [1] CRAN (R 4.1.1)
#>  colorspace     2.0-3   2022-02-21 [1] CRAN (R 4.1.1)
#>  DBI            1.1.3   2022-06-18 [1] CRAN (R 4.1.2)
#>  digest         0.6.31  2022-12-11 [1] CRAN (R 4.1.2)
#>  dplyr          1.0.10  2022-09-01 [1] CRAN (R 4.1.2)
#>  evaluate       0.19    2022-12-13 [1] CRAN (R 4.1.2)
#>  fansi          1.0.3   2022-03-24 [1] CRAN (R 4.1.2)
#>  fastmap        1.1.0   2021-01-25 [1] CRAN (R 4.1.0)
#>  generics       0.1.3   2022-07-05 [1] CRAN (R 4.1.2)
#>  ggplot2        3.4.0   2022-11-04 [1] CRAN (R 4.1.2)
#>  glue           1.6.2   2022-02-24 [1] CRAN (R 4.1.1)
#>  gtable         0.3.1   2022-09-01 [1] CRAN (R 4.1.2)
#>  htmltools      0.5.4   2022-12-07 [1] CRAN (R 4.1.2)
#>  knitr          1.41    2022-11-18 [1] CRAN (R 4.1.2)
#>  lifecycle      1.0.3   2022-10-07 [1] CRAN (R 4.1.2)
#>  magrittr       2.0.3   2022-03-30 [1] CRAN (R 4.1.2)
#>  munsell        0.5.0   2018-06-12 [1] CRAN (R 4.1.0)
#>  pillar         1.8.1   2022-08-19 [1] CRAN (R 4.1.2)
```

https://doi.org/10.1515/9783110704976-013

```
#>  pkgconfig     2.0.3   2019-09-22 [1] CRAN (R 4.1.0)
#>  purrr         0.3.5   2022-10-06 [1] CRAN (R 4.1.2)
#>  R.cache       0.16.0  2022-07-21 [1] CRAN (R 4.1.2)
#>  R.methodsS3   1.8.2   2022-06-13 [1] CRAN (R 4.1.2)
#>  R.oo          1.25.0  2022-06-12 [1] CRAN (R 4.1.2)
#>  R.utils       2.12.2  2022-11-11 [1] CRAN (R 4.1.2)
#>  R6            2.5.1   2021-08-19 [1] CRAN (R 4.1.0)
#>  rlang         1.0.6   2022-09-24 [1] CRAN (R 4.1.1)
#>  rmarkdown     2.19    2022-12-15 [1] CRAN (R 4.1.2)
#>  rstudioapi    0.14    2022-08-22 [1] CRAN (R 4.1.2)
#>  scales        1.2.1   2022-08-20 [1] CRAN (R 4.1.2)
#>  sessioninfo   1.2.2   2021-12-06 [1] CRAN (R 4.1.0)
#>  stringi       1.7.8   2022-07-11 [1] CRAN (R 4.1.1)
#>  stringr       1.5.0   2022-12-02 [1] CRAN (R 4.1.2)
#>  styler        1.8.1   2022-11-07 [1] CRAN (R 4.1.2)
#>  tibble        3.1.8   2022-07-22 [1] CRAN (R 4.1.2)
#>  tidyselect    1.2.0   2022-10-10 [1] CRAN (R 4.1.2)
#>  utf8          1.2.2   2021-07-24 [1] CRAN (R 4.1.0)
#>  vctrs         0.5.1   2022-11-16 [1] CRAN (R 4.1.2)
#>  xfun          0.35    2022-11-16 [1] CRAN (R 4.1.2)
#>  yaml          2.3.6   2022-10-18 [1] CRAN (R 4.1.2)
#>
#>  [1] /Library/Frameworks/R.framework/Versions/4.1/Resources/library
#>
#> --------------------------------------------------------------------------
```

Bibliography

Aden-Buie, G., & Warkentin, M. T. (2022). *xaringanExtra: Extras and Extensions for xaringan Slides*. https://CRAN.R-project.org/package=xaringanExtra

Allaire, J., Xie, Y., Dervieux, C., R Foundation, Wickham, H., Journal of Statistical Software, Vaidyanathan, R., Association for Computing Machinery, Boettiger, C., Elsevier, Broman, K., Mueller, K., Quast, B., Pruim, R., Marwick, B., Wickham, C., Keyes, O., Yu, M., Emaasit, D., ... Hyndman, R. (2022). *rticles: Article Formats for R Markdown*. https://github.com/rstudio/rticles

Allaire, J., Xie, Y., McPherson, J., Luraschi, J., Ushey, K., Atkins, A., Wickham, H., Cheng, J., Chang, W., & Iannone, R. (2022). *rmarkdown: Dynamic Documents for R*. https://CRAN.R-project.org/package=rmarkdown

Allison, P. D. (2001). *Missing data*. Sage.

Anscombe, F., J. (1973). Graphs in Statistical Analysis. *The American Statistician*, *27*(1), 7–21.

Arnold, J. B. (2021). *ggthemes: Extra Themes, Scales and Geoms for ggplot2*. https://CRAN.R-project.org/package=ggthemes

Bååth, R. (2018). *Beepr: Easily Play Notification Sounds on any Platform*. https://CRAN.R-project.org/package=beepr

Bache, S. M., & Wickham, H. (2022). *magrittr: A Forward-Pipe Operator for R*. https://CRAN.R-project.org/package=magrittr

Ben-Shachar, M. S., Makowski, D., Lüdecke, D., Patil, I., & Wiernik, B. M. (2022). *effectsize: Indices of Effect Size*. https://CRAN.R-project.org/package=effectsize

Best, H., & Wolf, C. (2014). Logistic regression. In H. Best & C. Wolf (Eds.), *SAGE Handbook of Regression Analysis and Causal Inference* (pp. 153–171). Sage.

Blair, G., Cooper, J., Coppock, A., Humphreys, M., & Sonnet, L. (2022). *estimatr: Fast Estimators for Design-Based Inference*. https://CRAN.R-project.org/package=estimatr

Brenninkmeijer, M. (2020). *DemografixeR: Extrapolate Gender, Age and Nationality of a Name*. https://CRAN.R-project.org/package=DemografixeR

Breusch, T. S., & Pagan, A. R. (1979). A Simple Test for Heteroscedasticity and Random Coefficient Variation. *Econometrica*, *47*(5), 1287–1294. https://doi.org/10.2307/1911963

Brostrom, G. (2021). *Event History Analysis With R* (2nd ed.). CRC Press.

Bruce, P., Bruce, A., & Gedeck, P. (2020). *Practical Statistics for Data Scientists: 50+ Essential Concepts Using R and Python* (2nd ed.). O'Reilly.

Brunson, J. C., & Read, Q. D. (2020). *ggalluvial: Alluvial Plots in ggplot2*. https://CRAN.R-project.org/package=ggalluvial

Bryan, J. (2017). *gapminder: Data from Gapminder*. https://CRAN.R-project.org/package=gapminder

Bryan, J. (2022). *googlesheets4: Access Google Sheets using the Sheets API V4*. https://CRAN.R-project.org/package=googlesheets4

Bryan, J., & Wickham, H. (2022). *gh: GitHub 'API'*. https://CRAN.R-project.org/package=gh

Chacon, S., & Straub, B. (2014). *Pro Git* (2nd ed). Apress.

Champely, S. (2020). *pwr: Basic Functions for Power Analysis*. https://CRAN.R-project.org/package=pwr

Chang, W. (2012). *R Graphics Cookbook* (1st ed.). O'Reilly.

Chang, W., Cheng, J., Allaire, J., Sievert, C., Schloerke, B., Xie, Y., Allen, J., McPherson, J., Dipert, A., & Borges, B. (2022). *shiny: Web Application Framework for R*. https://CRAN.R-project.org/package=shiny

Clarke, E., & Sherrill-Mix, S. (2017). *ggbeeswarm: Categorical Scatter (Violin Point) Plots*. https://CRAN.R-project.org/package=ggbeeswarm

https://doi.org/10.1515/9783110704976-014

Cleveland, W. S. (1979). Robust Locally Weighted Regression and Smoothing Scatterplots. *Journal of the American Statistical Association*, *74*(368), 829–836. https://doi.org/10.1080/01621459.1979.10481038

Cohen, J. (1988). *Statistical Power Analysis for the Behavioral Sciences*. Routledge Academic.

Comtois, D. (2022). *summarytools: Tools to Quickly and Neatly Summarize Data*. https://CRAN.R-project.org/package=summarytools

Cook, R. D. (1977). Detection of Influential Observation in Linear Regression. *Technometrics*, *19*(1), 15–18. https://doi.org/10.2307/1268249

Cortina, H. (2022). *hockeystick: Download and Visualize Essential Climate Change Data*. https://CRAN.R-project.org/package=hockeystick

Couture-Beil, A. (2022). *rjson: JSON for R*. https://CRAN.R-project.org/package=rjson

Csárdi, G. (2022). *gitcreds: Query git Credentials from R*. https://CRAN.R-project.org/package=gitcreds

Csárdi, G., & Salmon, M. (2022). *pkgsearch: Search and Query CRAN R Packages*. https://CRAN.R-project.org/package=pkgsearch

Cui, B. (2020). *DataExplorer: Automate Data Exploration and Treatment*. https://CRAN.R-project.org/package=DataExplorer

Davies, R., Locke, S., & D'Agostino McGowan, L. (2022). *datasauRus: Datasets from the Datasaurus Dozen*. https://CRAN.R-project.org/package=datasauRus

Dervieux, C., Allaire, J., Iannone, R., Presmanes Hill, A., & Xie, Y. (2022). *distill: R Markdown Format for Scientific and Technical Writing*. https://CRAN.R-project.org/package=distill

Dowle, M., & Srinivasan, A. (2022). *Data.table: Extension of data.frame*. https://CRAN.R-project.org/package=data.table

Enders, C. K. (2010). *Applied Missing Data Analysis*. Guilford.

Firebaugh, G. (2008). *Seven Rules for Social Research*. University Press Group.

Firke, S. (2021). *janitor: Simple Tools for Examining and Cleaning Dirty Data*. https://CRAN.R-project.org/package=janitor

Friendly, M. (2021). *HistData: Data Sets from the History of Statistics and Data Visualization*. https://CRAN.R-project.org/package=HistData

Gagolewski, M., Tartanus, B., Unicode, others;, Inc., et al. (2022). *stringi: Fast and Portable Character String Processing Facilities*. https://CRAN.R-project.org/package=stringi

Garnier, S. (2021). *viridis: Colorblind-Friendly Color Maps for R*. https://CRAN.R-project.org/package=viridis

Gelman, A., Hill, J., & Vehtari, A. (2020). *Regression and Other Stories*. Cambridge University Press.

Gohel, D., & Skintzos, P. (2022). *flextable: Functions for Tabular Reporting*. https://CRAN.R-project.org/package=flextable

Grolemund, G. (2014). *Hands-On Programming with R: Write Your Own Functions and Simulations* (1st ed.). O'Reilly.

Healy, K. (2019). *Data Visualization: A Practical Introduction*. Princeton University Press.

Henry, L., & Wickham, H. (2022). *purrr: Functional Programming Tools*. https://CRAN.R-project.org/package=purrr

Hester, J., & Bryan, J. (2022). *glue: Interpreted String Literals*. https://CRAN.R-project.org/package=glue

Hlavac, M. (2022). *stargazer: Well-Formatted Regression and Summary Statistics Tables*. https://CRAN.R-project.org/package=stargazer

Hodge, D. (2022). *ggblanket: Simplify ggplot2 Visualisation*. https://CRAN.R-project.org/package=ggblanket

Horst, A., Hill, A., & Gorman, K. (2022). *palmerpenguins: Palmer Archipelago (Antarctica) Penguin Data*. https://CRAN.R-project.org/package=palmerpenguins

Hothorn, T., Zeileis, A., Farebrother, R. W., & Cummins, C. (2022). *lmtest: Testing Linear Regression Models*. https://CRAN.R-project.org/package=lmtest

Hugh-Jones, D. (2022). *huxtable: Easily Create and Style Tables for LaTeX, HTML and Other Formats*. https://CRAN.R-project.org/package=huxtable/

Hvitfeldt, E. (2021). *paletteer: Comprehensive Collection of Color Palettes*. https://CRAN.R-project.org/package=paletteer

Iannone, R., & Cheng, J. (2020). *blastula: Easily Send HTML Email Messages*. https://CRAN.R-project.org/package=blastula

Imbens, G. W., & Rubin, D. B. (2015). *Causal Inference for Statistics, Social, and Biomedical Sciences. An Introduction*. Cambridge University Press.

James, G., Witten, D., Hastie, T., & Tibshirani, R. (2013). *An Introduction to Statistical Learning*. Springer.

Jeppson, H., Hofmann, H., & Cook, D. (2021). *ggmosaic: Mosaic Plots in the ggplot2 Framework*. https://CRAN.R-project.org/package=ggmosaic

Kahle, D., & Wickham, H. (2013). ggmap: Spatial Visualization with ggplot2. *The R Journal, 5*(1), 144–161. https://journal.r-project.org/archive/2013-1/kahle-wickham.pdf

Kahle, D., Wickham, H., & Jackson, S. (2022). *ggmap: Spatial Visualization with ggplot2*. https://CRAN.R-project.org/package=ggmap

Kassambara, A., Kosinski, M., & Biecek, P. (2021). *survminer: Drawing Survival Curves using ggplot2*. https://CRAN.R-project.org/package=survminer

Kearney, M. W., Revilla Sancho, L., & Wickham, H. (2022). *rtweet: Collecting Twitter Data*. https://CRAN.R-project.org/package=rtweet

Kuhn, M., & Wickham, H. (2022). *tidymodels: Easily Install and Load the Tidymodels Packages*. https://CRAN.R-project.org/package=tidymodels

Le Pennec, E., & Slowikowski, K. (2022). *ggwordcloud: A Word Cloud Geom for ggplot2*.

Leeper, T. J. (2021). *margins: Marginal Effects for Model Objects*. https://CRAN.R-project.org/package=margins

Lin, G. (2022). *Reactable: Interactive Data Tables Based on React Table*. https://CRAN.R-project.org/package=reactable

Little, R. J. A., & Rubin, D. B. (1987). *Statistical Analysis with Missing Data*. Wiley.

Long, J. A. (2021). *interactions: Comprehensive, User-Friendly Toolkit for Probing Interactions*. https://CRAN.R-project.org/package=interactions

Long, J. A. (2022). *jtools: Analysis and Presentation of Social Scientific Data*. https://CRAN.R-project.org/package=jtools

Lüdecke, D. (2022). *ggeffects: Create Tidy Data Frames of Marginal Effects for ggplot from Model Outputs*. https://CRAN.R-project.org/package=ggeffects

Lüdecke, D., Makowski, D., Ben-Shachar, M. S., Patil, I., Højsgaard, S., & Wiernik, B. M. (2022). *parameters: Processing of Model Parameters*. https://CRAN.R-project.org/package=parameters

Lüdecke, D., Makowski, D., Ben-Shachar, M. S., Patil, I., Waggoner, P., & Wiernik, B. M. (2022). *performance: Assessment of Regression Models Performance*. https://CRAN.R-project.org/package=performance

Lüdecke, D., Makowski, D., Patil, I., Ben-Shachar, M. S., Wiernik, B. M., & Waggoner, P. (2022). *see: Model Visualisation Toolbox for easystats and ggplot2*. https://CRAN.R-project.org/package=see

Makowski, D., Lüdecke, D., Ben-Shachar, M. S., Patil, I., & Wiernik, B. M. (2022). *report: Automated Reporting of Results and Statistical Models*. https://CRAN.R-project.org/package=report

Makowski, D., Wiernik, B. M., Patil, I., Lüdecke, D., & Ben-Shachar, M. S. (2022). *Correlation: Methods for Correlation Analysis*. https://CRAN.R-project.org/package=correlation

Mann, M. E., Bradley, R. S., & Hughes, M. K. (1999). Northern Hemisphere Temperatures During the Past Millennium: Inferences, Uncertainties, and Limitations. *Geophysical Research Letters, 26*(6), 759–762. https://doi.org/10.1029/1999GL900070

Martoglio, E. (2018). *rpivotTable: Build Powerful Pivot Tables and Dynamically Slice & Dice your Data.* https://CRAN.R-project.org/package=rpivotTable

Matejka, J., & Fitzmaurice, G. (2017). Same Stats, Different Graphs: Generating Datasets with Varied Appearance and Identical Statistics through Simulated Annealing. *Proceedings of the 2017 CHI Conference on Human Factors in Computing Systems*, 1290–1294. https://doi.org/10.1145/3025453.3025912

McBain, M., Carroll, J., Gelfand, S., Owlarn, S., & Aden-Buie, G. (2020). *Datapasta: R Tools for Data Copy-Pasta.* https://CRAN.R-project.org/package=datapasta

Meyer, F., & Perrier, V. (2022). *esquisse: Explore and Visualize Your Data Interactively.* https://CRAN.R-project.org/package=esquisse

Müller, K. (2020). *here: A Simpler Way to Find Your Files.* https://CRAN.R-project.org/package=here

Müller, K., & Walthert, L. (2022). *styler: Non-Invasive Pretty Printing of R Code.* https://CRAN.R-project.org/package=styler

Müller, K., Wickham, H., James, D. A., & Falcon, S. (2022). *RSQLite: SQLite Interface for R.* https://CRAN.R-project.org/package=RSQLite

Munzert, S., Rubba, C., Meißner, P., & Nyhuis, D. (2014). *Automated Data Collection with R: A Practical Guide to Web Scraping and Text Mining* (1st ed.). Wiley.

Neitmann, T. (2020). *ggcharts: Shorten the Distance from Data Visualization Idea to Actual Plot.* https://CRAN.R-project.org/package=ggcharts

Neuwirth, E. (2022). *RColorBrewer: ColorBrewer Palettes.* https://CRAN.R-project.org/package=RColorBrewer

O'Hara-Wild, M., & Hyndman, R. (2022). *vitae: Curriculum Vitae for R Markdown.* https://CRAN.R-project.org/package=vitae

Okal, T. (2020). *rtist: A Color Palette Generator.* https://CRAN.R-project.org/package=rtist

Ooms, J. (2022). *pdftools: Text Extraction, Rendering and Converting of PDF Documents.* https://CRAN.R-project.org/package=pdftools

Pearl, J., & Mackenzie, D. (2019). *The Book of Why: The New Science of Cause and Effect.* Penguin.

Pedersen, T. L. (2022a). *ggforce: Accelerating ggplot2.* https://CRAN.R-project.org/package=ggforce

Pedersen, T. L. (2022b). *patchwork: The Composer of Plots.* https://CRAN.R-project.org/package=patchwork

Pedersen, T. L., & Robinson, D. (2022). *gganimate: A Grammar of Animated Graphics.* https://CRAN.R-project.org/package=gganimate

Qiu, Y. (2022). *showtext: Using Fonts More Easily in R Graphs.* https://CRAN.R-project.org/package=showtext

Rajaretnam, T. (2015). *Statistics for Social Sciences.* Sage.

Robinson, D., Hayes, A., & Couch, S. (2022). *Broom: Convert Statistical Objects into Tidy Tibbles.* https://CRAN.R-project.org/package=broom

Rowling, J. K. (2014). *Harry Potter and the Order of the Phoenix.* Bloomsbury Children's Books.

Rubin, D. B. (1987). *Multiple Imputation for Nonresponse in Surveys.* Wiley.

Rudis, B., & Gandy, D. (2017). *waffle: Create Waffle Chart Visualizations in R.* https://CRAN.R-project.org/package=waffle

Schloerke, B., & Allen, J. (2022). *plumber: An API Generator for R.* https://CRAN.R-project.org/package=plumber

Schloerke, B., Cook, D., Larmarange, J., Briatte, F., Marbach, M., Thoen, E., Elberg, A., & Crowley, J. (2021). *GGally: Extension to ggplot2.* https://CRAN.R-project.org/package=GGally

Sievert, C., Parmer, C., Hocking, T., Chamberlain, S., Ram, K., Corvellec, M., & Despouy, P. (2022). *plotly: Create Interactive Web Graphics via plotly.js*. https://CRAN.R-project.org/package=plotly

Silge, J., & Robinson, D. (2017). *Text Mining with R: A Tidy Approach*. O'Reilly.

Slowikowski, K. (2022). *ggrepel: Automatically Position Non-Overlapping Text Labels with ggplot2*. https://CRAN.R-project.org/package=ggrepel

Solt, F., & Hu, Y. (2021). *dotwhisker: Dot-and-Whisker Plots of Regression Results*. https://CRAN.R-project.org/package=dotwhisker

Sood, G. (2020). *tuber: Client for the YouTube API*. https://CRAN.R-project.org/package=tuber

Spinu, V., Grolemund, G., & Wickham, H. (2022). *lubridate: Make Dealing with Dates a Little Easier*. https://CRAN.R-project.org/package=lubridate

Stephenson, A. (2021). *tayloRswift: Color Palettes Generated by Taylor Swift Albums*. https://CRAN.R-project.org/package=tayloRswift

Tang, W., He, H., & Tu, X. M. (2012). *Applied Categorical and Count Data Analysis*. Taylor & Francis.

Thorne, B. (2019). *posterdown: Generate PDF Conference Posters Using R Markdown*. https://CRAN.R-project.org/package=posterdown

Tierney, N., Cook, D., McBain, M., & Fay, C. (2021). *naniar: Data Structures, Summaries, and Visualisations for Missing Data*. https://CRAN.R-project.org/package=naniar

Ushey, K., Allaire, J., & Tang, Y. (2022). *reticulate: Interface to Python*. https://CRAN.R-project.org/package=reticulate

Vanderkam, D., Allaire, J., Owen, J., Gromer, D., & Thieurmel, B. (2018). *dygraphs: Interface to Dygraphs Interactive Time Series Charting Library*. https://CRAN.R-project.org/package=dygraphs

Waring, E., Quinn, M., McNamara, A., Arino de la Rubia, E., Zhu, H., & Ellis, S. (2022). *skimr: Compact and Flexible Summaries of Data*. https://CRAN.R-project.org/package=skimr

Wei, T., & Simko, V. (2021). *Corrplot: Visualization of a Correlation Matrix*. https://CRAN.R-project.org/package=corrplot

Wickham, H. (2016). *ggplot2: Elegant Graphics for Data Analysis* (2nd ed.). Springer.

Wickham, H. (2021). *Mastering Shiny: Build Interactive Apps, Reports, and Dashboards Powered by R*. O'Reilly.

Wickham, H. (2022a). *forcats: Tools for Working with Categorical Variables (Factors)*. https://CRAN.R-project.org/package=forcats

Wickham, H. (2022b). *httr: Tools for Working with URLs and HTTP*. https://CRAN.R-project.org/package=httr

Wickham, H. (2022c). *stringr: Simple, Consistent Wrappers for Common String Operations*. https://CRAN.R-project.org/package=stringr

Wickham, H. (2022d). *tidyverse: Easily Install and Load the Tidyverse*. https://CRAN.R-project.org/package=tidyverse

Wickham, H., & Bryan, J. (2022). *readxl: Read Excel Files*. https://CRAN.R-project.org/package=readxl

Wickham, H., Bryan, J., & Barrett, M. (2022). *usethis: Automate Package and Project Setup*. https://CRAN.R-project.org/package=usethis

Wickham, H., Chang, W., Henry, L., Pedersen, T. L., Takahashi, K., Wilke, C., Woo, K., Yutani, H., & Dunnington, D. (2022). *ggplot2: Create Elegant Data Visualisations Using the Grammar of Graphics*. https://CRAN.R-project.org/package=ggplot2

Wickham, H., François, R., Henry, L., & Müller, K. (2022). *dplyr: A Grammar of Data Manipulation*. https://CRAN.R-project.org/package=dplyr

Wickham, H., & Girlich, M. (2022). *tidyr: Tidy Messy Data*. https://CRAN.R-project.org/package=tidyr

Wickham, H., Girlich, M., & Ruiz, E. (2022). *dbplyr: A dplyr Back End for Databases*. https://CRAN.R-project.org/package=dbplyr

Wickham, H., & Grolemund, G. (2016). *R for Data Science: Import, Tidy, Transform, Visualize, and Model Data*. O'Reilly.

Wickham, H., Hester, J., & Bryan, J. (2022). *readr: Read Rectangular Text Data*. https://CRAN.R-project.org/package=readr

Wickham, H., Hester, J., Chang, W., & Bryan, J. (2022). *devtools: Tools to Make Developing R Packages Easier*. https://CRAN.R-project.org/package=devtools

Wickham, H., Miller, E., & Smith, D. (2022). *haven: Import and Export SPSS, Stata and SAS Files*. https://CRAN.R-project.org/package=haven

Wickham, H., & Müller, K. (2022). *DBI: R Database Interface*. https://CRAN.R-project.org/package=DBI

Wijffels, J. (2022). *cronR: Schedule R Scripts and Processes with the cron Job Scheduler*. https://CRAN.R-project.org/package=cronR

Wilke, C. O. (2019). *Fundamentals of Data Visualization: A Primer on Making Informative and Compelling Figures*. O'Reilly.

Wilke, C. O. (2020). *ggtext: Improved Text Rendering Support for 'ggplot2'*. https://CRAN.R-project.org/package=ggtext

Wilke, C. O. (2021). *ggridges: Ridgeline Plots in 'ggplot2'*. https://CRAN.R-project.org/package=ggridges

Wilkins, D. (2021). *treemapify: Draw Treemaps in 'ggplot2'*. https://CRAN.R-project.org/package=treemapify

Wilkinson, L. (2005). *The Grammar of Graphics* (2nd ed.). Springer. https://doi.org/10.1007/0-387-28695-0

Wolf, C., & Best, H. (2014). Linear regression. In H. Best & C. Wolf (Eds.), *The SAGE Handbook of Regression Analysis and Causal Inference* (pp. 57–81). Sage.

Xie, Y. (2016). *Bookdown: Authoring Books and Technical Documents with R Markdown*. Chapman; Hall/CRC.

Xie, Y. (2022a). *Bookdown: Authoring Books and Technical Documents with R Markdown*. https://CRAN.R-project.org/package=bookdown

Xie, Y. (2022b). *knitr: A General-Purpose Package for Dynamic Report Generation in R*. https://CRAN.R-project.org/package=knitr

Xie, Y. (2022c). *tinytex: Helper Functions to Install and Maintain TeX Live, and Compile LaTeX Documents*. https://CRAN.R-project.org/package=tinytex

Xie, Y. (2022d). *xaringan: Presentation Ninja*. https://CRAN.R-project.org/package=xaringan

Xie, Y., Dervieux, C., & Riederer, E. (2020). *R Markdown Cookbook*. Chapman; Hall/CRC.

Xie, Y., Lesur, R., Thorne, B., & Tan, X. (2022). *pagedown: Paginate the HTML Output of R Markdown with CSS for Print*. https://CRAN.R-project.org/package=pagedown

Young, D. S. (2017). *Handbook of Regression Methods* (1st ed.). Chapman; Hall/CRC.

Young, D. S. (2021). *HoRM: Supplemental Functions and Datasets for "Handbook of Regression Methods"*. https://CRAN.R-project.org/package=HoRM

Zhu, H. (2021). *kableExtra: Construct Complex Table with kable and Pipe Syntax*. https://CRAN.R-project.org/package=kableExtra

Index

Anscombe's quartet 161
API 353
arrange *see* dplyr
as.character 116
as.formula 299
as.numeric 116
assignment operator 24

boxplot 58
browseURL 338

c 27
class 31
colMeans 97
colors 204
column specification 116, 117
Cook's D 181
cor 64
correlation 65

data.frame 32, 119
DataExplorer
– create_report 59
– plot_bar 48
– plot_density 57
– plot_histogram 57
devtools
– install_github 20
– source_url 279
dplyr
– across 93
– anti_join 135
– arrange 73
– between 90
– bind_rows 357
– case_when 88
– distinct 294
– ends_with 76
– everything 93
– filter 71
– full_join 133
– group_by 79
– if_else 86
– inner_join 132
– intersect 135
– lag 364
– lead 364

– left_join 133
– mutate 76
– na_if 144
– num_range 76
– pull 76
– recode 91
– recode_factor 92
– relocate 81
– rename 121
– right_join 133
– select 74
– semi_join 134
– slice_* 341
– starts_with 76
– summarize 78
– transmute 78
drop_na 143
dwplot 189
dwtest 187

effect size *see* package effectsize
email *see* package: blastula
example 21
export data 114

factor 51
filter *see* dplyr
font type *see* package: showtext
for loop 304
forcats
– fct_collapse 150
– fct_count 148
– fct_infreq 151
– fct_lump 151
– fct_other 150
– fct_recode 149
– fct_relevel 148
– fct_unique 149
function 26

get 297
getwd 15
ggplot2
– aes 196
– aes_string 298
– alpha 224
– coord_cartesian 233

https://doi.org/10.1515/9783110704976-015

- coord_polar 232
- facet_grid 228
- facet_wrap 230
- geom_bar 221
- geom_col 221
- geom_density 218
- geom_histogram 218
- geom_point 196
- geom_smooth 222
- geom_text 371
- ggplot 196
- ggsave 215
- labels 197
- legend 211
- position_jitter 225
- scale limits 234
- scale_* 206, 223
- stat_summary 226
- theme_set 199
- themes 199
glimpse 44
glm 369
grammar of graphics 216
graphs
- alluvial 237
- bar plot 47
- beeswarm 238
- box plot 57
- choropleth map 239
- dot-and-whisker 172, 187
- dumbbell 240
- heat map 66
- hexbin map 241
- histogram 56
- lollipop 240
- mosaic 242
- pie chart 48
- ridge 243
- scatter plot 63
- treemap 244
- waffle 245
- word cloud 246

head 45
help 21
help.search 22
HTML 342
huxreg 171

if 310
ifelse 86
import data 112
install.packages 18
interaction effects *see* interactions package
is.data.frame 76
is.na 136

labels 52
lapply 97
length 29
letters 35
levels 50
library 19
linear regression *see* lm
list 35
list.files 318
lm 157, 164
lm_robust 186
logistic regression *see* glm

markdown 255
max 53
mean 30
median 53
min 53
missing values 136
mutate *see* dplyr

names 121
ncol 40
nrow 40

objects 24

package
- beepr 304
- blastula 313
- bookdown 373
- broom 176
- correlation 65, 298
- corrplot 66
- data.table 96
- DataExplorer 48
- datapasta 115
- dbplyr 343
- DemografixeR 353
- devtools 20, 279
- dotwhisker 188

- dplyr 70
- dygraphs 371
- effectsize 64, 161, 306
- esquisse 213
- estimatr 186
- flextable 267
- forcats 147
- ggalluvial 237
- gganimate 236, 371
- ggbeeswarm 238
- ggcharts 240
- ggeffects 184
- ggforce 235
- ggmap 239
- ggmosaic 242
- ggplot2 195
- ggrepel 371
- ggridges 243
- ggtext 236
- ggthemes 199
- ggwordcloud 246
- gh 282
- gitcreds 285
- glue 306
- googlesheets4 114
- here 303
- HistData 155
- HoRM 265
- httr 354
- huxtable 171, 269
- interactions 173
- janitor 122
- jtools 172, 187
- lubridate 364
- margins 370
- naniar 141
- pagedown 375
- palmerpenguins 40
- parameters 370
- patchwork 231
- pdftools 336
- performance 181
- ploty 371
- plumber 360
- PracticeR 20
- purrr 319
- pwr 166
- RColorBrewer 207
- readr 112

- report 307
- reticulate 254
- rjson 114
- rmarkdown 249
- rpivotTable 67
- rticles 264
- rvest 345
- shiny 372
- showtext 201
- stargazer 266
- stringi 336, 358
- stringr 325
- summarytools 46, 267
- survminer 236
- tibble 120
- tidymodels 368
- tidyr 126, 143
- tinytex 259
- treemapify 244
- usethis 283
- viridis 208
- waffle 245
- xaringan 374
pandoc 257
paste 299
paste0 302
performance
- check_collinearity 183
- check_heteroscedasticity 185
- check_normality 187
- check_outliers 181
pipe operator 79
plot_summs 172
power analysis 166
PracticeR
- show_linetypes 205
- show_link 21
- show_script 21
- show_shapetypes 205
predict 157
print 12
purrr
- as_vector 337
- map 319
- map2 320
- pmap 320

quantile 55
Quarto 373

R scripts 98
r2 174
read_* 112
regular expressions 326
relevel 165
rep 27
replace 144
replace_na 145
report
– report 307
– report_model 312
– report_participants 308
– report_performance 312
rm 104
rmarkdown
– chunk options 259
– chunks 252
– params 294
– reference_docx 264
– render 301
robust regression *see* estimatr package
round 30
rpivotTable 67
RStudio projects 102
rvest
– html_attr 350
– html_children 346
– html_elements 346, 352
– html_node 346
– html_table 349
– html_text 348
– minimal_html 347
– read_html 345

sapply 97
sd 53
select *see* dplyr
seq 27
setwd 16
shapiro.test 187
Simpson's paradox 169
snippets 105
source 105, 272
spineplot 62
split 319
str 45
stringr
– remove 341
– str_c 333
– str_count 334

– str_detect 334
– str_extract 325
– str_length 335
– str_locate 334
– str_replace 335
– str_sort 335
– str_split_fixed 333
– str_starts 334
– str_subset 325
– str_trim 339
– str_view_all 329
– str_which 338
subset 96
sum 29
summarize *see* dplyr
summary 54
summarytools
– ctable 62
– descr 55
– freq 46
system.file 114

t.test 312
table 46
tables 265
– descriptive statistics 267
– dynamic reports 296
– multivariate analysis 269
tail 46
tibble 33
– rownames_to_column 94
tidyr
– pivot_longer 129
– pivot_wider 126
tribble 33
typeof 51

union 135

View 46
vignettes 22

which 140
write_* 114
writeLines 327

XML 345

yaml 251